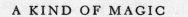

A KIND OF MAGIC

BOOKS BY EDNA FERBER

Autobiographies
A KIND OF MAGIC · A PECULIAR TREASURE

Short Stories
ONE BASKET · NOBODY'S IN TOWN
BUTTERED SIDE DOWN · CHEERFUL——BY REQUEST
HALF PORTIONS · GIGOLO · MOTHER KNOWS BEST
THEY BROUGHT THEIR WOMEN

The Emma McChesney Stories
ROAST BEEF MEDIUM · PERSONALITY PLUS
EMMA MCCHESNEY & COMPANY

Novels
ICE PALACE · GIANT · GREAT SON · SARATOGA TRUNK · DAWN O'HARA
FANNY HERSELF · THE GIRLS · SO BIG · SHOW BOAT
CIMARRON · AMERICAN BEAUTY · COME AND GET IT

Plays
THE ROYAL FAMILY (with George S. Kaufman)
MINICK (with George S. Kaufman)
DINNER AT EIGHT (with George S. Kaufman)
$1200 A YEAR (with Newman Levy)
STAGE DOOR (with George S. Kaufman)
THE LAND IS BRIGHT (with George S. Kaufman)
BRAVO! (with George S. Kaufman)

A Kind of Magic

EDNA FERBER

1963

DOUBLEDAY & COMPANY, INC.

GARDEN CITY, NEW YORK

Library of Congress Catalog Card Number 63-18030
Copyright © 1963 by Edna Ferber
All Rights Reserved
Printed in the United States of America

To Julie Goldsmith
and to
Peter and Kathy Klein,
a new young generation
in an old tough world.

E. F.

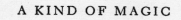

A KIND OF MAGIC

1

To be alive is a fine thing. It is the finest thing in the world, though hazardous. It is a unique thing. It happens only once in a lifetime. To be alive, to know consciously that you are alive, and to relish that knowledge—this is a kind of magic. Or it may be a kind of madness, exhilarating but harmless.

Hundreds of millions of people never once in their lifetime reflect on the stupendous fact that they are alive. They merely live. They walk talk work play love hate and die a little daily without marveling at these fascinating processes. Whether madness or magic, perhaps to do so is to possess a sixth sense. Having this, you must adjust to a double life in which you are both actor and audience. You are marching in the parade even though you stand at the curb watching the parade go by. Any writer whose work, as you read it or hear it, gives you a fresh and more dimensional impression of life and living, a keener awareness of the world about you, has that magic sixth sense.

It may be fortunate that this mildly schizophrenic state is not widely prevalent. Nature doubtless knows precisely what she is doing when she protects the great mass of humanity from conscious personal awareness of living in the kaleidoscopic and improbable world in which it moves. Yet, in a way, a pity. For our most fundamental acts, consciously noted, may seem miraculous.

Take walking as an example of ordinary performance. Here is this fragile, vulnerable and mobile box called the human body in which, with incredible intrepidity and good luck, we move around on the perilous planet Earth. A single blow, a misstep, can shatter the delicate piece of mechanism.

This body-box is your slave, ordinarily obeying your every reasonable (and frequently unreasonable) command. On the telephone you say to a friend, I'll meet you at the corner of Park and Fifty-seventh in fifteen minutes. Without giving the negotiation another conscious thought you are miraculously conveyed to your destination by your obliging body.

Perhaps on the way your slave may protest faintly, saying, "Look, I've been lugging you around all day. I'm tired."

You retort, "Tired shmired, you go on and do as I say." So off you go to keep your appointment, defiantly brisk in spite of that whimpering inner voice. On the way you are regaled with the sights and sounds of the human race in action; surely the greatest free show on earth.

The catch in it is that all this constant awareness of being alive may become a wearing process to you and a source of irritation to your friends. Wisely you refrain from mentioning it. Occasionally the numbed behavior of a fellow human being moves you to protest. This may be a workman performing badly and carelessly the services of his craft.

"I'm sorry, but you've made a mistake," you say. "Look, it's all wrong, here and here and here."

"I only work here, lady."

"But if you work here you're interested, aren't you! You can see it's wrong."

"I don't know about innerested. Talk to the boss. I only work here."

He is not living. The orbit of his being is walled by darkness.

To give the possible reader who has traveled thus far a fair chance to walk away from the printed page I must now state that I not only work here I live here I love it here. When I realize that I may not be here an hour from now and that it is absolutely mathematically certain that I shan't be here to celebrate that great round plump date, for good or for evil, January First in the year 2000, I am filled with a fury of frustration. While I cannot honestly say that I consider this the best of all possible worlds it definitely is the best of which I personally have any firsthand knowledge. This includes that rather tiresomely described haven known as heaven. Until the diligent scientists have completed comfortable tourist arrangements—including room bath and board, with air-conditioning—on another planet, this Earth is my favorite abode, grumble though I may. My chief criticism is that the entire production is frequently melodramatic, and the curtain uncertain.

Through the centuries we have arrogantly assumed that ours is the only habitable planet. We have named it the planet Earth and, arbitrarily, have bestowed the titles Mars Jupiter Saturn Venus Neptune Mercury upon various other planets. About Neptune we are somewhat sniffy. Rarely mention him, in fact. Yet he is third largest in the really stylish and important major group. Perhaps we are embarrassed to admit that Earth and Neptune are under-privileged planets. These two alone are equipped with only one moon each. The astronomers tell us that other planets are gifted with two—four—even nine lavish moons. Imagine the romantic possibilities of nine moons. Not to speak of the astronautic frenzy that these would entail. It is a prospect to give pause even to a Communist. And what names have these other-planet scientists given the tiny globe we call Earth? Do the three-eyed males on Saturn or the four-armed creatures on Mars refer to our planet as Bzzck? Or Mogwap? Or just Itsy Bitsy? Do their astronomers report that Itsy Bitsy is in the ascendant this week and some crackpots think it is inhabited by wee things that stump about on only two legs and haven't even the power of self-levitation? The air is too heavy.

Throughout my adult life until very recently a sort of naïveté perhaps prevented me from realizing that the world as I viewed it was as though seen through a double magnifying lens. If at times it seemed to me that I was more conscious of the minutiae of living than were others I assumed that this was due to the surroundings and training of my formative years. These included a troubled childhood, chancey, sometimes tragic, always fascinating, spent in various Midwestern small towns of the United States, with Chicago thrown in occasionally by way of variety; and a four-year period between the impressionable ages of seventeen to twenty-one when I worked as a newspaper reporter. Those years were to serve as an apprenticeship to a half-century of fiction writing but I definitely didn't know it then. Starting blithely at a minimal salary of nothing a week on the Appleton Wisconsin *Daily Crescent* I soared after a mere three months to $3 a week, then $5, then up the dizzy heights of affluence to $8 (and no Federal tax). Crazed with success and in love with my job I was the town scourge. A plump seventeen, my hair tied back in a bunch of wiry black corkscrew curls I daily ranged the news spots from the jail and courthouse to Pettibone's Drygoods Store. The advantages and perquisites attendant on the duties of a reporter working on a small-town daily afternoon newspaper were many and varied, ranging all the way from delirious to practical and including free theatre tickets, contact with every variety of human being extant, a rapidly growing knowledge of these humans as they functioned under stress, *sturm, drang,* ambition, terror, vanity, or any other known variety of emotion. Also, while I gained knowledge I lost some weight. If you were a reporter out on assignment you walked. Automobiles were those crazy new contraptions that scared the farmers' horses into fits when they came into town. There was a bee-shaped little yellow streetcar that buzzed and bumbled its way across town every hour or so, but the Appleton *Crescent* wasn't throwing its nickels around for any such nonsense and I definitely was not so sybaritic as to lavish five cents of my own on a mere two or three miles that could be walked, three dollars or no three dollars. To this day I am grateful for it, and whang out three miles without losing a spangle.

From this background it was only one great heartbreaking step to the big city splendors of the Milwaukee *Journal* and $15 a week. Room, board and all personal expenses came out of this. The nine o'clock police court, the Wisconsin Dairymen's Annual Convention, the opening of Gimbel's new furniture department, the latest city hall scandal —everything anything came under my typewriter keys. Certainly this must have strengthened any natural gift of observation with which I originally had been equipped. It was forced feeding. At eighteen, nineteen, twenty, everything registered; was retained. The eye became a trained eye, the photographic shutter of the mind clicked clicked clicked and thousands of pictures were stored away in the multiple vaults of memory. I worked like a horse, happily galloping the city from Lake Michigan on the east to West Allis (naturally) on the west; from the airy brilliance of Whitefish Bay to the sooty region in which the mill-workers perforce lived. You were sent out to get your story, you had to get it, you got it. You encountered all the kinds of people there are in the world, right there in the middle-sized city of Milwaukee Wisconsin.

So I charged on with it and over-dramatized everything—the job, the city, myself, the world, until one day I literally dropped in my tracks and was sent home to Appleton Wisconsin and the Ferber front porch to recuperate. But the four-year habit of feeling the typewriter keys under my fingers could not be dismissed.

Appleton Wisconsin was one of hundreds of Midwestern small towns, prosperous enough, conventional enough, perhaps dull-seeming on the surface. Sitting there on the North Street front porch while the town walked past to work, to school, to dinner (mid-day) to supper (six), to do the family shopping, I had a sense of living entertainment out of all proportion to the external picture that passed before my eyes. This may have been the result of the years of newspaper training. It may have been due to extra-sensory perception; or hyper-sensitivity or both. In any case I was choked with undigested ideas. Everything I saw and heard and felt interested me and I had no place to put it all. Here was the World. I was as blissful and disorganized as a child turned loose in a candy store.

Under a kind of compulsion I bought a battered secondhand typewriter for $17 and began, quite without plan or intention, the fifty and more years of novel writing, play writing, short story writing. And I knew—though all my life I have been stage-struck, and acting is my natural gift, if any—that I would rather be a writer than anything in the world. So that was all right.

But there was a catch in it. An extra-sensory perception or a hyper-sensitivity—though I did not know or name it then—became a technical nuisance. Practically every object that met my eye was endowed with a clarity, a brilliance that excited me. Three overblown adjectives would spring up in the path of my prose where a single one—or perhaps none —would have been more effective. Ruthlessly I would slash away two flowery weeds only to find them popping up again on the next page. With years of discipline this was overcome, or nearly. But I never have admired or striven for the me-go or early Indian-peace-pipe-grunt school of writing.

Glancing back over one's shoulder all this seems not only unimportant but trivial and perhaps even tiresome. In the days of those once-sprightly creators of stage comedies—Henry Arthur Jones, Pinero, Clyde Fitch—there usually were early introduced into the play two lines at which the listener's heart sank. One of these was, "Won't you— sit down?" The other, after a very gabby ten or fifteen minute monologue: "But why am I telling you all this!"

Why indeed. Plot—that's why.

So then, won't you sit down? And why am I telling you all this! There, over my shoulder, almost lost in the mists that have enveloped the world this past half century one can barely detect the hazy outline of a blundering stupendous futile cataclysm called the First World War. It wasn't tidily numbered at the time because at its so-termed finish it was supposed to have been the War to end all wars. To today's teenagers or even to the twentyish young, World War I is as remote as the Peloponnesian and less historically familiar than the American Revolution. They've heard of George Washington and Cornwallis and Lafayette but who was this Pershing and some old dodo called the Kaiser and, uh, von Hindensomething?

Only the very young—between the ages of six and perhaps twenty-nine—accept this world as a normal world. It's no use telling them that this is fantastic, that for hundreds of years no such chaotic state existed—a reeling universe of World Wars, of rockets, globe-destroying missiles, jet planes, machines which dominate man so that the very streets in which he walks are hazardous. Men and women between the ages of thirty and seventy, unless they are absolute clods, are bewildered and even deeply disturbed by the suddenness and violence of world change.

This is understandable and even normal in a fantastic way. For the 1920s, frantic though they were, and ending in a mass of rubble called the Wall Street Crash, could be termed idyllic in comparison with today's cosmic apprehension and insecurity.

Recently I tried, naïvely, to convey to an ordinarily intelligent young girl of eighteen something of the astounding changes that had come about in the United States during the past twenty-five or thirty years.

"You can't imagine the difference," I began, spaciously. "It's as if a hundred years—or even two centuries—had been compressed into two decades. It's a revolution in living and thinking. I don't mean only in personal behavior but in cosmic involvement. It's not only art and education and human relations that have changed; and clothes and sex behavior and science and religion and architecture and locomotion and health and the life span. There's an incredible change in pace, in actual climate, rainfall, humidity, topography, population. You can't imagine," I wound up, somewhat lamely, since she still appeared unimpressed, "how absolutely different everything was just twenty-five short years ago."

She wagged her pretty head politely in evidence of unfelt wonderment. "I know," she said. "You mean like not even air-conditioning!"

I could have been talking about the old covered-wagon days. Her generation had not been forced to cross a continent, a world, an era in one unwieldy leap. Roughly, North American world-terms of the 1930s would have summed up something like this:

RUSSIA: Czars. Siberia. Cold. Ermine, sables. Ballet. Troikas pursued by saliva-drooling wolves. Tolstoy. Caviar. Pogroms. Tschaikovsky. Dostoevsky. Kremlin. Snow.

CHINA: Rice. Floods. Empress. Pigtails. Porcelain. Chopsticks. Temples. Tea. Laundry. Chop Suey.

GREAT BRITAIN: The most. But they know it.

AFRICA: Jungles. Tom-toms. Safaris. Monkeys. Heat. Leopards lions. Missionaries. Savages.

INDIA: Elephants. Taj Mahal. Sacred cows. Beggars. Pearl prayer rugs. Hunger. Tigers. Maharajahs. Bazaars. Kipling.

MOON: Tides. Craters. Lovers. June. Man in (not on) the.

PRESIDENT: Elderly gentleman seated at orderly desk signing papers with important-looking pen. Group of other elderly gentlemen looking over his shoulder standing.

MISSILE: Stone. Bullet. Spear. Any small object hurled by hand or by hand-impelled mechanism.

Anyone who is old enough to get the long view must know how false, how meaningless is the hackneyed old philosophy of, "It'll all be the same a hundred years from now." Having lived just about three-quarters of one hundred years I can assure the blithe spirits who utter this blather that it won't be anything of the kind. Not only will the things you do now make a vast difference a hundred years from now, but the things you don't do will make a difference a hundred years from now. The fruity senseless old saying is purest miltown.

With a tremendous gesture of rejection those of us who still were young enough to adapt ourselves to the late 1930s tossed those past twenty-five years into the trash basket and started a new page. Living in the past is a dull and lonely business; and looking back, if persisted in, strains the neck-muscles, causes you to bump into people not going your way, and loses you your readers.

Still, fair is fair, and a writer should not begin a structure of daily 9 A.M. work on a basis of false premises. In the clean cause of soul-baring (and thousands of men and women are this minute paying psychiatrists fifty dollars an hour for listening to just this kind of blabbing) it should now be stated that I not only find it exhilarating to be alive but practically everything that comes within my notice or experience seems consciously amazing or depressing or wonderful or irritating or amusing or dreadful; even everyday things that normally should be taken for granted. I simply can't help it, but usually I manage to conceal this under a somewhat saturnine exterior.

Take flying (or leave it alone if heights terrify you). Airplanes are as everyday as trucks. I've flown in peace and in war; across oceans and continents; in tiny Plexiglas footbaths above bomb-ruined European towns; sipping champagne in turquoise-blue upholstered jets forty thousand feet up in the boundless sky. From my little terrace so high outside my New York apartment the aircrafts can be seen day and night, the decorous and matronly middle-aged 6s and 7s and 8s bumbling their way across the sky toward or from La Guardia or Idlewild; the jets streaking like demons across the high heavens, leaving their taunting screech miles behind them. Ya-a-a-a try and catch me!

I still don't believe it.

The telephone seems to me miraculous. The clothes-washing machine, the dish-washing machine, the deep-freezer, the electric typewriter (none of which I possess); the tape recorder (same); and—well—the sewing machine. This scant, this incomplete list, should include the wheel—or perhaps would if the automobile hadn't become such a nuisance.

Books, if they may be mentioned here without meaning to seem crass. Books, those great nourishers of man's mind and body and spirit. How sustaining, how comforting to be able to take with you, wherever you go, this friend, this counselor, this companion, this teacher, this entertainer, in whatever mood you chance to be; accompanying you when you walk in the woods or climb a mountain; when you are a passenger on train, plane or ship; in a lonely hotel bedroom or in your own living room; in bed, well or ill.

The body's functions—what an incomparable triumph of ingenuity, invention, performance; needing only a modicum of attention for their maintenance; persisting in spite of neglect, abuse, stupidity.

Seriously consider spit—that matchless marvel. Just stick out your tongue and lick a stamp handily; or slip a dry crust into that built-in blender, your mouth, and in a moment you have a palatable morsel.

Paeans have been sung about mountains trees flowers; rivers lake skies; yes, but what about a New England fence or stone wall with snow on it? Millions of people have seen a New England fence. But a poet, with his kind of magic, makes you not only see it but feel it; can so relate you to it that it is forever part of your life.

Most writers of any considerable achievement must possess this capacity. Oftenest the genuinely creative writer—the poet, the novelist, the playwright—has it. Otherwise there would be no poets, no novelists, no playwrights. No poems, no novels, no plays.

Perhaps because of this mysterious and somewhat fey quality the creative writer in the industrial-minded United States is regarded as in no other civilized country in the world. The general or over-all attitude is much like that displayed toward a precocious child. It is a mixture of resigned tolerance, puzzlement, curiosity, amusement and mild condescension. As for the United States Government, Federal Tax Department, this frolicsome and unpredictable organization regards writing not as a profession or a business or an art—all of which it is—but as a harmless and unimportant whim. This uninformed and patronizing attitude should deter any writer, no matter how dedicated, from the agonizing labor of putting down on paper, word by word, the idea that is struggling to be born. It doesn't. Even today, in a world of chaos, the writer suddenly is confronted by the past, the present, or the future, seizes it, makes it his own, and goes his way, fulfilled.

This book is meant to be as haphazard as the March day on which this page is being written; rain sun snow wind clouds; cold on the shady side of the street; unexpectedly warm, once you've crossed over. Your umbrella turned inside out on this corner; your winter topcoat too warm on the next. All kinds of weather compressed into a single day; all kinds of days jammed into a single quarter century between the years 1938 to 1963.

But first, as a disorderly start, I should like to record the day in the late 1950s when I chanced on a book by Aldous Huxley. It gave me one of the major shocks of my life. Entitled *The Doors of Perception* it seemed a prim slim little volume of a mere seventy-nine pages. Though originally it had been published in 1954 I had missed it until five years later. It proved a bomb to me.

Concisely and unemotionally the reader is told that Aldous Huxley, a writer of achievement and distinction, intentionally swallowed four-tenths of a grain of mescalin dissolved in half a glass of water and sat down to await the outcome. The pages of the little book calmly and scientifically describe the result of this premeditated act.

Mescalin is a drug made from the plant called peyote. Peyote is a mescal cactus found in the southwest United States and in Mexico. This was not news to me. I had come upon a living record of this plant drug when, in 1927, I went to Oklahoma intent on research for the novel *Cimarron* whose background was the melodramatic and incredible shenanigan of the Oklahoma Land Rush period in 1889. I learned that the Indian tribes living in Oklahoma had for decades known the use of the peyote plant and its derivative mescalin. The Indians did not distill this drug; they simply ate the little peyote bud or button. This allegedly non-habit-forming drug heightened the sense of perception, gave an exaggerated quality to sights, sounds, colors, textures. One had a sensation of serenity and exhilaration at the same time. The Osage Indians, for example, often held formal rites in which all participated in the peyote ceremony. The general effect was everything's-coming-up-roses, but the drug induced no craving for continued use. One could take it or leave it, unlike such drugs as alcohol, tobacco, and other narcotics or stimulants.

In Aldous Huxley's brief book, documented and written with simple clarity and observation, one could follow the effect of a dose of mescalin as experienced by a man of keen intelligence and scientific curiosity.

Under the supervision of certain scientist friends and associates he had deliberately and carefully swallowed a dose of mescalin sufficient to heighten his sense of perception. He spoke aloud as he experienced his reactions in the presence of the others. He walked about. He was driven from place to place, always under the heightening influence of the drug.

It was, one gathers, at once soothing and exciting. Patterns, sounds, textures, colors became clearer, sharper, brighter, more altogether splendid. A fold of cloth took on new depth and luster; a flower's petal possessed a vibrant glow; he noted a razorlike edge in the crease of a man's trousers; the pattern of a brocade came alive like a bouquet; the rung of a chair took on startling definiteness; music took on another dimension. But Huxley saw not only this. He perceived, briefly, the actual world complete and amazing as it was, with his own ego detached, removed. He was free. He was open to the world. He was experiencing a harmless and revivifying intoxication in which he became aware of the beauty and the wonder and the ugliness and the pretentiousness of that incredible and fascinating manifestation known as everyday life.

Stunned, I stared at the printed page. Slowly I put down the book and looked about me. I was scared. I never had taken mescalin nor any drug stronger than a Bufferin, perhaps, for a rare headache or a cold. Alcohol is not for me because it only makes me sleepy. Occasionally before dinner a cocktail or none—it doesn't matter. I smoke perhaps one cigarette a week or one a month or none a month. Simply, luckily, not a drinker not a smoker not a drug-taker. This has nothing to do with rules or health or moral behavior. Just not interested. It is, however, a bit of a handicap. Added to the fact that I sleep a natural eight hours nightly and walk a fast two or three miles daily (and talk about it) this has made me something of a social outcast. Like boasting about money, it simply isn't done.

I now realized that my everyday perceptions, in vividness and inclusiveness, were almost precisely those experienced by Aldous Huxley under the influence of mescalin.

Aloud I said to myself, "Why, this—this is the way I've felt every day, all my life!"

Those of you who are Dickens devotees will remember Mrs. Gummidge. Was I, then, a kind of Mrs. Gummidge? She who amused me and revolted me when first I came upon her in the pages of *David Copperfield* and whose remembered character will entertain me all my life. Mrs. Gummidge the lone lorn creetur who insisted that she felt things more than most.

"Yes, yes," Mrs. G. always boasted, "I feel things more than other people do, and I show it more. It's my misfortun'."

But mine was not Gummidgey bewailing. The condition I now perceived as being a normal one with me was a delicious one; always had been a delicious one, whether or not it was due to a certain chemical lack in my physiological makeup; or a profusion. Turning back to the Huxley book I remembered the author had stated that one of the effects of mescalin intoxication was that it decreased the customary amount of glucose to the brain. As all my life I have been congenitally a low blood-sugar type I thought now that perhaps it had been merely this state which had, all these years, served to give me that additional tang and relish in life? Was it just a lack of groceries, like sugar, that had made a walk on Madison Avenue, the rise of a first-act curtain, the timbre of a voice, so arresting, so enthralling? Was it this that had made boredom almost an unknown state to me? A conscious awareness not only of life but of living had somehow, miraculously, been mine. To live in this strange unpredictable world as a functioning part of it; to be able at will to walk talk travel hear see read; to sit with friends; work; oppose violence and injustice in some small measure at least; to type words on a blank sheet of white paper and to hope that they will come alive with meaning; to brush one's hair so that it crackles and stands erect; to fly across the Atlantic Ocean; to eat a ripe juicy pear; sleep, laugh, go to the theatre; pour and drink a cup of hot strong coffee; skate (no longer); pray quietly to the god which is whatever there may be of Good and of Strength in me; to buy a new dress and pay for it and wear it; to know love and friendship; the sound of a symphony, ignorant though I am of music; to note the plump succulent circle made by the bright yolk of a fried egg on a clean plate; the pattern and folds of silk as Rembrandt saw them with his kind of magic, luscious fold on fold, alive on the canvas; the bare bones of a tree etched against the winter west sky at sunset across Central Park. For that matter, a ride in a bus or the subway, those faces so vulnerable, so exposed that you are embarrassed to look.

Many people rather pride themselves on the promptness with which they can decide upon a dish in a restaurant. This, the psychiatrists will tell you, is good. Myself, I think they miss a lot of fun. They deprive themselves of the exquisite agonies of indecision, the hovering over the printed choice of this dainty or that as a honey bee weaves a moment here and there over the feast of flowers spread for his delectation. Are soft-shell crabs in season? Sauté meunière. . . . Oh, look! Shad roe. . . . Fresh asparagus with h— . . . no, cold. Vinaigrette. . . . Could I have just a little splash of Cointreau over the pineapple sherbet?

All this nonsense is not for the gulpers, they have little palate for food and possibly for living. Just take it as it comes, gobble the day the week the year the decade the life without savoring or even really tasting it. Shovel it in as fuel into a furnace.

It is a curious fact that people permit life to slide past them like a deft pickpocket, their purse—not yet missed and now too late—in his hand. They rarely undertake a conscious review of their past and their present as a steering chart for their future. They go through their clothes-closets to make sure that this garment can be worn for another season, that one must be discarded; this pair of shoes is down-at-heel, that hat passé. They review their finances, ruefully or joyfully. But not their lives. This may begin to fray around the edges, it frequently turns shabby and unbecoming, it even on occasion disintegrates. Mr. Wilkins Micawber was the flawless example of the something-will-turn-up boy.

That indomitable woman, Julia Ferber, my mother, used to go through a grubby but necessary formality following the crowded and hideously tiring period of the Christmas business rush in the thriving town of Appleton Wisconsin. She ran the jampacked general store by which she supported her blind husband Jacob Ferber and her two small daughters Fannie and Edna. After the merciless labor of the November and December business it was her invariable custom to value her remaining stock. An inventory was made. She called it stock-taking. If ever there was a human being who had early learned it was no good waiting for something to turn up, that one was Julia Ferber.

This stock-taking was much like counting the dead and the living after a battle. Literally it was the difference between victory and defeat. It proved success or failure for the year just passed; hope or despair for the year ahead. So and so many Limoges china dinner sets . . . black woolen stockings . . . sleds . . . dolls . . . lamps . . . kitchenwares . . . handkerchiefs towels glassware; notions novelties. Sold. Unsold. Cash on hand for new stock; or not enough for replenishment. The workers in the big Fox River Valley paper mills; the farmers' wives from the outlying districts; the students at Lawrence College; the comfortable middle-income citizens of the lovely little valley town of sixteen thousand; the college professors and their families; the moneyed owners of the handsome Victorian mansions on lower College Avenue and along the river bluffs—all these Appletonians had or had not tipped the scales in favor of the Ferber family's future. Julia Ferber had to know the concrete result clearly and precisely.

From counter to counter, from bin to bin she moved with her ledger and pencil, the two clerks aiding her. A black sateen apron protected her gray wool skirt from dust and bits of excelsior. She had the gift of being able to add up two and even three columns of figures at a time. Well, not so bad this year. No actual debts. The children are well, Jake's eyes are no worse, he can still tell the difference between day-light and dark, though the awful pains . . .

Inventory. A reckoning. That was the thing, I told myself, as 1938 stared me in the face. Stared me? *Hit* me in the face. That was the year of my first stock-taking. It had taken the form of an autobiography entitled A *Peculiar Treasure*, three words from a paragraph in Exodus (the Exodus of the Bible, I hastily add). The narrative took me—and, I hope, the reader—through the years from the day I was born in Kalamazoo Michigan to the ominous spring of 1938 in New York.

Writing that book proved to be a tonic, a catalyst. At the end of those months of work I felt refreshed, resolved, instead of spent and fatigued as usually is the case with a writer at the finish of a long pull of sustained work. A quarter of a century of writing had been one of the items summed up in this inventory of 1938. It had proved that I wasn't bankrupt mentally or physically or spiritually or financially. I was still a going concern. The planet Earth was soon to be rocked, torn, battered and very nearly shattered by a comic-looking character with the low comedy name of Adolf Schicklgruber, but who would accept that improbable eventuality even in the tempestuous year 1938?

1938 . . . 1963. In some miraculous way another quarter of a century had galloped by.

A half century of writing. Writing in all sorts of countries, in all sorts of rooms, under conditions good bad impossible; in sickness and in health, for better for worse—where had I heard that before? I sat star-ing up at a shelf in my workroom from which thirty-one books identi-cally dressed in neat dark green leather stared back at me with a sort of cold hostility like children who resent their parents. Don't stare at us like that! they said. Don't blame us if we didn't turn out to be the perfection you expected. We didn't ask to be brought into the world.

This came as an actual shock, though it had been creeping up on me unawares. For half a century I had sat at a desk facing a typewriter as

I put one little word down after another. The right word. The wrong word. The best word I could dredge up at the time. Last year. Next year and next year and next year. Fifty years of it. And for this.

Well, what of it, the taunting voices on the bookshelf yelped. The world is full of people—millions and millions of them—who have worked fifty years on the job. What's the fuss? What's all the beefing about?

Who's beefing! I've loved every m— well, every other minute of it. I was just thinking that, with all you children grown up and on your own I can't do anything more for you now.

Then what? What are you going to do for an encore?

I may go around the world. Everybody's going around the world. In the whole history of mankind there never has been such a procession of circumnavigators. They travel by plane, by ship, by train, by car. It is a bizarre parade of well-heeled compulsive tourists stocked against all contingencies with a load of nylons Dacrons Orlons barbiturates cameras tranquilizers anti-dysentery pills and credit cards.

We're going around the world, they say. We'll be back in May. The whirring sound you hear is Christopher Columbus, Jules Verne, Vasco da Gama, Magellan, Francis Drake and Captain Cook spinning in their graves.

But it wasn't that world I had in mind, tempting though it might appear with its present-day luxury; the giant jets, the modern hotels, motor roads into the once-impassable jungles; bottled water, Western dishes in Far-Eastern dining rooms for wistful palates craving steak, apple pie à la mode, corn on the cob. No travel bureau, no maps of Russia Germany Scandinavia Brazil India Australia Japan Africa Portugal Greece China were planning my devious route. No Little Tailor in Hongkong was to make me a Little Silk Suit for Little or Nothing. All these far-flung travelers—were they, unconsciously, intent on having a Last Look? A scramble to see the show before it closes?

No, the world I had in mind was my own circumscribed world of the past twenty-five years. Metaphorically, with ledger and pencil in hand and the remnants of the last quarter-century rush scattered in disarray all around me, I once more planned to take inventory of the small world in which I had functioned these past two and a half decades, and in which, with luck, I might continue to travel for a little while; savoring this, rejecting that, seeing the sights, listening to the sounds;

attracted, repelled, weary, exhilarated, amused, revolted; making, perhaps, the best of it if not always the most of it, until the passport date expires.

There has been so much one wished to see; to do; to be. So little time in which to accomplish this. It is like the plight of the visitor in New York or the too-hasty tourist amidst the wonders of Europe. You ask of one of these travelers: Have you seen this? Have you done that? Have you met those?

Regretfully he replies, "I'd have loved to. I meant to. But I didn't. I couldn't. There wasn't time. I'm just passing through, you know."

2

A house in the country—that was the thing. That was the place for Work. Get away from It All. No one stated definitely just what constituted It All, but whatever its gruesome ingredients they had not, one gathered, yet penetrated the verdant lanes, the leafy backroads, the hills and valleys of nearby Connecticut Massachusetts Pennsylvania New Jersey or more distant Vermont. Once possessed of that dream cottage (with three bathrooms an outdoor barbecue and two cars in the garage) and that magic chunk of solid land, symbol of security, nothing frightening or even faintly disturbing could happen to you. This was the year 1938, and the whole world was cataleptically frenzied. A house in the country—that was the thing.

A childish fantasy, this, imbedded for centuries in the human race. The feudal lord had had it as he looked down from his fortress castle on the hilltop. The peasant had it as he dragged his crude wooden plow through the sour land of his grudged allotment. Perhaps it had even been partly true once upon a time when distance still existed; long long before the planet Earth had shrunk to the size of a two- or three-hour air jaunt.

In this paradoxical state the world sat shivering, its gaze distended in terror like that of a rabbit transfixed by a cobra. The decade just passed had been catastrophic and the decade stretching ahead firmly promised to be worse. New York, exactly like the rest of the vast nation, was sitting scared. It had survived—though still twitching—World War I and the financial earthquake of 1929 which had reduced a nation's economy to rubble. The second temblor in 1933 was like a relapse fol-

lowing an almost fatal illness. The patient seemed lacking in the resistance to fight it. The flaunting night-lights ceased to blaze their
brilliant patterns from towers and man-made mountains that were hotels and office buildings. Radio City was a ghost town. The ruby and
emerald and sapphire hues that had glowed from the cupolas of the
Waldorf in bizarre resemblance to the Korean crown jewels now were
only dark blobs against the skyline.

From this shambles emerged a line of broken-spirited men standing
or shuffling four abreast in close formation around entire city blocks.
Their objective was any one of many soup kitchens where men whose
annual incomes might recently have been in the thousands of dollars
now drooped shivering in the cold or wet of the early winter morning
or late night mists, waiting for a bowl of tepid soup, a cup of coffee,
a piece of bread. This national state of wretchedness was called The
Depression of 1933 and was generally spelled with a capital D like an
actual historical event—which, doubtless, it was; the Pliocene Age—the
Civil War period—the Depression of 1929–1933.

By the time 1938 dealt the third financial blow in a period of ten
years the country was numb to that brand of shock. Now, with stunned
unbelief, it heard of the insane but highly effectual mass atrocities
committed in Germany by that comic character Schicklgruber. He now
operated with great success under the more imposing name of Hitler,
and he wasn't so funny any more.

England will stop him. France will stop him. They always have.
Those power-crazy nuts like the old German Kaiser and Napoleon and
Alexander and, uh, Genghis Khan. After all, it's their continent over
there, not ours. We can take care of ourselves.

But now in the United States of America, so snug behind its oceans,
you saw the swastika flaunting its zigzag madness on walls and fences
and shop windows and houses. In that section of New York's Manhattan called Yorkville whose citizens were so predominantly German-
born and now incredibly infected with the overseas homeland sickness,
a New York Jew was almost certain to encounter insult or even violence
if he walked there.

Things look bad, people admitted. They didn't exactly specify what
Things. Every Thing, probably; but Every Thing will turn out all right,
it always has it always will. Right will win. Just don't look and don't
get mixed up in it. If you don't look It will go away. This is one war

we won't be pulled into. Not again. Help, yes. Mix in? No. We're not a warlike nation, we never have been we never will be. We hate war.

This was gibberish—but understandable gibberish. An amorphous monster was breathing down your neck, its horrid horny hoofs were scraping your heels. The newspaper headlines and the radio commentators' voices were like daily hourly doses of poison whose names were Apprehension, Insecurity, Horror.

The Thing to Do was to Get Away from It All.

We're looking for a place in the country, your friends said. In a desultory way I had been doing this for years and years. It had become something of a joke among the people who knew me well. When spring came round my small-town Midwest background would sneak like a virus into my blood, made sluggish by a winter in New York. Then, annually and futilely it was ho! for the leafy lanes, the hideaway, the mythical refuge where one could Write in Peace. Those three words should be engraved on the tombstone (if any) of all dedicated writers who crave only quiet and privacy and the privilege of putting down on paper those thousand words a day. There at last, on the marble tablet, it should be granted them: *Write in Peace.*

Unbelievably, as I now look back on the period, I was living in a fantastic penthouse apartment snuggled behind a neat noise-repellent brick parapet atop the roof of a twenty-story building on Park Avenue. The Hanging Gardens of Babylon were a cabbage patch in comparison when it came to daring and botanical engineering. It had all been planned by a financial madman named Ivar Kreuger, its original tenant. With millions filched over the years from every gullible nation in Europe this criminal genius had bedecked his glittering world with every lavish whim and fancy that entered his sick and brilliant mind.

Some years previously, in my search for a quiet New York apartment dwelling, I had come upon this unbelievable country house in the air. Kreuger was dead, killed in a Paris hotel room by his own hand. It was offered me for rental at an unbelievably low figure. But then, this was 1933 in New York and money was practically non-existent; one could probably have bought Radio City and Brooklyn Bridge for a dime.

For five years I rented it and lived in it, always with a feeling of mingled delight, unbelief and considerable embarrassment. It was make-believe country dwelling. It was sybaritic simplicity. This some-what decadent conceit called an apartment I have previously described in the autobiographical book entitled A *Peculiar Treasure* which cov-ers the years up to 1938. Certainly I shall not, then, again lengthily describe it here.

Bordering the neatly paved paths of this sky-house willow trees fifteen feet high and as thick in circumference as an elephant's leg cascaded their liquid green branches over the parapet. Peach trees, espaliered apple trees, grape arbors and strawberry plants and rhubarb actually bore fruit in this bizarre Eden. Two fountains tinkled annoyingly. Jon-quils popped their golden heads in the spring, rhododendrons pro-duced gay little balloons of pink and white and mauve.

The times were mad and bad; the environment, too. But work was a habit, a release, a refuge, a fixed way of life; and, not so incidentally, a living. But deeply sustained writing was almost impossible in that time and place. Here I wrote *Trees Die at the Top* and *Nobody's in Town*, two long short-stories which might be termed novellas if I did not find this term pretentious. Here George Kaufman and I, working together daily for months, wrote the play *Stage Door*.

1933 . . . 1938. The agonizing pangs of the imminent World War II were wrenching the vitals of Europe. Even the United States, gulping health pills and shielding its eyes with dark glasses, began to feel aches and pains in its arms and legs and around the heart. It refused to utter the word War as a prospective victim refuses to utter the dread word cancer.

Uneasily, I worked and played in the Park Avenue penthouse, so un-real, so artificially remote, so typical of the lunatic period. And now the whole lovely mad eyrie with its view of the Hudson River and the East River and Central Park and the brilliant towers and pinnacles to the south seemed almost perceptibly to quiver and sway with the first warning winds of the approaching world-wide hurricane.

A little nagging inner voice that represented the fragments of my Midwest experience and wisdom now cautioned me. "Get out of here. A piece of land and a house in the country, that's the thing. Get out. There is no serenity here. Who can write in a climate of chaos? Writing is your job. Get out!"

I would resume that weekend search for the little dream-house.

Nothing could have been more unrealistic than my imaginary blueprint for this bosky abode. A small house, yet paradoxically roomy. I lived alone, but this house should be so elastic that it could, in case of emergency, accommodate my entire family. This vague emergency was not only indefinite but non-existent; but in this period of North American political and economic history emergencies seemed to lurk just around every corner.

A house, then, so simple that one could close the front door at summer's end and leave the entire shebang to fend for itself in cosy hibernation throughout the winter, returning six months later to find everything shipshape. A quiet spot, away away from New York—but not too remote. High, with a view—but nothing feudal. Neighbors close enough for reassurance but not too near, whose dogs never barked after 11 P.M. A close-clipped lawn of self-cutting self-sustaining green green grass all around. Twin wineglass elms standing sentinel, and an ancient giant oak that had been planted at least a century ago by a forward-looking pioneer. Plenty of bathrooms and fireplaces; no passing motor traffic other than an occasional barely purring delivery vehicle (dead-end road in splendid state of repair); apple trees in a constant routine of blossoming or fruit-bearing. Possibly, later, a cow and chickens and a weedless vegetable garden and live off the land. A station wagon; a bedroom for everybody, pink one blue one buttercup-yellow one; those little crisp dotted swiss curtains at the kitchen windows and what could happen to you then!

Compared with the planners of 1938 the ostrich was a model of prescience and vision. Not only little did we know; nothing did we know, including the extent and utter savagery of Hitler's genocide program; the gigantic treachery of Russia; the superhuman and glorious courage of the English people; the violent destruction of millions of young and useful human beings in the next seven hideous years.

A number of my friends had found and bought handsome old stone farmhouses built a century or more ago by the Quaker settlers in Pennsylvania and New Jersey. These houses, together with the land, were incredibly low in price considering the increasing desirability of that lovely rural countryside and the charm and solidity of the houses. George Kaufman and his wife Beatrice had bought there; Moss Hart and Kitty; the Howard Lindsays; Oscar and Dorothy Hammerstein; Alan Campbell and Dorothy Parker. The countryside was rolling, green, fertile; the stone dwellings spacious and dignified. But my northern

Wisconsin past nudged me, whispering that when I again settled in a green spot it must be up, up from New York, not down into Pennsylvania or New Jersey. My longing was for the cool Connecticut landscape with the Berkshire foothills undulating gently against the horizon; the salt breeze from the Sound, so soothing yet so tonic; the Sound itself glinting in the distance. An hour-and-a-half from the center of New York, just a whirl up the new Merritt Parkway. That was the thing for me. The vine-wreathed dream cottage must be so mild of maintenance that I might be able to keep the New York apartment for winters and use the Connecticut retreat for intensive writing and occasional collapses.

Now real estate agents' cars nosed almost automatically into places up for sale, though no sign notified the passerby. For months I looked at Connecticut farmhouses; colonial houses; ancient salt-box relics crouching by the roadside; square-fronted fretwork Victorian dwellings of substance, and modern atrocities called ranch houses where no ranch ever had existed, and no four-footed creature had ever grazed. Some of these I inspected thoroughly; from others I turned away without another glance. I intensely disliked the early American types which were what I termed quainties. Stumbling over uneven floorboards, unexpected craggy doorsills, into pinched low-ceilinged parlors, boxed-in narrow stairways leading to stifling attic bedrooms, I resolved that I'd never settle for less than big airy rooms with high ceilings and many windows from every one of which there was spread a View. The quainties not only faced the road, they were practically in the road. Built a century or more ago, there had been a sound reason for this.

These period pieces sat crouched by the roadside because in their day no one in his senses would deliberately have faced the task of shoveling by hand a long path leading to the main-traveled road. Connecticut winters were long, numbingly cold, snowbound. Small low-ceilinged rooms might at least partially be warmed by fireplaces or—in a later day—makeshift stoves. Besides, the cows and the horses were there in the barn opposite, just across the road. They must be reached and cared for, snow or no snow, cold or hot.

One year later the little vine-wreathed dream cottage turned out to be an enormous fourteen-room American Georgian stone house on one hundred and sixteen acres of rocky land, embellished with fields, woodland, swimming pool, orchard, walled flower-garden, vast vegetable garden, farmer-caretaker's house, barns, poultry house, tool house, croquet court, pool-house, terraces, driveways and no mortgage. Stone by stone, shovel by shovel, day by day, month by month, with the moxt exhilarating anticipation, it was built for me. My family and my friends said, you're crazy, and how right they were.

The explanation for this was that I had fallen hopelessly, inextricably in love with a gloriously handsome spendthrift stranger.

My meeting with the fascinating and irresistible stranger had come about by chance, as these fatal encounters so often do. I was spending an early spring weekend with Theresa Helburn and her husband at their country place in Weston Connecticut. Terry (no one ever called her Theresa) was a friend of long standing, dating from her days as one of the founders of the Washington Square Players, now historic in the annals of the theatre. Emerging from this early start to become one of the directors of the renowned New York Theatre Guild, Terry—a tiny, terrific and dynamic figure—was known to everyone connected with the theatre in the United States and most of Europe.

At dinner Saturday evening she said, with misleading guilelessness that gave no hint of giant purpose (unless you really knew Terry), "You've been looking at places all over Connecticut for years. I hear agents hide behind desks when they see you coming. I've found the ideal place for you."

Sourly I said, "It's always somebody else's ideal, not mine."

"Will you look at it? I'll drive you up tomorrow before lunch."

"After what I've seen I can look at anything. I suppose it's up on the Canadian border."

"It's actually about seven miles from here."

"Living room with vaulted ceiling made from a barn; wormy old oak beams, used to be a hayloft."

"No ceiling. No house. No nothing. Just heavenly hill with a view."

"I won't build a house. I'll remodel one if I have to. But build in these times! No, thanks."

"Wait till you see this. Perhaps you'll change your mind. It's about one hundred and sixteen acres, more or less—"

"Ideal? I'm looking for two acres. I'd settle for one."

"A whole hill, the highest hill in Easton, with fields and woods and rocks and rills—expecially rocks. It's owned by a sort of farmer. I don't think he actually can bear to part with it, though it's for sale. He's really in love with it. There isn't another view like that on the eastern seaboard."

"One hundred and s— why, I wouldn't take it if your lovesick farmer gave it to me with a brand-new house thrown in. An ideal white elephant."

You could almost hear Terry's mind clicking like a precision machine. "Just look at it. I've got a plan. Sumptuous."

"Sumptuous isn't for hard-working writers."

"But you can look at it, can't you?"

As Terry's car covered those seven or eight miles it was plain that we were climbing almost every foot of the way, hill after hill, sometimes a steep grade to be followed by a gentle incline; my spirits lifted with every inch of altitude. By nature and metabolism I'm a mountain dweller; the ocean depresses me. Given anywhere between five hundred and eight thousand feet, I'm likely to feel as most people do who have just had a very dry very cold martini; not gay, just exhilarated. To the right and the left of the road was woodland with dense green foliage. Higher and higher, the sky seemed nearer and clearer. Houses became rarer, sometimes there was a mile of field and woods between them. Now we were in almost open country of fields and pastures, grazing cattle and faded red barns. We flashed past the neat white steepled church on a knoll, so characteristic of New England. The whole had the look of Connecticut rural land unchanged for a century.

"Look, Terry, peace and quiet are what I've been shouting for— but a joke's a joke. I'm not a recluse."

"It's exactly an hour-and-a-half drive up the Merritt Parkway from the center of New York." We turned left and began the ascent of the steepest grade yet encountered. "This is the last hill. . . . Just wait. It's like a new world."

Darkly I considered this and rejected it. "There must be something wrong with it then."

"No, it's too far for daily commuting, and that's why no New Yorker has bought it. The nearest railroad stations are Westport and Bridgeport. But you don't have to commute. And you can buy the whole hundred and sixteen acres for what four acres would cost in Westport."

"I never said I wanted to go baronial. I just want a quiet high-up green place."

"Then you've got it."

At the corner of the next sharp left turn stood a handsome square-fronted Victorian house, two-storied neat and white behind its white picket fence. Facing it, across the road, the broad backside of the inevitable red barn shut out the valley below. (A few years later I wrote a short story entitled *The Barn Cuts Off the View*. Not bad.) As we passed the house a tawny Irish setter rushed out to bark us on our way.

"Who belongs to the white house and the setter?"

"The man who owns all this land, including yours. We're almost there. See that pond, right? That's about where your land begins. . . . There. That's it. There's the hill."

We had turned off the dead-end road and were jolting along the gullied dirt ruts of the old farmland itself. And what farmland! Eroded, weed-infested, barren. A tumbledown old stone wall marked it from the roadside. It was plain that not a spoonful of fertilizer had gone into this land for half a century. Rock-strewn and pebbled, sluiced down by a thousand rains, it was one of the geological corpses that litter the New England countryside. The glacier that had dragged its long tail over this part of the planet a million years ago had deposited more eggs in the shape of stones and boulders than anything since (and before) Stonehenge.

"Ideal," I said. "Ideal wasteland."

"Wait," said Terry.

Top of the hill now. Out of the car. We stood on the plateau. We faced south. And there it was.

There it was.

"See what I mean?" Terry flung a hand out in the general direction of valleys and hills and treetops and green and green and green and sky and sky. "Knock your eye out, wouldn't it?"

As I first saw it now, and kept it forever in my memory, it seemed to me the loveliest view on the eastern seaboard. Not only would it knock your eye out; it made your heart turn over. There are wider views elsewhere, higher views, more smashing views. The unique beauty of this landscape was its rise and fall, its valleys, its hills beyond; the feathery green of the massed treetops below; the little cluster of white house and red barn and tiny shed in the far distance, perched absurdly on the side of just one hill. And there—just there—distant and shining like a sword in the sun, was the silver glint of Long Island Sound. It was at once as spectacular and friendly, as soft and grand, as the heaven in which we believe in our childhood.

Terry was talking briskly. "About one hundred and sixteen—maybe one hundred and twenty acres, he said."

"Acres," I croaked, meaninglessly, like one in a trance.

Terry's tone became somewhat apologetic. "It's too much for one, of course. But for three or four—I mean—Oliver says it's ridiculous and impossible and he won't stir from our place, but maybe if two or three he would weaken on it."

Uncomprehending, almost unhearing, I still faced the picture spread before me. My face was lifted toward the hills and the distant sky. The trees feathered their leaves gently. "I've always thought lovely was a kind of weak adjective but it exactly—" Then something of what Terry had just said penetrated my consciousness tardily. "What? What are you talking about!"

"Well, I just wanted you to see it first. But everyone's got to be practical, these days. I thought it might be wonderful if three or four of us bought the whole thing together. About thirty acres each, d'you see. You'd build a house and I'd build a house, and maybe Sam Behrman, and I hear that Jascha Heifetz over in Redding is looking for a quiet spot, see what I mean? We'd each build a house and have our own place, big enough for privacy if you want it . . ."

(Privacy if you want it. A writer.)

". . . and of course weekends we'd probably all have our own friends up but we'd build a kind of community swimming pool big enough for all of us and . . . tennis court . . . croquet . . . one huge vegetable garden for the three or four households. . . . What do you think?"

What did I think. Dear Terry. Dear wonderful Terry. What did I think as I looked out across the view spread before me; the peaceful view that wasn't merely a view but a seeming continuation of the land on which we now were standing, so friendly it was, and yielding and gently gay. What did I think? What did Brigham Young think when first the Salt Lake Valley dazzled his eyes? What did Juliet think when first she saw Romeo; or Columbus when he sighted land at last?

Terry had brought me here out of goodness and helpfulness. How could I talk about privacy and solitude without sounding pretentious. What could I say as I mentally contemplated those tri-family weekends.

What piece of land, in co-ownership, is big enough to accommodate multiple families? Remember what happened in the Garden of Eden. What swimming pool, no matter how oceanic its dimensions, could accommodate the whims and foibles and moods of all those weekend talents? Martinis . . . foie gras . . . have another . . . oh, diet on your own time not mine . . . the music was pretty good but the book was awful . . . your serve . . . deuce again. . . . I read the script long before it went into production and I warned them. . . .

I shut my eyes and turned woodenly around and stumbled toward the car.

I had fallen in love. I had fallen in love at first sight with a good-for-nothing, a ne'er-do-well, a gorgeous profligate and wastrel who made all the others I had ever seen appear commonplace, loutish, grubby.

Terry said, "Well? What do you think?"

I shook my head slowly, sadly, even as I walked away. "There must be an easier way to ruin one's life."

3

I once knew a woman who fell in love with a drunkard. Today a victim of this illness is more tactfully and technically termed an alcoholic. This man was charming, drunk or sober; strikingly handsome, intelligent, and absolutely no good. She knew this and naturally he knew it; and certainly all her friends and his knew it. They rallied to prevent her marrying him.

"Look dear," they said, "we know he's fascinating and brilliant and of course he's terrifically good-looking, but he's—well, forgive me darling, but face it—he's a drunk."

"I'll cure him."

"You know perfectly well he's tried everything—religion and Alcoholics Anonymous and analysis and those pills and vitamins and compensatory diets and painting and tennis and it hasn't done a bit of good. He'll ruin your life just as his is already ruined."

"I love him."

"Why can't you love Martin or Giles or Greg? They're such nice sane boys and crazy about you."

"I love him."

So she married him. Her friends were right and she was right. She loved him, she wrestled with the hopeless situation for years, she tended him, enriched his life and it was like pouring Chanel Number 5 into the Ganges. So, having tried and failed (see adage re Loved and Lost) she left him and they both lived more or less happily apart forever after.

So, warned by friends and even foes, I tried to put the sour-soil hilltop out of my mind. Listlessly I again surveyed the old salt-box houses squatting by the roadside, the Connecticut early Victorians, the picture-windowed ranch houses whose windows pictured the picture-windowed ranch houses just across the road. The owners of these dwellings, rabid to be rid of them, said, variously, "We love the house we can't bear to give it up but my husband has been transferred to the California branch . . . our children are all grown up and married and gone away and now we just rattle around in this big . . . the doctor wants my wife to live in a drier climate, her asthma, we thought maybe Arizona . . . we've been very happy here we've been very happy here we've been very . . ."

"What's that noise?"

"Oh, that. That's—uh—that's nothing, it's just a small subdivision they're building across the road, it will be finished in another year and they say they'll sell only to the very nicest people, restricted."

So the morning would go by and the agent and I would stop somewhere for lunch and the afternoon would come to an end and I would say, "Look, my train doesn't go until four-forty, there's just time to run me up and look at that hill in Easton. It's such a restful view." Elaborately casual.

So we would turn up Judd Hill Road toward the soaring, the exhilarating hilltop. Each time it seemed to be more beautiful, more restful and less possible as a project for living.

I sought advice from People Who Cared. I brought my mother up to the hill, and my sister Fan. Julia Ferber, the practical, the experienced, who had learned about life the hard way, said, "You're too smart, you wouldn't be serious about this. A daughter of mine."

Fan said, "Mm, yes, it is absolutely wonderful but isn't it more for a village? a whole village?"

Now I began to bring loving friends and realistic advisers up to the hill. A lawyer friend; a contractor who knew all the intricacies of the building business; friends who liked views but were practical; hard heads; landscape experts; soil experts; tree men. The place boasted not one tree on the site that must naturally be the house location. There were the thirty-five acres of woodland to the east, but only scrub pine on the slope below the brow of the hill. One tree alone had caught my eye when first I had beheld the hilltop view. There, at the edge of the woods, stood a silver beech. How it had come there in the first place no one knew. Its kind is not native to the region. It was gigantic, it was almost awe-inspiring. Within a radius of one hundred miles there was nothing like it, surely. It must have been more than a century old. A natural and glorious wonder such as that, I told myself, would in itself be reason enough for buying a whole hilltop. This did not strike friends and family as being a sound purchasing argument. They all agreed that the view was priceless, was unique. They then said, in turn; don't under any circumstance buy it; it would cost you a fortune to begin to pull the land together, let alone the cost of the house; a road in here alone would cost you ten thousand dollars; is there water on the place I mean top of a hill how about artesian wells and so forth; this place would drink money like a thirsty elephant year after year, not just the original cost which would be astral; why don't you buy a little place you can turn the key and walk away from it whenever you want to; you're crazy if you buy this hunk of no-good land; why don't you buy or even build a little place, etc.

"I'm not buying a place in order to walk away from it."

"You'll be sorry."

Then, one day, after a morning and afternoon of looking at half a dozen houses and rejecting them all I slumped back into the car and said, as I had so many times in these past months, "Let's just drive to that hill in Easton, get a look at the sunset." It was late afternoon, I was weary, depressed, I had had a week of hard work in New York, a week of hard work lay ahead of me. It was autumn. Soon the search for this refuge from a world of city traffic and telephones and pressures and weariness and polluted air and doubts and fears and noise would have to be postponed until spring again came to the Connecticut countryside. I was feeling quite sorry for myself.

The car turned the corner of Judd Road into the dead-end Maple Road. There was the familiar solid white Victorian house that belonged to the owner of all this delectable indigestible land. And there ahead was the glorious hill and the view undulating away to the horizon. I could see it long before we came to it, as I shut my eyes on our way up the dirt road. I relaxed then and breathed the sweet air. A day of frustration and disappointment and rejection. Bad for a writer. Aloud I said, to my own surprise that amounted to shock, "It's good to be coming home."

"How's that again?" said the puzzled agent.

"Oh, I was just—nothing—"

But I knew. Unconsciously I had given it utterance. I knew I was going to marry the drunkard, not to reform him, but because I loved him. This was the place. Stones, rocks, weeds, sour land, neglected woods, hardpan soil, erosion, remoteness—this was the place.

But perhaps it couldn't be mine, after all. What if Terry Helburn really wanted it. The first chance at it was hers, rightly. It was she who had told me about it.

It now turned out she not only didn't want it, not only had she forgotten that she had ever considered it, but she tried to talk me out of considering it.

"Alone!" she said, as though doubting her senses. "You mean you want to buy it alone?"

"Yes."

"You're crazy."

"I know."

"You'll be sorry."

"I love it."

"So does the man who owns it. I'll bet he'll never sell it. I hope."

This almost turned out to be a shrewd prediction. The owner had put this land up for sale. Harold Stern, an astute and persuasive young attorney in the law firm directing my legal affairs, had succeeded in obtaining an option on the property. Legally, it was mine to purchase if I wished, within a stated time and by forfeiting a given sum if I decided in the negative. But when it came to signing the documents of sale the seller seemed never to be available. Date after date was agreed on, only to be broken. After weeks of this behavior stern measures were taken. We met at eleven in the morning at the office of the lawyer in Bridgeport. At three o'clock that afternoon we were still there —the owner and his lawyer and his son; my lawyer and I. The papers still were unsigned. . . . Could he have the use of the old barn down by the roadside for the storage of his hay for the next year? . . . Yes. . . . Could his cows be watered at the pond just below the woods hill? . . . Yes. . . . Could they graze in the meadow and on the slopes surrounding this? . . . Yes. . . . Could he cut and store for his own stock such scrub hay as the land still might yield this next summer? . . . Well—uh—yes. Still he sat there and did not sign.

Harold, a quietly effective person, now rose and seemed to tower as he stood. "It's almost three o'clock, we've been here since eleven. I must get back to New York. You gave us an option to buy this land. We've fulfilled all the required terms and many others that needn't have been granted. Legally, you're obliged to sign these papers. What do you want? What's wrong?"

We sat staring at the owner—this solid and personable man in his middle years. The muscular body bespoke strength. Silent, he sat there in his sober black suit, his Sunday suit. His color was ruddier than usual. Two bright pink circles, marks of repressed emotion, stood out on the broad cheekbones. His mouth was set with resolution beneath the tan mustache that swooped tidily downward. His strong hands, the fingers widespread, rested on his black-clothed knees as he leaned forward intently, still without speaking. The body was rugged and firm as a tree-trunk. The face as sound and rosy as an autumn apple. And as silent.

The young lawyer spoke again, quietly but insistently now. "What is the trouble? Why do you refuse to sign?"

The round blue eyes became bluer, brighter. He spoke slowly, evidently under emotion.

"I don't want you should make Nazi camp on my land."

There was a stunned silence.

That summer, in the village of Southbury Connecticut, only a few miles distant, a Nazi-American organization had actually contrived under an assumed name to buy a large acreage to be used as a Nazi training camp. The local newspapers and the New York newspapers had revealed this fact and had published accounts of the maneuvers there. The United States was not at war with Germany, we were still what is called a neutral nation. The land had been bought and paid for. Meanwhile the fair Southbury fields resounded to the tramp of heavy booted feet; martial German gutturals challenged the bells in the neat white New England church; and the swastika flaunted its menacing zigzags. The goose-stepping figures in the uniforms of the monsters who, in the next seven terrible years were so nearly to destroy the civilized world, now drilled in martial formation, contemptuous of the storm of remonstrance that arose from the outraged New England countryside.

My mind rejected what I had just heard. Until this moment I had taken no vocal part in these exasperating negotiations. But this was too much.

"What did you say! What's that you said!"

Firmly, he repeated it. "I don't sign because I don't want you should make Nazi camp on my land."

"Nazi camp! Me! You don't understand. I'm a Jew."

"Make no difference." He spoke with additional emphasis, and the outspread hands on his knees doubled now into fists. "I don't want you should make Nazi camp on my land."

Muddled though he was, but fundamentally so sound in principle, I found this astounding statement so endearing that, in the years spent on Treasure Hill, I never ceased to have a reassuring feeling that here was a neighbor and a friend.

Within the next hour we were able to convince him that my sympathies were not exactly with the Nazis. The necessary papers finally were signed. The big hunk of semi-wilderness that, in the next decade, was to be tamed and made tidy, was incredibly mine.

Only one utterly bemused could have contemplated the purchase of this glorious, unruly, stone-ridden wasteland.

There now began the gigantic labor of clearing the land, building the house, planting trees, laying stone walls, drilling wells, engaging a farmer-caretaker who had a practical knowledge of mechanics, agriculture and stock-raising. Curiously enough I found this man and, in the years to come, one other who succeeded him. I don't know if this type now exists in a world a quarter of a century older and a thousand times less possessed of a sense of responsibility. But the United States in the years just preceding the Second World War still boasted that invaluable Proteus who could mend a leaking pipe as a plumber; milk a cow as a dairyman; plow and plant as a farmer; bring forth roses or raspberries, asparagus and cauliflower, lettuce and apples and grapes, in the role of horticulturist. Not to mention the magic ability to clean and vacuum a swimming pool, lay a garden stone-walk, paint a red barn white.

I simply didn't know what I had undertaken.

When I think of it now, after almost a quarter of a century has elapsed, I always am freshly amazed at the indomitability of the utterly ignorant. This has been more aptly phrased by one who said, "Fools rush in, etc." I never before had built a house; but this wasn't a house merely, it was a stone mansion; I never before had owned land, but this wasn't land merely—it was one hundred and sixteen acres of scrub, hardpan, weeds, gullies, swamp and rock. Almost every element that

should be contained in productive soil was absent in this starved acreage. Evidently not a spoonful of fertilizer or chemical had been given
in refreshment of this barren sleeping beauty. In the rewarding thirteen
years of my life on Treasure Hill I never thought of money in terms of a
trip to Europe, a fur coat, an ornament, a personal luxury. You put one
word down after another on a piece of white paper stuck into the typewriter, and it was transformed into tons of lime, yards of fertilizer;
tractor, plow, motor; farm labor wages; cows, sheep; drainage, artesian
wells. I thought, much too grandly, that one day there would be at least
one hundred acres of Connecticut land which would be the better for
my having owned it. Everything remained to be done. The place was
as uninhabitable as though the native Indians had just left it—less
habitable, really, one should say in fairness to the American Indian. I
had learned that the American Indians for centuries had used fish for
the fertilization of their most sustaining crop—maize or corn. In each
hillock planted with corn they had slipped a fish and heaped it over
with a covering of soil. In the early spring of those past centuries the
Atlantic coast rivers had glinted with shad. It was a simple matter then
to catch them by the thousands, mingle them with the unfruitful New
England soil, and to wait confidently for the maize—the tall green
tasseled beauties—to emerge and to toss their silken locks in the breeze.
But the American Indian had long ago been herded into reservations,
his talents and his natural aptitudes wasted and lost. The fields and
meadows of Treasure Hill were not fish-fed. Tons of commercial
fertilizer were stuffed into it, not to mention all the cow manure and
chicken droppings into which we could lay a shovel.

The thing to do was to work at writing all that spring and summer
and autumn while the house was being built. This seemed to me a
normal and reasonable arrangement. Under these conditions, as the
book was to be entitled A *Peculiar Treasure*, I decided to name the
house and land Treasure Hill. I would temporarily settle down somewhere nearby (but not too near) during the process of building.

A professional writer is a dedicated person. I had trained myself to
write in any place that was reasonably quiet and even remotely comfortable. I have written, through this half century and more of daily
writing, in all sorts of places under whatever conditions. I have written
in bathrooms and aboard ships; on jet planes and in woodsheds; on
trains between New York and San Francisco or Paris to Madrid; in bed

at home or propped up on a hospital contraption; in hotels; cellars, motels, automobiles; well or ill, happy or despairing.

Settle down for six months somewhere nearby (but not too near) while the house is being built. Keep the schedule of working hours that you've held to since you were twenty-one; at the typewriter nine every morning, day after day. A thousand words a day, a thousand words a day—if possible. If, next day, they're not good enough pull them out and write better ones. (Here I should—but shan't—insert a brief and venomous paragraph on those people who say, "How do you write? Inspiration? When the spirit moves you?") I know of no professional writer who doesn't get to work every day as does a stenographer or a bus driver or a President of the United States. The difference is that the writer is accountable to no one but himself, which makes for a tough taskmaster; and the writer works as a rule seven days a week instead of the usual worker's five.

In that spring of 1938 I found myself trying to outline and fill in a sort of map or blueprint that might show me where I had been, not geographically, but mentally and psychologically; and in what direction I should continue that fascinating journey. I might even, by this method, dispel the mists and vanquish some of the monsters that imperiled progress along the tortuous path.

I began to write the book entitled *A Peculiar Treasure*. It was, to my amazement, an autobiography. Earlier I would have sworn that if I lived to be two hundred years old and found myself completely devoid of writing ideas, I never would turn to the story of my own life as a book plan. But here was my own country—and the rest of the civilized world—sitting by in a sort of horrified desuetude while Germany methodically and mathematically and with characteristic German thoroughness proceeded with the business of killing a preliminary six million Jews and, hopefully, all Jews, while conquering the countries of the world. Filled with a blazing sense of injustice and helpless fury and seething indignation I turned to the only weapon I possessed—my knowledge and experience as a writer. I would express my emotion in a novel. No. I would write a series of articles. Cold unpalatable. Well, then, I would write about the Midwestern middle-class American Jewish family I knew best, presenting them as typical—which they were. My own family. It would have to be an autobiography. Sit down in front of that typewriter and write it, plain. If you don't, this rage and frustration will kill you too (as a writer) and that will be another minor triumph for Hitler.

There were decades to cover. I had some sporadic diaries of my own; I had the touching and courageous diaries of my mother, begun when she was a high-spirited young bride. Fortunately, I had talked to her many times about her childhood and her girlhood in the Chicago of her pre-marriage days; of her young womanhood and middle age in small Midwestern towns with a blind husband and two small daughters to support. I never had talked at length in this way with my father. He had come to the United States from Hungary at the age of seventeen. Now that it was too late, how I wished that I had learned from him something of his childhood in Eperye, Hungary; his journey to the United States when still only a boy; his early struggles in a strange country, his young manhood, his marriage.

He had been a handsome man of medium height with a little Hungarian swagger about the shoulders as he walked; a skin so fair and poreless that any girl would have envied it; a gentle man with—paradoxically—a quick temper. He was the most inept man of business imaginable, and when darkness fell upon the bright brown eyes heaven knows how the blind man and the two small Ferber girls would have made out in the world if Julia Ferber had not taken over. She, too, knew nothing of business but she learned; triumphantly she learned.

Children don't talk with their parents about these things. Though bone of their bone, flesh of their flesh, dependent from birth to adult age upon these two usually benevolent monitors for even the most elementary sustenance, the young ordinarily have no interest in or curiosity about their parents as human beings. Mommy and Daddy. Then Mom and Dad. Then They. Necessary nuisances, soon to be dispensed with. I never have married. I have no children. I have grandnieces and a grandnephew who are intelligent and delightful. Will they, I wonder, ever be interested to talk to their parents about their childhood of the late 1920s and 1940s and 1950s; their struggles, if any; their triumphs if any; their part in the cataclysm called World War II. Practically everything these adult parents did and said and were must have had its effect on the unaware offspring. If only for financial reasons, let alone sheer entertainment, it might be cheaper to obtain this information now rather than have it painfully dredged up by an analyst twenty years from now.

If practiced in every land it might even help to instill in the young an abhorrence of the savage anachronism known as War.

Now then. Be practical, be realistic (I, who had just bought one hundred and sixteen acres of bald Connecticut hardpan). I rented a pleasant house, furnished, less than fifteen minutes by automobile from the Hill on which construction already had begun. The blueprints of the house and the detailed outline of the book had been painstakingly planned and revised and improved during the autumn and winter in New York. Now both book and house were well on their way. They had started off neck-and-neck. Their finish was anyone's guess. The book was the expression of my life as I had lived it and of the times as they had unfurled with the years. The house was, I suppose, an expression of the life I hoped to live in the future.

The spring and summer and autumn turned out to be one of the most exhilarating periods I had ever experienced, mentally and emotionally; and the most painful physically. Understandably, I had developed a quite splendid duodenal ulcer. I was working under intense pressure for I had, unwisely, arranged to have the book serialized in a magazine before book publication.

Up at seven daily. A brief walk down the road before sitting down in front of the typewriter to begin the hours of work. A talk with Mrs. Rebecca Henry about the day's meals, the household plans. What capability what serenity what quiet humor had radiated from her in the many years in which she so expertly had kept my house in order. What goodness and intelligence, what understanding and compassion dwelt in that dark madonna face. And, emerging magically from her kitchen, what crème brûlée, what corn pudding, what lobster aspic, what succulent chicken; what tiny golden pancakes or waffles for the more leisurely Sunday morning breakfast.

Eight-thirty, nine o'clock. Into the little makeshift workroom on the second floor, away from household sounds, road sounds, telephones, as is the way of all the neurotic tribe of writers. The typewriter on the small table by the window, the light falling over the left shoulder, properly. No view. Views are too distracting. (What are you going to do about the view from Treasure Hill? Never mind. You'll solve that when you come to it.) From this window could be seen only a bit of orderly lawn and a gigantic oak that must have been a century old. Its branches were the size of a full-grown tree and its trunk was a massive pillar measuring yards in circumference. A tree doesn't distract one; it soothes. At least this one had that effect until the great and disastrous hurricane of that September tore into the Connecticut landscape and set the noble patriarchal old tree to writhing and twisting in the antics of a rock-and-roll beatnik.

The hungry maw of the magazine in which the book was being serialized ate up twenty- or twenty-five thousand words a month for a six months' stretch. A thousand words a day, a thousand words a day. A nagging and down-breaking conversation with myself went on daily just before the work period began each morning. . . . It can't be done. . . . What do you think you are! A machine or something! . . . Well, Dickens did it and Thackeray and Stephen Crane and Sinclair Lewis and Hemingway and Marquand and de Maupassant and Sidney Porter. . . . So stop that doodling, you know what you want to say: say it.

Those early years of newspaper work doubtless had trained me to meet a deadline. So now, at the end of each month, the sheaf of type-written sheets went to the editor. I went nowhere I saw no one: I worked and walked and slept and worked and my diversion and excitement came daily at about three o'clock when I stopped work and drove up to the Hill. The distance between the rented house and the project that was Treasure Hill was just right. If it had been nearer, the temptation to dash up there early in the morning before commencing my own work, or at noon before my day's stint was finished, would have been harrowing. I had no guests. I went practically nowhere. This pattern of self-immolation is familiar to any professional writer worth reading. The writer does not look upon it even remotely as a hardship. It is a way of life. Every day he or she is shut up in a room with a company of chosen people created by himself. Witty conversation, dull dialogue, murder, love, marriage, violence, triumph, failure, birth, death—anything can happen in that room. Only one thing must not happen; that dread thing, interruption. This routine, this treadmill of work walk eat sleep read is the writer's heaven. Anything less than a holocaust is resented as an unnecessary interruption.

The progress on the book, the progress on the house, this seemed excitement enough for anyone; certainly it was for me. By this time Treasure Hill had been given the nickname of Ferber's Folly. A book to finish, a house to build, a large acreage to clear and landscape, trees to plant. I set my sights for autumn. This was, of course, madness, but like many mad plans, it worked out. Today I would no more plan a program such as that than I would attempt simultaneously to build the Taj Mahal and write *War and Peace*. Friends and family had sorrowfully but firmly washed their hands of the whole crazy business.

They waited ready and, I thought, a shade eager, to aid me when and if I should collapse. In this I failed them.

Now, a quarter of a century later, I realize that the vexations, the irritations, the disappointments, even the possible tragedies that usually plague the owner of a house a-building were much greater in this case than one ordinarily encounters. Curiously enough, aside from two tragedies, one major and one minor, the almost daily difficulties bothered me scarcely at all. Considering my low boiling point in matters of irritation and frustration this was a mystifying state of mind and behavior to my aloofly watchful family and friends. Not to me—or it wouldn't have been if I had thought about it, which I didn't.

I was having a wonderful time, pressure or no pressure, ulcer or no ulcer, progress or no progress on the two big projects. There was the land under my feet; there was the enchanting view daily as I visited the Hill; there was the house slowly taking the form of a habitation; there in the place that temporarily housed me were the pages marching tidily out of the typewriter and into the editor's office. The gruesome world of the shrieking paranoiac Hitler in Europe, the mounting unemployment and apprehension in the United States, took on a kind of unreality. Only the house was real and the land was real and the book was real. There they were, you could see them you could feel them, you knew where they were and what they were, you yourself were shaping them. Nothing unpleasant mattered if you had land of your own a house of your own a book to be published. What an ostrich!

There was another major reason for my cosy state of nirvana. All over the Hill, about the growing house and the grounds there swarmed a blithe and heartwarming crew of workmen. Perhaps I saw their perfection only through my love-bewitched eyes. I only know I can't recall one churlish word, one rude incident, one disagreeable or purposely careless act. These men represented American labor in a day and in a crisis that might have excused any number of resentments. There was no I-only-work-here spirit among them. Their backgrounds were Italian-American, Swedish-American, Norwegian-American, Polish, Czech, and native New England American. They were all citizens of the State of

Connecticut, Fairfield County. None lived more than twelve miles distant from Treasure Hill. They came to work in rather ramshackle cars, for this was the day, not merely of unemployment but of low and lower wages, no matter how talented the craftsman. There was an added zest for me in the knowledge that this Connecticut house in which I was to become a citizen of Connecticut was being built, inch by inch, by Connecticut citizens only, from the architect to the water boy. The architect was Phillip Sands Graham, gifted graduate of Yale University in New Haven Connecticut; the water boy was the teenage son of the contractor-builder Louis Forsell—the soft-spoken clear-headed Lou who lived just down the road two minutes distant.

All these men were careful craftsmen, they were glad of the work in these perilous times, they were interested. They were amused and mystified by the fact that a middle-aged woman was building, alone and evidently with no outside help or advice, a very large stone house on a very large tract of very high land in a very remote situation; all this for the purpose of living alone in this handsome house, and writing. Moreover, she came from New York. In the months to come I learned that if you moved to Connecticut from New York one thing was fixed and immovable; even though you had been born in Kalamazoo Michigan as I had been and never had owned an inch of New York land, you were to the New England mind a New Yorker forever; and a New Yorker, no matter how long the Connecticut tenure, was a foreigner; and not only was a New Yorker a foreigner but all New Yorkers (though I had worked as a writer for a living since I was seventeen and still was engaged in this chancey pursuit) were rich.

Carpenters, stone masons, plasterers, painters; landscape men; tree experts; plumbers, heating equipment men; road builders; farmer-caretakers; swimming pool contractors; electricians; interior decorators; bricklayers; wall-builders; insurance salesmen, car salesmen; tax collectors; artesian well diggers.

Artesian well diggers. Water does not flow uphill. Vaguely, quite remotely, I suppose I always had accepted this fact of nature without question. Now this fact became a monumental difficulty. The building site of the Treasure Hill house was a bit more than five hundred feet above the level of Long Island Sound that glinted so brilliantly in the distance beyond the rise and fall of the Berkshire foothills. But when you have planned and are building a house containing seven baths, with still another bathroom and a lavatory in the farmer-caretaker's cottage that soon would stand perhaps fifty yards distant from the main house; not to mention a swimming pool measuring fifty by twenty-five feet; and sprinkler pipes laid all over the place for the watering of vegetable gardens, flower gardens, trees, shrubs, you pray for an artesian well that will give you thirty gallons a minute and you hope blindly for fifteen because that is your barest minimum need.

After weeks of drilling in the chosen spot we got three gallons a minute. It was like a single drop of water to a man dying of thirst in the desert. Better none than that trickle. There on the crest of the Hill was the artesian well rig, its great hammer going *thump-bump thump-bump* as it drove the searching bore through the soil, through the hard-pan, through the glacial rubble and into the basic rock that was millions of years old. There, somewhere, there must be a crack, a cleft, a soft layer below the barrier of rock through which a secret stream of clear cold water flowed lavishly. Thirty gallons, please! Thirty—well, all right—twenty—fifteen . . .

Thump-clump thump-clump foot after foot through the sullen arid rock at just so many dollars the foot. Every day at about three-thirty I rushed up to the well site. Long before I turned into the Hill road I heard always the steady slambang of the giant hammer. Always I heard it with a sinking heart, for I knew that only silence would mean that the precious fifteen—twenty—thirty gallons had been yielded from the reluctant land. No Texas wildcatter hoping for millions to emerge in oil from the hole in the ground; no Alaska prospector peering into the perma-frost for the first glint that might prove to be gold, ever watched with breath more bated than mine as I prayed for nothing more rich than just plain clear clean water.

Each day I would leap from the car, sprint toward the sound of the *plunkbangplunk*. "What have you got?"

"Three, same's always." They were experienced workmen. Leaning against the well rig, helpless to do more than they were doing. The Thing itself must find the water. Their faces were expressionless but I knew their hopes and their sympathies were with me. They never urged me to continue, foot after foot after foot.

"Maybe tomorrow. Maybe we'll hit it tomorrow," I would say. It was like a gamble. I rather enjoyed it, foolishly.

Three hundred feet bored into the rock-bound earth. Three hundred and fifty. Four hundred.

"We hit four fifty today." There was an ominous note in his voice.

"How deep do you think we ought to keep on going?"

But he was too wise to commit himself. "Couldn't say, scarcely."

"Five hundred? Shall we go five hundred feet?"

Compassion moved him to a cautious warning. "They brought in thirty-five gallons at twenty feet down to that new Berringer place."

"Where's that?"

"Trumbull."

"That's wonderful. Maybe if we keep on—"

"The Berringer place is more low-laying."

Four fifty. Four seventy-five. Five hundred.

Three gallons.

A water-diviner, some of my more medieval-minded friends advised me. Get one of those fellows poke around with a willow switch and the thing jumps when it hits a water pocket deep down, and there's your well, no kidding, I've seen it done. The Blatzes over in Redding . . . the Cassaways in Fairfield, they went down six hundred feet and not a drop and then this guy comes along with a willow switch . . .

I believe in miracles as anyone must, in a measure, who has ever been alive on the planet Earth. So while the rig on the hilltop kept up its thumping and the faces of the men who tended it became even more impassive if possible, the man with the willow divining rod was sent for and arrived.

He was an appropriately damp and limp young man, pallid and dour, which seemed to me just right for a diviner. But he brought his mother with him, day after day; and she sat on a rock nearby while he stumbled hither and yon, divining. Each day she brought their lunch in a brown paper bag and she sat and sat and sat and I think that did it. No really self-respecting divining rod will work a miracle under such circumstances.

I feel certain that Moses, causing the water to gush forth as he smote the rock in the desert, never would have raised a trickle with his divine divining rod if his adoring mama, or even Pharaoh's daughter had been hovering on a nearby rock with a brown paper bag of lunch in her lap. It isn't the right atmosphere for magic.

Thump-thump-thump went the rig at the top of Treasure Hill.

The house was going up, the trees were being planted, the stone walls rebuilt. A mirage in the desert.

"Look," I said in desperation to Lou Forsell, "someone told me last week about a wonderful geologist who's the head of the geology department at Yale. Bailey or Bradley or something. He must know what's going on beneath all this rock. I'm going to call him."

"Yeh, do that. That's an idea." There was a startled look in the steady blue eyes.

Fools rush in, as everyone knows. It frequently saves a lot of wear and tear.

I telephoned Yale University at New Haven. I actually got my man. The voice was courteous, quiet, reassuring. He heard me patiently.

"I'm drilling a well in Easton for my new house there. We're having trouble. It's a big house. And a pool and farm and so forth. We've gone down five hundred feet. Three gallons. How much deeper do you think we ought to go? As a geologist, I mean."

As a geologist I mean. I later learned that the government of India, the governments of practically all the arid spots of the world gladly availed themselves of this great scientist's geological knowledge in order to relieve their needs or to abandon their projects as the case might be. He was The Authority.

Now his quietly authoritative voice came to me so logically, so reassuringly. "Have you a map of the place? And a survey? And an aerial photograph? Or all three, and if possible a plan drawing on which you can almost pinpoint the location of your well site?"

"Yes!" I trilled, as though this solved everything. Very thorough type I was.

"Just mail them to me, please."

"Couldn't you—uh—come and have a look at it?"

"Looking at it wouldn't help, really. It's the formation that tells the actual story."

Pooh, I thought. How do you know what's going on five hundred feet below the surface of the earth! Now the quiet voice was saying an astonishing thing, though I hadn't the intelligence then to know what it meant. "I'll try to come up if it's at all possible."

"When?"

A moment's hesitation. "I can't say, exactly. When and if I can. I can't promise. I am going away on Thursday." It turned out that this casual going-away term applied to a plea from some government in Africa or Asia or South America or Europe that he aid them in a waterless crisis. I don't remember which continent but I still recall my own eventual scarlet embarrassment. It was as though a blandly thoughtless mother had telephoned Albert Einstein to ask if he'd solve her small son's fourth grade arithmetic problem.

Two days later the reply with its firm findings came to me from Yale. The letter said: "The rock formation at the point of your present operation extends down approximately eight thousand miles . . ."

Miles!

". . . or more. Results in terms of yield will be the same as they now are. Regardless of how deep you drill you will not get more than three gallons per minute. My advice is to desist. . . ."

Desist. Eight thousand miles of rock. Damn right I'll desist, I said savagely to myself, unless I want to see eight million Chinese swarming up out of my artesian well.

". . . I suggest that you try the following operation. Have the well rig moved to the spot which I have indicated on the geological map of your land. If you decide to retain the present three-gallon well it probably will supply water sufficient for your house only. The site of the second possible water source is about fifty feet distant and at the base of a slope as you will see. It is a small hollow surrounded by gentle slopes. Drill there not more than fifteen feet. I have indicated the precise spot. This well should, at fifteen feet, yield a flow of twelve gallons per minute. It doubtless is not the flow you originally hoped to have but it should suffice for your needs. If, at fifteen feet, you do not get this flow abandon this second well immediately. It will be useless to drill further in this spot."

And he was, he wrote in closing, sincerely mine with best wishes, etc.

We moved the well rig to the spot indicated, though the operators were as skeptical as they had been in the case of the water diviner. More skeptical, really. They had known, they admitted, of a willow stick having magically dipped at a spot which later out-gushed Old Faithful. But this, they said, was sure a new one on them. Fifteen feet! they said.

The well rig was set up in the spot indicated. The *thump-bump* sounded afresh over the hills and valleys. They went down fifteen feet. We got twelve gallons of water per minute.

Not only was he sincerely mine; I have been sincerely his for these past twenty-five years, though I've never seen him. He is my notion of a hero and a knight in the shining armor of scientific knowledge. I'd rather meet him and speak to him than to the first man to reach the moon. I don't need the moon. But water is necessary to my survival, and yours.

4

"That's right, the stones are right here on the place," Lou Forsell said patiently. "All those stone walls, about a mile of them, and more. But I wouldn't do that. I'm just telling you because it'll be a whole lot cheaper if we go out and buy the stones. Outside."

"But I want the house built of the old stone walls on the place. They've been here a million years. They were dragged down by the glaciers. They were here before the Puritans, before the Indians, before the earth cooled, probably, and jelled them. I want my house built of the old stone walls on the place. The walls were built a hundred years ago—two hundred."

"But if you take a notion to sell off a piece of that land, back near your dividing line, I mean—"

"I wouldn't dream of having someone else on Treasure Hill. It will make all the difference in the world to me if I know that my house actually is built of the old stone walls that divided the pastures and the fields centuries ago. You can see that, surely."

Lou Forsell was a knowledgeable builder, a practical man, a kindly and a thrifty man. Now the steady blue eyes took on a look of compassion. "I get your notion. I thought you ought to know, anyway, the stones we'd buy, they'd come a good deal cheaper, though maybe that sounds unlikely to you."

"Certainly does."

"It's this way. Every stone off the walls—they're dry walls, of course—would have to be picked up by hand and selected for color, size, shape and so on. Some are dark and some are light. Some big others little. All kinds of shapes but they've got to be fitted or else cut by hand, every one, by the stone masons. You said you didn't want a dark stone house, you wanted a light one. Gay, you said. A gay stone house. Not gloomy looking, you said."

"Most stone houses look like miniature Sing Sings or fortresses with turrets and moats and boiling oil ready for uninvited friends. I want this stone house to be gay."

Lou always got the idea if you could just break down the practical side. He even began to look a bit dreamy now—with hard-headed Swedish undertones.

"Some of those old stones are pinkish cast, that's a fact. And some pure white and some pale kind of gray. Light color. That's where the catch comes in, you got to pick them one by one and leave the dark ones—the dark gray and the brown. That takes time. And time is what you're paying for by the hour. I'm just telling you. You got a right to know."

"All right. I know."

"And after they've picked the right ones they'll pile them on the stone boat, one at a time, and haul them down to here—and then Angelo—"

"Stone boat?" I wasn't prepared for this nautical transportation.

"Stone boat. You know. It's a kind of flat sled made of heavy timber, it's for hauling stones, they used to hitch it to oxen. Now you hitch it to the tractor."

"Not so picturesque—but more practical."

Lou permitted himself a fleeting but grim smile. "You're the boss. Long as you know what's ahead, it's all right with me. Now, about the cutting and shaping and fitting and so on. There isn't a better stone mason in Connecticut than Angelo, it takes the Italians to do that kind of job. Angelo and his boys, they'll have to chip and fit every stone, one at a time, just so. Sling in the mortar, set the stone, and then point the mortar by hand, in between."

"Point?"

"Pointing, it's called. Most stone masons, the general run, they won't do that. Don't even know how, and wouldn't if they did. But Angelo, he knows. He does it with his thumb, smooth as butter." He made a little motion with his right thumb, fist doubled.

Tidily, I ran this new knowledge through my mind. Old stone

walls half a mile back. White. Pink-tinged. Palest oyster gray. Stone boat. Tractor. Chip. Cut. Fit. Mortar. Point.

"There's a lot more to building a house than you think," I remarked idiotically, "when you first plan it all."

"That's the truth. But I wanted you to know why I said cheaper to buy the stone outside."

"Not gay."

"You're the one has to be pleased." Non-committal; but I thought there was just a tinge of approval in his voice.

"Tell him, will you, Lou? Angelo, I mean. He'll think I'm crazy. Tell him it's because I want a happy-looking stone house. Gay."

"Oh, he'll know ahead of you, Angelo will. Italian."

In an almost completely unrealistic moment I had decided that every room in the house, including the kitchen, must have a view of the View. This, it turned out, made the house just about one-third more costly than a compact house would have been. Lou Forsell had pointed this out to me and, airily, I had risen above it. The distance from the far kitchen wing at one end to the covered terrace beyond the living room at the far opposite end amounted, in footage or perhaps mileage to what actors—in the old days of the train-traveling road companies— used to call a sleeper jump.

To watch Angelo, the master stone mason, at his craft was to see an artist in action. I stood fascinated, as the small strong brown hands lifted and balanced each separate stone as though weighing it. He scanned it then, and looked again at its waiting mates, already imbedded in their mortar. Then he again scanned the stone in his hands, and turned it and chipped and hammered so that it would fit into the lines of its waiting neighbor stone. Then the trowel deposited its dollop of mortar, the stone nestled next its neighbor, a scrape of the trowel and the knife edge to clear away the excess; and then the brown thumb below the stone's base made the smooth curve of perfection. It was a performance intricately craftsmanlike yet simple-seeming; masterly, repetitious but infinitely varied. One watched it in utter fascination as the stone house—the gay stone house—went up inch by inch before my eyes.

Angelo lived in Bridgeport and he was life itself. He was Italy in sound and successful transplantation to the United States. His pride in his craft was deep and articulate. There was no I-only-work-here in

Angelo's philosophy. The big crew at work on Treasure Hill thought the house a fine example of building and that I must be what New England termed touched in the head to build it. They had pride in their work and were glad of the work itself. I was a strange specimen to them but they did not reject me, and as the months went by there developed a camaraderie which comes with a common interest shared.

They used to bring their wives and children up occasionally, Sundays, to have a look at this fine stone structure which was their handiwork, and perhaps to have a look at the loony lady who was to live in it, if it so chanced that she, too, had come up for a Sunday fond look.

One Sunday I drove up just in time to see the somewhat battered car just ahead of me turn into Treasure Hill and chug its way to the top. There it stopped in front of the house and disgorged its passengers. The car was small. Four people, or possibly five, could have sat in it none too spaciously. Now out of it spilled eight—ten—twelve—thirteen people. The effect was almost exactly like an amusing act that, just at that time, was part of the comedy routine being used in Ringling's Circus at Madison Square Garden. It was an hilarious act in which a tiny car drove into the tanbark ring, stopped, and out of which popped what seemed to be an endless and utterly improbable number of little passengers while the eyes of the audience rejected what they actually saw, knowing the infallible rule of nature that two bodies cannot occupy the same space at the same time.

Now it was Angelo's family—wife, children, sons, daughters, grandchildren—come to view the patriarch's masterpiece. As the patriarch was in his forties at the most, brown, wiry, tough as a sap-filled tree, this family group seemed to me much more an achievement than the edifice they had come to see.

When the final stone was in place and the roof serenely topping the whole, the old New England custom of the roof-tree was observed at Treasure Hill. Once the roof was firmly on your house you could defy even the New England elements. A lot they knew about the amazing series of hurricanes—beginning that September—which through the next decades were to send roofs flying through the Connecticut air like leaves in autumn. My roof, luckily, was not to be one of these.

A growing green-leafed branch now was plucked from a tree and fastened like a pert tassel to the highest point at the front and center-face of the roof. The roof-tree. A lucky symbol. A green flag of triumph, of well-done work completed, of life continuing to be lived in civilization. Perhaps the early Puritans started this pleasant custom. Perhaps it dated from the Stone Age. I don't know. (*Note to E.F.: Look it up.*) There was the house, there was the roof, there was the symbol of accomplishment. The owner, according to custom, stands the modest treat of beer and sandwiches to the entire work-crew once the roof-tree is in place. The cases of beer and the good thick ham and cheese and salami sandwiches went the rounds, while the sunburned faces were turned up toward the housetop, and the glasses were lifted toward the roof-tree. It was a good feeling; it was a good house. The handsome friendly stone structure stood in outline against the afternoon sky there at the crest of the hill and it did not quarrel with the New England landscape for its body had come out of the land itself, born through aeons of frost and sun and frost and sun. It was early autumn. I felt that the past six months had followed a pattern of actual accomplishment. Here were two tangible proofs.

The book—one hundred two hundred three hundred typewritten pages—was not yet finished but it had reassuring bulk as you rather childishly hefted it in your two hands. The house, solid and seemly, made Treasure Hill come alive. Never, before or since, have I felt so talented and so at peace with a world which, from that very September, was not to know peace again for decades; perhaps never again would know it.

In another two or three weeks I would be back in the New York penthouse whose sooty flowers and fountains now seemed to me so shabby and make-believe. Book and house were to be finished during these winter months to come.

The house was two houses, really; one inside the other. There was first a house of wood—a frame house, it was called—and enclosing that was the stone house. Between the two the space had been filled and packed with the solid steel wool padding of insulation material to shut out the cold in winter and the dampness of early spring and autumn rains. An uneven roof line. Two steps down into the living room, on the ground floor; two steps down into my bedroom on the second. American-Georgian, if one may describe its architecture in that way. A house of dignity and purity of line. The entrance foyer faced the hills and valleys and the feathery treetops, so coolly green in the summer, so gloriously scarlet and gold and tawny copper in the autumn. A thirty-four foot living room with a chastely carved pine dental, golden brown, between the high white ceiling and the French blue walls; pine paneling covering the west wall and pine paneling forming the walls and bookshelves of the library, and all the wood rubbed down painstakingly by hand with a waxen stain whose formula I had luckily procured from the head of the Metropolitan Museum's American Wing. This was no crude knotholed pine paneling. It had the color of luscious caramel. It looked as though it could be eaten with a spoon. A wood-burning fireplace in the living room, in the library, in the pale-green-and-white dining room; and, upstairs, a fireplace in my bedroom and in the workroom. All of these were set in facings and hearthstones of Vermont marble in pale green or delicate pink or white or darker green, in accordance with the decorating plan of each room. It was autumn. The exterior of the house was finished, but the interior would require another six months. All this waxing and rubbing down and electrifying and plumbing and tiling and flooring and plastering and painting must be done through the late autumn, the winter, the early spring. The book was not finished but it, too, would be—the painstaking rewrite for book publication, the proofreading in galleys and in page proofs.

Book and house, house and book, they had become inextricably woven into my daily life. The threads went back and forth, in and out, forming a glowing pattern.

Now Angelo took over with his warmly hospitable nature. "You come to my house," he said. "Eat spaghetti and chicken."

Spruced up for the occasion we drove to Bridgeport's Italian neighborhood section and stepped into the exhilarating atmosphere of Angelo's brimming home-life.

The quiet wife with the lively eyes; the sons the daughters the sons-in-law the daughters-in-law the small children of all these and, amazingly, Angelo's own additional very small fry, the latest of which actually was younger than any of the progeny of his own married sons and daughters. Here was the table set with the bottles of red vino. The toasts were drunk to the new house, to me, to Lou Forsell, to the world, all very heady so early in the evening's festivities. Vast bowls of glistening spaghetti and meatballs; succulent chicken, the oil-drenched salad, the bowls of fruit, and always the ruby glasses that seemed never to be empty. The huge new white refrigerator towered against one wall of the big kitchen-dining room. The strong overhead electric globes shone down on the lavish table and the vivacious faces. Angelo's startlingly young youngest offspring clambered into my lap. He was not quite two years old and altogether splendid in black velvet pants and a white satin blouse. He had just finished polishing off a heaping plate of spaghetti, a mammoth leg of chicken, a plump ripe pear and a glass of red wine. It was a good deal like holding a pony on one's knees. Very jouncy infant. Suddenly, with amazing quickness and deftness, the little hand reached up and plucked a minuscule pearl out of the brooch I was wearing and tossed it gaily to the floor. There was a scramble for it but it never was retrieved among the crumbs, and by that time it didn't much seem to matter. I've never had a finer evening.

Sometimes I wonder—almost twenty-five years later—where now is this doughty lad? Pitching for the Yankees? Pointing the bricks or stone carefully, skillfully, as his father Angelo did before him? Not likely, even if people now built houses such as that, which they don't.

As though intent on offering a truly varied program to one who would later return as a voting citizen of the commonwealth, Connecticut now rather outdid itself. A few days after Angelo's party, as I glanced out of my workroom window in the house I had rented for the summer, and was so soon to leave, I noticed that something peculiar was going on. It was Mrs. Rebecca Henry's Thursday off and she had left for the Westport station and a brief holiday in New York. She never made it.

It was raining. It was raining very hard but the unseemly thing about it was that the rain wasn't perpendicular as is normal in rainfall. It was horizontal as though picked up and driven by a giant draught. The oak tree outside my window was performing weird contortions. Great branches two feet in circumference were wrapping themselves around the parent trunk like strips of elastic. And over and through and above all this there sounded a whining shriek, demoniacal and dreadful.

The hurricane of Wednesday September 21st 1938, unheralded destructive and death-dealing, was upon a shocked and defenseless New England state.

Rebecca! I thought. And then, The House! The House! The roof

61

the new trees the farmer's cottage the pool-house the wells. There was no getting out, there was no telephoning, there was no driving. The power lines were down the roads were blocked with great trees prone across them.

The United States Weather Bureau of twenty-five years ago had no hurricane warning service in Connecticut. Hurricanes were products of the tropics, they did not grow in New England. This one did. It took the lives of 682 persons; it destroyed dwellings and property in terms of five hundred million dollars. Human beings, livestock, houses, bridges, roads, fields, crops, trees, fences, communication wires were picked up and swept into oblivion by flood and wind.

I was alone in a stranger's rented house in a hurricane. There was no way of reaching anyone. Treasure Hill. Was the house still standing, I wondered, as I saw strange objects sailing unseemly through the high air. The fiendish shriek of the hurricane continued. I asked myself, as I watched the great oak bending like a willow wand before the blast, were my trees—so carefully so professionally planted and suckled in their deep soft beds of horribly expensive black soil (brought by the square yard) and rich fertilizer and precious water lavishly applied; the twin wineglass elms that framed the glorious south view; whose exact position we had so painstakingly discussed and argued; whose size had been so long debated; whose cost had seemed to me so astral—were they flattened now to the ground? Was the big new maple now a shambles of wide-split trunk and drenched autumn leaves? The slim little dogwoods that surely—I had promised myself—would next May against the background of the long stone house, take on the look of a company of ballerinas in fluffy pink and purest white tulle tu-tus; were they kindling wood strewn on the newly seeded lawn? In a way these were like children that I had cared for and nourished. But over and above even these I thought of the great old silver beech on the edge of the big woods facing the drive halfway up to the house. This was no johnny-come-lately, stuck in as you would pin an ornament on the front of a handsome dress. It had stood a hundred years there at the edge of the wood. It would be there a century later.

Well, nothing I could do. The shriek was dying away now; became a wail; was gone in a last derisive yelp. The eerie horizontal rain became properly vertical, then ceased altogether. No telephone no lights no heat no reassuring whir of the refrigerator. I lighted a fire in the fireplace, hoping the chimney hadn't fallen in without my having noticed it; brewed coffee over an improvised trivet, and then, warmed and refreshed, ventured gingerly out of doors to peer at a devastated world; tree limbs dangling, sheds flat as playing cards tossed on a table; the road, impassable, was Burnham Wood hurled into the face of Connecticut.

Mrs. Rebecca Henry, the serene, the indomitable, returned to the house a few hours later, having luckily been marooned at the Westport railway station with scores of other would-be passengers there to board a New York-bound train which never came. Railroad tracks were under water and crisscrossed with fallen tree-trunks, battered cars, piled-up debris.

Twenty-four hours later I was able to reach Treasure Hill. As I turned into the dead-end road and came then to my own soaring acreage I was torn between averting my eyes from the massacre I foresaw, or looking straight at it at once, and getting the full shock and over with it.

Lou Forsell was there, Phillip Graham was there, the crew was there. The lovely stone house stood, serene and whole, its roof much firmer than my own spinning head at the moment. The twin wineglass elms stood before it, untouched; the big maple, the handsome pin oak in the center of the circular entrance drive; the bevy of dogwood trees, the mountain ash, the apple orchard, the cherry tree, the peach tree espaliered against the gray-white southwest wall—these trees I had so painstakingly planted all were there to greet me, unscathed, sprightly. It was a miracle. But the century-old beech at the edge of the wood— the vast, the unique, the irreplaceable specimen of arboreal grandeur, lay now with its silver head in the dust.

This was the first tragedy that had come upon Treasure Hill, and realizing with what great good luck I had escaped an infinitely worse punishment, I decided there should be no whimpering about the death of the fallen giant.

October came, with winter in the offing, so back to the New York apartment until May, when I would gather up my household and say goodbye forever to this rooftop imitation of a garden house. I knew that every weekend during the winter I would rush up to Treasure Hill for a day spent in gloating over the week's progress. The interior of the house took on a fascinating aspect of its own. The electric wiring, the plastering, the painting, the floors. The smooth beautifully grained wood of the library walls and the fireplace wall at the west end of the living room were being stained and waxed and rubbed down. There were brilliant Saturdays or Sundays in December January and February when, eager to see what progress had been made during the week, I would make the brief trip from New York to Treasure Hill, there to sit outdoors on the terrace in the glorious midwinter sunshine of the hilltop at noon time, eating my little packet of sandwiches and gathering a miraculous measure of energy and hope and even serenity as I breathed deep and looked long at the hills and valleys that undulated away to Long Island Sound. I told myself, perhaps fatuously, that this was like the winter sunshine of Switzerland.

Indoors the house was without furnishings of any kind, but its atmosphere was incredibly cosy. The dimensions of the rooms; the vista from room to room; the fluid curve of the stairway; the light through the sun-drenched windows, had the effect of a habitable whole. On the practical side the rooms were exactly right in temperature, for the oil-burning furnace had been turned on early in the autumn for the workmen's comfort and for the drying of the walls and the safety of the plumbing. Then, one morning, for no reason I ever understood, someone had lighted a fire in the living-room fireplace. I was, as usual, at work in New York. The luscious pine paneling at the west end of the room was being waxed and rubbed in a finishing coat.

One of the young Scandinavian workmen, busy with his oils, his wax, his expert polishing, threw a soiled wax-and-turpentine-soaked rag into the low flames. His overalls, his hands, his shoes, had been spotted and smeared as he worked with the highly inflammable stuff.

Now, with a hellish leap, the flame sprang out at him as the rag met fire. His clothes, his head, his hands—he was a pillar of fire. Screaming he ran through the house and out of the door and rolled in the snow and rolled and rolled and lay there. He died of it. And sometimes, during the years of my life at Treasure Hill, as I started up the stairway to bed, and glanced back at the living room dim in the moonlight, he would come alive again and I would shut my eyes and turn my head away in pain; one of the few deep pangs of pain that Treasure Hill ever brought me.

Perhaps even as early as this, before I actually occupied the house, I sensed that already the house the land and all that went with it actually had become an anachronism. The times already had outgrown it. Exactly as the vicious and unexpected flame had leaped out at the handsome industrious young workman, just so had all Europe become the tortured victim of insensate fires of destruction. What, I asked myself, was I doing, wallowing in comfort, luxury, veneered with false serenity while whole nations were screaming in horror and pain. It was 1939. It was 1940.

Perhaps, just as blue appeared bluer and peaches more delicious and the sound of a voice more grating and the play at the theatre gayer or duller than to the less acutely keyed (or more glucosed) brain and nerve centers, so now, in the midst of comfort and anticipated security in house, land, sustenance, my feeling of guilt in these possessions was greater.

Puzzled and often deeply uncomfortable emotionally in these thoughts from time to time, it wasn't until some years later, by a slow and unconscious and certainly unpremeditated form of self-analysis that I realized my fundamental reason (this is pure conjecture) for my having bought this huge eroded hunk of rocky and sour land; built this large and handsome house; planted its acreage with grains and fruits and vegetables and trees and flowers in lavish profusion and converted it into a dream house, a dream garden, thriving pastures and fields and orchard—all this against the considered counsel of those who cared about me and wished to protect me.

I realized, vaguely at first but more and more definitely as the years went on at Treasure Hill, that this was only the fulfillment of a childhood dream. I'm certain that a brief stretch on an analyst's couch could have spared me an enormous amount of time, energy, money; and deprived me of deep satisfaction, much actual knowledge of the land, an enormous source of self-expression, and a lot of fun. When I stood with my feet on my own land and said to the farmer-caretaker, "Perhaps if we plant that sour south meadow to rye and then plow it under for fertilizer, maybe we'll get a decent crop of hay for the cows—" I was aware of a feeling of security and belonging. Though a small derisive voice deep within me cackled cynically, "Who're you kidding, Ferber!"

To my own astonishment I seemed somehow instinctively to know quite a lot about the soil, about planting, about trees, weather, crops, even livestock. This may have stemmed from my Midwest childhood in Iowa and Wisconsin, or, more mysteriously, it could have been a throwback to my Grandfather Ferber who, before coming to the United States, had owned a sizable acreage of farmland in Hungary.

It is difficult but, to me, fascinating to try to trace the emotions that motivate this sort of behavior.

All my life I had been a reader. Reading was as much a part of my daily existence as breathing or eating or sleeping. A child who was an habitual reader in small Midwestern towns of decades ago—one of those naturally quick readers who could encompass a page in a flash—I frequently read two or even three books a day. Mr. Andrew Carnegie had contributed one of his ornate Greek columned temples dedicated to literature (this is equally ornate writing lingo for stating that there was a Carnegie library) in Appleton Wisconsin. There were the hot summer afternoons during school vacation time; there were the long winter evenings when I should have been doing my school homework. I read. I read and read and read; and now when I contemplate today's children squatted bug-eyed in front of the television's violence, indecency, and crime I am anguished by the thought of what they are missing.

Not that my reading was always of a lofty type. It was haphazard, omniverous. The printed page fed me, whether nourishing or pallid in content. The words were there and I was acquiring, among other things, a vocabulary.

English novels had a prominent place in that haphazard childhood reading. I know I was reading Dickens at nine because we had a full set of that robust writer's novels in the bookcase. Thackeray came later, and the yellow-hued paperbacks of that day, many of which were published under the author's pseudonym of The Duchess. To this day I don't know who The Duchess really was—possibly a sex-starved spinster in some damp Northern English shire. But certainly her novels and those of many other English authors followed a pattern that cast a roseate glow over my Midwest American schoolgirl existence. I had only to open a book to Page One. Immediately under the influence of these flowery confections I was transported from the humdrum daily life of Ottumwa Iowa or Appleton Wisconsin to a land of blue-blooded and riding-booted nobility and gentry. They dwelt in ancient and extremely solid castles vine-covered, towered; amid a mass of flowers, chintz, damask, tea, port, and bedrooms with fireplaces. They were crawling with butlers footmen parlor-maids (always pert, these last) cooks scullery maids and housekeepers with jingling bunches of keys dangling somewhere at the waistline.

The crunch of carriage wheels on gravel announced the arrival of the Young Master from travels heaven knows where, with his pale and tragic-eyed young bride seated beside him, sulking like anything.

That graveled and winding drive particularly impressed me. In my part of the globe you walked perhaps five steps from the sidewalk and there you were on the front porch. No such humdrum entrance for these entrenched characters. They proceeded in carriage and pair up a mile-long majestic winding drive under majestic old beeches (beeches!), the pedigreed setters barking their welcome, and the uniformed, capped, and aproned servitors bobbing their knees and heads off.

The impressive thing was that the Young Master, and his father the old Duke before him, and his grandfather and great-grandfather and way back to Egwald the Red (this refers to his beard not his politics) were brought up and securely habituated to ancient beeches, winding drives, casements, portcullises and crumpets. Oh, well, perhaps Egwald hadn't gone in much for crumpets, he was more the raw meat type, but at any rate all these established characters on which I fed so hungrily were indelibly impressed on my childhood consciousness.

The American world of my experience was forever on the move. Certainly the Spaniards had come trooping through, across deserts and jungles and plains, sweating or freezing in their plumes and their cuirasses and their plush and metal; the French, too; one lot intent on finding the golden Seven Cities of Cibola, the other on the Fountain of Youth. Certainly the North American Indian followed the fish and the buffalo for his food and clothing, erecting his temporary tepee or hogan and, when the season changed or provender became scanty, left these behind or wrapped them up, and off to richer pickings.

The Pilgrim Fathers and Mothers—that misleadingly soft-sounding Mayflower lot—no sooner set foot on Plymouth Rock than they were off in all directions, up and down the New England coast and inland. If the Connecticut or Maine winters were too rigid even for these granite-visaged pioneers, why, off to Indiana or Ohio, if not for them then for their descendants of the next or the next or the next generation. There was the limitless (or so it seemed then) land to be had for the taking. Let the stay-at-homes wrestle with the rocks of the Connecticut soil, the snows and frigid temperatures of the Vermont winters. The English came, and the Germans the Scandinavians the Poles the Irish the Russians the Chinese the Dutch the Hungarian. Into this new and lavish land, and on across it to anywhere the grass is greener just there—or there—or there. On to the Midwest, the Southwest, on to another gigantic ocean called, misleadingly, the Pacific. California! Well, that was more like it. Here actually was the gold for which their ancestors had been scrabbling. Here actually was the sunshine, the year-round summer; the bracing fogs and winds of the high-hilled north coast; the heat of the southern desert on which, if you dropped a wild-fruit seed a tree sprang up.

On and on they moved, and then backward and forward; up to Canada, down to Florida. First by covered wagon; then by stagecoach, by railroad, by automobile, by airplane, by jet.

Where do you go for the winter? Where do you spend your summers? My husband likes to hunt fish swim. . . . My wife enjoys the mountain air she's the low-blood-pressure type. . . . We just pile the kids into the car and make for the heigh-ho open road. . . . They say Alaska is fascinating we thought we'd try it. . . . Chicago's all right but we thought we'd spend the winters in Arizona, Steve can get work anywhere.

A continent habitually on the move these past four hundred years. The Ferber family had traveled, too. But they did not travel for fun or through a whim. They traveled and shifted through necessity. Certainly the Chicago-born Julia, a bride in her early twenties, was surprised to find herself living in Kalamazoo Michigan; an improbable-sounding town of which she never before had heard. The surprise became consternation as the next few years proved that the seemingly prosperous and handsome Jacob was no businessman at all. So off, then, to Chicago again, the young wife—apprehensive now—with her husband and the small child Fannie and the infant Edna. Then, unhappily, into the bigoted little town of Ottumwa Iowa, and the same story repeated. Again the move back to Chicago. Now Chicago to Appleton Wisconsin. By now the young wife, still in her thirties, knew that she must take hold, inexperienced though she was, or the little family would go under.

When the blind and suffering Jacob died it was again Appleton to Chicago. Then, with the relenting of the Fates, and prosperity, it be-

came Chicago to New York, New York to Chicago to New York to
Europe to Chicago to New York to Europe . . .

But it was always back to the United States. Here was Home, amorphous though that establishment was in my case. A hotel here, a furnished apartment there, always comfortable, frequently luxurious, but
always there was the weaving back and forth without the assurance that
comes of a firm foundation.

If all this did not make for assurance it definitely did give variety and
tang to existence. In these ever-shifting scenes there were the elements
of excitement, of drama. As the English saying goes, what you lose on
the swings you gain on the turnabout. All this shifting geography meant
that constantly I was leaving childhood playmates, girlhood friends,
having to form new human contacts, make fresh adjustments, fitting the
viewpoint to the new view. With this the child and the girl and the
young woman frequently knew loneliness and sometimes fear and a
nameless depression. But just as frequently it was challenging, and
toughly educational. While I wasn't precisely a woman of the world
at twenty-five I had seen quite a lot of it. All this uprooting and
readjustment may have been frightful for my psyche but it was fine for
my later life as a writer. A child of six eight ten twelve fourteen knows
terror and loneliness if she shifts in adolescence from place to place,
leaving friends, accustomed home, this schoolhouse, that church or
synagogue behind. Yet these emotions furnished me with a rich store-
house of memories and experiences I would use in the next fifty years
as a writer of short stories, novels, plays. The towns of my early childhood provided me with the terror and loneliness of Selina Peake in the
novel *So Big* when she came as a schoolteacher to the little Dutch
settlement of High Prairie just outside Chicago; Sabra Cravat of the
book *Cimarron* when she came with her melodramatic husband Yancey
Cravat to the wild strange life of the Indian Territory's opening as
Oklahoma; the child Magnolia Hawks of the floating theatre in *Show
Boat*; even the ruthless-seeming Clio of *Saratoga Trunk* and certainly
Leslie Benedict of the novel *Giant* when she came, a young bride, from
her Virginia home to the fantastic Texas ranch of her husband Bick
Benedict—these apprehensive insecure women of my imagination all
carried in their bloodstream and their unconscious something of their
forebears Julia Ferber and her daughter as the pattern of their life had
shifted and broken and reassembled; Kalamazoo—Chicago—Ottumwa

—Chicago—Appleton—Milwaukee—Chicago—New York—The World. Strange towns, new faces, new risks. It was wonderful it was enriching. Today's child seems to me to be having a thin time of it in comparison. Lamb chops and string beans and applesauce. Chicken and spinach and Jell-O. Television. Movies. The Park with Nana. The Park with Mommy. To school in the car. To everywhere in the car. The analyst's couch at twenty-five. I must be wrong. I wouldn't swap my chancey childhood for their shielded one.

Perhaps it was in those long-ago days that the big gay stone house on Treasure Hill came into shadowy existence. Land and a house of one's own.

Now the exterior and interior of the house on the hill were almost completed; but there was no possibility of moving permanently from New York to Connecticut until next spring—April at the earliest.

In these past few months the tree men, the nursery gardeners, the road builders had concentrated on the work that must be done before the winter months closed in. If the gay brilliant faces of jonquils and tulips and delphinium and gladioli were to glow up at one in the late Connecticut spring the practical brown bulbs must be bedded in the autumn. An apple orchard that would bear (I hoped) crackling juicy McIntoshes, bouncing red-cheeked Rome Beauties, Golden Delicious, and even old-fashioned russets—nostalgic memory of an Appleton Wisconsin backyard tree—had magically appeared in the bare field just beyond the rear drive. Perhaps this was not so entirely magical if one considers the hours spent in reading orchard lists, consulting apple-tree specialists and neighboring farmers, testing soil, spreading fertilizer, putting up wire shields against the possible damage from field mice; and writing checks.

Albert the caretaker and his young bride were installed in the neat white cottage that sat so snugly between the main house and the big new white barn. Young Albert, native to the region, strong, intelligent, enthusiastic and jobless in these times of wide unemployment, took on as a challenge the management of this half-wild one hundred and sixteen acre chunk of New England beauty known as Treasure Hill (or Ferber's Folly). It was he who laid the handsome flagstone paths with the soft green frames of grass growing between each slab of stone leading to the front entrance and down to the walled garden and over to the swimming pool. It was he who planted and tended the vegetable garden, the asparagus bed, the strawberries, the raspberry bushes; milked the cows, tended the chickens, the sheep, put in hundreds of mountain laurel up the long drive from main road to house; put up sturdy hardwood fences; cut hay, raised rye and alfalfa to be plowed under for land enrichment; discovered a gold mine of topsoil that, in past years, had been washed down to the foot of the barren eroded land; hauled this treasure by truck and tractor up the hill to be spread before hungry flowers, vegetables, shrubs, lawn.

Ordinarily, at the end of a long siege of furnishing or redecorating a house or an apartment, the interior decorator and the client are, at the worst, engaged in a lawsuit or, at the least, are not speaking to one another. As in other relations that had to do with this vast (at least, vast to me) project, such a condition did not exist between me and Elizabeth Peacock. Sketches had been made of each room in the house, and the ideal and logical place for each piece of furniture intended for that room had been indicated in the drawing. Our taste in fabrics and colors was almost identical. I hated all muddy colors; visceral liver-like magentas and fuchsias and purples and oranges and mustards. I loved clear fresh pink, and the dusty pink called bois de rose; clear pale yellow, heaven blue, rich prune brown, golden brown. I liked a flash of well-rubbed brass; authentic old good English and French furniture; carpets or rugs, unpatterned, on which one heard no footfall; English or French chintz; waxed and softly polished wood; porcelain; crystal; a single splash of clear crimson somewhere, for audacity. I have absolutely no paintings of the least beauty or value. Perhaps this can be traced to the same reason as that which accounts for my never having married; perverse perfectionism. The white-plumed knight never really showed up, or perhaps I missed his passing because I had my face always in the typewriter. The enchanting Renoir I secretly craved for that space over the fireplace mantel always became a living picture instead, needing a solid frame for its background. Besides, writers can't buy Renoirs (Somerset Maugham to prove the rule's exception).

As I returned to the New York penthouse to remain there until spring I think I did not yet realize that all this construction of the house, draining the marshy lowland, fertilizing the fields and pastures, clearing the neglected woods; the talk of plans (all later carried through) for vegetables flowers cows sheep chickens berries grapes rye hay alfalfa apples—all of it was the fulfillment of a childhood dream. And having

71

fulfilled it I would waken to reality and face it. Having lived out a romantic dream that was, perhaps, a concrete evidence of a sort of success, I would no longer need the evidence itself. Certainly I needed no mansion. A workroom a bedroom a kitchen a living room would fill my needs amply. I needed no swimming pool though it proved to be a fine health-agent for one who crouches over a typewriter for hours daily; I needed no orchard, as I'm the citrus type; no cream and butter, being wary of fats.

But all these were things created. You could see them you could feel them. And they were beauty. When, years later, the time came to leave it all I went without a quiver or a backward glance. I had it always. There was nothing trite for me in the timeless words—a thing of beauty is a joy forever.

The book was completed, the house was completed. Neck and neck, it was what racetrack people call a photo finish. I don't know whether the final clack of the typewriter keys or the last slap of the paintbrush was the ultimate effort. But either had a sweet sound in my ears.

May 4th 1939 was moving day. We were up early. Everything had been removed from the penthouse apartment and sent on its way to Connecticut. Boxes and crates and barrels together with house-furnishings down to the final dish-towel had been sent up during the week and placed as definitely as possible. We had spent the night at a hotel and now we returned to the empty penthouse for a last look around before leaving it forever. The bare rooms that had seemed so charming to me five years ago now appeared drab, spiritless and sordid to my Treasure Hill enamored eyes. How spindling how soot-strewn the rhododendron and privet that once had seemed miraculous on the rooftop. How paltry the little fountain and shallow pool. Even the willow tree, bravely ballooning its May plumage over the parapet, was a sickly sprig to a tree-proud Connecticut landowner.

Goodbye and good riddance I thought, disdainfully. The car was waiting. We were ready now for the drive up the beautiful new Merritt Parkway with its May finery of trees and shrubs and smooth-cut lawns.

"That's that," I said to Mrs. Rebecca Henry. Then, in alarm, "What's that!" A crash. The building was shaking. Another crash.

The sounds come up from the street eighteen floors below. I opened a terrace door and peered over the parapet to the south. A private dwelling, only five stories high, had been my nearest neighbor, unseen unheard unheeded from my eyrie these past years. Now I could discern great machines drawn up in front of the place; the sound I had heard was their initial roar and thump-stamp-crash of destruction. Workmen swarmed in the street below.

The wreckers had arrived to tear down the fine old house in order to make way for an apartment building whose construction in the months to come would sift clouds of dust and plaster and all the debris of building over and through the rooms that had been my home in New York. The insufferable noise of riveting and hammering and the chugging of machinery would continue daily all day. Six months later my erstwhile penthouse was as though at the bottom of a well. I had known nothing of this contemplated building when I bought Treasure Hill. If I had remained—if I had not gone my foolish headstrong way with the glorious wastrel known as Treasure Hill I would have withered away in the atmosphere of the blighted penthouse. By the following autumn I was told that a battery of windows and brick walls glared down upon what had been my sunny clear-viewed living room and bedroom and workroom. Radios and, later, televisions blared across the roof-garden. No privacy now beneath those many-eyed windows; the eyrie was now seemingly a cave; no quiet, no south sun, no fun. All this discomfort I had escaped.

The Fates, so often despised and maligned, are really darling girls once you get to know them.

The big moving van was drawn up at the entrance as we arrived at the Hill, and its contents were being unloaded. We had timed our appearance exactly. A few days before this the carpets and the rugs had been placed, the curtains hung—the creamy English chintz with its muted flower pattern, the ruffled organdies, the sheer net. The chandeliers and the old crystal sidelights caught the spring sun in an explosion of rainbow colors. Fabrics, textures, colors, patterns, all gladdened my eyes. Pantry shelves had been lined; china, glassware, cooking utensils placed.

By evening, incredibly, all was in order, each object in its foreordained position. There is a brief passage in the diary for Thursday May 4, 1939:

Moved to the new house at Easton. The new household couple seem fairly good. Rebecca wonderful and a great comfort as usual. Movers arrived just as we did. Little if any damage. Pretty well settled, orderly

enough, and everything looking dazzling to my eyes. Got up at midnight to go downstairs and look at my lovely house. I can't believe it
is mine.

This bleak entry quite fails to describe that midnight prowl. I was alone
in the big house except for Rebecca and the new couple soundly
asleep in the far end of the house as well they should be at the end of
this long and tiring day. All was quiet, quiet. Wide-eyed, I now lay
staring into the midnight black bedroom: the gay pretty bedroom in
the gay handsome house which had been a dream and had become a
reality. I, whose greatest gift was the delicious habit of sleeping a deep
and natural eight hours every night without the aid of potions, pills,
or athletic sheep, now remained absolutely sleepless and, curiously
enough, not the least weary after nineteen hours of working planning
deciding; rushing out to confer with workmen busy outside; men who
were planting or hammering or digging; painting the barn (white);
mending the ancient broken-down stone walls. Now, not a sound as I
lay there in the black velvet May night.

No sound? Wait a minute. Yes, a muffled rhythmic sound that was
scarcely a sound at all. It was more like a beat. *Beat. Beat.*

Pulse? But it couldn't be. You don't hear pulses. Heart? The ebb and
flow of the blood through the veins? Was this going to keep me awake?
Whoosh. Whoosh. Whoosh. Yet from the world outside there was not a
sound. This was me. Perhaps, as the closed eyes sometimes convey to
the brain a clear picture or outline of a sight one has just now gazed
upon, so the ear, too, might possibly convey to the brain the ghost of
a sound recently heard. Was this the ghost of New York's Park Avenue
traffic, etched on my consciousness these years and years and years? As
the city's mechanical sounds had irked me all these decades was I now
to be made sleepless by the complete absence of noise? Quiet. Quiet.
Beat. Beat. But strangely alert, exhilarated, gay.

I got up, and in nightgown and robe and slippers at one A.M. I
went into every room and every bathroom and every hall on that floor
except, of course, those of the sleeping household workers. I turned on
all the lights—my bedroom, dressing room, bath; my workroom; the
yellow bedroom, the pink bedroom, the blue. There was one master
switch that turned on all the outside terrace lights upstairs and downstairs, and all the entrance lights. I went slowly down the stairs, I had
all the time in the world. On went the lights—lamps, sidelights, every-

thing—in the entrance hallway, the living room, library, dining room, pantry, kitchen. Any neighbor, distant though he was, must, if he were awake, have thought that a madwoman had come to live amongst the peaceful hills. I stood in the doorway of the big high-ceilinged living room savoring its colors, its quiet, the curves and glow of its eighteenth-century mahogany and brass. The big black piano at one end of the room was a final period at the end of a well-rounded sentence.

I went down the two steps into the big glowing room and passed a hand, slowly, sensuously, over the lemon yellow brocade of the twin chairs placed so artfully just at the side-front of the eggplant-brown satin couch. I then padded over to the twin blue armchairs by the fireplace, and I sat in them. In both of them, quietly, judiciously. I sat for half an hour, just so. Across the room, then, and up the two steps, and a long backward glance. I looked and I fed on the colors I love—the pale yellow, the muted French blue, the soft dusty pink. The William and Mary secrétaire, the polished side-tables gave back the glow of the shaded lights. My gaze went then to the dining room just opposite, all white and green and crystal like a crisp head of lettuce with the dew on it.

I opened the front door and peered into the night. There were the twin wineglass elms, on sentinel duty. One o'clock in the morning and the neighbors' dogs aren't barking. No sound. Nothing.

The sky was lavish with stars, they seemed to swing low and singularly brilliant against the purple black, and I, too, had a curious sensation of swaying a little, of rocking gently with the planet on its journey as it went weaving its way among the other glittering planets; passing them smoothly, effortlessly. Hi, Jupiter! Out of my way, Mars!

A deep breath. Another another. So that was what they meant by the trite air-like-wine. Better—much better than wine, I thought, arrogantly. Air like next summer's apples on the trees. Air like next summer's clover and July hay, fresh-cut, and new-mown grass, and salt breeze from the Sound but cooler cooler cooler. No gas. No fumes. And actually a sliver of moon (this was a quarter of a century before moons and planets and stars were cluttered by monkey tourists and dog tourists and man tourists in capsules whizzing through space and peering through keyholes at the infinite).

Another deep breath, and another. All right all right, you're thinking like a writer, with phrases. Better go in before you catch cold. I closed my eyes a moment, stood there, opened them and came back into the house—the house that actually was finished and furnished and habitable and beautiful. It was mine and I was living in it and it was paid for— house and land and trees and garden and pool and roadway down to the very last dishcloth. Month by month, as the typed pages rolled off the typewriter, it had been paid for by the autobiography A *Peculiar Treasure*. A bourgeois plan of existence, mine; a compulsion always to pay immediately for anything purchased; a horror of owing money, born, doubtless, of the hazardous days of my childhood.

I stood a moment more, gloating. A last look around from the big square entrance hall into the living room, invitingly open and softly glowing. The crisp dining room, cool and fresh. I began to cry, quietly, with my eyes wide open. The tears coursed down my face and I did nothing to check them except occasionally to stick out my tongue and catch one that was tickling my upper lip. I was crying tears of joy, I was enjoying crying. Or perhaps, I thought, cynically, you're just dead-tired and a little hysterical. But I rejected that.

The book, A *Peculiar Treasure*, was finished. The house, Treasure Hill, was completed. Suddenly I was sleepy; drugged with sleep. I turned out the lights, quickly, and padded up to bed.

And slept.

5

The ideal view for daily writing, hour on hour, is the blank brick wall of a cold-storage warehouse. Failing this, a stretch of sky will do, cloudless if possible. Every professional writer knows this to be true and, beset by nature's visual beauty, is likely to pull down the shades, draw the curtains and work by artificial light. They have even been known to plan workrooms with windows placed so high that one must climb a ladder to see out.

A room with a View is not a room in which a working writer can write. From the southwest second floor window of my workroom in the house on Treasure Hill there was merely—or nearly—a view of the Western Hemisphere. Once the gaze was caught by it you were lost, hypnotized. The scene changed and shifted with every breeze that ruffled the plumage of a thousand trees that billowed downvalley and uphill to the Sound. The colors shifted with the sun and the clouds; now purple, now blue, now green, silver, gold.

There was the workroom, looking exactly as it should; the Study it would be called by anyone who wasn't a writer by profession. Caramel carpet, soft green walls, fireplace, bookshelves, armchair, desk-chair, desk, typewriter. Wall sidelights from the old Roosevelt (Theodore)house in New York's Sixties; original drawing, framed, of the charming illustration that had decorated the jacket of the first edition of the novel *Show Boat*. Windows windows windows, three of them, each presenting its own enthralling and special view.

The east window. Thirty-five acres of woodland—birch maples oaks elms cedars. . . . Must clear all that underbrush next autumn, maybe

Albert can make woodland paths, quite a job, better not think of that now . . . Get to work.

The south window. The Big View the glorious view, the view I had first seen when Terry Helburn, with a wave of her hand, united it and me. Don't look.

The west window. Albert vacuuming the swimming pool? No, that's the lawn mower, I hope he isn't going to cut the grass again in the morning just when I'm working. The noise. Who would have thought so much machinery around a farm, well, you bought it all didn't you, all those plows and tractors and seeders and mowers and harrows and trucks and everything and stuff. You're living on a farm, remember? A peaceful expensive heavenly farm. Get to work.

Heroically, I moved the desk, tugging it inch by inch; I brought the chair round and placed it in front of the typewriter, my back to the windows. Stoically, I viewed the soft green wall of my workroom; the wall, and nothing else. The beguiling landscape dipped and soared away to the silver Sound but it made the journey without me.

It was easier to turn one's back to the View than to the world. Luckily, my New York morning newspaper and the mail did not arrive by rural mail delivery until noon or later. Albert could have driven over to the nearby Stepney Depot post office to call for it in mid-morning, but this would have demanded from me a gigantic daily test of character. I missed *The New York Times* with breakfast each morning, I missed reading the early mail though the absence of both was all to the good. Nothing could have been more distracting and dis-organizing than the 1939–1940 newspaper headlines. In New York it could, I suppose, have been remotely possible to set aside both news-paper and mail until, say, two or three o'clock, when the bulk of the day's writing has been done. But what ex-newspaper reporter could ever achieve such an act of renunciation? The will—the resolve—might be there. I-won't-look-at-the-*Times*-until-after-lunch. Well, I'll just take a peek at the front page headlines, after all the world may have come to an end overnight and I won't even know it. Just one look. Just one— like a drunkard. Then I gulp the whole paper including the obits and Bergdorf's ad. The War News. It was like tossing down a glass of prussic acid daily with breakfast. But one couldn't evade it.

Now, if the paper wasn't there until after lunch—and it wasn't—you simply couldn't read it. So that was better. To my surprise I learned

that irksome and baffling city noises and distractions, so gaily left behind me, now were replaced by country distractions, equally baffling
though quite different in origin.

Someone must be drilling an artesian well over on Judd Road, poor
devils I don't envy them. That thumpthump is driving me mad how
long will it last I wonder . . . there's the telephone again, why doesn't
somebody answer and stop it . . . Albert's cutting the grass outside my
workroom . . . there's a bluejay on the dogwood twig, no it isn't, it's
actually a bluebird you hardly ever see them, bluebird for happiness
happy happy happy get to work don't be maudlin Ferber . . . now
he's got the tractor going it sounds as if he was in the south meadow
. . . south meadow how wonderful that sounds . . . we're cutting hay in
the south meadow today . . . well, pooh! to the Young Master and
His Pouting Bride in the English novels, they've got nothing on me!
I guess that's merely amazing. Of course you had to buy another cow
to eat the hay though there's all that fresh grass and clover which is so
much better for it—uh—for her. Never mind. What of it! If you were
to turn around this minute you'd see the most beautiful damned view
on the eastern seaboard but you're not going to turn around you're
going to put those words on paper before lunch or work straight through
the afternoon and you know how you hate to work after three because
it's never any good what you write then I mean after three that's be-
cause you worked on an afternoon paper and it's a habit to quit then,
your brain quits your imagination quits the flow dries up.

These superficial things could be managed, they could be thrust out
of one's consciousness. But one monumental and awful obstruction
to normal work, normal thought, normal life, could not be evaded.
Though one tried to escape it there it stood, menacing, inescapable,
hideous beyond imagining. South meadows and bluebirds, dogwood
trees and fireplaces, swimming pool and walled garden, delphinium and
white lilies eerily lovely in the moonlight, all these were a sentimental
and childish evasion of a brutal unreality called World War II.

Spasmodically, I kept a diary. Sometimes entire weeks were left blank
in the disorderly little books. Perhaps 1939 and 1940 held days which
were too difficult to pin down on a blank page. Diaries are written for
various reasons. Sometimes they are meant to be a terse record of one's
daily waking hours. Sometimes they are an unconscious relief from
the day's tensions. There it is on paper, you say, plainly to be read, so it

couldn't have been so unendurable. Diaries sometimes are written by people who fancy themselves another Pepys; by exhibitionists whose eyes slide round as they write, hoping that one day while the writer still is alive other eyes will read the ornate and specious thoughts and comings and goings (with profit to the writer), though a diary is supposed to be the most personal and private of records. Then there is the diary kept as an orderly attempt to set down the thoughts and acts of one who seeks to make some sort of guiding path in a trackless world.

Perhaps nothing could present a more concise picture of one writer's state of mind than a handful of lines dredged up from a sparse and spasmodic diary dated 1939–1940.

April 10. Worked. It didn't make sense. Everything normal seems so silly now with all Europe gone mad. The Germans are in Norway.

April 16. A fine nine-hour sleep. Worked on Saratoga Trunk. The news from Norway continues to be bad. . . . The Germans are said to be within three miles of Sweden.

May 2. Drove to Westport and marketed. Dreadful news of the retreat and failure of the British troops in Norway. The Nazis continue to triumph . . . Cleaned my workroom . . . Not getting enough sleep.

May 23. The new mowing machine arrived . . . The Nazis are at the channel port of Boulogne. . . . Churned my first pound of butter.

May 25. News of the war continues bad. Things look very dark. Talk all of Europe and America. The Pembertons in to lunch and the Kirbys too, they left at 4. Had a walk. The outer stone wall finished. . . . Found three lovely blue robin's eggs in a nest in the cedar just at the front door. A foolish place to build a nest. Perhaps the world is a foolish place to build a nest.

May 30. The British are escaping from Belgium via Dunkerque. A hideous situation since Belgium has capitulated. . . . Little accomplished on Saratoga Trunk . . . To Westport for vinca vines, sweet alyssum, and ageratum for flower boxes and garden borders. . . . The English are succeeding in getting their troops out of Flanders but the Nazis continue to win. Deeply depressed. Must pull myself out of it.

June 3. The sun came out. . . . Suddenly warm . . . Stone masons began work on the new cowbarn. Paris bombed from the air by Nazis. Italy about to enter the war.

June 7. Picked up lobsters at Fisherman's Wharf. Germany is attacking France with the most gigantic ferocity.

June 8. Odd jobs. Some work on S.T. Drove to Westport to meet Peg Pulitzer for lunch at Cobb's Mill. Kit Cornell came up to the Hill, having had lunch with Helen Keller . . . Terry Helburn and Oliver to dinner. We talked endlessly about the war. Didn't get to sleep until 2 o'clock.

June 16. France ceases to fight.

July 7th. Worked on book. The Malcolm Johnsons arrived about 1:40 having lost their way. . . . Morris Ernst telephoned from Nantucket asking to bring his daughter Connie here for the night and to meet them at Bridgeport airport. . . . Waters Turpin, dear Rebecca's son, now a professor in Lincoln University, called up, I sent the car to the station for him. Then the Ernsts had to be called for. Took all the guests and mother to Cobb's Mill for supper.

June 8. Up at 6:30 to get the Ernsts off. How I long for peace and quiet.

July 11. The delphinium in the walled garden is so lovely. The blue against the white lilies in the dusk. . . . The world outside the Hill is so horrible.

September 14. Worked A.M. Played medicine ball. Swam. Walked. Drove to postoffice. Did every damn thing to escape from myself. No good. Early to bed. Slept badly. Poland. Three million trapped and helpless Jews waiting for the German slaughter.

Well, there was the work of writing to be done daily; sick or well, troubled or tranquil, hot or cold. Here is your world, good or bad, here are your materials, here is your equipment; you are trying an experiment like a chemist in a scientific research laboratory. You are the glass retort into which this and that and those and these must be poured and mixed and blended. It may fuse to achieve the result you hoped for; it may fall flat and be nothing; it may blow up in your face.

There were days, there were months, there were years of happiness and unhappiness on Treasure Hill; of productiveness and sterility in writing; of fun and tragedy; of hope and disillusionment; of war and peace. In short, there were years of normal living for one whose work it is to write about life. Certainly that escape, that sense of security, that ivory tower existence of which I foolishly had dreamed did not materialize, and this was a great stroke of luck for me. Far from being a simplification of life Treasure Hill had introduced complications hitherto undreamed of for me; but they were enriching and productive. I felt rather smug as I realized that I was not only putting down on paper my own emotions and observations; I was, at the same time, responsible for the production of some vital material products. It was as necessary to follow through with these as it was to get those words somehow down on paper. When the apples were ripe they must be gathered before they fell, over-ripe; when it was time to cut the alfalfa it must be cut; when the furnace needed cleaning the suction-cleaner must be summoned from Bridgeport; when the snow fell—ten feet of it, sometimes, in the drifts—the snowplow hitched to the tractor must clear our private roadway. Cream must be churned into butter; berries made into jam and preserves or stored in the freezer. Trees must be pruned; sheep sheared; cows milked. Fields must be drained. Eggs gathered. All this proved to be enormously exhilarating and reassuring, even though sometimes exasperating. Temporarily, at least, it gave one the feeling of self-sufficiency, of roots. In another year or thereabouts, when the United States finally was hurled into the Second World War (by a handful of Japanese boys who, buzzing overhead, were themselves surprised to find how easily they could cripple the sleeping giant), it was good to know that farm food produced on the Hill was providing food not only for one household but for others.

Treasure Hill, it turned out, was not to be a refuge. And that was as it should be. Compared to a New York existence it had superb advantages. It possessed glorious beauty; the fresh clean slightly salt air was tonic; each night's sleep was balm incense and myrrh. I don't really know what myrrh is but the Biblical connotation is soothing, certainly. There was triple work now—my own exacting job of writing for hours a day, daily—the over-all conduct of farm, garden, household—the actual business detail that automatically follows a career as professional writer, and which takes the form of protecting book rights, serial rights, foreign rights, motion picture, stage, radio and television rights, though television at that time was only a gleam in the broadcaster's eye. Not quite enough time was left for family and friends and fun, all of which I cherished. My mother spent a large part of the summer months up there, but Treasure Hill was a bit on the dull side for the life-loving life-giving Julia Ferber. She did not approve of this white elephant which had been caught and partially tamed by her daughter (and how right she was though she never gave voice to her dissent). She liked to be driven briskly about the lovely green Connecticut countryside, she battled the Japanese beetles in the walled garden; she enjoyed my friends and they her; she played gin rummy or bridge with any or all comers; she read and read omniverously as she had all her life, anything and everything from Hemingway, whom she didn't care for, to *Variety*, which she did; and including the Bible and Mary

Baker Eddy's *Science and Health*. In her thirties, years ago, when tragedy and deep apprehension came upon her, she had learned of Christian Science, and though Julia Ferber certainly was neither Christian nor scientific this creed's philosophy had immeasurably sustained her through the years.

There was no lack of available gayety and companionship in the region. The roster of long-time friends who had summer homes in nearby Westport, Weston, Fairfield, Southport, Newtown would, if listed here, read like outrageous name-dropping.

The War was still called The War in Europe but the clouds were plainly gathering closer and closer to the western side of the Atlantic shore. By now it had become a sort of extra-curricular career to every civilian who had any interest in the human race. The sheer madness of the German Hitlerian attack had seemed at first to make its continuance impossible. We knew better now, in 1940. The unavailing attempt at help for England France Belgium Holland Norway Finland, while abstaining meanwhile from actual participation in the wildly monstrous conflict itself, went on month after month. Bundles for Britain. Food for France. It was absurd it was hopeless.

Heartbreaking pleas poured in faster and more and more frantically from the doomed Jews of Germany, of all Europe.

What with trips to Washington, affidavits, endless cables and letters, and with the noble help of friends in England I managed to bring four children and three adults out of Germany before the gas chambers and the incinerators had reduced six million Jews to dust. The four children were of one family living in Berlin. Though I had previously known nothing of these children's existence they were the grandchildren of my mother's cousin, a stately old lady at whose beautiful house in Berlin's Tiergartenstrasse I had dined when I visited Europe for the first time in 1914, just before the outbreak of the First World War.

The brief history of these four children's pilgrimage from Berlin to London to Kent to New York to Chicago to the wide United States might read much like any number of similar case histories of refugee Jewish German children, but emotionally its inner content should have some record here.

The detail of bringing these seven out of Germany before the door should be forever closed upon them was endless and will not be recounted. The oldest boy was brought out about a year before his two younger brothers and the sister. The three young children were flown from Berlin to London actually in the last minutes before that escape means was closed to refugees. It was Charles Evans, head of Heinemann, Limited, of London, who triumphantly brought about this last-minute miracle. Heinemann's was my English publisher and I had enlisted Charles Evans, the gentle, the firm, the indomitable Charles, to help me in this difficult and critical adventure. Without him I could have done little or nothing. It was grimly ironic that though the four children escaped to the United States Charles Evans' death could be attributed to the shock which so shatteringly disrupted his entire nervous system when a German bomb fell in the garden of his home outside London.

The children's family name was Hollander. Their father was a judge in Berlin, their mother a lawyer. Help us, help us to get the children out, this father and mother wrote as did so many others in the same terrible plight. Just get them out first, we will manage for ourselves later and join them in London.

Perhaps they thought, privately, that this horror they feared would not actually happen to them, perhaps they said to themselves or to each other, after all are we not a judge, a lawyer? Our family can be traced back centuries in Germany. Besides, their own elderly parents were living in Berlin. How could they leave them to an unknown fate?

I wish I could say that all seven turned out to be brilliant additions to the country that adopted them. One actually did—but he is dead. Of the adults, one (a woman) is a physician on the staff of a New York hospital. Two became businessmen. The girl is an invalid. The history of the four children rescued while the United States was not yet actively involved in the Second World War can be briefly told. It is perhaps interesting because of only one of them. The father and mother vanished from Berlin and never were heard from again after it was reported that they had been seized in their home, herded into a sealed car and sent to one of the many concentration camps, there to end with millions of others in the Nazi gas chambers or incinerators. The grandparents were blotted out without trace. Myself, I haven't been back in Germany lately but I hear the country is booming along very well indeed. Better off than England, one hears, with some bewilderment. Big Business and all that. Industrially, economically, financially doing just fine. Steel mills and so forth. But the mills of the gods seem to be in reverse gear, somehow.

When I was overseas as a war correspondent in the early spring of 1945 before the end of the Second World War I wanted to go to Berlin and tried desperately to get permission.

But I didn't make it. The Russians would not permit American war correspondents to enter Berlin. Among other things, in the course of my proposed (and prohibited) work there I should have been interested to know just what had become of the handsome old house and garden in Berlin's Tiergartenstrasse. Is it a garage now; or a gloomy restaurant; or a dwelling for some Russian official of rather high degree?

But before these tragic sequences it was the fate of the four children that concerned me. Then, one day, I had a cable from Charles Evans. The plane bearing the children had landed safely at an airport outside London. He had met them there. With him at the airport was Jerome Weidman, the American novelist and playwright, whose books also were published by Heinemann of London. It had been arranged (again through the services of the angelic Charles Evans) to have the children entered as students in a private school in Surrey until such time as they could somehow be brought to the United States. Later, in New York, Jerome Weidman related to me an incident which serves to illustrate the early psychological effect of Nazism on Jewish children.

"At the airport we all piled into the car," Jerome said, "the kids and Charles Evans and I. They were very quiet children—too quiet. They didn't talk unless we talked to them, though they all spoke excellent English with the English accent you hear spoken by Europeans who have had English tutors or who have attended very good continental schools. At any rate, off we went. Charles was pleased and relieved. You know it had been touch and go as to whether they'd ever make it. Suddenly, as we drove toward London, a sharp gust of wind blew up and a spatter of rain. I reached forward quickly to close a window. As my arm came forward so suddenly the smallest boy— Gunther his name was—instinctively ducked and shielded his head with a raised arm as though to defend himself against an expected blow . . . That's all. . . . Gives you a rough idea though, doesn't it?"

After a maze of legal and statistical procedure it finally became possible to bring the children to the United States. They were to go to

Chicago, there to live under the supervision of a near relative who had married a prosperous Chicagoan.

Gunther, the youngest, turned out to be a mathematical genius. In less than a year after his arrival he was the mathematical wonder on the weekly Quiz Kids panel, at that time an enormously popular radio program.

He was a singularly winning lad; quiet, self-contained, purposeful; handsome, blue-eyed, fair-haired. He had the good manners of a boy who has been well brought up in a family of taste and intelligence. His slight English accent was attractive. His eyes were unusually clear and luminous.

Whenever I visited Chicago I looked forward to Gunther's company at lunch or dinner. He knew what he wanted of life. He would study to be a physicist, he said. This was in the early 1940s when the mouthing of the word physicist had not yet become a fad. His was an appealing but slightly aloof quality. I suppose it could all be summed up in eights words. Gunther Hollander was a brilliant and manly lad.

As I saw him and talked with him I thought, well, Hitler, here is one you didn't destroy. He will live and work to defeat you and your bloody plan of destruction long after you are dead. Actually, at fifteen he was the youngest student ever to be awarded a scholarship entitling him to enter the University of Chicago as a freshman student. The announcement made quite a newspaper furore but a later announcement eclipsed it.

One afternoon in November he stepped off a bus on a Chicago street, skirted the vehicle swiftly in order to cross the street, was run down and killed by a second bus which was supposed not to proceed until the first bus had moved off.

One rather macabre feature of his death was that *Variety*, the famed periodical that publishes the weekly news of every form of legitimate entertainment in the United States, carried this refugee child's death notice as its leading obituary, thus:

Gunther Hollander, 15, member of radio's Quiz Kids team, was killed in an accident in Chicago Nov. 15. A first-year student at the University of Chicago, brilliant young star of the ABC Network, he was fatally injured when he stepped from one bus into the path of another. Gunther was an orphan, having escaped from his native Germany . . . His father, Ernst Hollander, was a prominent judge in Germany, his mother, Cecelia, an attorney. They were imprisoned by the Nazis in 1941 and are believed dead. One brother is in the United States Navy and another brother was recently discharged from the RCAF. . . . Gunther was the Quiz Kids' mathematics shark and was ambitious to become a physicist. The War Bonds he won for his appearances on the program this year were used for living and educational expenses. He also worked at football games as a candy butcher, and he had a job in the hospital library.

The University of Chicago set about establishing a scholarship in the name of this fifteen-year-old refugee lad. Books on the subject of Physics were bought and placed in the University Library with a book-plate stating that they were bought in memory of Gunther Hollander.

Not a bad record for a boy in his early teens. Had he lived he would now have been a man in his thirties. Definitely, he was a genius. Perhaps the history of the world tomorrow would be different if this one valuable and beautiful young creature had lived. He had traveled far, this German-born boy; but not quite far enough to escape the fate that had so long before been set in motion by the Nazi of all Nazis.

6

It is the way of writers and of actors to use their book titles or their play titles as sign posts and time recorders on their autobiographical journey through life. Emotions, events outside the perimeter of their careers are barely mentioned or entirely disregarded as they recount the triumphs the catastrophes encountered while engaged in the unpredictable occupation of writing or of acting.

Though world turmoil may be raging, nations collapsing, floods and starvation decimating millions, they are likely to record, "That was the year I wrote *Red Ashes* . . . I remember I was playing in *No Lady* that year . . . *Dazzle* was the longest novel I'd ever written, I had worked on it—on and off, that is—for fifteen years . . . Imagine a musical called *North Dakota* being a success but it ran three years in New York alone, I was so identified with the part of Hulda that it became a professional handicap, really . . ."

These facts fascinate no one—not even the Federal Tax Agent. The process—the long painful gestation involved in the writing of a legitimate book—probably would interest few. But the curious contretemps or the unexpected happening or the chance glance that could be the seed which germinates into a five-hundred-page novel might, if not ponderously dealt with, prove rather beguiling as a record of deviation from the norm—like Picasso's three eyes.

Delving thirty-five or forty years into the past I might here briefly dredge up the novel entitled *Show Boat* and the musical play of the same name which followed. That novel is still being published and read in all sorts of languages, including the English; and the musical play is presented constantly in improbable places such as Fort Worth Texas; Stockholm Sweden; Tralee, County Kerry Ireland; Sydney Australia. Yet if I hadn't merely glanced in passing at three old men sitting on a bench in the watery spring sunshine of Washington Park, Chicago, I never would have written the novel *Show Boat*. The three old men became a short story entitled *Old Man Minick*. This in turn became a play by George Kaufman and myself entitled *Minick*; produced by Winthrop Ames at the Booth Theatre, New York, September 24th 1924. During the road tryout in New London Connecticut it looked awful though it turned out to be not bad; the producer, the authors, the company were understandably depressed as we all sat in a sort of midnight post-mortem following the tryout first performance.

"Never mind, boys and girls," Winthrop Ames said soothingly though fancifully. "It'll be fixed and everything will turn out all right, and some day we'll charter a show boat and just drift down the rivers and forget New London tryouts and New York openings and everything—"

"Charter a what?" I said.

"A show boat."

"What's a show boat?" I said.

He told me. And I spent the next two years, exhausted and happy, researching and writing *Show Boat*.

Now, in 1940, it was *Saratoga Trunk* that was eluding me, deviling me as it had for years during which I had wooed it, discarded it, slaved for it, wrestled with it.

Unlike the *Show Boat* procedure, I had first thought of *Saratoga Trunk* as a play. At that time the now outmoded terms Watering Place and Spa still were in use in describing the allegedly healing waters of Saratoga Springs New York; the bizarre architecture, the madly gambling atmosphere, the unbelievable mixture of visiting gentry and over-all high jinks that somehow melded to form a notably sporting resort. During July and August, in that day of no air-conditioners, Saratoga Springs was the hot spot of the East, both as to temperature and temperament. The fantastic United States Hotel, the Congress Hotel, the Grand Union, whose verandas could be computed in terms of acreage, were crammed to the cupolas. Eventually, in the novel, I tried to describe the atmosphere of this melodramatic spot in the years of its heyday, before I was born. Much of this I had read in old newspapers, old letters, dusty volumes of reminiscences; much of it I had imagined. In a later day I had seen it on frequent visits. Too many adjectives went into this:

Here, in July, were gathered the worst and the best of America. Here, for three months of the year, was a raffish, provincial, and swaggering society; a snobbish conservative Victorian society; religious sects meeting in tents; gamblers and racetrack habitues swarming in hotels and paddocks and gaming rooms. Millionaires glutted with grabbing, still reaching out for more; black-satin madames, peroxided and portly, driving the length of Saratoga's Broadway at four in the afternoon, their girls befeathered and bedizened, clustered about them like overblown flowers. Here were invalids in search of health, girls in search of husbands. Every incoming train disgorged politicians, speculators, jockeys; dowagers, sporting men, sporting women; middle-class merchants with their plump wives and hopeful daughters; trollops, railroad tycoons, croupiers, thugs; judges, actresses, Western ranch-and-cattle men. Here were gathered for two blistering months the prim, the bawdy, the vulgar, sedate, flashy, substantial, tawdry. Here was Saratoga.

When first the idea for this background rose mistily in my mind it took the form of a romantic and colorful play in this setting, with a sombreroed Westerner for the male lead (Texas, perhaps; Texas had not, twenty-five or more years ago, been belabored into fictional pulp), and a dark-eyed languorous adventuress for a heroine. A foreign woman, perhaps, of some vague European background. This, baldly put, seems a tinsel background for a play, but it was not. Its reason for being was this; in entertaining terms I hoped to present a play about a phase of the rape of America; that part of North America which was the United States. The land grabbers the forest grabbers the metal and waterways grabbers, the old-time railroad millionaires who had helped themselves with a long-handled deep-scooped ladle to the riches that lay ready at hand to feed the voracious.

Two impecunious rascals, a man and a woman, both bearing a grudge against the world. Meeting by accident. Combining forces, without sentiment, without love, without marriage, to fight and defeat a horde of moneyed rascals in a ruthless world against a ruthless background. Saratoga.

Who were the ideal actors to portray these two schemers? Who could make these characters appear plausible pitiless charming?

Alfred Lunt and Lynn Fontanne, of course. What's the fun in flying if you don't fly high! Immediately I telephoned them and rushed over to speak to them. They lived just around the corner in East 75th Street. This was when I still was occupying the penthouse apartment of the make-believe gardens and the fountains and the skyscraper views in New York.

In a sort of babble I outlined the idea. The two adventurers. The underlying theme. The railroad tycoons of about 1885 their victims; these old-line money grabbers of the past century being taken by two wily outrageous smoothies disguised as a drawling Westerner and a sultry beauty of vaguely foreign background. All poured together and brought to a boil in Saratoga.

The Lunts loved it.

Actors—by which I mean men and women who have genuine talent for the art of acting—are dedicated people. They must be or they could not endure the uncertainty, the hazard, the nervous and physical strain of their precarious profession. I have known many such dedicated men and women to whom the theatre was life itself. I never have seen two such sacrificial worshipers at the altar of the theatre as Alfred Lunt and Lynn Fontanne. They talk breathe live the theatre. They carry it with them throughout the months they spend (when not playing) at their farm in Wisconsin. It is the center of their existence, it is the core of their conversation. It is with them in their house in New York; in a London hotel or in Cleveland or Omaha or Milwaukee or Kansas City if they're on tour.

Within a week Alfred had produced a detailed drawing of a Saratoga hotel bedroom, that incredible example of grim walnut furniture, liver-colored marble, cabbage-rose carpet and brass spittoons. He now began work on an actual miniature set for this room and an adjoining sitting room. He had a definite talent for this and could have been a brilliant scenic designer. As for directing, he does undertake this intricate task at times, and successfully.

Now the important thing was to interest George Kaufman in the idea of these characters, this theme, this background for a play. Together George and I had successfully written a number of plays; *Minick* the first one, which was followed by *The Royal Family*, and *Dinner at Eight* and *Stage Door*. No two people could have been more unlike in temperament, style, habit, taste, emotional and physical reactions. Yet our collaboration in the writing of plays was pleasant and productive. Two or three traits or habits we had in common, and they were important in this relation. Both were work worshipers; both stage-struck; were punctual; were politically and humanely liberal; were neat to the point of fussiness. If George said, "I'll see you at eleven tomorrow morning," he appeared at eleven, shoes polished but not glittering, tie handsome but restrained; shaved pink; spectacles sparkling. He would glance hungrily at the outer covering of my morning mail which I cannily had thrust back into the envelopes. He then would sit down, untie his shoelaces, and tie them again, neatly. To any psychoanalyst who is interested in this last detail I now state that I make him a present of it. There, too, was I, with two hands practically poised above the typewriter keys. If a fleck of white paper, a tiny bit of thread, appeared on the workroom carpet we both pounced on it. George disliked food, sentiment, walking (or any form of exercise); any expression of emotion; declarative and purposeful women (like myself); sauces, travel; being interrupted while speaking. Myself, I was more or less given to all these things. Added to all this, George was at his liveliest at night, having been trained on a New York morning paper. I was crisp as celery in the morning, my newspaper background having been an afternoon paper.

We worked mornings and into the afternoon.

George seemed mildly attracted to the Saratoga idea but not really steamed up about it. I was astonished to learn that he never had seen the town, so nearby and so dramatic.

"Come up and have a look at it with me, just for a day."

"Oh, I don't know. I don't really think—" Travel. That was it, no matter how brief.

"But you must, to get any idea of the crazy place. Of course this isn't the time for it—December. No one there. Everything closed. But at least you'll get a sort of idea of the thing."

So up we went in December. By train. The Gideon Putnam Hotel, modern and comfortable and empty. It being up-state New York there had been snow followed by rain followed by freezing. Green-black ice coated Saratoga Springs. George was uncommunicative.

I never have written a play alone. This I can't explain. Novels, short stories, articles, but never a play alone. It isn't a matter of structure, it isn't a matter of dialogue that baffles me. Perhaps it's the casting that tears me to bits—the hopeful young actors, the case-hardened middle-aged, the quietly resigned elderly, standing there on the bare stage under the cruel light of that single blasting electric bulb, reading expertly or fumblingly from the manuscript thrust into their hands. Then the moment's silence. The hurried whispered consultation down there among the empty seats. Thank you so much. . . . No, don't call us. We'll call you.

Perhaps it is the out-of-town tryout. The midnight to 3 A.M. sessions after the performance in New Haven or Philadelphia. The rewrite next morning. The rehearsal. The performance. The midnight session. The rewrite. . . . All these can be faced and they can be, in a kind of terrible way, challenging and even exhilarating. But it's better to face them, not alone, but in twos.

Up to Saratoga Springs, then, at the wrong time of year.

Born in Michigan, inured in my childhood and girlhood to the rigors of Iowa Wisconsin and Illinois winters, certainly Saratoga in December had no terrors for me. The Gideon Putnam Hotel, modern cosy, was situated a short distance outside the town itself. We planned to stay perhaps twenty-four hours. Two of the vast hotels and the red plush Casino, all closed, locked and hibernating for the winter, had agreed to open their doors and their public rooms and private bedrooms for our brief inspection. The arrangement had entailed coaxing, wire-pulling, influence, affluence, time, energy, patience.

George and I had arranged to meet in the lobby of our hotel immediately following a brief unpacking and washing-up interval. Ten minutes. Oh, make it fifteen, won't you, George?

A tall somber figure awaited me, leaning morosely against a pillar. George's trouser-ends were tucked into heavy high galoshes whose tops met the hem of his overcoat. He wore earmuffs. A thick woolen scarf. Wool gloves.

"Mr. Peary, I presume?"

"No cracks, please."

Into the depths of the cold car awaiting us. I began to prattle, always a bad sign. Nerves. "Of course you'll have to imagine what it's like in the summer . . . wineglass elms lining the streets simply lovely . . . horses and carriages in those old days, tandem and high coaches and everything . . . Lillian Russell . . . Diamond Jim Brady . . . Jay Gould . . . President Chester Arthur . . . hops—"

"Hops?"

"I mean dances kind of hops, not the beer kind. And for fire escapes they actually have—wait till you see it you'll die—they have coils of thick rope hitched over a hook at the side of the bedroom windows, you're supposed to throw out the rope and slide down it in case of fire, can you imagine!"

"If they're closed for the winter are the hotels heated?"

"Uh—no. No, not heated."

This proved to be an understatement of almost epic dimensions. There is, in outdoor cold, a kind of challenging freshness—oxygen, probably—that makes it bearable and even stimulating. There is nothing that so strikes to the marrow of one's being as the mordant cold of the interior of a long-closed wooden dwelling in a Northern midwinter. The United States Hotel in December.

I have visited the crypts of St. Peter's. The Roman Catacombs. Point Barrow Alaska on the Arctic Ocean in January. A theatre on the closing night of a play that is a failure. Any of these would seem cosy—even tropical—compared to the mortuary atmosphere which engulfed us as the waiting caretaker opened the door with a clanking and squeaking of chains and bolts and we stepped into the charnel marble halls of erstwhile gay Saratoga.

The caretaker was a grayish man behind grayish spectacles, and the face that one glimpsed as little more than a pie-slice between the cap pulled down over his forehead and the coat collar turned up over his chin, seemed inadequate as a repository for usable features.

George turned up his own coat collar over the muffler and thrust his gloved hands into his coat pockets. Our breath froze on the indoor air.

A sound emerged between the caretaker's cap and his collar. "D'you want to see the whole place!" He carried a flashlight.

"No," George said distinctly.

"Look," I said very sprightly. "It's so good of you to do this—show us, I mean—we wouldn't think of the whole place—I mean—how about the main dining room and maybe the ball room and a couple of typical bedrooms and maybe the cottages—"

"Cottages!" George croaked.

"They're not really cottages, they just call them cottages, they're a kind of balcony addition facing the garden—more private than th—"

"No cottages."

The dining room of the old and now non-existent United States

95

Hotel had, roughly, the dimensions of New York's Pennsylvania Railroad Station's grand concourse. It was a proverb that hot dishes became cold, cold dishes hot, no matter how speedy the waiter on his long journey from the kitchen to the dinner guest seated at the far end of the room. As we stared into its darksome reaches it seemed incredible that human beings could ever have survived in these surroundings, much less have willingly gathered in this murk to engage in gustatory gayety while china clattered, crystal tinkled, silver clashed. It was like viewing the moon, minus its craters, through an icy telescope on a frosty night.

Back to the sepulchral entrance hall, up the creaky stairway, into the frigid bedrooms, sheeted, ghostly; the stout loops of the rope fire escapes actually hanging in coils at the side of the windows; the liver-colored marble tabletops dim with dust. The gruesome black walnut beds and cupboards—George Kaufman sneezed. Sneezed again. Again. It was quite a production.

Emerging from this he now turned toward the waiting caretaker. There was a gesture of exchange in which his woolen hand paused briefly over the caretaker's woolen hand and the pie-slice uttered the monosyllable "'Anks." Behind the glittering spectacles George's eyes were frosty with dislike and discomfort.

That was all. That was it. George took the late afternoon train back to New York. It would have been useless to say . . . but in the summer . . . the satins and laces . . . the jockeys in their silks . . . the big black dollar cigars . . . the French perfume . . . the battle for the railroad, ruthless, savage . . . the Gould and Vanderbilt and Fisk men rocking gently on the vast front verandas while their thugs . . .

Useless. Stubbornly I stayed until the next day, moused around in the Saratoga Public Library (ancient yellowed newspapers and periodicals); had a soothing and mysterious sulphurous Saratoga Springs hot bath and massage; dinner (including cocktails, gossip, and laughter) with Frank Sullivan the Sage and Wit of Saratoga; and slept as angelically as though I had not just been hit over the head with an empty idea. Oh, well, I thought, probably it was a no-good try, anyway. Besides, it is spread too thin. What is the background of these two people—this man and woman? How did they get to Saratoga? And why? What was their past? Why are they embittered against the world, both so young and handsome? What do they want? If he is just a Texas gambler that's dull old stuff. If she is just a sloe-eye on the make that isn't attractive. What of it! Maybe George is right.

Practical. That's the thing. Be practical. You have been thinking about *Saratoga* as a play. That is ended unless you do it alone, and you're scared. Why not first as a novel? But it doesn't seem to take that form. Then leave it. Go away somewhere, see something you haven't seen before. You've been hearing a lot about a mythical place called Texas. Why not go to the Southwest, you haven't seen anything of it since Oklahoma and *Cimarron*.

I put the play *Saratoga* into temporary mothballs from which it emerged later as the novel *Saratoga Trunk*, and later still as a rather dashing motion picture; and much later still as an unfortunate musical play that was born sickly and that died on Broadway. I had no active part in these two materializations of *Saratoga*.

Even in that day—twenty-five years ago—it was slightly eccentric to take a train for a journey as long and as potentially tedious as this jaunt to Texas. To fly was considered The Thing, but in 1940 it was not taken for granted as it is today—just a routine form of locomotion. Flying was thought to be definitely adventurous, though chic. As a general thing I flew, but for this journey I wanted no sudden whirl into another region of the United States—another civilization altogether, I had been told—this Texas which I never had seen. For years there had been for me a feeling of freedom from responsibility on a train. You were snugly ensconced in a room no one could enter unless permitted; books, papers, magazines, typewriter at hand if you wanted them; you needn't go to see the sights because the sights obligingly came to you, sliding past your window, mile after mile; your meals in your room if that was your preference, though I rather liked the drama of the luxury-train dining car—even the vague discomfort of finding oneself seated at a table for four in the intimacy of dining with three total strangers.

This, though, was almost the last of that. One chance plane trip taken a year or two later converted me forever to plane travel. It was a daytime flight from San Francisco to Boston; smack across the country. It happened to be a rare day as clear as transparent as glittering as a pearl and crystal necklace. From start to finish it was like that. I've never again encountered anything like it. It was before the day of jets. We were high, but not astral. There were pink-tinted baby clouds now and then, but not an inch of overcast. There, for your delectation, was the

United States of America; mountains, towns, rivers, forests. California's incredible mountain ranges; the flat lands of the South with their sluggish streams; the desert; the vast plains and prairies of the Southwest and the West; the farms, so precise and geometric; the forests and prim white church steeples of New England. My face pressed to the window hour on hour I was, I suppose, just short of hysterical, partly due to the fact that being a low-blood pressure type I am affected by seven or eight thousand feet of altitude as I would be by one oversize very dry very cold martini. My fellow passengers sat reading (as they properly should) or just staring at the back of the seat in front of them, their eyes wide open and unseeing, like sleepwalkers. I barely restrained myself from shouting, "Look! Look! It's like a map drawn by angels who were Michelangelo and Velázquez and Corot and Grandma Moses, you can trace them all the way from the Pacific to the Atlantic. Look! You'll never see the like of this again."

Walden Pond or no Walden Pond, I still think Thoreau missed a lot. Travel—anywhere, any time—always has been for me the most refreshing form of recuperation from hard work, tension, repetitious tasks of living; escape from social life family life business cares, professional involvement. A new country, a new city—new, at least, to me—no matter where—Oregon, Africa, Canada, Texas, Egypt. It isn't the actual travel that is exhilarating; one encounters lumpy mattresses, hard pillows, strange food, indifferent cooking, fatigue, scrambled schedules, hours lost hours gained, baffling languages and customs—to name only the irksome features. But out of this welter of discomfort comes a curious feeling of refreshment once you are home again.

But most of all, I love to travel in the United States. Anywhere; the rickety New Haven to Westport Connecticut. A jet to Seattle. Even today, when every city in the United States seems to resemble Detroit, a mass of neon lights, factories, motorcars and apartment houses, I still have that sensation of release, of almost childlike curiosity as the plane or the train or the automobile or even the taxi begins to roll into or above those American streets so much alike now, yet in color and sound and movement and vitality and background so unlike any people any streets, good or bad, to be found in any other country in the world. Rome — Berlin — Paris — Vienna — London — Amsterdam — Prague — Budapest — Lucerne — Brussels — Cairo — Tel Aviv — Athens — I have looked at them with great interest and entertainment and even wonder because of their beauty or strangeness or historic background but it is almost as though I were looking at a play or a motion picture. I get less emotional impact, less feeling of kinship and deep understanding than I do when walking down a street in, say, Ashtabula Ohio. This isn't merely provincialism. I've been whirling around this planet since I was two years old, or younger. The faults and failings of the people and the towns of my own country are as obvious to my observant gaze as are their admirable qualities. I do not know why I am interested and stimulated by walking along the main business street of Bridgeport Connecticut, certainly one of the least glamorous cities in the world. But I am. Good or bad, I am attracted and fascinated. And why this is true I do not know.

The train Texas-bound was hot, stuffy, and an hour late. The journey began to seem interminable and I thought of the old joke about the Englishman who, on his first long trip across the United States, said, "I wonder why such a fuss was made about Columbus discovering America. I don't see how he could have avoided it."

Because of the difference in East-West time our arrival in Dallas was inconvenient. Arrivals are almost always inconvenient to hotels; and morning arrivals always. This was morning, and early morning. Though you've made the reservation and verified it, and, as a final precaution, reaffirmed the reservation, it's all a surprise to the room clerk. After two nights spent on a train there is nothing more revolting than to walk into a hotel bedroom to find the bed unmade, a mass of soggy towels strewn on the bathroom floor, empty whisky bottles, dregs in glasses, cigarette stubs, grimy soap, wads of paper, drifts of newspapers. I went for a walk. It was late March. Dallas, to my astonishment, was like a Northern town. An unexpectedly worldly city, geographically flat but pleasantly lively. A drive around town, a saunter through that fabulous bazaar which is the institution known as Neiman-Marcus. One had heard of it, of course; crammed with porcelains and linens and laces and silks and furs and jewels for the delectation of the multimillionaire oil men's wives. Here, on the desertlike plains of Texas, was lavish luxury rivaling anything in New York or Paris. It seemed an anachronism; or a mirage. Back at the hotel there was awaiting me a young man who introduced himself as Joe Linz of the *Dallas Journal*. He turned out to be full of charm and New York conversation, having lived there for some time after his college years. The pleasant effect of this was canceled by a dinner interval with three Texans whose talk was dull and dirty. Perhaps they were sadistically interested in the possible reaction of a spinster novelist whose work was unknown to them. They were like nothing so much as a trio of small boys who have tied a firecracker to a cat's tail, lighted it, and were waiting for the explosion.

I had met an engaging young member of the Neiman-Marcus firm. A warm sunny Friday this was, and as we walked along the teeming street I said, partly in curiosity concerning Texas leisure hours, "After all this rush and bustle I suppose you're going away over the weekend." I had envisaged a cool green oasis not too distant; fifty miles, seventy-five as New York City dwellers escape for refreshing weekends in New Jersey, Westchester, Pennsylvania, Connecticut, Massachusetts.

"No," he said. "We're not going anywhere. There's no place to go."

This shocked me. A week or ten days later I myself could verify the startling statement. There were ranches and comfortable ranch houses outside the busy towns and cities; there were country clubs; but these sat starkly on the desertlike plain with here and there a mesquite grove or even a painstakingly planted Northern tree, imported and as unsuited to the climate as the Paris gown of the ranch-owner's wife.

Houston next. That's the big one, I told myself, that's the brash one, that's the one about which the Luce magazines are always publishing incredible articles of improbable people named Glenn McCarthy and Jesse Jones and Ima Hogg.

It was March. I had left New York in late February, deep in snow and hard winter cold. I now began to feel rather odd. Perhaps it was the effect of that rocket streamliner from Dallas, very hot and with a side-to-side motion that now made your early Dallas breakfast a cause for apprehension and regret. I did not admit it to myself, but already I had begun to reject this region as a background for any creative work of my own.

Twenty-five years ago the Shamrock Hotel had not yet risen to stare blankly at a thousand miles of flat Texas range land. The Rice Hotel, slambang in the center of the city, was the place. This was before the day of air-conditioning. The hot hotel lobby was milling with men all of whom appeared to be seven feet tall. They wore sand-colored clothes and big creamy Stetson hats and their faces were sherry brown or Burgundy red from the smiting sun and dust-laden winds of the Southwest plains. Their voices were strangely gentle and even musical emerging from those giant bodies; their eyes had the far look of seamen's eyes, the eyes of men who daily gaze across endless empty spaces; somewhat hard, those eyes, yet strangely childlike, too, like those of tough big boys. They stood in little groups, talking quietly except for an occasional volley of Homeric laughter; or they sprawled silent, like collapsed behemoths, in the lobby's huge leather chairs.

In my bedroom that seemed unimaginably hot, a huge fan contrivance attached to the ceiling above the bed was equipped with four long lazy arms like oars and these revolved slowly, with a nightmarish dreaminess, shoving the heat from one corner of the room to the other.

Unpack the necessities; get a car for an hour or two and have a first quick over-all look at this hot noisy rich town sprawling fungus-like on the plain, almost as unbelievable a manifestation as the mythical, heroic but actual giant Sam Houston for whom the city was named. Into the car at noonday, up one section and down another; into the Mexican quarter, then along streets of fine houses where grounds, open to the street, were ablaze with azalea blossoms in feathery masses of pink and white and orchid and orange and purple. But by now I was feeling odder and odder, my face burning, my clothes a burden, my head a conflagration. You had to come to Texas, I thought, acidly. New York and Connecticut in February weren't good enough, h'm? Ill and alone in the Rice Hotel in Houston, Texas, that's what you wanted, was it? with a long-legged slow-dragging nightmarish fan revolving over your bed. You had to come to Texas to get some strange tropical disease.

I re-entered the Rice Hotel lobby and tottered up to the desk for my room key. The lobby was still swarming with the big men of the big hats and the high-heeled smart-looking neat boots and the spurs and the great sunburned faces. As I picked up the key one of these said genially to the desk clerk, "Getting along toward spring, sure nuff. Ninety-five in the shade today—if you can catch yourself any shade."

Cured, I handed back the key and went into the hot dining room for a cold lunch.

Houston days were spent in spade-work for a possible novel whose background had piqued my interest for years. I talked to many people; vulgar people, charming people; literate, ignorant, bigoted, liberal; white brown black; rich, poor. And I walked the stifling humid streets and drove to giant ranches squatting starkly on the plain; and accomplished some research in the library and spent a day in nearby Galveston on the naïve notion that, being a seaport, it would be cool.

Like most Midwesterners born and bred, intense heat and biting cold do not much bother me. I was early accustomed to extremes in temperature. But humidity destroys me. Here in Galveston the humidity was like a clammy hand held over your face. Yet the city had a ghostly charm. The scent of the tangled gardens hung heavy on the muggy air. The houses, pock-marked by the salt mist and the sun and heat and mildew, seemed built of ashes. Here was a remnant of haunted beauty —gray, shrouded, crumbling. What did they resemble? Of what did this city remind me? Miss Havisham, of course. That was it. Miss Havisham the spectral bride in *Great Expectations*.

San Antonio next, all dressed up for tourists with the old town restored as La Villita; the festooned lagoons; the Governor's Palace, so-called; relic of a long-gone period in San Antonio's history. It was a little like a movie set representing a Spanish town. But the Alamo was real enough; and the centuries-old missions, golden brown and crumbling in the sun, were touching and historically fascinating though the winding high ancient stairways to the steeple crippled your leg muscles for a week. And Maury Maverick, forceful, courageous, dramatic—a born actor as are all good politicians, including Fiorello La Guardia, Franklin D. Roosevelt, Theodore Roosevelt and Abraham Lincoln— certainly Maury Maverick was real and convincing.

In and out of Texas towns. Talking to scores of Texas people. Amazed by their viewpoint, their braggadocio, their seeming unawareness of the world outside their own vast commonwealth; beguiled by their easy charm, grateful for their spontaneous hospitality, touched by their lavish giving of time, energy, thought, to a tourist stranger. Appalled and fascinated by turn.

It was a superficial tour, certainly. But the years of trained observation and the natural ability to assimilate even the indigestible sights and sounds and personalities encountered served me here in this Texas which was at once so American and so unlike the rest of the United States. What was it? What was it that made me feel so alien in this vast vital expanse of throbbing plain and range? Egypt, perhaps? An atavistic throwback to that blood-drenched desert land and the arrogant emperors and the young Jew Jesus, so many centuries ago?

Miles—hundreds—thousands of miles of flat roads, flat fields, flat plain, stretching away to the always distant horizon with nothing on which to rest the sun-weary eye. Vast herds of cattle, many of which were strangely humped and mythological creatures imported from India and bred to the local Herefords to produce the famous Santa Gertrudis stock; ranches that were kingdoms; towering men; shrill-voiced women; blazing sky; fried food; oil rigs; millions millions millions. A violent climate, an atmosphere potentially violent. A tropical climate that was ignored by the Texans. Any other land in the world, under this heat and glare, would have been shuttered, slow-paced. Not here. They rode they drove at breakneck speed. They ate huge hot platters of fat-drenched food. They moved swiftly, dressed in canvas and leather; drank alcohol prodigiously. Everything they did would seem to have brought swift sure death in any similar climate; but not here.

South to Brownsville on the Mexican border; to Corpus Christi on the bouncing wind-driven bay that was an inlet of the Gulf of Mexico; to Austin, capital of the state of Texas; to Lubbock, thriving cow-town; Up. Down. Up again to Dallas.

It was larger than life. Too big. Too massively male. Too ruthless and galvanic and overpaced. Too blatant. Too undiluted. Too rich. Too poor. Cattle and Mexicans and oil and millionsmillionsmillions. Braceros laboring for twenty-five cents an hour in Brownsville. This was no book for me. Work is work, I told myself, and fun is fun, and you thrive on both these, and sometimes they seem almost interchangeable—not often, but sometimes; but this novel of Texas life is not a book for a woman to write. It would kill you. This is a novel for a man to write—a man who is a combination of Hemingway and Faulkner and Thomas Wolfe and Sinclair Lewis. Let that Proteus write it. Go on home.

The fact was that neither the Texas novel nor the Saratoga novel was ready for writing. Often, I reminded myself, a novel or a short story idea had lain dormant in my mind for years before the actual task of writing was possible. Like wine, they must be stored away in a dim cool cave of the brain to mellow, to ripen, until they are palatable.

At the moment of this rather elaborate decision a telegram arrived:

JULIA SAYS YOU TEXAS HOW ABOUT MEETING ME NEW ORLEANS.

LOUIS

It was from Louis Bromfield.

Goodbye Texas. Goodbye forever. Some tougher sturdier writer will have to undertake the feat of bulldozing you. Little (as they used to say in the old-time novels) little did I dream that, in the next twelve years, Texas was to have a staggering effect on my life—my health, finances, emotions, work; or that weeks—months—of my time would be spent in Texas.

7

I never had seen New Orleans; had the most romantic idea of its character. Balconies of iron lacework. Creoles, part-Spanish part-French; food to swoon over at Antoine's; the Vieux Carré; banjos on the levee; the Mississippi, that tawny lion, king of rivers; ancient cathedrals; the French market, brilliant with the hues of fruits and vegetables and flowers. I had heard.

And it was true. This was 1940, just before our entry into the Second World War sent every established United States order crashing into actual or psychological or emotional rubble. It was 1940 and it was still true. I was so bewitched that I even managed to forget the fact that New Orleans is a city below sea level, a topographical statistic which ordinarily would strike terror to a low blood-pressure type like myself. The subject never came up.

That New Orleans has vanished as the Paris of a past day has vanished; and New York as it was, and even London and San Francisco and Rome and all the great colorful distinctive cities of the world; a mass, now, of neon lights, and motor traffic like rivers streaming the streets; of gas-and-soot-blackened buildings and littered gutters; of roaring noise and jostling crowds, and over all, like an unseen formless cloud, the poison of world-wide apprehension.

But New Orleans a quarter of a century ago was still New Orleans; romantic, evil, curiously foreign; careless, delicious. In the novel *Saratoga Trunk* there is a brief description of the New Orleans of a much earlier day, but that still was true of the New Orleans of 1940 when first I saw it. That New Orleans is gone now, never to return.

This was Clio Dulaine's first impression of the city in which she had been born and from which her mother and the infant girl had been banished two decades earlier.

> Over all New Orleans there hung a pungent redolence that was the very flavor of the bewitching city. First, as always, the heavy air bore the scent of coffee pervading everything like an incense wafted from the great wharves and roasting ovens. Over and under and around this dominant odor were other smells, salty, astringent or exotic. There were the smells of the Mississippi, of river shrimps and crayfish and silt and rotting wood and all manner of floating and sunken things that go to feed the monster stream; of sugar, spices, bananas, rum, sawdust; of flower-choked gardens; of black men sweating on the levees; of rich food bubbling in butter and cream and wine and condiments; the sweet dank moldy smell of old churches whose doors, closed throughout the week, were open now for the stream of Sabbath worshippers. The smell of an old and carnal city; of a worldly and fascinating city.

And there it still was in 1940, the old enchantress. There were the wrought-iron balconies and the Cabildo; the Vieux Carré and the Pontalba Apartments and Royal Street; the levee, the sugar plantations, the Negro cabins, the sazarac cocktails, the vast Mississippi, the oysters Rockefeller at Antoine's—and Louis Bromfield. Gone now, or changed, never to return. It was enchanting, it was gay, it was hot and delicious and steaming. There was good talk with Roark Bradford (gone, too); and the leisurely ride on the throbbing old riverboat down the Mississippi—actually an old stern-wheeler of the kind I had described in the novel *Show Boat* written fifteen years earlier, though I never had seen one at that time. For that matter, I never had set foot or boat on the Mississippi until this moment.

Here were color, variety, drama; good music, food, tragedy, comedy. Here, on the surface at least, was just my dish. There was, obviously, violence here too; and the ancient shabby plantations were pitiful in comparison with the vast high-powered ranches I had just seen in Texas. The men here definitely were not the two-fisted ten-gallon-hatted giants of the Southwest plains; the tempo was lethargic, there was none of the high-powered whooshing up and down the highways. This was the deep South, this was quite another facet of a country so diverse as to make it unique among nations.

The city was rank with the odorous political scandals that still emanated from the regime of the notorious Huey Long, dead these five years by assassination. The conduct of this tyrant-buffoon had been wildly obnoxious, the city had rocked with it, the entire country was aghast at it. It had seemed somehow to have touched the population of the entire state of Louisiana.

This sinister undercurrent in the character and life of the city of New Orleans was strangely akin to the hidden dangers of the great river itself with its perilous eddies and shoals and sudden bursts of disastrous flood. I said something of this to the intelligent and altogether delightful young New Orleans man who acted as a sort of friendly guide to Louis Bromfield and me as we roamed the levees the bayous the plantations restaurants shops courtyards.

With appalling righteousness and lack of tact I said, "It's unbelievable that a city such as this—historic and unique—should tolerate this wholesale dishonesty. New York is bad enough, heaven knows. But this! They seem to encourage it. Why, I was told that the proprietor of this restaurant is out on bail, walking around town after being indicted with all that crew."

"Yes," the charming young man said sadly. "I know. He's my uncle."

There never was anyone more exhilarating as a traveling and sightseeing companion than Louis Bromfield. For decades he and Mary Bromfield had been my friends. Together, side-by-side in rented chalets we had spent gay hard-working summers in the little Basque fishing village of Socoa in the Basses-Pyrénées. Just across the Bay of Biscay was St.-Jean-de-Luz with its Casino and *plage* in case we wanted a bit of night life.

Louis had an unparalleled zest for life and the gift of communicating this excitement and relish to those about him. People fascinated him, good and bad and all intermediate shades; he worked hard, played hard; was gay, humorous, perceptive, compassionate; knew and appreciated music, food, color. If I were asked to name four friends, now gone, whom I'd love to see and talk with for a day an hour a minute, Louis Bromfield would be one of them.

Together Louis and I ranged the city and the surrounding countryside—the restaurants, the bayous, shops, night spots, private homes to which we were lucky enough to be invited. The old side-wheeler down the Mississippi, the plantations crumbling and ghostly; Lake Charles nearby; and Lake Pontchartrain. The city itself was shabby and romantically beautiful in a decayed sort of way; and touching, like an aging though still lovely courtesan who is living on the last of her jewels.

The position of the New Orleans Negro was appalling. Yet in their faces there was something at once composed and brilliant. Perhaps there was, in those faces, enough French and Spanish blood to lend them that look of insouciance. Certainly it is on record that out of the original musical talent of the New Orleans Negro was born the rhythm known as jazz. Back in the 1870s they had roamed the streets on holidays and in the dusk of the sultry southern evenings—little groups of them equipped with haphazard odds and ends which served as musical instruments—a paper-covered comb, an upturned pail or washtub beaten with two sticks, a battered mouth-harp, a banjo, perhaps a horn or crude whistle. With these they beat out a tantalizing exciting strangely broken rhythm that made the pulses pound and the feet taptap and that set a world a-dancing. It was the mother of American music today.

It was known as ragtime.

All this chance New Orleans holiday would have been only a pleasant but passing gay interlude if an astounding stroke of luck had not emerged from what had started as a mere romp in a colorful American deep South city.

The elusive first half of the novel *Saratoga Trunk* was there, awaiting me. The contrast between the lush Latin background and atmosphere of New Orleans and the absurdly rakish sportiness of Victorian Saratoga seemed to me like a piquant dish that was sweet-and-sour; appetizing; and composed of two incredible sections of the always incredible United States.

The riddle that had eluded me was solved. This city was the natural birthplace of Clio Dulaine, the important female character in the unwritten novel *Saratoga Trunk*. The first meeting between Clio Dulaine and Clint Maroon, the Westerner, must be in the French Market of long-ago 1870 with its rich scents and sights and sounds and colors that would have seemed improbable in any other city in the United States. Here, even now, were the relics of the romantic balconies and gardens, the narrow foreign-seeming streets, the foods, the faces, the very language with its mixture of French and Spanish and English and a bastard dialect called Gombo.

The early spring jaunt was finished, I was so eager to return to Treasure Hill and the workroom that Texas—which had been the reason for this trip in the first place—was wiped from my mind at least temporarily. A journey that had seemed a practical failure had been magically transformed into a potential success. I wanted only to settle down to work.

Back in New York the streets looked sodden and gray with the sooty dregs of last winter's snow. It was late March, that ugliest sister of the family of months, neither spring nor winter but partaking of the worst family features of both. The wind was clammy and cold, the trees bare; street traffic was a snarl of trucks, taxis, private cars. It actually took longer to drive from Newark Airport to Park Avenue and 75th Street than it had taken us to fly from Atlanta Georgia to Newark.

Ordinarily this would have made me impatient and vocal with annoyance. I saw it only with an eye bemused by triumph. I had New Orleans of a past century in my mind's eye, I had Clio Dulaine's background. I knew her now, and her mother and her father and the texture of her life and theirs, though I never had seen her or dreamed of her before now. It simply didn't matter that New York was bleak, gray, wet. An avalanche of news, good and bad, met me after these weeks of absence. Piles of mail, the usual problems that accumulate in the life of any working adult after a month's absence from the home base. Now I headed joyfully for Connecticut and Treasure Hill. Months of work on the novel lay ahead of me—a year probably, if I was lucky. The prospect did not dismay me.

Albert, the young farmer-caretaker, met me at the Westport station. We swooped up the hills toward the farm. The March air was sweet and cold. Albert, as a usual thing pleasantly chatty (for a born New Englander) with news of the spring planting, the livestock, the house, the neighborhood and the village, was noticeably silent.

"Something wrong, Al?"

An intelligent and composed young man, trained in agriculture and forestry and general husbandry, he knew his work, he was not a word-mincer, good news or bad. Still he said nothing. I turned to look at him. Horrified, I saw that there were tears in his eyes.

"Al! Your wife! The baby!"

He shook his head. "The trees."

Two days earlier a freak March sleet storm had encased every branch and twig in a sheathing of ice. Now, as we drew up in front of the house, I saw the carnage. My twin wineglass elms, so graceful, so symmetrical, planned and planted to form a frame for the view of valley and hills, sky and Sound, were mangled almost to their basic trunks. The big pin-oak in the circle drive had been neatly sheared of its entire top half so that now it was a squat thing of meaningless planes. The dogwoods were split. Later I was told that throughout the night and day of the freezing ice storm Albert had run from tree to tree with improvised props made of poles, of old branches, of boards, notched to support the cracking branches. He had saved many, but the sheathing of ice was too heavy for some. The ground was littered with the casualties.

A stricken tree, a living thing, so beautiful, so dignified, so admirable in its potential longevity, is, next to man, perhaps the most touching of wounded objects.

The budding springtime was just ahead. We had looked forward to the leafy shade of the newly planted trees on the crest of the once-bare hilltop.

"We'll put in new ones, Al."

"Cost a lot of money."

"I know." Then, at sight of his anguished face, I said, virtuously, like a horrid little character in a Victorian Elsie Dinsmore sort of novel, "Maybe if I work hard I'll earn a lot, we'll put in new trees and by next summer we'll forget there ever was an ice storm."

"Always something on a big place."

"Always something in a big world."

"The lambs came in."

"Came in! You mean came out."

He grinned. "Eight of them so far."

"Lovely. That cancels the trees."

You had only to look at the lambs in the pale spring sunshine to experience (foolishly) a surge of reassurance. They were real, their antics were absurd and utterly winning. Tiny, their ridiculous hoofs and spindling lower legs as black as their upper coats were white, they scampered the fields, they leaped into the air and came down in a bunch on all four feet. They were as idiotic and winsome as children, and as refreshing.

April. *Turn your back to the view and get on with it.* So I sat there in the lovely house on Treasure Hill resolved to conquer the novel. I knew what this would mean, inured as I was by now to writing daily, using the accustomed discipline to clear my mind of events, people, troubles, joys, anything that might divert the writer from the task of writing; hour on hour, day after day, shut off from the distracting world. . . . Thanks. I'd love to but I can't . . . I never lunch out . . . Just a bite of something on a tray in my workroom . . . In bed by eleven . . . Up at seven . . . the right word the right word . . . a line a paragraph a page two pages three four . . . discipline . . . discipline . . . no clock to punch, no clients no patients awaiting your services, no students no fellow workers no boss no organization no director no audience. Just a pencil or a typewriter between you and a day of freedom. A writer's working hours are his waking hours. He is working as long as he is conscious and frequently when he isn't. A dream, a subconscious thought that wells up in the hours of sleep may magically solve yesterday's hopeless word-block.

I don't know what it is that makes a writer go to his desk in his shut-off room day after day after year after year unless it is the sure knowledge that not to have done the daily stint of writing that day is infinitely more agonizing than to write. Also, there is that slight item known as earning a living. So, hot or cold, sick or well, weary or fresh, young or old, a disciplined writer writes. In the United States, according to reliable statistics, there are just two hundred and fifty writers who earn their living by writing only. The hundreds, the thousands of others who write and are acknowledged professional published writers earn a living at some other job profession or business and write in whatever spare time they can manage. Many people who speak hopefully or wistfully of writing do not actually want to write. They want to be writers. They may actually possess a talent at least for the art of writing. But the drudgery, the loneliness the daily discipline of driving oneself to that closed room and that yawning desk is too much.

The questions encountered are mildly maddening.

Q. Do you write by inspiration or what?
A. I go to work and I write every day.
Q. You mean like a stenographer or something?
A. As regularly as a stenographer; but usually I work seven days a week.
Q. Why?
A. Because I am a writer and I would rather be a writer than anything in the world. Also, I earn my living by writing.

111

Q. How many hours do you work? A day, I mean.

A. About twenty-four.

Q. No kidding, I mean actually.

A. I mean it, too. Even after the hours of putting words down on paper some part of my mind is thinking about writing. This is true, in a measure, of everything I do or see or feel or hear. It's compulsory or habitual or perhaps it comes under the head of an occupational disease. All writers have it.

Q. Are you still writing?

A. Are you still breathing?

Q. Don't you get tired?

A. I'm tired practically all the time.

Q. Why don't you stop?

A. Why don't you stop living?

Q. Well, say, I like to be alive, don't I?

A. Even when it's tough?

Q. Better tough than dead, anyway, it isn't always tough. Sometimes it's wonderful.

A. That's what I mean.

So I sat there in the lovely house on Treasure Hill and turned my back to the View and wrote the novel *Saratoga Trunk*. It might have been much more difficult to have written the book in New York during that year of increasing horror and apprehension. The world was poisoned and writhing. Just to glance at the hideous front page news wrung the vitals; the certain knowledge that worse was to come proved so depressing that planned work seemed futile; writing an impossibility. But one wrote.

Not to write was to admit failure and defeat.

This book was not to be (and was not) a story merely of New Orleans and Saratoga romance; of lacework iron balconies and swooningly scented Southern gardens; and high jinks among the rich and ruthless in a Northern spa. All this was part of the book, certainly; but it was sugar-coating on the pill.

On the surface *Saratoga Trunk* gave the effect of liveliness, color, romance. Like every novel I have written (except *Show Boat*, which never was intended to be more than an authentic and romantic novel of Americana) this book had an underlying theme and purpose. Ever since my early days when, at seventeen, I had become a newspaper reporter, the theme of the background and growth and fundamental spirit of this country—this fantastically rich and spectacular—this gorgeously electric and vital country—had exhilarated me beyond anything. I don't know why this was true, but true it undeniably was. It also sounded foolish if mentioned and I never talked of it, coward that I was. I just wrote about it with all the writing power I could summon and all the frustrated actress emotion and all the newspaper reporter's training and all the creative energy I possessed. These were considerable I do not hesitate to say.

Perhaps I had imbibed some of this in my very early childhood when my sister Fan and I were taken on an annual visit to my grandparents —my mother's parents—in their home in Chicago. They lived in one of those four-story brick-and-stone houses on Calumet Avenue when Calumet Avenue was a good Chicago street in which to live. There was a little area-way of courageous grass in the front and a genuine back yard with a bordering garden at the rear, and I loved it. Louis Neumann will not be even sketchily described here. He was a rare and gifted and lovable character but I covered all that in the autobiographical book A *Peculiar Treasure*; and only the senile repeat in their writing.

Louis Neumann had come to the United States a young man in 1848 with the great liberal Carl Schurz. The son of a conservative Berlin banking family he had left his native country forever because he had shocked his people by becoming one of the intellectual and articulate group that hoped for and politically fought for a constitutional government in autocratic Germany.

Something of this I must have heard when I was three—four—five— six. I could not have understood it, nevertheless some tiny seepage of this rebellion and courage, this admiration for the potentialities of the new country in which these freedom-lovers had found refuge, must have trickled through to my childish consciousness.

I could not have been older, for Louis Neumann died at that time. Perhaps there had been newspaper obituaries read aloud in the family household following his death and through this spoken word there may have filtered through to the child's mind some inkling of his rebellion and courage; his love of freedom; his belief in the new country. It could have been this. Or it could have been an inheritance.

Whatever it may have stemmed from, my hero-worship had early turned to certain national figures whose crusade was defiance of the despoilers of the United States. Perhaps my newspaper reporter's background had given me a knowledge of political skulduggery, of the ruthless Great Grabbers; of those who, years later, were to be so brilliantly and courageously described in the book by Matthew Josephson entitled *The Robber Barons*—a new-minted term which became part of the language.

Certainly the Appleton Wisconsin *Crescent* on which I worked from the time I was seventeen until I was about eighteen-and-a-half, was a cocky liberal little afternoon newspaper in a cocky liberal little Midwest town. The Milwaukee *Journal*, also an afternoon sheet, on which I covered everything that wasn't labeled Men Only, was and is a dynamic and courageous paper. I suppose there is no conversation or comment that is freer, more debunked, less cautious than the relaxed and world-wise talk of the reporters on an American newspaper as they lounge around the city room after the last edition has gone to press. This was the kind of talk I heard daily in my most impressionable years. The rich, the poor, the snide, the motivated; good bad, high-minded or double-dealing—none was sacrosanct.

Certain figures out of the past had the respect and admiration of the nation; Washington, Jefferson, Lincoln; but these were History, these were Text Book Pages, interesting and even stirring, but indubitably dead. Now new figures of achievement and courage had begun to emerge whose names, as the years whisked by, loomed larger and larger in the all-too-brief roster of those who cared more for the freedom and integrity and open guardianship of their country than for caution, wealth, position or power.

Robert La Follette, Governor of Wisconsin, and later United States Senator from Wisconsin, was the first of these to impress me. For centuries the Grabbers had gone their way, unchecked. The Land Grabbers the Forest Grabbers, the Grabbers of the minerals and the waterways. There it all lay in this fabulous virgin continent, and no one to stop them; no one who cared enough or had courage enough or sufficient foresight to sense the inevitable result of this ravaging.

Four national figures have influenced my early political thinking and broadened my social sense. Four are dead. Of these four only one, probably, is an actively dimensional name to Americans aged twenty or less. That one is Franklin D. Roosevelt. Robert M. La Follette of Wisconsin, Governor and Senator: the fiery and dramatic little leader, waged war against the Railroad Big Grabbers. He was the outspoken antagonist of the ruthless men who were—in reverse one might say—the builders of the country even while they despoiled. A frustrated actor, as are so many dramatic politicians, he was a powerful stocky figure, short, broad-shouldered, his hair en brosse perhaps to give the effect of height. He made up in drive and purpose what he lacked in inches. He spoke forcefully and in fresh terms, he was not to be bought or cajoled. It was due to La Follette that state laws were passed for taxing railways according to actual valuation. The Wisconsin and Michigan men of power and great wealth, and scores of others of the same ilk in other states throughout the nation had taken over the timber lands as right-of-way as they built the railroads; had diverted and polluted the waterways, claimed the land for thousands of miles and the mineral wealth underneath those lands. The tax on all this was bitterly opposed. The doughty little Wisconsinite won. This was one achievement only in his long list of constructive measures. He was overwhelmingly rejected as President in the year that elected Coolidge. It is interesting to conjecture what the history of the United States would have been in the past forty or more years if he, rather than the meager and vinegar-veined Coolidge, had been President of the United States in the fateful Twenties and Thirties. By this time the fiery little fighter for the rights of the average man had become a pacifist. Certainly all war, no matter how modern and scientific, is a throwback to the savage and brutal in man. And just as certainly the First World War, had the United States been a solidly pacifist nation, would have been won by Germany. At the thought of what this might have brought about the senses reel.

William Allen White, rotund, gloriously human and humorous; editor and owner of a tiny newspaper in the little town of Emporia Kansas whose wise and humane editorials were copied and read through the United States—here was probably the most character-forming influence in my life. In his adult lifetime there was no national political combat which was not influenced by this man's thought and principles; yet he never ran for office or took office. I used to go to California in those days just as an excuse for a twenty-four hour stopover in this little Midwest town; just for the fun, serenity, wisdom and peace to be gained by sitting on the front porch of the big house on Commercial

Street, Emporia Kansas, rocking gently and eating home-made peach ice cream and talking talking talking about the world with Bill and Sally White. That twenty-four-hour period was, in effect, a sort of mixture of a brief Catholic Retreat, a Jewish Yom Kippur, two weeks at Elizabeth Arden's, a sea voyage and a month in Europe, all condensed into a single day and night.

It may be that many young people in the United States today are not familiar with the work of William Allen White. But he influenced their lives today as surely as the minds and bodies of their parents and grandparents have affected them through the recent decades.

Then, striding down the road into our lives came the wielder of the Big Stick, Theodore Roosevelt, President of the United States. Both these men (and they were friends and fellow-workers) were Republicans with democratic souls. It has now become the fashion to speak of Theodore Roosevelt in belittling terms. Theodore Roosevelt was a Republican President politically; a democrat in the large social sense; a born aristocrat, as was Jefferson; and a born charmer. An actor when necessary; but a doer, too, of terrific proportions.

Here was the man who dispelled in this country the cynical assumption that there was one law for the rich and another for the poor. A rather shadowy figure now, perhaps, in spite of the courage, the originality, the utter freshness of attack which characterized his every moment throughout his political lifetime. It was he who introduced conservation into the common language and into the consciousness of a country grown careless with plenty. He had seen the timberlands stripped; the grazing lands, minerals, oil, all in the hands of the few. It was he who worked and fought for the preservation of the national resources in a country whose citizenry thought fatuously—if they thought about it at all—that the vast natural bounty of the land was inexhaustible.

It is only insecure and snobbish people who are afraid to fraternize with people less secure than themselves. The Theodore Roosevelts invited a Negro to be a guest in the White House. The United States of America, the greatest republic the world has ever known, was so undemocratic in its large social sense at that time that this gesture was a bomb. The Negro guest was Booker Taliaferro Washington, educator, reformer, head of Tuskegee Institute in Alabama. To read the account of this man's life is to realize in some degree at least the dimensions

that may be achieved by the human mind and soul and spirit. In a
written chronicle of his life there is a last line of chilling brevity.

"He died at Tuskegee on Nov. 14, 1915, as the result of overwork."

Overwork is not recommended as a desirable cause of death, but it is
a stark sentence that comes to mind as one sees the gilded young of
today step into the car at the curb to drive down to the corner store in
the next block to purchase that pack of cigarettes.

The phrases of this President Theodore Roosevelt stirred the imagination and enthusiasm of the young people of that day. One no longer
hears them, they are outmoded, but they were then as effective as vitamins. A country that saw him enter into the thoughts and problems
of the worker, the so-called Little Man found in him a hero to emulate,
to idolize. Teddy, they called him. Dee-lighted! they said, in fond parody
of his own famous grin and greeting. The White House became a sort
of Open House. People came and went in droves.

He said, and was the first to say it, "This is your house. You're paying
for it." Here was a President who seemed a great elemental force. He
was a leader of what he called The Strenuous Life, a phrase so widely
adopted that it became trite. He was author of more than two score
books; naturalist, soldier explorer, historian politician, statesman. He
seemed to hear, see, read, know, understand, appreciate everything.

Himself a writer and a respecter of writers, here was the first United
States President in decades who did not think of books as something to
be interred in libraries like bodies in a catacomb. Perhaps one would
have to go back as far as Benjamin Franklin to find a statesman who
regarded writers as human beings. Certainly it was more than a mere
trick that enabled him to dazzle an author, encountered unexpectedly,
by quoting at first meeting entire paragraphs from the writer's published works, together with comment, criticism, approval or condemna-
tion. Sometimes he seemed to know more about the book than the
author himself remembered. He coined phrases that fitted the period.
They were endlessly quoted, perhaps because they were minted exactly
for the country's need of the moment.

Walk Softly and Carry a Big Stick. Certainly he laid about him with
this peacetime weapon, it crashed down on the thick skulls of those who
were despoiling the country Theodore Roosevelt knew and loved.

Malefactors of Great Wealth. Hastily the world turned to the nearest
dictionary for the definition of this somewhat pompous-sounding word

and learned to its astonishment that it meant an offender against the law; a criminal; one who does evil; and that this word was being applied to the heretofore privileged and money-mighty.

Conservation. For the first time in the country's history a voice of power and high authority proclaimed a national truth that cast some doubt on the future of the vast rich country's natural resources. This land of ours, he said, belongs not only to you but to your descendants. The great lakes, the rivers, the creeks, the water under the earth; the forests, the minerals, the soil itself belong to your children and your grandchildren and their children and grandchildren forever. There never was a nation so naturally bountiful. This bounty will not last forever if you continue to waste and squander it as you have in the past. Replant the forest for the one you've just destroyed. Revitalize the soil for the field or pasture you have just denuded. Harness the rivers. Cherish the mountain streams. You have defaced, plundered, ravaged, stolen, grabbed for centuries because no one has ever warned you that this great bounty would not endure such treatment forever. A Maharajah cannot eat his pearls, nor an Emperor his porcelains nor a Czar his gold and emeralds. This land of ours is for all and for always.

The Strenuous Life. The spindling and weak-lunged lad, Theodore Roosevelt in his teens, had pulled himself and doggedly trained himself into husky manhood through sheer determination to possess health and energy necessary for the accomplishment of his lifework. The sickly youth went West. He lived the life of a ranch-hand. He rode. He worked. He breathed the air, felt on his body the sun and wind and rain and dust of the plains and the prairies. Muscles and blood and bone responded. He returned to his home in the East a man, sturdy, primed for the battles which, even then in his youth he must have sensed, lay ahead of him. He had conquered the battle of ill-health. Now nothing he would encounter could terrify him.

These Rooseveltian utterances were not mere catch-phrases. They were not empty words. They changed and immeasurably improved the thinking and the mores of the greatest and most democratic republic in the world.

Oh, yeh, they say today. Theodore Roosevelt. The fella with the Big Stick. Related, wasn't he? Yeh. Big-mouthed guy, too, wasn't he? Always talking, and his fist out. Wasn't for him, my grandfather used to say, our family would of owned the whole damn state.

It is interesting to note that an accusation made against Theodore Roosevelt, President of the United States, was identical with that made against his cousin Franklin D. Roosevelt three decades later. It was only one of a number of parallels in the lives of these two kinsmen. Both had known and conquered grave illness. Each had served as Assistant Secretary of the Navy; had been Governor of the State of New York; and President of the United States. The social outlook in both men was broad and compassionate; and deeply opposed to the mass accumulation of great wealth by any individual. Both came of a distinguished and "good" family; highly intelligent, dedicated to the service of their country; possessed of seemingly boundless energy and enthusiasm; of great personal charm; of sufficient but modest wealth.

In the ranks of the privileged and the power-seeking the cry went up against President Theodore Roosevelt in 1901 and against President Franklin D. Roosevelt three decades later: *ROOSEVELT HAS BETRAYED HIS OWN CLASS.*

A strange protest it was, coming from citizens of a democracy.

Franklin D. Roosevelt. Here at last is one at least that they still know today, almost two decades after his death. Even the young careless ones have some knowledge of this almost incredible natural phenomenon. Here was a man who actually transformed himself from a tragically paralyzed and helpless victim of polio to the functioning position of the foremost public figure in the world of his day. What he was and is lives so vitally in our world that his great deeds for humanity and his great human mistakes are not only history; they are a living part of our lives today. That magnetic and civilized voice on the air waves in the 1940s heartened and united a nation. His uttered phrases gave fresh courage to millions.

"We have nothing to fear but fear itself."

So there they were—the four men in the life of the young woman from Kalamazoo Michigan and Appleton Wisconsin. By the time Franklin Roosevelt loomed large on the horizon of her thinking the young girl was an old girl indeed. But certainly her thinking had been formed, her emotions touched, her horizon broadened by the public performance of these four great men. It had been my good fortune to have met all four and to have been guest, briefly in some cases, or for a period of days in others, at the home of each one of them. Good conversation and roast beef hash at lunch in the Oyster Bay home of Theodore Roosevelt while the stuffed trophies of his safari days in the jungles and on the plains of Africa Australia and America grinned and goggled down on us, fang and claw, from the walls. Days and nights of peace and friendship and illuminating talk in the big comfortable William Allen White house in Emporia Kansas. More than one visit to the White House during the Franklin Roosevelt administration, but one that stands out radiant as a sunrise. It was a twenty-four hour stay at the White House. On the way there at four in the afternoon I had said, "I wonder if I can ask to see the Lincoln bedroom. Of course it's part of the private section of the mansion and perhaps I shouldn't ask. But if I could just have a peek, I've always wanted . . ."

Ten minutes after we arrived, and while we were still drinking tea and eating cakes before being shown to our rooms in which we were to be quartered as guests, Mrs. Roosevelt spoke in a quiet aside to me.

"I want to ask you if you would prefer to have any other guest room. I had planned to put you in the Lincoln bedroom for your stay. Is that agreeable to you?"

I remember being late (inexcusable behavior) for cocktails in President Roosevelt's study before the big dinner that preceded the evening's reception and musicale, because after I had changed for dinner I just sat rocking rocking in the rocking chair facing the big walnut bed and I thought about Abraham Lincoln and I thought about myself, and I thought about Julia Ferber and Jacob Ferber and the world, so strange and so terrible yet wonderful at this time, and I came downstairs late, apologetic, red-eyed and happy.

Seated behind his desk in the study or office sat President Roosevelt vigorously shaking up a container of martinis. There were only a half dozen of us in the room, all house-guests. So we sat sipping and talking, cosy and relaxed and informal as we might have been in any friend's house before dinner; the great formal dinner and reception and musicale lost their vaguely forbidding aspect.

After dinner, and just before the guests were to congregate for the evening's concert we stood aside to form a sort of aisle down which President Franklin Roosevelt walked, leaning on the arm of his son James. That walking passage of this man was one of the most painful and glorious examples of human courage I have ever witnessed. His physical condition was that of a hopeless cripple and his spirit was that of an indomitable and functioning human. Each step was impossible and he took it, and the next and the next until his goal was gained. On his face was a gentle smile that actually had in it something of humor, and perhaps a small glow of boyish triumph. With no thought of disrespect there came to my mind a paraphrase of that boastful shout of the kid on the bicycle, "Look Ma! No legs!"

Many guests had arrived for the concert after dinner. The music room was crowded. We had not yet taken our seats. Across the room I saw the brow and the eyes of a tall woman. I am very short—hardly five feet. I didn't know and couldn't see the lower face of this woman in the crowd. The features that had attracted me were her eyes. She evidently was engaged in a conversation that deeply interested her. I stared, dazzled. I never had seen such beautiful, compassionate and intelligent eyes.

The crowd now began to move toward the seats. Groups broke up. I saw that the eyes were those of Eleanor Roosevelt.

There were, during that autumn visit to the White House, one or two additional glimpses of family life in that historic, yet curiously cosy mansion. Or perhaps it was the Roosevelts that created the cosy quality. The kitchen, for example. One doesn't somehow think of a kitchen in connection with the White House. Food magically appears, but nothing as mundane as a stove or a sink or a refrigerator comes to mind—at least, to the guest's mind. But there it is, I had so wanted to see it, being a kitchen fancier myself. Smaller, somehow, than one would have imagined. Vast stove surfaces; plateaus of table. To myself I thought, "No marble halls for me, thank you. How I'd miss being able to help myself to that late snack if I felt like it—glass of milk and a couple of crackers and maybe a small hunk of cheese."

Mrs. Roosevelt caught my eye. She knew. It was as though I had spoken aloud. "The boys used to complain those first years. Just about everything is locked up at night. I suppose the custom of raiding the icebox is a strictly private home institution."

Somewhere along the halls and corridors and passages that led up from the kitchen Mrs. Roosevelt opened a closet door whose shelves were laden literally with hundreds of small packages all wrapped and tied with holiday trappings of colored papers and ribbons and tinsel.

"Some of my Christmas packages," she said. "I try to collect them and tabulate them all through the year. Otherwise I'd never finish the shopping."

Her smile was a touching blend of pride and tenderness. This was another facet of the gemlike character; this was not the First Lady; or the shrewd and knowledgeable political figure; or the world-traveler; or the columnist; or the courageous wife of a hero. This was the plain and lonely young girl of so many years ago who had known rejection and had loved the world in spite of this; and who, you knew, as you surveyed the scores of little gay boxes, would have liked to give a special and separate Christmas gift to every living human being in the world.

During these same earlier formative years, too, four women strongly influenced my thinking and my conduct of life. Three of these were spinsters; three were old enough to have been my mother. Two of the older women were Jane Addams, sociologist, of the famous Hull House, Chicago; and Ida Tarbell, author of the trust-busting and muck-raking Standard Oil articles which caused an economic cyclone in the United States. The third was Lillian Adler, a Chicago social service worker of my own age. The fourth (definitely not a spinster) was Julia Ferber, my mother.

Certainly Jane Addams, of the settlement house known as Hull House had, without in the least meaning to, established the sociological model (for her day) of the Social Service Center throughout this nation. There it was, a smoke-blackened red brick pile on the far West Side, Halsted Street, Chicago, in the midst of the smells and dirt and teeming tenements of the old Chicago stockyards district. Even today, more than a quarter of a century after her death, I never see a group of youths, vacant-eyed, restless, lounging on a New York rundown neighborhood street corner, full of pentup energy and no legitimate place in which to expend that energy, that I do not think of Jane Addams' book, *Youth and the City Streets*. This could have been called West Side Story before *West Side Story* ever was thought of for the stage or screen. Her *Twenty Years at Hull House* is, in effect, a sociological textbook. To spend an observant day at Hull House and its environs was practically a university seminar course in applied sociology. A quiet gentle woman, Jane Addams, her face etched with the lines of the perpetually overworked; eyes remarkably soft, clear and merry like the eyes of Eleanor Roosevelt; and behind this a determination, a purpose, of steel.

Ida Tarbell's name is little known today. Her *History of the Standard Oil Company* and her series of magazine articles that were more explosive than any roaring oil well just bursting through the crust of the earth, may now be all but forgotten. In their own period they were potent enough to shake the economy and the politics of a nation. She was one of the editors of the *American Magazine* (now extinct) in which my first short stories appeared. Though I saw Ida Tarbell rarely, owing to the difference in our ages, our background our interests and temperament, I was influenced sociologically by this quiet, soft-spoken powerfully intelligent woman. She was one of the first women of consequence that I met when I came to this bewildering dramatic New York in 1911. And immediately one of my first lessons in long-term conduct was casually taught me by Ida Tarbell. She, with two or three others of the magazine world, were having dinner with me. I was living at a pleasant sort of family hotel called the Belleclaire at Broadway and 77th Street. Potted palms in the lobby; red plush; apple pie; middle class, clean. There I could manage a winter of work comfortably enough in the little rear sitting room and bedroom apartment.

We were to have dinner downstairs in the hotel restaurant. As we left my apartment Miss Tarbell and I were the last of the little group. I was about to shut the door. The lights were all cosily ablaze in the two rooms and hallway.

"You've forgotten to turn out the lights," Miss Tarbell said.

"Doesn't matter," I said. "I leave them on. This is a hotel."

"It's you—not the hotel—who'll have to pay for them," Miss Tarbell said gently. "You are the ultimate consumer."

I didn't really know what she was talking about. But I learned. I learned. And certainly the tens of millions of wasters in the United States today are, in a sense, leaving the lights burning contemptuously or carelessly in the form of food fuel clothing air soil luxuries necessities of every sort with never a thought of the economic penalty they inevitably one day must pay.

Lillian Adler. Here was a friend who was to be a friend for forty years. In her very young womanhood she was the daughter of well-to-do parents, as the homely Midwestern term then went. Yet, perhaps influenced by that same Jane Addams, she became an amateur settlement worker or social service worker in the old Jefferson Street Settlement House on Chicago's West Side. It was a district of Russian and Central European Jewish emigrants. Later she became a professional social service worker and she successfully continued in this through the decades until her invalidism and death. There never was such a merry worker in the slums; or a more understanding and compassionate one. The combination of these qualities made her one of the most effective workers in this Chicago field. This was no Pollyanna. Lillian Adler was an intelligent and psychologically adjusted woman who was using her potentialities. Chicago's West Side wasn't merely a slum to her. It was the teeming stockyards-smelling section of the sprawling city. Into it there must be introduced light cleanliness occupational opportunity; hope fun education. And so, wherever she went, they were.

Julia Ferber. There is a book in itself—a book which never will be written. Gay, enormously entertaining; shrewd, intelligent, possessive; intuitive, courageous, here was a protean character who, often to my surprise and sometimes annoyance, flung open the door and marched lifesize into many novels as I wrote them. Full of small and irksome faults, possessed of almost all the great human virtues, she appeared in one guise or another in *Fanny Herself*; *The Girls*; *The Emma McChesney Stories*; *So Big*; *Show Boat*; even *Giant*. She represented squarely the type of mother who went out of fashion when Freud came in. Heaven help any well-known figure in today's political, artistic, or industrial life who might utter the once-admired statement: All That I Am or Ever Hope to Be I Owe to My Mother. They'd have him on the couch in no time.

It is difficult to say whether Julia Ferber was a help or an obstacle in the course of my life as a writer. Probably a great deal of both.

Now, decades later, as I survey the appalling waste—the almost criminal carelessness—that is an ingrained characteristic of the North American way of life I recall and marvel at the prescience of these named men and women of another day. They knew and loved the country which can only be described by a spate of paradoxical adjectives—the vast splendid immature generous naïve rich colorful dramatic lavish childlike careless wonderful United States of America. Curiously, these people sensed what was coming. They spoke words that went unheeded. Conserve. Save. Replant. Wastefulness. Waterways. Oil. Land. Food. Money. Cars. Clothes. Crops. Youth. Youth. Youth.

They had extra-sensory perception, these vanished ones. They were among the first to denounce the ruthless Grabbers. Yet I think that if I were to say today to the first hundred people I might encounter between the ages of sixteen and twenty-five: Jane Addams; Robert La

A KIND OF MAGIC

Follette; Theodore Roosevelt; Ida Tarbell; William Allen White; ninety out of the hundred would say: Who?

From all this it may be deduced that mine was the life of a writing do-gooder. Not at all—or almost not at all. I took no actual part in all these worthy lives or in any group devoted to this uplifting effort. I just sat for fifty years with my face in the typewriter and wrote and wrote and wrote and looked and listened and felt and enjoyed and wrote and wrote. But the observation, the emotions, the impact, the significance of all that I had seen and felt and learned was inherent in the majority of the books that emerged from that typewriter, page by page.

I was industrious but frivolous, too. I had a reluctance against being part of committees, organizations. A lone vixen. I was an almost complete non-joiner. Probably this was born of my newspaper days when I had had to cover meetings, clubs, committees, conventions. Politics, too, I am sorry to say, come under this head. I am a registered member of no political party. Though I have voted the Democratic ticket for years and years and years I like to feel that when a Republican Congressman (for example) in prospect seems more liberal, more intelligent, altogether more desirable as a candidate than does his opponent, I can cast that out-of-the-fold vote without experiencing the twinge of guilt that goes with disloyalty to an affiliation.

Added to this, I loved (and love) the theatre, travel, walking, working, reading, having dinner with friends, in and out; privately taking part in public movements. This may be a form of vanity, or, worse still, an inability to yield to the majority against one's personal convictions. Frivolously serious, one might say.

The books I wrote and write had, and have, the qualities of vitality, observation, characterization and readability. But—with perhaps one exception only—they had and have more than that. If this were not true they could not have persisted as they have for twenty-five, thirty-five forty years after their birth. In their very core there lay something more solid, more deeply dimensional than mere entertainment or readability. They had power they had theme they had protest. Readers perhaps were rarely conscious of this, and book reviewers scarcely referred to it. Perhaps you couldn't see the woods for the trees. They were and are books of the American dream, of the American nightmare, of the smallness and greatness and beauty and sordidness and romance and tragedy of a people in the United States of America. I am not at all embarrassed to say in deep and quiet satisfaction that these books have been read by four generations. Sometimes the letters are from writers of seventy; sometimes from students of sixteen. The books will be read in the next fifty years by another four generations if this world still manages to pick its way out of the path of the missiles and the space ships. Make of this what you will.

8

A gentleman farmer, no matter how gentlemanly, is a farmer if he owns, lives on, and is actively interested in the workings of a working farm. Victorianly speaking, then, a lady farmer is a farmer; and certainly a farm is a farm is a farm. True, Al and his two helpers milked the cows, planted the fields, raised the vegetables, cut the hay, fed the chickens, tended the sheep—not to mention the more elegant and vexatious chores such as cutting the lawn-grass (acres of it); vacuuming the swimming pool; kneeling for hours in the walled garden, the cutting garden, the rock garden, cultivating the sun-baked soil, feeding it, watering it so that the roses the lilies the delphinium the Canterbury bells, the chrysanthemums the poppies gladioli tulips jonquils pansies would oblige; even the fluffy double pompons of the hollyhocks, once so bourgeois, now pretending aristocracy in the pride of their pale lemon yellow and clear salmon blooms. There was the orchard to be pruned and cultivated and protected from small-winged and four-footed invaders. Farm machinery to be cared for. Wood chopped, cut, stacked. Inside the house, rooms and rooms to be tended, furniture polished, beds made, food cooked and served, bathrooms scrubbed, floors waxed, guests made welcome. Up in the second-floor southwest corner sat the zany instigator of all this, her back to the view, putting one word down after another so that a novel eventually would emerge from the typewriter. Not at all incidentally, she earned her living and all the above-named goodies by this same daily effort. It left her little time for what New York City cockneys would call terling in the serl, but she did manage a spot of delving off and on. She also learned that, though you turn your back to the view, you are still facing the world.

Happiness had taken on a curiously different angle. Often, now, it had nothing whatever to do with gayety or satisfactory writing or even the news from Europe of a temporary triumph over the Nazis. The 1940 diary, old reliable, proves that. It is May. And it says:

Happiness means a steady downpour after a drought. Raining very hard at night. Thunder and lightning. Lovely! Milked one of the new twin Jersey cows for the first time. Looks simple. Isn't. They are cream-color like their cream. Helped churn too. Tricky stuff.

Even my bedtime reading had taken on a new trend. *Steps in Home Churning. The Principles of Vegetable Gardening. Flowers of North America. Soil Feeding. The Story of a Thousand Year Pine.*

When, in September, Al won blue ribbons at the Easton Fair for our gladioli, assorted vegetables and apples (McIntosh and Delicious) I was puffier about it than when I had got the Pulitzer Prize for *So Big* in 1925.

It was, in a nice way, madness. It was psychologically sustaining. And very expensive.

It was incredible that the work could go on, day after day, week after week. But it did. This was June 1940 and there were times when the World of Terror took over and at such times writing, farm, garden, even superficial serenity, all but vanished.

June 14. At ten the ghastly news of the Nazi occupation of Paris. All France's population streaming along the southern roads to nowhere. Sat staring at the typewriter. Writing seems silly.

But the book did manage, somehow, to get itself down on paper. Always, at the start of a new piece of work, the pages loom up ahead, a blizzard of blinding white emptiness. This particular novel was, perhaps, even more difficult and elusive than its older siblings. Not only were they older but so was their mother. But she was well enough; swam daily in the pool, walked the quiet green aisles of the unpaved road that lay unbelievably untouched just a quarter of a mile to the west of the house; ate three balanced bountiful meals daily; slept eight hours nightly. Tried not to boast of these almost spectacular accomplishments; hugged them to herself, in fact, in the superstitious secret belief that to boast of them would be, somehow, to have them snatched away like one who brags of her jewels and is promptly robbed of them.

There were, about this big lavish new dwelling place, some aspects that I could scarcely credit. Fourteen miles from the sprawling brawling industrial city of Bridgeport; barely one and a half hours distant from New York by motor up the Merritt Parkway. Yet walking almost soundlessly down the woods road one could actually, now and then, glimpse a plump little red fox cub skittering briskly into sudden hiding, or even its tawnier mother pointing a sharp muzzle in staring alarm before shunting her new offspring to safety. Intruders on this road were so rare as to be almost non-existent. No one in Easton walked—that is, for the pleasure of walking. No one, in fact, seemed to walk anywhere except on the paved cement of the city shopping streets of the United States. To enjoy walking merely as walking was—and is—considered an eccentricity in the United States. Children ride to school. Men and women drive to work. Golfers ride from hole to hole around the golf course; housewives drive to the supermarket; their children sit in the little metal compartment of the shopping wagon with the other vegetables as the cart is pushed up one aisle and down the next. In Los Angeles California this anti-walking trend has been carried to the last absurdity. In Beverly Hills, for example, one who walks on the quiet residential streets is municipally regarded as a potential criminal. To stroll at five in the bright sunlit afternoon past the costly comfortable dwellings that line either side of the street is to be as alone as though one were walking in the snowy wastes of the Arctic or on the sands of the African desert. No one. No human thing moving or visible. Then suddenly a car appears. It is a police car. It stops.

"Heh! Where you going?"

"What!"

"You heard me. Where you going?"

"Nowhere."

"What you doing here?"

"I'm walking."

"Where to?"

"Nowhere. I just like to walk."

"What's your name?"

"Soandso."

"Where d'you live?"

"Suchandsuch."

"Get in."

"*Get in!* Listen, I certainly—"

"Get in, lady."

You are taken to and deposited at the address you have given, where your information is verified. That is, if you are lucky. You could be taken to the nearest police station. The charge: Walking. Loitering.

After two or three days at a luxurious hotel in Bel Air, surrounded by exotic flowers, swans, swimming pools and patios I approached the uniformed attendant who reigned over the car parking space.

"Tell me, is there some place where one can walk? Near here, I mean."

The broad paved road lay before us. Cars cars cars whooshed past at fearsome speed. There was absolutely no provision for walking; not even a footpath.

"Walk!" echoed the man, in a low voice as though I had queried him about some ancient obscene rite.

"Yes. A place that isn't so full of traffic—where one can walk, you know." It somehow began to sound foolish, even to me.

"Nobody walks," said the man, "except Europeans and people from New York."

But here in Connecticut, walking along the leafy unpaved path called Maple Road was to know a brief period of peace and serenity though every newspaper headline, every turn of the radio knob proved this to be a completely false state of mind. France. Italy. Germany. Belgium. Holland. Austria. Russia. England. Above all, England. This was the country which, after my own country, I thought best in all the world. Its people, so quietly humorous, so self-respecting, seemed to me actually the most civilized people on earth. How could this little dab of an island stand against the onslaught of the barbarians.

Next day, glancing out of my bedroom window at the early fresh Connecticut morning I might see a deer with her tiny doe at her side, standing a moment like statues on the lawn near the little pool in the walled garden. Another moment and they were away with a bound over the low stone wall, and into the woods. For a moment I would forget about England—the War—the world.

Of course the deer definitely did nibble the choice young greens in the vegetable garden, and so did the plump rabbits but no one was permitted to shoot them while I was around. Even the foxes had a heyday during my years on Treasure Hill. North Americans do a lot of shooting in the movie Westerns but not much otherwise as a sport. Through the centuries, from bow-and-arrow days to the present moment the British have had an obsessive craze to shoot any feathered or four-footed wild thing within sight. An ancient food atavism, probably.

Slowly, day by day, inch by inch, page by page, the novel was creeping its way toward completion. Slowly I was settling into the countryside, into the neighborhood. The postmistress at the Stepney Depot post office said, "I see by the Bridgeport *Post* you're writing a new novel. I suppose we'll all be in it, life-size."

"No. Not my neighbors. That would be cannibalism."

Jim Hitchcock who ran his own chicken farm at the far foot of the hill just across the road came up in his sparse spare time to give Al a hand with the mounting farm chores. And chance illness or a bit of unexpected trouble would find Mrs. Hitchcock stepping up the drive, looking, in her freshly starched gingham, as crisp as a pink carnation. In her hands she would be bearing a dish covered by a glistening white napkin. The community threads began to make a pattern . . . Tickets for the Firemen's Fair Benefit? Thought you'd like to contribute to the Easton School baseball team's uniforms . . . Lou Forsell returned from a hunting trip upstate and appearing at the door with a venison roast as neighborly proof of his prowess . . . town meeting at the school Friday night . . . see where they're talking about forming a committee . . .

At the little roadside corner grocery a couple of miles distant you easily had a first-hand lesson in Americana as you chose your list of flour sugar salt cereal delicious tangy "rat cheese." A Czech couple were owners; a hard-working pair, in the store early in the morning, late at night. She was a woman perhaps in her forties; teeth missing, high cheek-boned face; resolved, strong, hearty. First generation Americans. A second generation son and daughter; the daughter a student in a commercial art course at the university; the son majoring in executive management; interested in music. You got a vicarious thrill out of this.

You experienced the gustatory pleasure of plucking an ear or two of Golden Bantam or Country Gentleman corn from the garden cornpatch, ripe and warm from the sun; rushing with it to the kitchen where a pot of boiling water was hissing a welcome; popping the shucked ears into the pot in anticipation of that first delicious chin-buttering bite into the sweet kernels. How could one ever have eaten the stale and starchy ears that masqueraded under the title of fresh green corn in the New York grocer's vegetable bin?

You learned that you could, if you chose, daily eat fresh string beans or baby peas or tomatoes or lettuce or even spinach cucumbers or broccoli or cauliflower or cabbage or corn; but asparagus, always considered something of a delicacy, was a sometime thing, mysteriously enough. Once a week—twice at the most—did it. Asparagus simply wouldn't go down daily. Yet there it was every morning thrusting its green spears out of the earth, never tiring, popping up overnight, too profuse, too accommodating, too flavorous like a human who wants too eagerly to be loved and repels one by its insistence.

At that period I must have possessed (or been possessed by) a demonic energy. Within a period of less than two years I had written the autobiography *A Peculiar Treasure*; built and put into practical operation a whopping big house garden and farm; written the novel *Saratoga Trunk*; assumed my small part in the civilian effort that was being made by the citizens of the United States to assist Europe in its struggle against Nazi Germany; and was now deep in plans to collaborate with George Kaufman in a play entitled *The Land Is Bright*: a title taken from a poem by Arthur Clough. It was a strangely optimistic choice on our part, considering the mess the world was in.

> *And not by eastern windows only,*
> *When daylight comes, comes in the light,*
> *In front the sun climbs, slow, how slowly,*
> *But westward, look, the land is bright.*

It was almost a year later before westward took the hint.

The novel finished at last I deliberately did something that all my life I had wanted to do. For one week that August I played a leading part in a professional theatrical company presenting a play that I myself had written in collaboration with George Kaufman. All professional playwrights privately think of themselves as potentially gifted actors, as all drama critics regard themselves (not so privately) as potentially talented playwrights. Both are almost invariably wrong.

The play was *The Royal Family* which had been produced at the

Selwyn Theatre in New York in 1927. It was a comedy about an eccentric and famous theatrical family—mother daughter son grand-daughter. George Kaufman and I assured everyone that definitely the play was not patterned on the brilliant Barrymore family, but we succeeded in convincing no one, including possibly ourselves. The play was a success, is still being done in stock and in amateur performances, and I always had had a mad yearning to play the part of the actress-matriarch, Fanny Cavendish. In the original New York company the role had been magnificently portrayed by the frail and indomitable English actress, Haidée Wright.

The hastily assembled summer stock company for the presentation of *The Royal Family* had one week's rehearsal before opening for a week in Maplewood New Jersey. As I had practically all my life thought of myself as a frustrated Bernhardt, and as I had, with George Kaufman, written every line of the play, I blithely assumed that all this would come naturally. It had taken us the incredibly long period of eight months to write that play, way back in the '20s; we had worked week in week out, I had thought that every line of dialogue in that comedy was clearly engraved forever in the memory cells of my brain. Not at all. I had to learn them almost as though I had never before heard them. Always I have had the deepest admiration and respect for actors and the art of acting. Certainly I had sat through rehearsals of many plays and agonized as a playwright through many a road try-out. Now I thought with awe of these past performances on the part of professional actors. The terms "on cue" and "pace" and "projection" took on different dimensions. I wasn't coming in quickly enough on cue, my pace was too slow, I wasn't projecting.

A very long part to be learned; costumes to select; fittings; rehearsals. Character make-up for the Fanny Cavendish part; hair style too. We opened in *The Royal Family* in Maplewood New Jersey in mid-August 1940. The blighted Bernhardt wasn't bad but she wasn't good. Her performance could be—and was—described by the gruesome adjective "adequate." I was adequate; the most damning phrase in the language of the theatre.

The drama critics of the New York daily newspapers—the *Times,* the *Tribune*—all of them—journeyed out to Maplewood, to my consternation. George Kaufman and Beatrice, many other friends, and a wholesome leavening of enemies showed up; not only showed up, but the Kaufmans and a sprinkling of other theatre-wise ones actually came backstage to see me *before the performance*, when I was making up. This was, naturally, in order to evade the awful moment when they might otherwise be obliged to go back after a probably disastrous performance to tell me how dazzlingly I had carried the whole thing off. Pre-performance visits are strictly taboo. They knew and I knew that to pay this pre-curtain call was as unheard of and as nerve-rackingly dreadful to the victim as a cosy social call on a young prospective mother in labor with her firstborn.

The reviews damned me with faint praise; not bad not good. To my amazement I found I was bored. Bored by the routine of coming down to the theatre nightly and twice on matinee days; making up, putting on and taking off those clothes; going on stage to say those same lines, night after night. I thought of actors who play two years, three years, in the long run of a successful play. The monotony of it, I thought. Petrifaction must set in. I realized now why gifted playwright-actors such as Noël Coward refuse to stay more than three months as actor in a play they have written.

I thought Saturday night would never come.

On the Friday night before closing Louis Calhern, playing the dashing Tony Cavendish, dropped me on the stairs. Louis Calhern was about six foot four in height; handsome, husky; and a successful actor these many years. But at that time I definitely was twenty-five pounds heavier than I am today. The onstage stairway was steep and winding.

After a terrific bravura speech all about the theatre and the Cavendish clan and the art of acting, I was supposed to faint; then to be gathered into the arms of my stalwart though wayward son Tony Cavendish and to be carried by him up the stairs and ostensibly into second-floor offstage bedroom; no mean feat. Halfway up the stairs he dropped me. As I thumped to the steps the audience sat petrified. So did I. I toyed with the idea of fainting in reality but the Ferbers are not a fainting family, Louis Calhern and I managed, by a mishmash of scrambles, hobbles, and a second herculean effort of lugging on his part, to get me through the upstairs exit and presumably into an offstage bed. At the end of this accomplished feat there issued from the audience a burst of hysterical applause interspersed with helpless shrieks of laughter, that even the Divine Sarah (who, I am told, always insisted on making her own exits under her own steam, even when she had but one leg) would have envied.

Saturday night finally came round, as Saturday nights always do. I wiped off the make-up, packed up the dresses, said goodbye and thank-you to the company, and so back to Easton and the comparative peace of the heavenly hill. Still stage-struck, still in love with the theatre, in a way, like an erring wife who has strayed for a fling with that dangerous strangerous heart-breaker and home-wrecker, the Theatre; and who now, all contrition, comes creeping back to her tried-and-true love, her love of a lifetime; the dependable, stimulating, accustomed, understanding husband—Writing.

It had been a curious year, coming now into its autumn. An exciting and productive year; an industrious and a terrible year, too; a year through which—over and above and through everything that happened —there was the feeling of waiting for something awful and inevitable. It was an oppressive sensation like that one has when waiting for a hurricane to burst—the dreadful stillness, the ominous mammoth clouds in the distance, the jagged thrust of far-off lightning, the rumble and roar of approaching thunder, nearer and nearer, louder and louder. You sensed there would be a feeling of actual relief when finally the thing burst. The house rocks, the thing beats against the walls, the windows; you must fight its ravages and repulse it as best you can.

Physically, the United States was lapped in comfort. A huge thing called the Atlantic Ocean (which no longer really existed as a barrier and which, in the next twenty years, was to shrink to the size of a hop-skip-and-jump puddle) lay between us and England; between us and France Italy Germany Belgium Holland.

Dunkerque had reared its massive monument in history; one of the most heroic achievements—if not the most—the world had ever known. Throughout the United States, wherever you were, whatever you might be doing, you changed your course, you temporarily dropped your occupation to listen to one of two voices, whichever was scheduled to be on the air waves at the time. You listened to the civilized and deeply informed thoughts, spoken with assurance and passionate con-viction, with which President Franklin D. Roosevelt, President of the United States, addressed his millions of hearers. You listened to the curiously compelling voice of Winston Churchill as he seemed, almost singlehanded, to be battling the shrieking psychotic who threatened to destroy England and the world. Churchill's was an astonishingly flexible and utterly convincing voice; sometimes a nasal snarl that expressed withering contempt; now stormy, now reassuring, always resolved. There was wit, astoundingly enough (considering the somber subject of his message) in what he said, and heroic exaltation without heroics, and on occasion a colloquial pungency that caused the stricken world suddenly to roar with laughter.

Perhaps George Kaufman and I would be seriously at work on Scene I Act II of *The Land Is Bright*. We worked daily from eleven in the morning until three—four—five in the afternoon. But then, as writers almost invariably also work when they're not working, it might well have been called a roughly round-the-clock job, as usual. While actively at work in our regular hours of collaborative writing no interruptions were permitted—no telephone calls, no messages slipped under the door announcing that the house was on fire; no lunch, even, unless one or the other decided that we must choose between an immediate sandwich and coffee or death from starvation. No interruptions, then—except two. One was the voice of Franklin Roosevelt, the other the voice of Winston Churchill. An announcement that Churchill would speak next day over the radio aroused, perhaps, a shade more anticipation than a Roosevelt announcement. Roosevelt's was a voice of reassurance and even of hope; Churchill's was the difference between the life and the death of the human spirit throughout Europe and perhaps the world.

Winston Churchill on the air at noon. We quit work. The voice came to us, the man was there, the spirit was there, filling the room with courage and a kind of defiant gayety. Hitler speaking in German from Germany had screamed his latest boast:

"We shall wring the neck of England as you would wring the neck of a chicken."

England had retorted with a gloriously effective bombing of Germany that night. And now Churchill's incredibly clear youthful Eton-student voice came to you, you seemed actually to see the cherubic pink face, the sternly resolved eye, the contemptuous curl of the lip as he said, jovially:

"*Some* chicken! *Some* neck!"

There is an interesting resemblance in the speeches of dictators, no matter what country they may hail from or what language they may speak.

Just about twenty years after this charming boast by Hitler, the guttural and rasping voice of a dictator again came to us as we listened, horrified, to the message on the air waves (television this time. Wonderful, isn't it, how civilization has made its gigantic strides!). The voice spoke in Russian and it issued from the metallic throat of Khrushchev. He was speaking to the United States of America in general, and to Dwight D. Eisenhower, President of the United States, in particular.

"We will destroy you," he said, "as we would pick up a cat by the tail and dash its brains out against a stone wall." A pretty thought. A graceful phrase in diplomacy.

Tiresome, these boys are and repetitious. But terribly dangerous, too, as are all psychotics behind a weapon.

So then, the Kaufman-Ferber play entitled *The Land Is Bright* opened at the Music Box Theatre, New York, October 28, 1941. In three incident-and-character-crammed acts it presented the rise and fall and rise of three generations in a fabulously new-rich American family in New York City from 1896 to 1941. It was, in genre, a melodrama I suppose. Powerfully written, in parts, by two people who wanted terribly to say something that they deeply felt should be said. Perhaps that was its chief fault. Certainly the play was not a success. But even now, two decades after its birth and death, I believe it was prematurely born. Its theme was not a popular one at the time; it was not even understood, really. It was like trying to get the attention of a giant lying asleep as though drugged. In dramatic (and melodramatic) terms the play said Wake up! Wake up! Wake up! And the giant mumbled gowaydonbothermecantyouseeImbusy. It was a play that might even have had a better chance today than it had in October 1941.

When Japan struck its fearful blow on December 7 1941 it was, in a fantastic way, almost a relief. Here was the hideous Thing, here was War, the festering monster, turned loose in our midst. It was the awakening of the sleeping giant. There was a fearful task to be done, the country aroused itself to do it.

Bridgeport Connecticut was about ten miles distant from Treasure Hill. Bridgeport became an arsenal. Airplanes, guns, brass equipment poured out of its vast factories. So did smoke and oil fumes from its chimneys. The surface of the swimming pool at Treasure Hill bore an iridescent glaze. The dust-cloth came away black after it had passed over the white-and-green dining room. Fine. Tangible evidence that the giant was stoking his furnaces against the enemy.

As one reads of it today the four years that followed seem as quaint and old-timey as the days of the Civil War cannon or the Indian bow-and-arrow. The good Americans were good and the bad Americans were bad and the selfish were selfish; but then there turned up the good-bad and the bad-good and the selfish-unselfish and so on. War is a psychological electric blender.

What to do? we said, the one to the other. What sort of work can I best do? we said; those of us who certainly were not actual combat material. Food and guns and planes and bombs and ships. That was the idea.

Food rationing. Certainly we were better fed even under rationing than any other country in the world. But we took it hard. Overfed overweight United States of America had, in this past century, got into the habit of accepting luxuries as necessities. Beef butter eggs cream milk sugar cheese whisky gasoline steel; all these poured out of the farms and factories and into us and onto the roads of the countryside and had for decades and decades. In the West or Southwest a T-bone steak with two fried eggs on top was not considered an unusual luncheon dish for a trucker in a roadside diner. Exotic fruits filled the grocers' windows.

In a perverse way you almost envied the men in the troopships, the bomber planes. At least they knew the job they had to do and they did it. At home one felt lion-hearted and capable of anything but the world realistically saw just a gray-haired woman in her fifties; energetic, but what of it?

The black market was flourishing. It brought into existence some of the weirdest examples of the smallness of the soul under stress. A prosperous and not-too-distant neighbor lived in that region of pleasant well-kept homes. Just past middle age, the owner of the house was a quiet and highly intelligent professional man, married, as so often is the fate of quiet husbands, to a waspish woman.

Periodically we of the town of Easton, as in all other localities, were required to call at the local headquarters of the Food Rationing Board to declare our stock on hand of this or that rationed commodity. It might be oil, fats, grain, butter or many another item. Our ration books were more valuable to us than our jewels, if any.

So as their turn came in the line this husband and wife stood now before the rationing board.

"Sugar?" the rationing official asked, her pen poised. "How many pounds on hand?"

The wife spoke up quickly. "Ten pounds," she said. "Our five each, of course. And the maids have their ration, naturally. Two maids."

The official began to enter this in her papers. Quietly the husband said, "There is an entire barrel of sugar in the attic of our house."

There was a moment's awful silence. If he had said his wife had committed a murder and had stowed the body in the attic, it could not have been more shocking. He did not say, my wife has an entire barrel of sugar in the attic.

One of the infinitesimal acts of unsung heroism in the course of the Second World War.

9

It would be pleasant to believe that the abhorrence of war—a state of mind so prevalent in the United States—is due to a high spiritual quality inherent in the citizens of this exhilarating and fortunate country. It is true that North Americans are deeply opposed to war as a means of settling national or international problems or crises. They are peace-loving members of the human race. This commendable state of mind and emotion may partly be due to a civilized way of living and thinking. But it also could be partly a matter of geography. A large and wealthy family, dwelling in a handsome and commodious house surrounded by rich and extensive acreage is not likely to pick a quarrel with a less opulent and lucky neighbor; nor does it willingly participate in a quarrel which that neighbor may be carrying on with yet another neighbor. Free people with plenty of breathing space and the wherewithal to enjoy it rarely are war-loving people. They are likely to be good-natured, somewhat naïve, with a live-and-let-live philosophy.

For more than four centuries the big bounding Atlantic Ocean and the vast tumultuous Pacific Ocean had successfully barred marauders from our wide open doors. From the security and richness of our ocean and mountain fastness we could stand on the front porch and safely shout, "You can't catch me! You dassn't touch me! My father is bigger than your father. My daddy can lick your daddy, only he doesn't even want to."

But that was before Science had completely banished the distance that once existed between the borders of the Atlantic the Pacific and all the oceans and mountains and lands of the planet Earth; and had filled the air of the universe with potential death deliverable to millions of people at any moment in a single gesture.

Viewed from the disadvantage point of today, World War II, in spite of its then modern equipment and its endless lists of uselessly dead men women children, mounting into the tens of millions, was really just a sort of bow-and-arrow shindig. Today Science says what about all that nonsense in the 1940s, putting all those young fellows into uniforms and hauling all those men and the food and guns and equipment and stuff around in ships and trucks and planes and so on, when all you have to do now is press a button and bingo! all fall down.

To the free citizens of a democratic and liberal country the face of the dictator of an enslaved country almost invariably seems to be cast in comic mold. The destructive potentialities of the Power Monster are under-estimated by the world because his outward aspect is misleading. Usually he has the aspect of a clown or an ape or a rat or a fox or a pig. Certainly this is true of Hitler Mussolini Stalin Khrushchev. Look at that Charlie Chaplin mustache we said in the mid-'30s. Get a load of that falsetto. The guy is a nut. And how about the other one with the stickout jaw and the bulging eyes. Look at those pudgy paws. Look at those mean little eyes. Get those whiskers. Again and again we seemed unable to realize that these clowns, apparently cast for comedy, were performing as the leads in world tragedies.

Now the knowledge finally was borne in on us that these Funny Faces were playing for keeps. So then, the millions of men were mobilized and trained and sent about their dreadful business; and thousands of factories, shops, production plants, poured out the planes the guns the equipment. A country so accustomed to plenty that lavishness was merely taken for granted now was sternly ordered to observe a system of rationing. Food, gasoline, clothing, travel, white paper, fuel, electricity—all the things we had carelessly regarded as necessities, suddenly now became luxuries; frequently unobtainable luxuries.

Middle-aged gray-haired non-combatants like myself stumbled around rather blindly saying What to Do? How to Help? No good sticking your head out of a window like Barbara Fritchie and waving a flag. The Government of the United States replied by saying, "Use the tool you are best equipped to handle. You're a writer. Write."

There followed three or four years of sporadic and ineffectual writing, punctuated by two major events that affected the future years of my life. The first was on the tragic side—or so I at first believed. The second was enormously dramatic with a mingling of the terrible and the exhilarating.

There was formed a tremendously capable and hard-working group called the Writers' War Board. I was not an executive member of this organization (I am bad on Boards) but I, like scores of other writers, was directed by it. You, as a professional writer, were ordered to write an article, a short story, a sketch, a play on a given subject or against a stated background, depending usually upon whether you were a playwright, a writer of factual articles, a novelist, a short-story writer. The over-all results were sometimes superb, often pretty good, frequently terrible.

Writing to order is something I simply cannot do well. This may be due to vanity, stubbornness or (I hope) a purely creative urge to write only as I please. It accounts for the fact that I never worked in pictures in Hollywood as a paid writer; never was able to accept a suggested idea as a background for a novel or play of my own. The idea had to come from within me. The process must be always a kind of chemical fusion. Letters come to every writer, people come to every writer, and they say, "I've got the most wonderful idea that only you could write. The background is the Midwest and this fellow—"

"No!" you say. "No! I don't mean to be impolite—but no!"

Certainly in the years during which I had worked as a newspaper reporter—from the time I was seventeen until I was twenty-one—I had to cover whatever assignment was given me. If it was a factual assignment I wrote it factually, trying at least not to yield to the temptation to be fancy. Fanciness in news stories was frowned upon by the tough-minded expert city editor of the Milwaukee *Journal* which was the hard-hitting bulletin afternoon paper on which I worked for fifteen dollars a week. Sometimes I was permitted what was then called a "feature" story; usually based on a situation or an idea I myself had dug up. Then I really squared off and gave it my all—adjectives, characterization, humor, tears (I hoped) in a pent-up burst of creative and definitely fancy verbiage. May no eye, including mine, ever again fall on those early effusions.

It is just possible, psychologically, that it was this experience in early writing frustration that later caused me always to rebel at being told what to write. Perhaps I subconsciously felt that to write to order would signify a throwback to my beginning years as a writer. Vanity, insecurity—whatever it fundamentally was—there it was, unsurmountable.

So, then, I wrote whatever the Writers' War Board ordered me to write and the result was, at best, commonplace.

"You're to go to Kokomo on Tuesday," the Writers' War Board would say. "Here are your plane tickets."

"Kokomo!" feebly. American town names containing the letter K and especially those beginning with K—Kokomo; Kalamazoo (where I was born); Kewaskum; Kewaunee; Kankakee; not to mention Oshkosh which carries the K in its middle—these are for some obscure reason considered mildly comic and always were good for a laugh in the old days of vaudeville.

I love geography on the hoof; travel, that is. But geography, map-wise, was one of my weak points at school and still is. At this moment I don't think I could bound New York State.

So then, "Kokomo! Where—I mean—what—?"

"Kokomo Indiana," accompanied by a shuffling of papers meaning get going, now. "There's a plant there that manufactures lifeboats. That's what I said. Lifeboats. They want a story on the manufacture of lifeboats, how they're made and so on, and They want it to be in the form of fiction. Attractive. They're having trouble getting workers to stick. They all want to make airplanes. You know—lifeboats—wonderful—necessary to the winning of the War—heroic weapon of construction not destruction, see. *Cosmo* says they'll use it."

So off to Kokomo and into the lifeboat factory and around and everything, my old reporter's knack put to good use again; and out by way of the Indianapolis airport via a bumpy little low-flying plane in which I proceeded to be very sick indeed. Throughout the little trip I found myself thinking of Booth Tarkington, that superb writer hailing from Indianapolis; and recalling that heartbreaking and funny novel *Alice Adams*, the poignant story of a wallflower whose agonies I so well understood, having often endured them in my Appleton Wisconsin ugly duckling school days.

The story was written, *Cosmopolitan* magazine published it, I never have seen it since and I can only hope that it served the purpose for which it was intended, but I somehow doubt it. The story was entitled, not very brilliantly, *Life Boat*.

"Write a short story about older women working in airplane factories. Certain operations can be performed by older women and that will leave men free for the tougher jobs, see." That was easy. Bridgeport was a mass of airplane manufacturing and Bridgeport was only about twelve miles distant from Ferber's Folly (Treasure Hill to you). Older women delightedly working in airplane factory. Doing their War bit. Now independent of grudging son-in-law. Don't have to take any sass from grandchildren. Get new dress, have hair done at a beauty parlor; rejuvenation. Title; *Grandma Isn't Playing*.

Rehabilitation story. Ex-telephone-lineman used to work on those high poles. Injured in the war. Can't remember anything. Badly smashed up. Months. Gets a letter from his girl back home. It doesn't matter how badly smashed I love you. Magic. Cured. Marriage.

Far far back in the deep-freeze compartment of my mind I found myself thinking of a novel-idea that had been tucked away and half forgotten in these past busy years. Actually, no arresting and legitimate idea ever is forgotten by a writer, once it is conceived. It may be ignored, it may be pushed back into a remote corner of the memory, and there it lies, sometimes perhaps kicking and even whimpering until one day it bursts into yells and will no longer be ignored. It has grown into surprising dimensions as though thriving on neglect. You lavish time and care on it, you write it finally because you must—to get rid of it.

I had once, on a brief visit to California, made a hasty and unpremeditated trip to Seattle Washington. No reason, really. Vaguely I knew about the explorers of the Northwest Territory. I knew and loved San Francisco but San Francisco wasn't Northwest, it was West. I had taken a train from Los Angeles, bound for Seattle. We rode and rode and rode and I stared and stared and stared at the United States of America going by the car window. The forests of Michigan and Wisconsin were not new to me, but they were matchsticks compared to this Northwest region. Forests mountains lumber camps; forests forests forests. This was Gargantuan. This was Paul Bunyan country. This was old Mother Nature at her most colossal. You want a river? Here's the Columbia, just for example. You want bays mountain peaks, forests, ocean on a scale to be seen nowhere else on the continent of North America? Here they are. Help yourself. Make yourself at home. Don't let it scare you. Just pull a deep breath. You'll get used to it.

Here was the city of Seattle built like an amphitheater that slanted steeply down to the Bay. Facing it was its worshiped and unpredictable goddess, Mount Rainier, now coquettishly hiding her face and form behind folds of gray chiffon, now blazing forth in cloth-of-gold and purple velvet.

There had been an exhilarating ten days; roaming the Farmer's Market or prowling Skid Road on the waterfront; up to the University on the Hills. The people were hospitable and interesting; the social life, scenery, conversation, history a source of daily delight; the hotel luxurious the food Olympian (if you haven't combined rock crab with ice-cold beer or Columbia River salmon with a dry cold martini you come under the head of deprived); the boat trip to Victoria British Columbia, and Victoria itself, with Hindus dashing about on bicycles, their robes billowing out behind them; school girls in black woolen long stockings, business and professional men in striped pants, black bowlers, umbrella, as British as London City; the Japanese, Chinese, East Indians on the streets of Seattle; and always the forests the forests the mountains the mountains in the near distance and the air all iridescence; all this, all these, and a thousand others.

Strange people turned up; sometimes wonderful, sometimes bizarre. Conversation with them was almost invariably refreshing, frequently rewarding, always thriftily stored away, through force of habit, in an untidy notebook or an equally untidy mind.

Dave Beck, for example, though I never did have that conversation with him; never tried. He took the initiative. Dave Beck, now serving a Federal prison sentence, was at that time not only the local Labor King but famous as the National Overlord of the Teamsters' Union, one of the most powerful if not the most powerful union in the United States. His canny eye espied me one day at lunch in the Olympic Hotel, surrounded though he was by a group of hand-picked henchmen. He sent a message via the head waiter. He would be delighted, the message said, if I would go to the afternoon races with him today, and to dinner afterward. It was tempting. A chance at least to get a surface knowledge of this strange product running amok in a democratic society. But the voice of the young girl reporter of many years back now whispered cautiously in my ears—and I wish I hadn't heeded her.

"They'll arrange to take photographs of you at the races with Dave Beck, and photographs of you at dinner with Dave Beck and his crew. They'll send them out through the newspapers of the country. It won't be bad for Dave Beck to be photographed with a respectable middle-aged woman writer. But some day when they catch up with him it won't be so uninvolved for you."

I didn't go to the races, I didn't go to dinner and I wish I had. Writers can't afford to be cautious. Better to be misunderstood, if necessary.

Bafflingly, the Seattle Washington reaction as it developed on the sensitive plate of my writing sense was almost identical with that I had after the Texas trip. Too vast a canvas; too overwhelming. Too much of everything. It was like a table so laden with rich and varied food that at contemplation of it your appetite vanishes. Nature and history and the teeming present combined to make this a man's job of writing. This, like Texas, was a man's world, I told myself; but I didn't actually believe it. This sort of reasoning, I felt sure, had limited women for centuries. You can write about anything that interests you. It will be tough work. Well, you're used to hard work. What are you sniveling about! Besides, you won't be writing about a region, this will be about people—people who are in every way remote from the Eastern sea-board where you live. You came here in the first place because you had a book-idea about a family that had lived for generations in this gigantic Northwest and who had turned out to be little or big or both. And the effect of this War on them. You simply are unhappy writing little ineffectual pieces about this and that, on assignment. It's no good and you know it. This is something you want to write because you want to write it; you thought of it, it popped into your head. Write it.

Forget it. Too long. Take months maybe years. Do as you're told, They know what They want you to do. But I'm no good at it, I whimpered. Maybe later. Let it simmer. This can't go on forever. . . . Oh yes it can. And worse can follow if whiners think they know better than They.

Back in New York, back at Treasure Hill, that View seemed some-how smaller but as lovely as ever. It didn't overpower you, it just took you tenderly in its arms.

Write as you're told to write, and shut up.

An astounding thing happened. There came a communication from Washington and it wasn't the State of Washington. It was Washington D.C. And two young Air Force officers—a major and a colonel—came a-calling. You are asked, I was informed, to go abroad as correspondent for the United States Air Forces. You will be expected to fly over the Hump. Because of the altitude necessarily involved you will first go to Washington for a complete heart checkup at Bethesda Hospital in Maryland. Planes at that time were not expertly and completely pressurized as they are today.

Well. That was more like it. Edna, you're shot with luck.

Heart checkup. A mere formality. Aside from those routine stethoscope formalities I never had given any particular attention to that important piece of physical machinery. Certainly I had given more time, thought and financial help to the electric pump cosily tucked away underground at Treasure Hill where it somewhat grudgingly forced the necessary water into the main house, into the swimming pool, into the farmer's cottage. It was a temperamental and unpredictable organ, that underground electric pump, insatiably demanding attention and given to fits of hysteria when denied it.

My own physical pump, tucked away behind a barrier of protective ribs, was taken for granted by me at least. I was walking and working and sleeping and eating and occasionally playing. What more?

Washington was an orderly madhouse as was any capital of any nation in wartime. Hotel accommodations were practically unprocurable. Streets were packed. Taxis rare as golden coaches. Blithely I plunged into the maelstrom, swimming with the crowds; battling against them. Here was the powerhouse of the horrible but now inevitable thing called the Second World War and I was to be a purposeful agent in it at last.

The heart specialist at Bethesda Hospital turned out to be a man I had known in New York, which was his home in peacetime. I knew he stood high in his field. This was reassuring. The butterflies that had been beating their wings in my stomach quieted down.

"I was jittery," I said. "I suppose everyone's jittery in Washington. But I feel better, now that I know it's you."

The usual routine. Then a thing gaily called the Twostep which turned out not to be so very gay because it actually was two steps; two up two down, like the sort one sometimes sees in private libraries in aid of out-of-reach bookshelves.

Up two, down two, up two, down two, up two down two, uptwodown twouptwodowntwouptwodowntwo. A bit winded but who wouldn't be!

Lie down on this cot. Relax. . . . Now this machine will give the effect of the altitude you will experience on flying over the Hump.

"I've climbed," I boasted, "to the top of Long's Peak in Colorado on my own feet and that is an altitude of fourteen thousand two hundred and fifty."

"Really!" the doctor said politely. He was busy with gadgets and things.

"Everything all right?"

"Just stay there another minute. Then you can get dressed."

So I bustled into my clothes and came out and he quietly showed me a cardiogram on which all the little peaks that should have been pointing up were pointing down.

"You can't go."

"Can't go where?" Idiotically.

"You can't fly over the Hump. Sorry."

It was a cold and snowy day and I remember stumbling rather aimlessly around the streets of Washington; the suddenly empty-seeming streets. I felt very sorry for myself followed by a surge of wholesome fury at the Fates who for the second time had played me a shabby trick in wartime. Twenty-five years earlier, in World War I, they had prevented me (for a quite different reason) from fulfilling a Red Cross writing assignment in Europe. The remembrance of this added now to my deep disappointment and frustration.

Back to Treasure Hill and the Writers' War Board assignments. The novel of the United States Northwest, whose theme was the mythical Melendy family of Seattle from their pioneer beginning to the present day, now began of its own volition to take form and to demand attention.

Write me! Write me! it said.

I'm busy. I haven't time. Go away.

Write me! I'm Peace and I'm War and I'm the helpless refugees of Europe against whom your doors are closing tighter and tighter. I'm your lifeblood. What's it matter whether you fly over the Hump and write about it or not? I'm here, waiting, hearts don't count with me.

So there was another journey to Seattle (Is This Trip Necessary?) and research and notes and the beginnings of a skeleton form. Technique and imagination had irresistibly taken over again. But I fought against it and it was not until 1945 that the novel was published. It turned out to be pretty good, I thought, but not as good as I had hoped. Perhaps it had lacked pre-natal care. Perhaps it was one of those unwanted offspring. It was called *Great Son* (See Shakespeare: *Coriolanus*). "Thou know'st, great son, the end of war's uncertain."

Incredible though it now may seem (or does it?) the people of the United States were being a little nonchalant about buying War Bonds. These were the things necessary to keep afloat the great and complex plan of war against the enemy. You bought War Bonds, you were paid interest on these bonds, you placed them comfortably in your bank box or your safe or whatever your cache for hoped-for security and you knew that if these were not a sound and dependable investment then nothing in our world was sound and dependable. But the sales, incredibly enough, lagged. I think that perhaps we, as a whole nation, hadn't yet actually accepted this hideous war as inevitably our concern. War haters, accustomed through the centuries to a habit of security fostered by well-being and geographical remoteness, many still thought, perhaps privately, that if you didn't look, if you ignored it, it would slink away.

So the War Bond selling groups were formed; glamour pitchmen recruited from the ranks of Hollywood; writers of a less dazzling appeal, certainly, whose books had (it was hoped) been read by solid cash customers. The glittering young motion picture stars and some no longer so young or so effulgent but still solid in the affection and admiration of a vast American public; the virile and the durable male stars of pictures; the well-known men and women of the legitimate stage; all these now were called into service as salesmen.

It may have been a bit exhausting at times, but it was competitive, it gave the performer a feeling that something tangible was being done by a team of which he or she was one.

You went from town to town, from city to city. You went to Gary Indiana and Chicago Illinois and Kansas City and Milwaukee and Boston and up and down, speaking in theatres, school auditoriums, halls. Four or five speakers made up a team.

An example might be composed of Clifton Fadiman, Carl Sandburg, Fredric March, Oliver La Farge, S. J. Perelman. There was an air of excitement and even festivity about the proceedings. One had something resembling a feeling of guilt because the whole thing was fascinating and unpredictable. In the first place, you were, day and night, in brilliant and amusing company. Talking and laughing with the Fadimans the Marches the La Farges and the Perelmans of the world definitely is no hardship. Then you read the newspaper accounts, you heard the radio commentators as the dreadful news from England France Belgium Holland poured in. You felt a slacker.

To promote the sale of War Bonds. That was the job. The team would be given the fanfare on arrival in a city because this was good salesmanship. Police escort, sirens screaming, pennants and flags flying, we swept down the streets toward the hotel, the hall or whatever. A meeting at noon, in the afternoon, and the big blast at night. You spoke and spoke and spoke. Carl Sandburg played the guitar and sang. We tried to hold our audience and usually did. But the chief actor, the real puller-in of Bond money, was the auctioneer.

In every town our platform was dramatized by the performance of the local hard-headed and popular citizen who made what we called the pitch.

There is no denying the fact that writers should be read but not seen. Rarely are they a winsome sight. Women writers do not usually run to glamour. Men writers rarely look like movie stars. We made our speeches as best we could knowing that the patriotic audience wouldn't walk out on us but hoping that what we briefly said was entertaining or convincing or practically and dramatically effective—or, with luck, all four. Then the spell-binding auctioneer would take over and the faces of the audience lighted up as with incandescence.

Before the start of these carefully planned programs each writer had been asked to contribute to the common cache of prizes a large number of his or her own published books, autographed; and also notebooks, original manuscripts, corrected galley sheets. In any University Library, Historical Society Library or Museum of manuscripts these books, these notebooks, scraps of paper, these galley or page proofs all hen-tracked with the writers' corrections or additions would, in terms of literary history or of market value, be worth important sums.

Now the auctioneer stood up. He cleared his throat. On a stand by his side were piled the books, notebooks, original manuscripts up for bidding.

"Here we have . . . who will name the first bid for . . . what do I hear for this rare First Edition autographed by none other than . . . do you realize ladies and gentleman that this is actually the original manuscript, with hand-written corrections . . . this is an entirely hand-written first manuscript of . . . notebook containing the complete out-line and original notes on . . . my fellow Americans you have read the book made from this original manuscript, your children will read it and your children's children . . . imagine actually possessing the origi-nal manuscript of this great . . ."

They weren't *Hamlet* and they weren't *War and Peace* or the Guten-berg Bible. "Ten thousand dollars' worth of War Bonds for this priceless original work. . . . Who will make it twenty thousand . . . thirty . . . fifty . . . fifty . . . fifty . . . Gone for fifty thousand dollars' worth of War Bonds and worth a hundred . . . Now, my fellow Americans, we have here . . ."

Seated up there on the platform we needled each other jokingly as our children came on the block. No one of us would have admitted to that pang of anguish when a first manuscript or a complete notebook came up. The autographed books didn't matter. First edition or no first edition, it's possible to come by a book somehow if one really wants it. But it would be false to say, even under the circumstances, one did not appreciate something of the way the Uncle Toms and the Elizas felt when they saw their children and their grandchildren carried away by strangers, never again to be united with their mother or father or broth-ers or sisters. That paragraph—that page—you remember writing them twenty times before they came right. That chapter. It absolutely stuck there in the typewriter. Weeks went by, over and over you had rewritten it, trying for the perfection that never came. Perhaps I, a spinster, thought that these pieces of paper were my only tangible tie to the movement of the world I lived in and loved.

Sometimes, even now, I find myself wondering where they are—these children these time-yellowed bescrawled manuscripts and notebooks of novels and plays written forty—thirty—twenty-five years ago; *So Big*, done with a feeling of inner compulsion but with no hope of success; *Show Boat* whose actual writing was the nearest I ever came to enjoy-ment of my particular craft; *The Girls*; *American Beauty*; *A Peculiar Treasure*; *Come and Get It*; *Saratoga Trunk*; *The Royal Family*; *Stage Door*; *Dinner at Eight*; *Cimarron*. Sometimes I wonder where they are. Perhaps long ago cast into the dust bin; or brown-edged and crackling in an attic, if attics still exist.

There were times when these speaking engagements were ludicrous and even painful. Some misguided committee had assigned me to a between-curtain bond selling speech at the Winter Garden Theatre in New York. The Winter Garden is a huge Broadway playhouse in which big musical plays are presented. The play that season was Michael Todd's production of a colorful noisy scamper called *Mexican Hayride*. The theatre was packed with a war-weary audience that wanted only for an hour or two to forget the grim terror that now encircled the world. The curtain descended on the first-act finale of pretty girls, bare shapely thighs, stamping feet, flashing eyes, brilliant colors. The audience sat a moment, reluctant to awake to reality. From the stage right emerged a gray-haired character in navy blue and a definitely stern un-Mexican hat.

"Perhaps you've come here," I began, with less than engaging candor, "to forget about War and War Bonds. But—"

Truer word never was spoken. The audience rose as one man and surged up the aisles. The speech was concluded to more empty seats than have been seen since Samson put his shoulders to the temple pillars. It wasn't lack of patriotism or even shock at being jolted from the romantic to the commonplace; from fantasy to reality. They wanted only for a few moments to know the surcease of forgetting.

Sometimes, in these past distraught years since the so-called end of World War II, I have wondered why the writers, composers, players of this troubled country could not be effectively organized for what is termed peacetime. Then I remind myself of the Russian enslavement of the creative artist. Write this. Write that. Write and perform thus and so. Discipline is a primary necessity for the writer; but it must be self-discipline. Spontaneity must be the urge or the product is born dead.

Behind the heavy curtain of frustration, anxiety, apprehension, tragedy born of the War the life of a young ebullient nation went on, miraculously. Work, food, exercise, friendship, even fun somehow proceeded in almost orderly fashion. My little private world of family and friends was almost uncannily fortunate. The two nieces, Janet and Mina, had married and their husbands were off as part of the United States wartime forces in Europe. Janet was a member of one or another of the many theatrical companies organized under the USO, playing in the South Pacific or in Europe; with Moss Hart at the head of *The Man Who Came to Dinner* company. Mina whose work career was magazine advertising and publicity was in effective organization including canteen programs at which servicemen were served with food, entertainment, music, companionship. Sister Fan was an air-raid warden. Julia, now in her mid-eighties, did valiantly what she could, but now even that indomitable spirit, so triumphant in her early days of work and tragedy, occasionally was forced to submit to the weight of years.

Friends vanished and sometimes returned, having been to strange places that, until now, had been to us little more than tiny pink or blue dots on the map of an unpronounceable far-off region. Or you saw them gratefully performing tasks equally foreign to their accustomed career. Alfred Lunt, his shirt-sleeves rolled up, an apron tied around his waist, washing dishes daily at the Stage Door Canteen. Lynn Fontanne serving as waitress. On an errand in Washington I emerged from the White House main entrance one day just as one of the rare and coveted taxis pulled up at the steps. I said to the guard, "Do you think I can have that taxi if it isn't going to be held?"

"You sure can, Ferber," said a voice from within the taxi. And Robert Sherwood stepped out. War chores were no novelty to Bob. Famous as a playwright, he now was part of a staff whose work it was to discuss, to assemble, to dramatize the magnificent speeches with which President Franklin Roosevelt was charging the spirit of the country. In the First World War Bob had tried to enlist in various branches of the United States Armed Forces but his giant height—he was more than six feet seven inches—was against him. Desperate to serve he had enlisted and was accepted in the famous British-Canadian Black Watch regiment. He was almost incredibly thin for his height. The regiment's dashing uniform of plaid kilts, jaunty tunic, cocky cap sat almost ludicrously on this towering meager frame. The haunting El Greco face, the mournful compassionate eyes, so deeply beautiful in their intelligence, regarded unresentfully the amused glances of the passerby. That towering shambling figure with its Lincolnesque face may, on the surface, have appeared somewhat comic, but they knew—and he knew—that in World War I a man in the uniform of the Black Watch meant the reverse of comedy in 1917.

10

Recently I stumbled on a statistic that startled and fascinated me. Ordinarily, statistics have little fascination for the imaginative mind. When my eye comes upon one of those charts or graphs—especially the lightning-struck kind—proving the number of thousands of this that mingle with the tens of thousands of that, combining to produce the millions of those in countries whose names I cannot pronounce, I skip it. My mind simply doesn't work that way, which probably accounts for the fact that I just barely didn't flunk in arithmetic, algebra, geometry and physics at school in Appleton Wisconsin. But this particular statistic was about writers and I found it not only fascinating but incredible.

There are, the proven statistics said, only two hundred and fifty writers in the United States whose art or profession is that of creating original books, plays, short stories, articles; whose complete working hours are spent solely in the task of writing; and who earn their living by this means only. I, in my ignorance, had thought we numbered many thousands. If only from reading the book reviews and the publishers' advertisements I knew that books were written by college professors and taxi drivers; doctors, lawyers, actors; merchants, politicians, prize fighters, ex-kings-and-queens, insurance salesmen, murderers, strippers, whorehouse madams. But, the statistical article went on to say, these do not primarily earn their living as writers; perhaps because they couldn't. They may be one-idea people; they may lack the iron discipline necessary to drive themselves to a seat at that desk for hours daily, year in year out, with no taskmaster no time-clock standing over them saying, be here at eight, be here at nine, be here at ten; and sit there. Sit there whether you are able to write ten words a day or ten pages a day. Let nothing distract you, let nothing tempt you, let nothing lure you away.

So then, college professors may—and do—write books, but usually teaching is their means of livelihood; taxi drivers drive for a living; lawyers practice law. Writing is a precarious and unpredictable art or profession. A book, a play, may take one—two—five years in the over-all producing, from the time the actual idea is conceived until the final page proofs are read and the completed work is launched on the choppy or glassy seas of the vast reading public which may promptly cast the whole thing up on the beach and leave it to rot there. Even a single short story may require weeks in the writing, or months. But a novel may be published, may be adequately advertised, and may actually sell two or three thousand copies only, bringing the writer less than an unskilled laborer would earn by digging ditches. A play, after months and perhaps years of writing, weeks of rehearsal and preliminary touring, may open on Broadway Monday night and close the following Saturday; may, for that matter, close on Tuesday night. It has happened hundreds of times, and to playwrights of established reputation.

This is a risky means by which to support oneself and one's family. For the thousands who are ambitious not only to be writers but to write and who cannot afford to take this economic risk, writing must be a sometime thing; an avocation. They may write effectively, even magnificently, on occasion, but not as a daily yearly life-long career. They must write only after their accustomed daily work is finished; at night, during weekends, on holidays, in whatever spare moment they can contrive. It is a heartbreaking situation for a would-be writer of integrity, it explains why many potentially gifted writers have been twisted into strange literary distortions; hacks turning out scripts which they despised, pouring fodder into the maw of mechanical choppers such as radio, television, motion pictures in order, they hope, later to be able financially to write as they long to write. Unfortunately, this doesn't seem to work out well. A writer who has debauched his talent rarely makes the stiff grade back. His muscles of writing integrity have gone slack. Many years ago a writer named Gelett Burgess put it succinctly into ten words. He had heard a talented but unscrupulous writer say that he intended deliberately to write what he knew to be trash solely for money until he had what he considered enough to enable him to write the kind of thing he really longed to write. Gelett Burgess said, with terrible perspicacity, "You can't go on the street to earn a trousseau."

Compulsive and dedicated writing is the most purely creative and the most enduring of the arts. Painting and music are, perhaps, its closest rivals. But the canvas is a visual form, it can be copied but it cannot be reproduced; it must depend on talent or genius, on color, form, meaning, technique for its impact. It can be destroyed by a single gesture, never again to be seen. Music is limited by the scale and the conveying instrument, whether it be the human voice or the man-made device. Acting is an interpretive art. Deeply though I admire and love the theatre, when I hear it said of an actor that he created this or that part in a play I resent the statement. The actor may have been the first to interpret the character on the stage but he did not create it. The character was created by the author. Without the author there would be no character for the actor to present. Dancing is of the spirit and the emotions but it is the slave of the human body, and limited by it. It can soar just so far. Then muscles and flesh and bone rebel. Perhaps only Nijinsky ever was able to defy the law of gravity.

In the written word there is no voice or musical instrument to woo you or lull you or excite you as in music; no color or visual line or movement to puzzle or dazzle or exhilarate you, as in painting; no visual character or spoken dialogue as in the art of acting, so that the beholder may identify himself or his experience with a character or a situation; there is no motion, color, music, rhythm, as in dancing. In writing there are only the little black marks on white paper, but those marks must become living things, so charged with power and passion and imagination and truth that they are capable of transporting the reader into any world, any mood, and to influence him perhaps for a lifetime.

Come with me, the little black marks say. Or I will come with you, anywhere. Tuck me in a corner of your knapsack. Slip me into your pocket. Place me on your bedside table. I will keep you company as you eat your solitary dinner. I will serve you anywhere, everywhere; ill or well; happy or wretched; old or young; rich or poor. I require only that you bring with you tools of your own, and these will grow rusty if you fail to use them. You must read. You must think.

Read. Think.

The written legend, saga, story mysteriously manage, somehow, to survive through the centuries, through the thousands of years. Temporarily lost, rumors of their once having lived still persist. They are transmitted, sometimes in garbled form, by word of mouth from generation to generation. Many hundreds of years may pass over a lost manuscript before it is again found, defaced by time and the elements; almost, but not quite, reduced to dust, but bearing still in its heart the wisdom, the beauty, the truth which have persisted through the ages.

The written word has lived when most of its period has perished. Massive edifices built by man have crumbled and, through thousands of years, have again blended with the soil from which they came. Entire nations have vanished leaving almost no trace.

We are astounded by the emergence of the Dead Sea Scrolls after aeons of cave-hidden existence. Runic stones confound us like messages from another planet. Even the Dark Ages managed to hoard and preserve whatever feeble light they had in the form of laboriously wrought scrawls painstakingly cut into the walls of caves and crypts. Some writer, a thousand—two thousand—five thousand years ago felt the burning urge to communicate that which was in his mind, his imagination, his emotional being. Merely to utter the thought was not enough. It must be set down, it must not perish. So he wrote it, crudely on rock, on baked clay, on parchment contrived from the dried skin of animals.

The architecture of ancient Greece is a fragment only. Where are the rich and powerful citizens of Greece and Rome and the storied East and the land of Jesus and the Prophets? Who were the Big Business Men? Who were the oil millionaires of that day? Name me the stock market boys. Their names are obliterated as though they had never been. Yet the Apologia of Socrates lives today, Plato is here for the young and old to read; Euripides speaks, and Aeschylus and Horace. The Songs of Solomon; the compassionate and loving words of the great Jew Jesus; the wisdom and teachings of his Apostles in the faith of Judaism; all shine forth from the printed page, they are as lucid and as sound, philosophically and sociologically and humanely, as though they had been new-minted today by the wisest man in this tormented universe—whoever that may be.

Of a century now past the Tolstoy and the Chehkov of Russia, among others, are brilliantly alive today. Whatever became of that

Russian Grand Duke who gave those lovely parties? Catherine the Great and Peter, Tiberius and Pontius Pilate, Henry the Eighth and Hitler and Mussolini stormed and raged and brutalized and decreed, but that which they thought to accomplish is only black history; or worse has come to take its place as a result. Would you care to read or see a play by that hard-working lower middle-class English chap named Will Shakespeare? The books are just there on that shelf, all of them. And the theatre in which one of his plays is showing is just around the corner.

Perhaps it doesn't really matter; but through the decades of my life as a writer I have increasingly wondered why the millions of book-readers in the United States and the vast procession of government officials ranging from the President of the United States to the least of the tax-unit officials, have shown little or no curiosity concerning the actual labor attendant on the production of the written word. Vaguely the average person knows that in order to paint one must apply to canvas a brush with paint on it. In order to produce music some one arranges the notes of the scale and this comes out as sound through the human voice or a horn, a violin, a piano or some other instrument. But a book is a collection of printed pages on which words somehow have appeared and that's all there is to it. The hours days months years spent in seclusion, choosing these words from among the hundreds of thousands of words and trying to fashion them in relation to one another so that they will come alive with meaning or purpose or entertainment—these rather statistical matters do not ususally interest a reader, and perhaps this is a good thing. But to the writer there often is an irksome aspect to the reader's utter misunderstanding of, or indifference to, the art of writing.

The United States Government, and most readers, if they consider it at all, think of writing, not as an art, a profession, a craft or even a business. They seem to regard it as a kind of hobby or whim, like needlework or china painting or home-carpentering. Anybody can write, they say, and practically everyone does. They "take up writing" as the phrase goes.

"The children are all married and now I've got a lot of time on my hands—Wilmer is always off playing golf, seems—so I thought I'd take up writing. A book."

It turns out not to be writing but merely printed words on pages bound between hard covers. This is not actually a book. It has come to be known as a non-book, and thousands of these are published yearly, and it is dreadful to think that even the smallest sapling in the largest forest has been cut down to make pulp for the paper on which is printed this collection of jokes; this ghostwritten account of a sordid life; this crackpot religious fulmination; this deathly diet program. A plumber must serve an apprenticeship before he can become a member of his union; a teacher doctor lawyer engineer architect musician actor dancer scientist politician printer cook must spend months, even years, in the learning of his craft. But thousands blithely "take up" writing.

The writer is a writer because he cannot help it. It is a compulsion. Sometimes it is called a gift, but actually it is an urge for expression that simply cannot be denied. The born writer goes to his desk daily and remains there throughout certain fixed hours each day. Sometimes ten words manage to get themselves down on paper, sometimes a page or two, sometimes (rarely) five or even more. Even though he is economically entirely dependent on writing, a fiendish whining little inner voice immediately begins to devil him.

"What are you sitting here for, you dope! Who says you have to? You could be out playing tennis . . . Why'n't you go out to lunch? . . . There's the telephone, it must be the pantry extension, the other two are turned off if some one doesn't answer it after four rings I will . . . now it's stopped . . . I wonder . . . get to work . . . reread what you wrote yesterday it certainly sounded terrible when you looked at it then . . . mmm not so bad pretty good in fact . . . uh . . . where are those notes on . . . let's see . . . page 226 . . ."

You're off at last. Four hours later you look up at a discreet knock on the closed door. Lunch! But it can't be lunchtime!

If, after months and sometimes years of research, of notes, of a first rough copy, you begin to try to assemble this amorphous body into some semblance of form, begin the actual long process of writing in order and in sequence, it is better (for me, at least) to think of it only in terms of one day; today's work only. Each day three pages, two pages, even but one on a bad day; and sometimes all of it to be rewritten next day and often rewritten and rewritten. It is better to think of a novel or any long piece of work as a day to day task to be done, no matter how eagerly you may think ahead (when you're not actually putting words on paper) to the chapters not yet written. It is a long journey, to be undertaken sometimes with hope and confidence and high spirits; sometimes with despair. If one thinks of it in terms of four hundred—four hundred and fifty—five hundred pages one can drown in a morass of apprehension. So, one step after another, slowly, painfully, but a step. And so it grows. You have felt or observed in life something that you want terribly to say, and you want to say it more than you want to do anything else in the world.

It is finished, it is published, it is reviewed. And a reviewer may say, "Evidently this was written in the hope of making a movie sale."

One encounters strange comment:

"Look, do you write when you have the—uh—inspiration, or what?"

"It must be fun to be a writer."

"I'd like you to read a thing I've written—of course I only write for my own amusement . . . I don't publish."

"That novel about Texas—is that the story of your life?"

"That novel about New England—is that the story of your life?"

"That story about Alaska—is that the story of your life?"

Possibly they would not believe that all the characters, situations; the theme, the dialogue, the color, the movement are purely and solely created in the imagination of the writer. Cap'n Andy, Magnolia, Gaylord Ravenal, Julie in *Show Boat*, and the great Mississippi itself, for that matter, which I never had ever seen except from a train window in my early childhood; the three generations of spinsters in the novel called *The Girls*; the farm woman, Selina Peake and her son Dirk, of *So Big* (I never had spent a day on a farm and certainly never had borne a son); Clio and Clint of *Saratoga Trunk*; Yancey Cravat and Sabra of *Cimarron*; all these people of the crowded novels and all the characters of the plays were born of the imagination.

Yet when readers of these books write or speak to me, asking if this is the story of my life, I am far from irked or resentful. I am flattered. It means that these fictional lives, these characters that never existed except in my imagination, actually have taken on such proportions of reality that the reader believes them to have been formed on fact; and that the tragic and comic and everyday events described in the novels took place in real life. Not only that—in the story-teller's real life. What can a writer wish for more splendid than to know that by putting those little black marks on a sheet of blank white paper there have been accepted in the mind of the reader human beings with three dimensions who walk talk breathe live suffer exult die, much as the reader has done or will do, or has observed in his fellow men.

Is this, they ask, the story of your life?

Yes. My inner life. The life of my imagination and creative ability.

Writing is lonely work but the creative writer rarely is lonely or alone. The room in which one works is peopled with the men and women and children of the writer's imagination. Often they are difficult—but rarely boring—company. This is a fortunate thing, for they are with one day and night, they never leave while the book or play is in progress. One wishes sometimes that they would go away. Just leave me alone for an hour—a minute—won't you! Often they are so much more fascinating to the writer than the living people one actually encounters that to go to a party, a dinner, even to the theatre is an anticlimax. Every day for hours one is shut up in a room with a company of chosen people created by oneself. It is a pattern of self-immolation familiar to any writer worth reading. The writer does not even remotely look upon this as a hardship. It is a way of life; a necessary and chosen way of life. Witty conversation, purposely dull dialogue, love, murder, marriage, birth, violence, triumph, failure, death—anything can happen in that room. Only one thing must not happen; that dread horror, interruption. This routine, this treadmill of work, walk, sleep, eat for months on end is a writer's heaven. Anything less than a holocaust is resented as an unnecessary interruption. If a writer doesn't mingle much in society it is, perhaps, because he or she is surrounded by hordes of people throughout the working day, daily.

This makes for a reputation as a curmudgeon. For a practicing writer living in New York life can be as precarious, in its own way, as that of the early pioneer living in the stockade. The woods are full of Indians. Spartan though one may be, there definitely are temptations. I love the theatre, I love and value my friends, I like pretty clothes (but hate shopping); am sustained by contact with my immediate family wherever they may be (this is a familiar Jewish trait, doubtless, born of centuries of religious persecution and enforced isolation). I enjoy walking—not ambling, but walking a few miles. Shop windows on Madison and Fifth Avenues fascinate me. Whatever meets my eye, whether human or fabric, interests or stimulates me. To spend a day or a few days in the green countryside of nearby New England—or anywhere—is enormously reviving. I am, as I have said, almost neurotically conscious of being alive and living.

All this is time-and-energy consuming; and time-and-energy rewarding. Torn between a guilty conscience and the compulsion to work, small wonder that writers age and die before their time. Myself, I am, to my astonishment, quite ancient, so this does not apply to me.

Then, too, New York City is one of the crossways of the world. Everyone, it seems, comes to New York at least once a year. They come from California, Texas, Illinois, Alaska, Oklahoma, Maine, Massachusetts, Arizona; from France, England, Switzerland, Italy, Israel, Austria. They are friends, they have been hospitable, you want them to come to dinner, to go with you to the theatre; for cocktails; lunch. But you are working, you are bound to this treadmill, oftener than not. If you were reveling in one of those rare free-times it would be wonderful. Male writers I know have wives who cope with all these situations. The writer himself merely is present, practically a guest-host, at the festivity which has so carefully and tactfully been arranged with little or no help from him. Unfortunately—or fortunately—I am interested in, and appreciate, food and furnishings and flowers and comfort, and perhaps perversely I find it impossible to leave these details of hostess-ship to others, no matter how capable. This may be a form of vanity, but there it is. Melon and prosciutto ham to start? Or do you think they'd like that lovely crab bisque, after all the weather's pretty cold . . . entrecôte, or maybe a filet but they're so horribly expensive, of course there's no waste as there is on all those rib bones in a roast beef . . . vegetables . . . salad with a Camembert or maybe that heavenly Italian cheese—what's it called?—Fontina or Fontana or something . . . and could you give us a crème brûlée? With fresh strawberries. I saw some as I passed Ferrari's yesterday . . .

Cooking gives one a sense of achievement but I no longer have time for it, and perhaps, too, the infinite patience and energy required now are lacking. But the interest is there, and a sort of instinctive cook's knowledge of how it should be done. . . . Just pass a clove of garlic lightly over the leg of lamb, and a faint sprinkling of ginger, before you put it in the roasting oven, and add about two tablespoonfuls of black coffee to the basting gravy . . . What has this to do with writing! Nothing, unless living has to do with writing.

Perhaps the friends I love and cherish have been neglected, to my sorrow, for the work which is more demanding than they, who understand. They know, if they are members of the creative arts (and they usually sense the situation if they are not) that to stop or to be diverted from work in hand at a critical moment is likely to be fatal. It is like trying to arrest the progress of a skier in full speed down a hazardous mountain slope.

"Stop!" the bystander may say. "Stop and look at the sunset . . . Look at this enchanting field of snow-flowers. . . . Let me introduce you to Thomas Jefferson to Winston Churchill to Eleanor Roosevelt . . ."

"Me! Stop!" you yell as you whiz by. "If I stop I'll break a leg or be killed."

It all depends, I suppose—and one must make the decision—on whether you prefer to have some one say, "Did you know Ferber? She was a dolling. And such parties!" or: "My grandson at school brought home some books he has to read in English course. *So Big* and I guess *Cimarron* and *Show Boat*. I remember reading them when I was his age."

So then, to be a professional writer one must be prepared to give up almost everything except living. Amateur writers are not included in this rule. (I loathe loud-talking amateurs of any walk of life. An amateur is an apprentice and should conduct himself as such, keeping his mouth shut and learning his craft.) The first lesson to be learned by a writer is to be able to say, "Thanks so much. I'd love to, but I can't. I'm working."

All this does not mean that I believe a writer should forego travel, change, variety, gayety, fresh experiences. A writer, like the snail, takes his house—his workhouse—with him wherever he goes. A writer is, or should be, an explorer and a discoverer of the human race. If he is on the pinnacle of Mount Everest, the highest known point, or on the shores of the Dead Sea, the lowest known spot on this planet, the writer need only open his typewriter or lay out paper and pencil—and he's in business. When a writer stops work the shop is closed completely. The machinery stops, except the wheels that keep on revolving in his brain. If it isn't set down it escapes. When the president of General Motors leaves his office for three months all those cars still roll obediently off the assembly line and appear at the curb outside your house. The most obscure as well as the most important workman in the factory can be replaced and the work goes on. In the theatre, if an actor for some reason fails to appear for a performance he is replaced by an eager understudy. A soprano at the Metropolitan Opera in New York cannot go on, she has a cold; she is replaced and the new young singer is made by her next morning's notices. The famous architect dies, but his plans, his notes, his blueprints are there. The vast structure is completed by his assistant.

When a writer ceases to write for one day or one year, the works are silent, the shop is closed.

Wherever he is, is his workshop. Certainly a writer should have roots, but these should be limited strictly to the planet Earth—for the present at least. Perhaps even now one should say, the planet Earth and its environs. But roots, in the strict sense of the word, are for rutabagas. Every normal human being, including the writer, needs not only a house but a home. He needs a fixed place in which to keep his books, his household effects, his family if any, his clothing not in present use; and where he receives his friends and his mail and those bills. But to be front-porched there can be fatal. Writers are, for the most part, roamers. This is instinctive and good. Traveling, even uncomfortable traveling, is a refresher course. The publicity picture of the famous writer walking down to the post office daily for his mail, this constituting his only foray into the great world of today, is a mistake if true. Thoreau was a home body. He just sort of sat there at Walden Pond and mused. It is *lèse-majesté* for me to hint that perhaps he could have been just as wise and more exhilarating if he had, now and then, turned the key in the door, asked his nearest neighbor twenty miles away to look in now and then to make sure that no beatniks had taken over the place, and had roamed the world for a bit, if only to experience the exquisite happiness of returning to Walden.

It isn't that the writer writes about his far-off travels. It is only that the known, the familiar, the writing project that is hammering at the door of one's consciousness, becomes clearer, sharper, deeper, as one superficially sees and appreciates and enjoys the interesting or even enthralling unfamiliar sights and people.

I have written for weeks and months at a time in France, England, Austria, Germany, Switzerland, Italy, Holland, Belgium, Monte Carlo, Hungary, beside brief side-steps into many other foreign countries. I never have written a fictional line about any of them other than two or three unconvincing short stories done decades ago. Why this is true I do not know; but on my return from these diverting or glamorous or uncomfortable faraway spots I have been able, always, to write more satisfactorily about the people and the background of, say, Texas millionaires or Oklahoma Territory pioneers, or Illinois farmers or Michigan lumber barons.

Curiously, it happens now and then that in writing about the person, the people, the background that will emerge as a novel, a stranger will appear on the typewritten page and try to take over. A battle ensues between the writer and the brash character who frequently is vital and dimensional. It can happen that, in the heat of the fight for supremacy, the writer kills the character, strictly in self-defense, it is thought. A mistake, almost invariably. Midway in the book I killed Luz Benedict in *Giant*, Barney Glasgow in *Come and Get It*, the spinster (what *was* her name?) in *American Beauty*. A crime that was almost fatal to the story structure.

There is the danger, always, of trying to write better than you can. The next book, the one you are just beginning to cope with, must be better than the one before it, or before that, you say (but not consciously). It must be more seriously conceived, more entertaining, more adult; fresher, more vital. This naturally raises up a hideous structure known in writers' psychological language as a block, and as a result you can't write anything. Rarely does a human being achieve his or her highest potentialities. But for a short person to try to walk as a giant results only in a strut which is ludicrous to behold.

The finished work rarely is what the writer has striven for; has hoped and prayed and thought about during almost every hour of the day. All this perhaps unattractive shoptalk is not peculiar to one writer only. It is the daily struggle of every writer I know. In the early years of my writing life I used to think that this *sturm* and *drang* this insecurity and self-searching all were due to the fact that I had had no formal education after graduating—with some sensationally low marks—from the Ryan High School in Appleton Wisconsin. Of college I had none and I felt that this must be a handicap. I once regretted this lack keenly. Knowing what I now know I am certain that if I again were obliged to choose between a formal and solidly constructive education, with a minimum of four years at college; or four years as a reporter on the Appleton *Crescent* and the Milwaukee *Journal*, I would choose, without a pang of hesitation, the unplanned course of my rather haphazard life.

Great areas of ignorance are mine. I don't know where the Euphrates flows. I have infinitesimal knowledge of Greek mythology, I am helpless when confronted with the square or cubic foot, let alone root. But in the years of my newspaper life between the ages of seventeen and twenty-one I learned an awful lot about the subject known as people.

I can read about Greek literature, Greek mythology and history in the enthralling and delicious books of the amazing Edith Hamilton. I can engage some one to cope with a cubic root if I have a cubic root to tangle with. But a writer can't be taught about the human race merely through the medium of books or of lectures. People must be experienced at firsthand. A lively liberal tough newspaper city room—if you have the wisdom and the strength to escape it after four or five early years—should sustain you and give you awareness of life and the living for the rest of your own natural life. Or even unnatural. So then, there is no denying that such a life is demanding, often solitary, relentlessly workaday; crammed with apprehension; absorbing beyond belief. One is haunted by the fear that this golden gift may suddenly be snatched away; is certain that everyone and everything is conspiring to prevent one from working; and knows that one wouldn't change places with any living or dead human being.

The work and the years etch early lines on the face of a writer. Inside, a writer remains somehow mysteriously young—or perhaps not so mysteriously, for one is drinking deeply at the fountain of curiosity about the human race, and this source has magic powers. Sometimes the years are betrayed only when, at close quarters, in spite of the springy walk, the alert eye, the agile mind, one notes the fine crepey film of lines etched on the mask from brow to chin. Many things have helped to trace this pattern indelibly; the tens of thousands of hours the writer has spent hunched over a desk or a typewriter indoors; intense concentration; the necessary solitude; the strain of evolving believable human beings and situations out of one's imagination, experience, emotions. Frequently, after an absence of a year or two or three, writers may appear to each other, on again meeting, like a fuzzy carbon copy of the face we knew so well.

From all this whining and complaining it must not be deduced that writers don't have fun. They have, probably, more fun than anyone because they so relish it when they are free to enjoy it.

I am impelled to say that at this moment I am hard at work, but reasonably happy, content and serene (for me) in a comfortable gay chintzy (those three adjectives again) room in a hotel in Switzerland. I've ordered lunch to be wheeled in within the next hour because I don't want to stop work until then, if then.

Here at the wide window, and just below my balcony, is a grass-covered, tree-shaded, flower-scented park whose green is so rich and lustrous that it seems, in spots, coolly black. At the foot of this park, and lipping its low parapet, is a postcard blue lake, and just beyond this is a pink and green and white and purple Alp, and above all this the sky. Five serene and precious weeks of this. President of General Motors me eye!

All this does not make for such a rugged life, once the day's work is done. Mountains and lakes; a fondue for the first course and let the calories fall where they may; sweet air; quiet sleep. A writer's life is not entirely one of drudgery. Incense and myrrh, whatever that is; milk and honey; sweetmeats and roses are also part of the regimen.

Still, a fly or two are to be found in the ointment. There is no disputing that the acknowledged and accepted writer in the United States occupies a unique and often unenviable position as compared to the writer citizens of other civilized countries.

The United States, the greatest and certainly the largest and richest of the democracies, alone of all the liberal lands of the world denies its professional writers the rights to and the income from their own published work still existent in the later years of their lifetime. The rights to a novel, play, short story, historical, biographical or autobiographical work belong to the author of such a work from the date of copyright to the termination of a period of fifty-six years. In the meantime, according to law, the original copyright must be renewed before the end of even the twenty-eighth year after copyright or the penalty is lapse of copyright and complete loss to the author.

In the liberal countries outside the United States of America the original copyright grants the author the rights to his work for lifetime plus fifty years. Thus the writer may enjoy for a lifetime whatever profits accrue from the labor of writing; and the heirs to such properties may benefit from them for whatever period up to half a century after the writer's death. An appeal against this unjust and unique copyright law in the United States now is being made by the Authors League of America, the largest and most active of professional writers' organizations in the United States. Little progress has been made at the time this page is being written, and the prospects are not rosy.

No writer whose work is in demand expects that this work will remain his property and the property of his heirs forever. Though I can't imagine why not. If you were the fortunate owner of Rockefeller Center it certainly would stick around in the family for more than fifty-six years. First built in 1932, how would you like to lose it in 1988! If New York City calls the Metropolitan Museum its property, or City Hall, it definitely would expect to have claim to these edifices for more than a mere fifty-six years.

But now, at the end of fifty-six years, whether you are alive or dead, your written property may be used, republished, distorted, sold in any desired form in the marketplace by anyone who cares to present the novel or play or other written matter in a theatre; as a motion picture; on television or radio; from a platform; in a tent; anywhere, anyhow. All this may be done with taste and intelligence by the producer, the actor, the publisher, the editor. Or its treatment may be crude, vulgar. It may yield them profit, it may represent financial or professional loss. But in any case, whether it be tasteful or vulgar, the author, if alive, will writhe; if dead, he will be whirling like a dust-storm in his urn of ashes; his heirs will experience the frustration of a child whose taffy-apple has been snatched away before the first delicious bite.

My first volume of original creative writing was published in 1911 by the Frederick A. Stokes company. It sold ten thousand copies the first year and wasn't very good, though readable. It went on selling for a surprising number of years but is now, I am happy to say, not only gone but forgotten. May it never be exhumed. The fact is that, as I've been a professional and published writer for more than fifty years this early flower, now withered on the vine, will find itself in the public domain four years from now. It is doubtful that any necrophile will care to snatch this corpse; but its livelier and still winsome or sturdy brothers and sisters, older, more adult, will before too many years also be food for the vultures. There is new meaning for me in that death-where-is-thy-sting query. I never expect or wish to witness that public domained hopped-up version of the novel *Show Boat* or the musical to be evolved from it (with Jerome Kern's enthralling score way-outted like anything).

To complete the flight of fancy, just suppose, then, that the edifices I've mentioned—Rockefeller Center, City Hall—were, after fifty-six years, by law thrown into the public domain, quite out of their owners' hands. Or, to bring it nearer home, your own house which you may have built with your own hands; or your factory, your business, your practice, your invention, your hotel, oil field, cattle ranch. Rockefeller could be a public hall or a house of prostitution if the necessary arrangements could privately be made; City Hall a hotdog stand; your house a gas station or a morgue; your oil field free to the first wildcatter to grab it off.

No. Writers in the United States are considered eccentrics. Their art or profession, though it may bear in its wake a complicated and highly profitable business, is not regarded by the government as a business at all—or scarcely at all. A writer, sardonically enough, can find himself propertyless and penniless in his old age (what with all these life-prolonging high proteins, vitamins, hormone shots, health rules and gadgets); and his heirs baffled, while the whole world is enjoying, not only the hard-earned words on the printed page but the other profits of years of the writer's work.

For that matter, the writer of integrity who would, invariably, rather be a writer than anything in the world (or he wouldn't and couldn't be a writer of integrity) is given rather shabby treatment in the United States in terms of everything but money. Certainly no one in his senses, writer or artisan, would argue that money is unimportant. It is the prevailing medium of exchange, it is necessary to existence. A writer whose work is widely read is handsomely rewarded for his labors in terms of money. Sometimes these rewards are fabulous. But aside from this he is in many departments given the status of a second-class citizen. This is true, too, of other purely creative workers such as composers and painters.

As has been stated, the business that results normally from the conduct of his work is not considered in ordinary terms of business as business at all—or scarcely at all. A Southwest oil-well owner can annually withhold 27½ per cent of his entire oil income as tax-free because of a mysterious element known as depletion. A wildcatter, drilling for oil and coming up with a duster after months of searching, can deduct this time-and-money-consuming venture from his income tax. A writer who manages to exist as best he can on whatever he may possess at the time, while he spends two or more years in writing a novel or a play, may—to use the oil-field terms—at the end of that time find that after all his labor he has come up with a complete duster or a mere trickle. As for depletion—the fact that the creative and imaginative brain suffers definite depletion through the years is not acknowledged by the government. The lake of oil beneath the surface of the land is getting lower and lower. That is depletion. The lake of ideas, of invention, of emotion, of imagination that lies hidden there in the place called the brain-spirit or the spirit-brain is draining away with the years. Depletion? No. The old boy's getting kooky. His stuff isn't so good any more. He hasn't written anything in—let's see—must be five six years, isn't it? The Somerset Maughams the Edith Hamiltons the Robert Frosts the Carl Sandburgs the Ernest Hemingways the Willa Cathers and the Mark Twains and the Moss Harts and the Robert Sherwoods haven't merely, like the Southwest drillers, made your car go and your oil burner and your plane. They have powered your thoughts your will your imagination your hope your very life. They were, or are, writers in their sixties, seventies, eighties, even nineties.

In a less material way, there is, too, in the United States, a curious social attitude toward the writer. It may often amount to actual derision, not because of anything the writer is, or has written, said or done. Simply because one is a writer and therefore looked upon as different; unpredictable; an odd ball.

The accomplished and acknowledged writers of France, Italy, Belgium, Holland, Spain, Japan, India, Germany, Switzerland, Norway, Sweden, Denmark, Finland, the South American countries, England—even England, that pricker of the pompous—have known a solid appreciation not only of the thoughtfully written word but of the creator who wrote it, from Shakespeare to the latest and sulkiest Angry Young Man. Hungary, Poland, Czechoslovakia, before they became Communist-controlled, had this same attitude of respect—amounting sometimes even to reverence—for the dedicated writer.

American writers definitely do not want to be revered. Too wearing. Too embarrassing or ludicrous. They want to be free to write as they wish; to be readable and read; to be able thus to come by sufficient on which to live; and to have such respect from the reading public as their work and their person deserve.

Often these reasonable expectations are not forthcoming. I have read New York first night reviews of plays in which practically the entire review was based on the personal life of the playwright. The reviewer discoursed on the playwright and the play, not in terms of writer and written product, but in terms of a fellow he disliked and of whom he disapproved as a human being. Needed a psychoanalyst; concerned only with perversion; didn't pay his taxes they say; afraid of people; bad breath; alcoholic; doesn't know women; doesn't know men.

When people go to the theatre, when people read a book, the fact that the writer likes to paint himself pink, green and yellow and live on a diet of bananas and pickles exclusively may mean that he is an exhibitionist and a phallus-worshiper. If the novelist lives in a tree and writes on birch bark, this is really irrelevant. The audience comes to see the play, not the playwright. There once was a playwright—wasn't there?—who said, the play's the thing. And a book writer who said, by the work one knows the workman.

The writer, one would think, is a kind of comic garbage collector, going about picking up such scraps and oddments as he can fish up out of the gutter, or overhear in a plane or train or ship's lounge. If he goes to Madagascar, Keokuk Iowa, or Honolulu, he encounters the inevitable, "You writing a book about this place?"

"No."

"Who d'you think you're kidding! Don't forget to put me in but good, will you."

A writer, as a person, may warrant or earn or deserve special and personal articles or interviews written by a reporter or a writer of magazine pieces, and these may be approving, disapproving, flattering, malicious, highly admiring, near-libelous and even libelous. The writer can take them or leave them. Once the article is published he must bask or fume or sue. None of these does the writer much good; or any.

All this lengthy and unscholarly dissertation on writers and writing is definitely not based merely on my personal experiences in a half-century and more of daily writing. On the contrary, I have had what I consider an enthralling time of it. The world owes me actually nothing. I've had a—to me—thrilling ride. Bumps, yes, and dangerous curves, and spills; but a rich, fulfilled and enchanting journey nevertheless.

Perhaps one shocking example of the manifestation attendant on a display of personal vituperation against a book of fiction might be of some interest to a reader. It interested me. I was the author of the book.

The book was entitled *Giant*. Its background was the State of Texas. Its characters were built on no human being I had ever known or seen. The book was based on months of research and personal observation. The novel was successfully published and the motion picture made from it was successfully produced. *Giant* was a well-written novel. *Giant* was an excellently produced picture.

Texas, that virile and dramatic commonwealth, is a region of extremes. Vast, exciting, irritating, fascinating, overdrawn, underdone, to view it for a day a week or months is a crashing experience. I had been delighted by it, shocked and startled by it; revolted and enthralled. It was Texas; like nothing and nowhere else in the United States of America.

Well. The blast of insult, vituperation; the published scatological and libelous outpouring that followed the magazine serialization and the book publication of this novel was something I never before had witnessed. There had been minor regional blasts after the publication of *Cimarron* and of *American Beauty* and even *Come and Get It*. But this was savage. It sickened and saddened me. I had written truthfully, seriously, and with purpose. The book contained no errors of statement, no exaggeration of conduct or character. I had, in fact, felt it necessary to play down or even to eliminate some of the facts and situations and behaviorisms encountered in the violent mores of this unique society. In Texas the truth often is too strange for fiction.

Headlines in black letters two inches high streamed across the pages of Texas newspapers. This Ferber is a liar and a criminal. We think she ought to be caught and hanged here in Texas and we'll arrange the hanging and choose the people to hold the rope. The drop should send her through a sheet of glass below the scaffold so that she'll be cut into hamburgers when she falls. She's an idiot. She doesn't know Texas. She'll be shot if she ever dares to show her face again in Texas. Letters. Telephone calls. Animal rage.

I had—and have—dear friends in Texas. There was little they could do about all this. There was little that I or my publishers could do other than to ignore all this filth as best one could. It comforted me often to think of what Eleanor Roosevelt, that magnificent example of courage and humane endeavor for the good of the world, had all these years endured in the way of verbal brutality; and had managed to endure in quiet dignity.

The Lively Arts have a lively time of it. But they survive and they help the world to survive. They survive in spite of the scorching fires of criticism; the bludgeoning of disapproval or misunderstanding; the indifference of a hoped-for public. They seem even to thrive on neglect, abuse, derision.

What manufactured or commercial product would survive (or for a moment tolerate) the sort of treatment dished up to the creative worker? Just suppose that Wotnex Household Appliance Company were to come out with a new gadget called the NEXWOT Clothes Washer. Previous to its birth it is introduced to the public by a blasting ad in the, say, New York newspapers. Housewives Throw Away Those Detergents Those Flakes Those Powders Those Crystals. You'll Never Need Them Again. You Never Have Known the Wonder of Washday Until You've Owned and Used a Nexwot Washer.

That appears in the Monday papers. On Tuesday we read the review:

Yesterday we attended the first performance of the Nexwot Washer. We never will feel really clean again. This thing is not only the spirit of tattle-tale gray—it is the raven-tail black of all washers. After watching this first demonstration we can only assure you that the whitest robe of the neatest angel on the puffest-ball cloud in the azurest sky would emerge sable somber after one dip in the Wotnex Household Appliance Company's Nexwot Washer.

The Wotnex Company doubtless would sue the paper for one billion dollars and probably win.

The practitioners of the Lively Arts are the world's aristocracy, they are the Chosen People. They persist in spite of misunderstanding, persecution and even violence. Though their sense of insecurity is everpresent their well of hope and their self-respect are deep and enduring. They know they are the founders of the spiritual laws of mankind. No matter that their work is distorted by others, and their motive misinterpreted. They will persist as long as mankind inhabits the earth—and perhaps after.

11

Life in wartime, even for a non-combatant, is an exhausting thing. Hope and apprehension and frustration battle for inner supremacy. You envy your secretary who is going to the South Pacific area as an office worker in the WAACs. You envy the farmer's helper who is whisked away into the Remington Arms Works in Bridgeport. The laundress is working in the airplane factory. Al, the farmer-caretaker, his wife his small boys have vanished.

But the everyday life of a lady farmer, complicated and even hazardous, had an excitement of its own, and of a different sort altogether—stimulating, constructive excitement. Sometimes the small and perhaps unimportant aspects of daily life at Treasure Hill in the State of Connecticut, so bosky and warm-cool in the summer, so ethereal with dogwood and new foliage in the spring, so blazingly brilliant in the autumn, so diamond-white in the winter, seemed more truly exciting than world-stirring and gigantic events.

The amazing changes that magically took place overnight, for example. In New York the gray stone or cement or red brick twenty-five story apartment building across the street is just as it was yesterday. Grim, staring out from its hundreds of soot-streaked windows, there is about the pile no noticeable change since yesterday or since last year or the year before. Maybe just an additional film of the black coating that is exhaust gas, chimney fumes and soot. Perhaps, in the street, they have dug up, by drill and shovel, a twenty-foot section of paving, and a helmeted crew of workmen is descending and disappearing into the bowels of New York on some mysterious surgical task that has to do with the circulatory system or the lungs or heart or liver or intestines of these disease-ridden innards. Though it must grudgingly, in fairness, be admitted that occasionally, at the end of April or the beginning of May, on a brief whirl of a walk into Central Park and out, you may come upon an astonishing flowering of Japanese magnolias near the 69th Street entrance; or a haze of pink-and-white flowering cherry trees in full bloom at the East Drive of the reservoir walk. A gentle spring rain overnight has produced a miracle. It is a brave and splendid show against the gray asphalt prison; gay banners flaunting their defiance in the face of smog acids gas and dirt. As you walk you say, gravely, thank you and bravo bravo bravo, and you even incline your head and never mind the passerby who thinks the old girl is off her rocker.

But in the country! The grass, as you step out of doors in the early morning shouts Look! Look! Look! I've grown an inch overnight. Tight little green marbles have become pink roses. Asparagus spears are full-grown where yesterday only a tiny tip pierced the black loam. The baby robins actually have learned their lesson of aviation and have flown away after being subjected to alternate moments of scolding and pampering from their mother. There are enough ripe red raspberries for a bowl. The tree man is here, the furnace-cleaning man is here, the Lenhacker boys want to know if you'll buy tickets for the Firemen's Annual Benefit.

But best of all, the lambs and the calves; the ludicrous four-footed leap into the air of the new-born lambs as they scamper the meadow, the sloe-eyed calves whose creamy coats presage their future yield.

It is time to shear the sheep. Now there's drama for you. In sheep-shearing, one of the most elemental acts of husbandry, known and recorded all the way from the Bible to Cornell University, the hand has given way to the machine. The sound is *bzzzz* instead of *clipclipclip*. Disillusioning when first seen and heard, especially for an erstwhile city dweller turned farmer.

The sheep, bleating, held in the vise of the shearer's two muscular knees. The snarl and whine of the instrument mingled with the bleating. It is, actually, a shave not a shearing. Sheep-shaving would, I suppose, be the modern ugly term. No pain is attached to the process, the shearer (shaver?) is quick and deft. Shorn from hoofs to ears, the animal is released and clatters off in a final yammer of protest to join the other members of the outraged flock, all looking extremely embarrassed by their new nakedness. Perhaps that is where the word "sheepish" comes from.

The pile of oily grayish wool on the barn floor mounts higher and higher. There is about the sight of this something atavistically reassuring. Wool. Spinning. Garments. Covering. Warm.

This same feeling of security, absurdly enough, came at sight of various farm processes on Treasure Hill. Cows. Milk. Cream. Butter. Cheese. You had only to glance at a couple of Jerseys chewing tongueily away in a field to know reassurance. Earth. Food. Sustenance.

In an elegant, costly, and idiotically satisfying way the barren rocky hill I had so rashly bought a very few years before this now could, if necessary, have sustained us in all but such dry grocery staples as sugar coffee tea salt. We never did get down to vinegar and cider from all those bushels and bushels of apples, but we well could have.

So then, milk cream butter cheese chickens eggs strawberries blueberries raspberries blackberries; corn peas beans tomatoes spinach cauliflower lettuce cucumbers broccoli; even peaches and melons which don't thrive in that northerly Connecticut climate. Not to mention hay alfalfa rye potatoes. The list of bountiful foods that the erstwhile starved and rocky soil of Treasure Hill produced is too long to enumerate. Most of this yield was due to the magic of the farmer-gardener that I miraculously came by after the gifted Al was snatched away.

Harold Curtiss had been a farmer for a couple of hundred years more or less, and in Connecticut. The Curtiss family came of that early Connecticut stock that stemmed from England. The reluctant and frigid New England soil had no tricks which they could not outguess or circumvent. During the years of the tenancy of Harold in the white cottage that nestled perhaps a hundred feet from the main house Treasure Hill bloomed and proliferated like the Garden of Eden. Our patriotic vineyard, for example. It was an amusing and defiant gesture of food culture on Curtiss's part. He told me nothing of it until it was in fruit. It was a smallish vineyard of red, white, and blue grapes. The red was Catawba, the white Niagara, the blue Worden, sweet and yet tangy varieties all. The tricolor globules ripening in the sun were absurdly heartening. Perhaps the whole hill farm idea was basically simple, innocent and not a little foolish. But certainly not as foolish as the penthouse garden atop the roof of the apartment building on Park Avenue, New York.

While Curtiss's farming blood ran deep and true his actual craft or trade was that of carpenter. At this he was masterly. He could construct anything and everything, and did; from a violin (which he played) to a two-story house, which he built later for himself and his wife, unaided. He was past active army age when he came to the Hill.

There is a rare characteristic inherent in men whose guild or craft is that of carpenter. I have occasionally known and remonstrated with surly, unreliable and careless workmen of just about all other crafts and trades. I never have known a genuine carpenter who was not prideful in his work; gentle, forthright and humane in his nature. Carpenters are mysteriously likely to be men of intelligence and integrity; they are at once visionary and realistic. Perhaps the working with wood has something to do with all this. Sawing, cutting, hammering, nailing, the scent of clean wood is always in his nostrils. Perhaps still lurking in the wood is something of the quiet fragrant forest whence it came. It just could be that the still living tonic of the long-felled trees clears the workman's brain and steadies his nerves and makes his hand sure and deft. Carpenters talk little above the tap of the hammer, the buzz of the saw, but when they do speak they are likely to be unloquacious and dryly humorous. All this fancied explanation could be false, and probably is. Doubtless the fundamental explanation for the characteristics of the genuine carpenter is that he is descended from the carpenter who possessed all these qualities—the carpenter craftsman, Jesus Christ.

Those of us in United States who were born and have continued to live in the Temperate Zone of this many-climated country are, I think, the fortunate ones—and let the West Coast yell as it will. I had little choice in the matter of the place of my birth, but certainly in the past half century I could have lived in Southern California, in Florida, in Arizona in Puerto Rico, in Mexico, South Carolina, Virginia—any of the warmish, or tropical or semi-tropical sections of my own country, let alone the balmy countries of other continents. These are not for this Kalamazoo-born and Iowa-Wisconsin bred character.

The four seasons of the Temperate Zone are a perpetual adventure, a dramatic entertainment, assured yet unpredictable. The four seasons on Treasure Hill were, each in its way, enthralling. Autumn adjectives such as gold and scarlet and orange-flame, though these blazed away from the front terrace to the distant Sound against the horizon, are too tired and worn to do service once more here. The indescribable needs a stern hand at description. Sometimes, in the winter, when an ice storm had coated the tree branches in crystal overnight you found yourself living in a glittering fairyland when the sun shone. When, after a blizzard, our snowplow had made its way down the hill to the main road and back again we took pictures of the newly formed white mountains against the blue sky. There is one of Harold Curtiss, a tallish man, leaning with a triumphant grin against a shoveled snow mass ten feet high at the side of the driveway.

Spring came late to Easton. Always, down below at Westport just about thirteen miles distant the green had already burst into bud while the trees and even the forsythia in our district were seemingly winterlocked. It was like beholding the marvel of spring in three distinct acts; was, in fact, just that. In New York, where I was likely to be at least part of the time in those unpopular months, February and March, spring, such as it was, came early and soon was over. The trees in Central Park showed their pale yellow-green in early April, or even in late March if the season happened to be a mild one. Three weeks later, as you drove up through Westport on your way to Easton and home, there was the brilliant new green of spring once again, to delight the eye and the spirit. At Treasure Hill, higher in altitude, and always cooler or colder, spring did not come until still another two or three weeks had gone by, the early buds were tight little knots after the Westport's tree-lined streets were in full green. The delight of witnessing this threefold magic was almost too much.

So the house, so big, and the land, so many-acred, and the labor and the time and the money and the fruits, dairy products, vegetables, grain and meats produced on this acreage did not seem so spendthrift after all. It was wartime. Food was rationed.

With the exception of the lambs, the wool, and an occasional calf and a few tons of hay, we did not sell the products of Treasure Hill. We used them and we gave them away to family, friends, neighbors. Meat was, of course, very strictly rationed but no lamb or sheep or calf was killed on the farm. I could not physically have downed a mouthful of one of these, no matter how skillfully cooked and garnished, no matter how scant the meat ration. I would as soon have eaten a neighbor's baby. I remember bottle-feeding a couple of the lambs who, at birth, had turned out to be less sturdy and aggressive than their tougher cousins. As for calves and cows, once they've looked at you with those great soft brown eyes you can never face them on a platter. This was, of course, mere sentimental evasion. Some one ate them eventually so that the rationing effort wasn't, at least, cheated. As for chickens, that was different. Chickens are silly creatures at best, tiresome, un-amusing and not friendly. I was not emotional or neurotic about broiled chicken or succulent fricassee.

If all this sounds dreamy, it wasn't. The times were tragic, and what was worse, they were nerve-racking. One can summon courage and fortitude to face tragedy; irritations and frustrations are a cloud of mosquitoes that nip and sting and drive one frantic.

Farm-help was practically non-existent—not to speak of household help. Any man or woman who could stand up (or sit down) and use one arm was needed and welcomed for war-weapon work. Nearby Bridgeport was a fountainhead of guns, planes, ammunitions, metal parts of all kinds needed in the grim resistance against the enemy. Lads who had been working for twenty-five dollars a week in peacetime were getting one hundred—even two hundred—a week in war work. They took their girl to New York—so near and, until now, so far to them—and went dancing and night-clubbing at the Gold Slipper. Being a compulsive perfectionist I could not bear to see the land, the stock, the trees, the house neglected; even, I am somewhat embarrassed to say, the lovely gardens and the pool.

"Harold, don't you think we ought to get those berries into the deep freeze before they're over-ripe?"

"Another two days won't hurt them. They haven't gone by. I want to get the hay in out of the south piece before it rains, the radio says thunder-showers."

"The apples are dropping like flies."

"The sound ones stick. Thursday for sure."

"I hate even to mention it, but the pool needs vacuuming, doesn't it? Not important but—company coming Saturday from New York."

"Tonight, after chores."

"Do those two front elms need water? They look so kind of blah—the leaves, I mean."

"I've already got the hose on, just a trickle at the roots, but it does it. Take a look. We're water short, you know."

He was a monument of patience and resourcefulness. He was a one-man band, working hand and foot. Jim Hitchcock, the chicken-farmer in the neat white house at the foot of the hill, gave us a hand when his own mounting chores had been disposed of. William, seventy at least, no teeth, his left arm useless, his asthma like the clatter of gravel, painstakingly weeded and cultivated the more fragile of the flowers— the lilies, the delphinium, the roses, the Canterbury bells, the salmon-pink poppies, the tulips, the peonies, the chrysanthemums, as they came in seasonal rotation from April to December on that heavenly high hill which somehow evaded the frost after all the flowers in the gardens of householders in the valley below lay blackened and dead.

You played a kind of exciting game with the rationing program and it was rather fun, especially if it came out in your favor. You were allowed the maximum-minimum of gas for necessary farm implements —plow, tractor, truck. But passenger cars got short shrift. We were thirteen or fourteen miles from the nearest satisfactory shopping center. But as we were five or six hundred feet in altitude one could coast the hills practically all the way down to Westport and sea level. This was exhilarating but somewhat dangerous on those narrow curving country roads. Of course the way back was a different story but at least the downhill gas-saving was tucked away under your belt. A cheese soufflé and green salad and fresh raspberries constitute a perfect lunch both tastewise and healthwise. Local fish or lobster (non-rationed and—in a glaze of aspic—celestial) and chicken (home-grown) with a crème brûlée or a strawberry meringue to follow (eggs cream courtesy of Treasure Hill) made a midsummer dinner not only fit for but too good for a king. And no ration stamps.

Meanwhile I went where I was sent, did as I was bidden to do as a writer; and worked hours daily at my own task of writing because— for one thing—this was the way in which I earned my living, shouldered my responsibilities, kept Treasure Hill in motion.

Julia Ferber was ensconced there during July August September surveying all this pomp and circumstance with an appreciative but mildly sardonic eye. It didn't fool her for a minute. She sat on the cool screened north terrace and read after she had had her breakfast in bed, mastered her daily Christian Science lesson, bathed, dressed and descended to view the sparkling green countryside. She was, inexplicably, a city-born tree-worshiper. Her love and appreciation of these giant plants is something I've never seen equaled. Cooly comfortable on the terrace she would read and read and read—Bromfield, Sinclair Lewis, Dickens, the Bible, *Variety*, the *New York Times*, the Bridgeport *Post*, Willa Cather, Arnold Bennett, Maugham, the *Cosmopolitan* magazine, the *Saturday Review of Literature*, the stock market reports, Woollcott, the fashion pages, and practically anything about the theatre. She had the Neumann-Ferber love of the theatre.

Daily she went forth to wage war in the garden with the hordes of Japanese beetles that infested the land like a Biblical scourge. They hung like grapes in obscene clusters from every slender branch and bud, gnawing and champing their horrid way through tender leaf and flower. An open pail of beetle-destroyer liquid hitched over one wrist, Julia reached stoically with the other hand for the bunched enemy, clutched them, doused them, defeated them. Incidentally, all this reaching with her right arm in the hilltop's violet ray sunshine cured her shoulder of a bursitis that had been bothering her for months in New York.

Julia dearly loved to bounce around the countryside in the station wagon—anywhere, at any hour of the day or night. Gregarious by nature, she must have been bored for days on end, but she never indicated that this was so. She made small tasks for herself; oiling the leather-bound books in the library; mending a torn napkin (she hated sewing); chatting a moment with the cook in the kitchen and shelling peas as an excuse. The keen alert mind had not enough to feed on in this sylvan though busy retreat. She loved people.

"I think I'll go to Chicago week after next and see Josie." Her only sister. "I've got a feeling she isn't well. She doesn't say so in her letters, but I always know."

Josephine Neumann, spinster sister, lived in a large comfortable hotel on Chicago's south side—city of her birth—facing Jackson Park and the glorious Lake Michigan. There lived buddies of Julia's own age and often younger (she was popular with all ages and sought by them). There was bridge, there was gin rummy and good gossip on the terrace facing the Park. People came and went; laughter; music; the bus downtown. She refused to take a taxi. Here was life moving and at hand for a life-loving woman in her eighties. She packed, resolutely, she took the *Twentieth Century* for Chicago, she wrote that welcome letter that began as informally as though she were carrying on a momentarily in-

terrupted conversation from an adjoining room. At times her letter
even began with a conjunction. No punctuation marred the brief
page.

"Well everything is fine here Josie was a little under the weather she
didn't write to me foolish as always but she is all right now I played
last evening bridge with the girls . . ."

The farm and all Treasure Hill was held together and prospered
mildly, no mean feat in wartime. It took a maximum of effort and a
minimum of available material, but there it all was in full bloom in
1943 and 1944; the sleek stock, the hay, the alfalfa, the orchard, the
vegetable garden. And miraculously, too, the cutting garden, the walled
flower-garden dazzling with color and scent; even the swimming pool
for health; that early morning dip, a brief swim before lunch, a longer
workout in the late summer afternoon. Having learned to swim only
in my late thirties I never quite got the hang of it, I never trusted the
fluid stuff actually to hold me up. But I exercised grimly, enjoyed it in
a self-congratulatory and approving way; and just barely didn't drown
daily.

Everyone on Treasure Hill was busy as a bird-dog. The days flashed
by like scenes on a movie screen. Curtiss never walked; he ran. A
strange physiological trend had slowly come to our notice on the Hill
and perhaps it could be traced to something in the soil—an element
which affected the X and the Y chromosomes in the unborn infant,
whether human or animal. The fact is there. Al's two infants, born
on the Hill, were boys. Curtiss's son had been a hearty lad of twelve
when he arrived with his parents, so that couldn't count. But definitely
our new-born ducks were drakes, our chickens roosters, our calves bulls,
our sheep rams and that is the truth. Perhaps the bees fetched the
proper pollen from other sexy apple trees to pollinate our own he-
apples. They did proliferate. Privately I decided that if writing failed
me I'd turn the place into a clinic guaranteeing male birth; I thought
of Eddie Cantor, still youngish then and brilliantly entertaining, five
daughters and no son; Louis Bromfield in his forties, three daughters
and no son; King George of England, two daughters and no son.
A summer on Treasure Hill, drinking of the magic artesian well (courtesy of Yale University and that dear geological wizard); eating of the
farm's miracle fruit and vegetables at some fabulous sum a week and

satisfaction guaranteed or your money back. To quote a bawdy phrase, nice work if you can get it.

In the morning, from 8:30 or nine until half-past one I worked rigidly and consequently not very well, at the novel which I was resolved to do. It was *Great Son*. All around me, close at hand, the details of the household, the business of the farm, the lives of my immediate family, were in full movement. But permeating everything—pressing into the workroom where I sat writing—in the air—in the sound of the mower cutting the hay in the south field—in the village—throughout the nation—in all of Europe—strangling and torturing the entire world—was the omnipresent monster, War.

The sparse notations of the diary outline the days one by one, making somehow a fairly clear picture of the whole for one who could read between the lines. That one was I.

> *March 3.* Berlin well bombed by Flying Fortresses. Splendid!
> *March 8.* Working on the novel. Shall I ever finish it. I wonder.
> *March 17.* Worked on article needed for British War Relief: Seeds For Gardens in England. This, reread, sounds more idiotic than it actually could have been, otherwise I wouldn't have been assigned to write it.
> *April 14.* Spoke at New York Stage Door Canteen. Midnight. Those boys' faces. Sitting so polite and uninterested as this gray-haired woman prattled on about what! I wish at least I could have looked like Marlene Dietrich just for those ten or fifteen heavy minutes.

Those two years were made up of layers of good and of bad; hope despair exhilaration apprehension fun tragedy work play. I was alive. That was all to the good so far as I was concerned, certainly. Not only that, I was equipped with that inexplicable perception which made everything larger than life. And I was solvent, and comfortably—even luxuriously—housed; I was working. War or no, the machinery of living was in motion.

For just a minute there—or at most, a few weeks—it might have slowed down. But that too, was interesting as is any first. Off to Medical Center, New York, for my first operation. It came, as I'm told they always do, at an inconvenient time. But, They said, it had to be, it might be serious otherwise; gall bladder, appendix; duodenum leaning like the Tower of Pisa—out with it all, They said, brandishing an imaginary knife before my reluctant eyes.

Being a girl who was all for drama I didn't confide in the family, particularly because of Julia who was seemingly none too flourishing herself at the moment and doing nothing medical about it, being a Christian Scientist. So off I cantered in a taxi to 168th Street and Medical Center, fortified with a bundle of books and a box of work-sheets and notes, and even a typewriter, like a fool. A nasty trick to play on a fond family, and served me right if I had come out the wrong door. That first night I slept like a babe (slightly depraved), having been given the first sleeping pill I'd ever taken.

So the novel went, for the time at least, unwritten; the futile dabs at war work, so-called, went undone; Treasure Hill was left to the de-vices of others, but as Curtiss was devisor-in-chief that was nothing to worry about; but it was disappointing to realize that my dear English friend, Victor Cazalet, aide to General Sikorsky in Europe, now was due in New York any moment and that he would come and go unseen by me. I was never again to see him. A short time after his brief New York assignment he, with General Sikorsky, took off from Gibraltar, their plane rose, soared, dipped abruptly and dived perpendicularly and directly into the ocean, lost forever with its passengers and crew. Sabotage, the brief accounts stated.

Waste. Idiotic war Waste.

Displaying enormous strength of character I never have written that awfully amusing cliché-infested hospital operation short story or article. A weird experience, hospitalization, for one who never before has known it. Suddenly to find oneself the hub of a tiny monotonous ro-tating day, bounded by four smallish walls, peopled by beneficent strangers in starched white who poke with scientific and detached in-terest into your most private parts and you do not mind much, knowing that you are for the moment to them faceless and nameless. Small in-cidents take on the proportions of vast events. The screams of the man in the next room become almost routine in your ears; but the failure of the corridor attendant to deliver the morning *Times* is a catastrophe. I did mean to write that hospital short story, perhaps, of the day that lay between the reading of the morning paper and the evening paper. I even had the titles for it: It was called *Morning Sun, Evening Star*. But it all went into immediate and permanent eclipse.

There was the trip later that winter with Peg Pulitzer, to visit the Nelson Doubledays in their lovely and somewhat anachronistic planta-tion at Yemassee, South Carolina. The sun and fun; the friendly warmth of Nelson and Ellen Doubleday; the companionship (and gin-rummy, at which I invariably lost) of Somerset (Willy) Maugham and Glenway Wescott and Monroe Wheeler; and the witty and perceptive talk of Peg Pulitzer mingled with all these, made for a perfect post-hospital recuperation. The days were lively yet restful; the evenings cool and refreshing, with a huge fire snapping in the fireplace, savory food interlarded with those irresistible and deadly Southern hot breads of every description; good talk during and after dinner. Of those rare carefree war days three items not exactly carefree stay fresh and vivid in my memory.

Peg and I had adjoining compartments on the southbound train, very ease-taking, and my diary for that February journey states that I breakfasted in bed after having slept merely nine straight hours; and that I had a guilty feeling about the whole lovely situation because the world was in frantic turmoil (neurotic Jewish emotionalism, I told myself sternly, stemming from two-thousand-year inherited history).

We lunched in the diner which was stifling and crowded, this being before the day of the ubiquitous air-conditioner. A waiting lunch-hungry line stretched from the dining-car doorway to the end of the vestibule. They watched each bite as it disappeared into the guilty maws of the lucky early lunchers. Peg and I, too, had of course stood our turn in the line. Just behind us had stood two Negro young men in the uniform of the United States Army. Neat, intelligent-looking, quiet. By the time we had ordered our food and the waiter had brought it the other two passengers just opposite us at our table rose and left. The dining car steward then ushered to our table two young white men in the uniform of the Army of the United States. The two colored soldiers who had been next in line still stood in the doorway, quietly. So we dealt with that steward, quietly, too, but in unmistakable terms and the two young colored soldiers came to the table and sat and had their lunch. There are times when you long to take hold of your fellow-countrymen and shake them until their bones rattle.

Some time later there was a superb and excruciating short story by Irwin Shaw in *The New Yorker* magazine. It was about a troop-train that stopped for lunch at a railroad station restaurant of the short-order eating-house type.

The horde of hungry uniformed young men poured into the railroad lunch-room and seated themselves at counter and tables. Two Negro soldiers were of the company. They were told that they were to go around to the kitchen back door. There they were handed a sandwich each and a container of coffee which they perforce consumed standing in the garbage-strewn back yard.

Incident ✗2. Merely a brief little run in the car from the Doubleday plantation to the nearby town that was a sardonic sort of movie set in real life, with its white-pillared mansions set back under the shade of moss-hung oaks and green satin magnolia branches. Below, in the bare fields, were the black shanties and the broken fences speaking a silent language that now is understood by the whole civilized world.

Incident ✗3. A heartening one. The guests who turned up for lunch March 7th were an impressive lot including Colonels, assorted Majors, and a clutch of Captains and what with all the buttons, insignia, stripes and straps the dining room glittered like Macy's window at Christmas. Surprisingly, seated at table in the midst of all this pomp and hardware was a smallish red-headed chap in the uniform of a private of the Marines. Parris Island, famed Marine training station, was nearby. The dazzling officers, too, hailed from there. The little Red Head who had been introduced as Mr. Smith had a nice wit and a manner that you felt must have a basis of security, humor, intellect and experience.

You were right. The little private was merely Paul Smith, famous erstwhile managing editor of the equally famed San Francisco *Chronicle*. He had been commissioned a Colonel soon after our entrance into the war. It turned out to be a cushy job and he deliberately quit it of his own volition. He had gone into this thing because he wanted to fight as a soldier in the hideous struggle and he enlisted as a private in the Marines, getting his boot-training at Parris Island. As tough and hazardous a job as you'll find in World War II or any other numbered or unnumbered war. Winston Churchill, Franklin Roosevelt, Sergeant York and a couple of other fighting boys have rated pretty high in the affections of this girlish heart, but for a while there in the Doubledays' dining room I could gladly have bumped my head on the floor in front of the shining boots of Marine Private Smith.

Certain inexplicable nonsenses jotted down in a period now twenty years past, bob up in my diary and my memory. Considering the war-torn world of two decades ago the following brisk notation is now bewildering to its writer:

Had a party of twenty-eight to dinner in the Victorian Room of the Carlyle Hotel. Can't imagine why.

And to this very day I can't imagine why.

Or perhaps I can. It was escape; legitimate escape if one desired to function on a sane basis in wartime. There is reassurance and an easement of the spirit to be found in the company of one's friends. All over the world agonized men and women were going to parties and giving parties and dancing and laughing if they could; and going to the movies and to the theatre; and making love and bearing children and managing as best they might their households and their business and their souls. They were earnestly and wisely trying, in fact, to behave like ordinary civilized human beings in the midst of such barbaric events as the world had never before known. The theatre in wartime was medicine relieving pain. Almost any amusement, any legitimate entertainment magically gave one new work-energy, fresh ability to go on. . . . Saw Van Druten's play *The Voice of the Turtle* . . . Saw Eddie Chodorov's play *Decision* . . . Wrote brief piece for Writers' War Board on Bond Drive not much good . . . Went to ice hockey game at Madison Square Garden . . . Saw Jed Harris's production of *Dark Eyes* . . . Saw Janet in *Junior Miss* she was good. The old Ferber blood . . . Dinner at Dinty Moore's and to see Helen Hayes in *Harriet*, a moving performance in a mediocre play . . . to see Noël Coward's picture *In Which We Serve*. Fine and moving. . . . Sent out article for British War Relief. Not good. . . . Julia's birthday eighty-four remarkable in her clearness of mind and her strength and all her functions. With her and all the family to dinner and to see *Over 21*. . . . Worked on Board article for TransAtlantic not good . . . With Max and Millie Gordon to see *Jacobowsky and the Colonel* Karlweiss's a fine performance the rest dull and unconvincing . . . With War Bond team to Meriden Connecticut to Kansas City to Des Moines. . . .

Life in the countryside was spiced by city life during the toughest winter months.

Having successfully, I had thought five years previously, removed myself and my working hours from the impact of big city scramble and pressure and social goings-on I now discovered that never in my absorbing and industrious life had I been so jostled and crowded with Things To Do. Daily I made long written lists entitled Things To Do and I did them, doggedly or happily as the case might be. Not only was life less simple, it was enormously more complicated. My own work as a writer consumed the entire morning and part of the afternoon as it had for decades. The house and the farm alone could have constituted a second career. Such work as I could accomplish in the war effort was puny enough but it, too, took its toll of time, thought, energy. Family. Friends. Fun. All important and necessary.

Alice or Jean would come in from the kitchen to ask, quite within reason, "How many for the weekend?"

"Weekend! Today's only Wednesday."

"Thursday."

"Oh. Well. I haven't done anything about weekend guests."

"Then no one?" They seemed disappointed. Household workers in country houses like weekend guests, I can't think why unless it is a kind of liveliness after a dullish week especially when employed by a weekday hermit of the writing type; the prospect of tips (loathsome practice); or a quite understandable urge to display the cooking, butling and serving ability which is their art and their justifiable pride.

"I didn't say no one. Look. I'll start telephoning this afternoon, or just before dinnertime, when people will be home."

A feeling of horrid guilt suffused me, especially when the days were hot or particularly beautiful or the berries ripest or the moon fullest.

"There they are in New York, sweltering," I reminded myself, reproachfully. "Working their heads off in war work and their own living to be earned. And here you sit, cool and wallowing in comfort. Dandy friend and citizen you are!"

You began to telephone. "This weekend? . . . Thanks, Ferb, but I'm going to be at the Rodgers' this weekend they asked me a month ago . . . Love to but we're at Terry's this weekend . . . Any other weekend, but this week we're up at the Lawrence Langners'. See you, I hope. Maybe they'll run us over to your place."

Two weekenders finally; maybe three. "We could come up Friday in time for dinner—unless you'd rather we waited until Saturday lunchtime. I'll have to take the train. Pete's got the car he's off on some mysterious . . . well, do I get off at Bridgeport or Westport or what? There're taxis, aren't there, they'll know the road, won't they? . . . you will! How sweet of you! I haven't got a New Haven timetable . . . The 6:03? Isn't that a bit latish? I thought a delicious dunk in your pool before dinner . . . We'd love to come but we haven't any gas of course . . . It'll be heaven, it's ninety-three here in New York today and hot-soup humidity."

As the weekend loomed you wrote with one eye on the clock. Another half-page and the day's stint—no, can't make it. Torn between two compulsions, writer's frenzy and hostess's vanity you zip the page from the typewriter feeling like a murderer and rush up and down the second-floor hallway placing yellow towels and yellow soap in the yellow bedroom and blue towels and blue soap in the blue bedroom and pink towels and pink soap in the pink bedroom and you cut and arrange flowers flowers flowers in the living room, the library, the bedrooms, the hall. The years and years of long ago when you lived in boarding-houses, in hotels, in strangers' furnished apartments take hold of you and will not be denied. "This is what you've been yelling for, now you've got it. Enjoy it."

"For dinner Friday night . . . For lunch Saturday . . . We're having dinner at the Rodgers' Saturday night, they're all coming here for dinner Sunday night, we'll be fourteen."

The Lord and Lady of the old English manse had nothing on me when it came to weekends, except that they weren't trying to write a book; but in a perverse way I loved it. I know and enjoy good food, I enjoy selecting it, hovering over its preparation, seeing that it is not only properly but deliciously cooked and appetizingly served. Never have been able to trace this trait. My sister Fan has it, too, and even wrote *Fannie Fox's Cookbook*, a triumph of culinary guidance, and a published success. I have had strangers come toward me with a light in their eyes, while I preened in anticipation of a flattering speech, only to hear them say, "Aren't you a sister of Fannie Ferber Fox? Say, that cookbook of hers is our food bible, we'd rather starve than do without it. Is she here? I'd like to meet her."

Julia couldn't cook worth a cent. She hadn't that particular kind of patience.

A second occult gift for possibly earning a living (the male-birth-properties of Treasure Hill was the first) if writing failed now was discovered. I was a rain-maker.

The governments and nations of the world could profit by this price-less and rare gift of mine; especially India, the Southwest section of the United States, all farm lands in dry areas, the Sahara, Mojave and any other deserts, parts of China and Africa and, in a year or two, the moon.

I need only have a house in the country, fairly remote, and an electric kitchen range. Let me invite ten, twelve, or more guests to dinner. Arrange to have me place a twenty-pound turkey, a fourteen-pound beef roast or four capons in the oven.

Immediately there descends a sizable cloudburst that settles into a determined five-hour downpour; ferocious booms of thunder resound over hill and vale—especially Treasure Hill—together with zigzags of lightning that connect heaven and earth and an accompaniment of semi-hurricane winds. Roads are immediately blocked by fallen trees of gigantic circumference, overhead telephone and electric wires are sent crashing with their poles. Turkey, roast or capons remain as cold in the oven as they were on the day they emerged from the butcher's refrigerator. Guests never appear. Can't. Roads blocked. It practically never fails to work. My services are not at the moment available, being otherwise gainfully employed. But who knows? It isn't a bad idea to let this magic gift sort of get around.

But on weekends when I withheld my witchlike powers and the weekenders arrived and then the dinner guests arrived one forgot momentarily the horror that seemed about to destroy Europe and the world; personal tasks, daily work, took on less gigantic proportions; never mind the silent typewriter upstairs in the workroom and the pile of blank white sheets of paper.

The nights were always cool up on the heavenly hill, no matter how hot the day. Toward the end of summer, often as not, a fire snapped and sparkled in the fireplace, good dry tangy wood cut in our own woods and properly seasoned in the woodpile. They were there—friends I had known for five, ten, twenty, thirty or more years. The talk was good, whether grave or gay; the food, I state without false modesty, delicious (how about that first course of trout in aspic, arranged fan-shape on the platter, decorated on its surface with sly vegetables and savories, then glazed with the golden aspic?).

After dinner, what went on in that company of the hard-working and gifted? Well, for example, Noël Coward, momentarily here from England, played the piano, mostly Richard Rodgers' music because Noël is like that, while Dick Rodgers beamed and we all sang with the gusto and innocence of the fifteen-year-olds who, back in the Appleton Wisconsin days, used to stand bawling around the battered old organ in the Sunday school room at a church sociable. What a relief for pent emotions group singing can be.

Moss Hart, a raconteur gifted especially in recounting his own incredible mishaps, regaled us with the latest and most outrageous of these, himself laughing as helplessly as anyone at his own terrific gaffe. His wife, Kitty Carlisle, sang for us. Mary Martin, not quite the great star then that she is today, proved that she could play the lead in the road tour of *Annie Get Your Gun*, by singing the whole score and with a characterization thrown in that was stupendous. Josh Logan and Nedda. Oscar and Dorothy Hammerstein. George Kaufman. Kit Cornell. Margalo Gillmore. It is strange, since I am primarily a writer of novels, that it is the theatre and workers in the theatre that have been the long-lasting loves of my life. Come to think of it, I know few novelists intimately. Perhaps in the enforced loneliness of our life-job we lose the capacity for public charm and performance and outgoing warmth. Perhaps writers of novels are so busy being solitary that they haven't time to meet one another. But then, a writer learns nothing from a writer, conversationally. If a writer has anything witty, profound or quotable to say he doesn't say it. He's no fool. He writes it.

As neighbors sometimes available for an occasional revitalizing talk and dinner there were the incredible wonder-woman, Helen Keller, and her companion and friend Polly Thompson; and Giles and Janie Phillips, all in Easton; and Bob and Harriet Pilpel in Newtown not fifteen minutes distant (if you had the gas); and Terry Helburn and the Lawrence Langners and Dick and Dorothy Rodgers in nearby Fairfield; the Creens and the Leopold Godowskys in Westport.

War was raging, but the Atlantic Ocean and the Pacific Ocean still were there in that day, though so soon to vanish as barriers against horror, and to become merely water. War or no; work, worry, apprehension —there still existed clean air and sun and flowers and friends and healing innocent spontaneous fun on Treasure Hill in that grim year 1944.

It is a curious fact that writers can write even under stress of their own private problems. Usually they can put down those words in spite of personal tragedies, disappointments, major emotional upheavals in their own lives. But when the whole world is in eruption—when gigantic catastrophe is upon the human race—their work almost invariably collapses around them. For the world is their subject and when it is distorted beyond recognition it ceases to be usable. It cannot be molded into cohesive form. Dimensional writing rarely is produced when the world is in frenzy. It is then that you hear the unavailing squeals of the Angry Young, and the possibly maundering reminiscences of the autobiographers. The ideal atmosphere for the pursuit of writing can be stated in paradoxical terms only. Writing, to be memorable, must be done in a state of impassioned serenity.

12

Those two young men in uniform were here again. Their first visit had resulted in semi-tragedy for me following that non-terpsichorean two-step in the heart specialist's test room at Bethesda Hospital a year or so previously. There now was something reassuring and revivifying in the manner and appearance of the two young officers. One was Colonel Corey Ford of the United States Air Force, a friend of many years, a writer of reputation; handsome, droll; regarding war intelligently as a dirty job that must be finished, once confronted by it. The other was Major William Hodapp, United States Air Force, erstwhile radio producer and director; quiet, confident, debunked.

"No flying over the Hump this time," they said reassuringly. "It's just Europe."

"Just Europe," I repeated after them idiotically.

"It's like this, Ferb," Corey explained, gracefully glib; and little characteristic imps of sardonic humor in his eyes. "They want this special stuff and they think you can do it, see. Just the air bases in England and France and Italy and Belgium and Germany."

"A mere jaunt," said Major Hodapp.

"In uniform, of course," said Corey.

"Silly. I'm too old and short and unmartial for a uniform."

"You'll be commissioned a captain, temporarily of course."

"Why! I don't mean why a captain, I mean why me commissioned?"

"Because, if you're captured by the enemy, you'll be entitled to receive the treatment of an officer in the United States Air Force."

"Naturally," I croaked.

"Then it's a deal."

"Look. Wait a minute. Who? I mean—with you two?"

Corey shook his head as at a not quite bright child. "What do you think we're doing here! Inviting you to go to dinner and the theatre! I'm slogging it out up in the Aleutians. Hodapp here is all over the place—half the time I bet he doesn't know himself where he is—Italy or England—unless he happens to get a glimpse of Trafalgar Square or St. Peter's as he goes by. Ain't, Major?"

"Sure is," agrees Major Hodapp, looking surprisingly like one of those rosy angels peering down at you from the Vatican ceiling. You could picture him peering over the edge of a Plexiglas cockpit and saying, "Ooh look! Westminster."

"The doctors—"

"Oh, sure, you'll have to get the shots and stuff—typhoid and small-pox and so on. Mere detail. Get fitted for your uniform—I bet you'll look real snappy in it the boys will be saluting the hell out of—uh —O.K.?"

"O.K."

"Permitted to take a secretary with you, if you want to. Sort of aide."

"Real stylish!"

Dr. Alvan Barach, when informed, looked not only doubtful but definitely disapproving. "That cardiogram at Bethesda, remember?"

"I feel great. They say most of the planes are pressurized now, any-way. And thousands and thousands and thousands of perfectly sound people are being bombed and gassed and burned and buried alive all over Europe this minute. Let them move over. There's always room for one more."

"Smarty—what?" Alvan said.

It was characteristic of Julia Ferber that when I told her I was going to Europe to have a look at the war and maybe write some pieces she said, "That's lovely. I wish I could go." She didn't mean it. She merely did not want to seem disturbed.

I took with me my niece Mina.

Uniforms. Papers. A thousand last-minute tasks. Yes, I'll cable the minute I can after arrival. No, they don't say where but we'll come down somewhere and I'll let you know. There had been a minimum of fuss and talk. I only knew we were headed for Washington D.C. and would take off from there.

Washington was bedlam. Mina and I were comfortably housed at the Carlton Hotel, we were to be there overnight, all the next day and night, and were scheduled to leave for Europe late the following day, after a briefing and various other technicalities, such as, look, Aunt Ed, I think I'll take these shoes to a shoemaker, see if he can give them a stretch or something, after all, we'll prolly be walking our legs off, you've got to be comfortable in the shoes.

Next morning's briefing was brief enough but slightly morale-jolting. *If plane is ditched in midocean read these instructions before taking to life-rafts.*

The following instructions were long enough and (to me) complicated enough to have provided me with a long cosy winter evening's reading before the fireplace—and I'm a quick study.

Also, the text went on, thoughtfully, do not drink salt water or urine in case of long period adrift without water. Mina and I did not meet each other's gaze owing to incipient hysteria. The briefing officer went into other necessary and wise details, and when the period was finished Mina and I staggered out into the cosy and accustomed security of Washington's mad traffic. We then leaned against a lamp post and laughed a little, weakly.

Errands. Shoes. Important. We stopped at the shoemaker's recommended to us. The shop door was open to the street, but no shoemaker. His bench, his tools, shoes, but no shoemaker.

"Hello!" we called toward the little open door at the rear of the shop. "Hi! Anybody home!"

No sound. We peered. Empty. We went to the shop next door, seeking information. But that shop, too, was open and empty of any human thing. What goes on here, anyway!

Out into the street again. It was not until then that we noticed the strange aspect of people on the street. They were walking rather oddly, their faces grim or shocked and they stared ahead with curious fixity, unseeingly; or they were gathered in little stricken knots, but quietly. At that moment a young actor I knew—now in uniform—passed by. He had played in *Stage Door*. "Bob!" I called. "What's going on? Has something awful happened? We've been at a briefing and we don't—"

"President Roosevelt's dead," Bob said.

That night at dinner at the hotel I beheld one of the most gruesome sights that could be witnessed. Here and there, in the big luxurious dining room, little groups of men and women at dinner were hilariously drinking toasts to the death of the great and gallant President. They were the reactionaries and the suet-brained who had reviled him in life and who now, the necrophiles, could rejoice over him in his death. Sickened, unable to eat, we left the room.

The Europe-bound plane was a big (for that day) C-54 absolutely glittering with Big Brass including Lewis Douglas, kindest of men; soon to become United States Ambassador to Britain. I had known him slightly, having sat next him at a dinner once upon a time. There was to me something reassuring about his presence on the plane, especially after his kind and cordial greeting and his immediate efforts for our welfare.

The plane was not entirely filled. When darkness fell and the motors throbbed through the night Mina and I were dazzled to discover that we could have an entire double seat each in which to curl up comfortably. For the first time in my life I took a self-administered sleeping pill and slept my luxurious way to the War.

The stop at Newfoundland, again at the Azores; and then, instead of a Scotland landing we knew to our relief, that we were headed straight for England. Now the pilot invited me to come into the cockpit and have a go at bringing the C-54 into England. A euphemism, of course, but there against the pink and blue and rose of a sunset sky loomed the White Cliffs, closer and closer as I stared enthralled through the cockpit window. Columbus may have had a finer moment back there in 1492, but I wouldn't have swapped places with him.

If this was war, I thought, in my innocence and ignorance, then death, where is thy sting?

England it was, then. A midnight arrival in London and roughing it in the red plush and gold and smooth linen elegance of the Savoy Hotel.

"Who said it was hell?" Mina inquired.

We had eaten nothing for hours. We were bone-weary. Tentatively, I rang the waiter's service bell. "Yes, Moddom."

"I know it's late. But we're starved. Could we have something? We're too hungry to sleep, really."

"Certainly, Moddom." He withdrew. Our memories roamed over the

succulent savors of the roast beef of old England. The waiter returned
with tea and two of the most transparent slices of bread I have ever
beheld, palely verdant with hairlike strands of unborn watercress. Snow
in the tropics never met with a quicker fate.

A cold spring morning after a blissful sleep between clean soft linen
sheets. A bath in a tub roughly the size of a municipal swimming pool
back home. I rang for the waiter. Surprisingly, the same waiter. I stifled
the old reportorial instinct to ask him how he managed to get on without
sleep. "Could we have some breakfast? Quite a lot, if possible. We
seem to be hungry again." It was only ignorance on my part, not
crudeness.

"Yes, Moddom," he said. "Very good, Moddom." Withdrew. Breakfast arrived for the famished. We made a rush for it. On the tray were
tea and two plates on each of which reposed two large flat black mushrooms on thin toast. The waiter withdrew.

At that crashing moment there was a firm tattoo at the door. I opened
it to be confronted with Alfred Lunt, towering tall in a smart maroon
dressing gown. With a yelp of rapture I threw both arms around him
but he half-withdrew, discreetly.

"Careful! Care—full. Precious freight here."

He advanced into the room, surveyed the breakfast tray, and held
out to us the little basket in his hand. Nestled in it were four objects
more precious in wartime London than diamonds emeralds and rubies.
There lay two uncooked eggs and two oranges. And a little nosegay of
English spring flowers.

"I was afraid of that," he said, his gaze flickering over our mushrooms.

From Mina and me there came somewhat incoherent screeches of
rapture and unbelief. But how did you know we were here! Who told
you? Janet's husband is here somewhere—he's in the Intelligence and
even he doesn't know we're here and we've no idea where he is. How did
you know, dear darling Alfred! And eggs!

"I know everything. Me and Winston. Wait a minute, I'll give these
to the waiter, he'll boil them in the pantry in a jiffy."

"How is Lynn—where is Lynn—what—how—who?"

"Would you like to see the play tonight? I've put seats aside for you."

Thoughtfully, as I stood there, I picked up one of the coolish black
mushrooms in my fingers and I ate it, reverently. "There will always be
an England."

Lynn Fontanne and Alfred Lunt were playing in the theatre in London in wartime and through bombtime. To the not-far-off boom of destruction, and with backstage plaster loosened and falling to the floor from time to time, they had been playing in the comedy *Love in Idleness* at the Lyric Theatre; to the applause and rapture of English audiences—the most appreciative theatre audiences in the world, peace or war. And from the countryside, theatre-goers grateful for the two magic hours of entertainment that made them forget the danger and tragedy that had been their lot throughout the past six or more years, brought them gifts that money could not find or buy: eggs, fresh chickens, English fruit and vegetables, cream, butter. Often—in fact almost invariably —the Lunts did not even know the names of these donors. "From one to whom your performance brought lovely hours of happiness," an accompanying note would say.

A year later, in so-called peacetime, this play was produced at the Empire Theatre in New York under the title of *O Mistress Mine*, with the Lunts again triumphantly starring.

Here in wartime London, as we saw the play, we were stirred, not only by the performance but by the electrifying current that flowed out from the audience and over the footlights to Lynn and Alfred and back again from these two into the hearts of the viewers. The theatre. If ever it vanishes we, too, of the civilized free world, will have been lost.

After the play there was none of that supper-party business. The Lunts went off to a Servicemen's Club to take part in an entertainment for Wisconsin Servicemen temporarily in London. The Lunts have a farm in Wisconsin, it is the state of Alfred's background, they deeply love the place—Lynn as much as Alfred, English-born though she is.

Most of the men and women whose ages ranged from nineteen to fifty-five or more and who were sent to or through Europe at any time during the Second World War had seen and heard and experienced sights and sounds beyond anything they could have wildly imagined; horrible or wonderful; painful or exhilarating; tragic, frequently comic; certainly the greatest adventure of their lives. They didn't want to talk about it and they didn't talk about it, even if prodded to do so. A war-weary world, combatant or civilian, wanted only, if this nightmare ever came to an end, to sit back quietly, eyes closed, mouth slightly open, and let peace wash over them. This must, too, have been true, not only of this holocaust called World War II, but of the American Revolution, the Civil War, the Spanish-American War, and the First World War. Torn, bone-weary, shattered, the world says, "Forget it. Let's pretend it never happened. I don't want to hear about it."

It is not that the world underestimates the horrors of wholesale combat or fails to appreciate the magnificence of conduct which war can call forth. But in those weeks overseas in 1945 during one of the most bitterly cold spring periods known, flying in C-54s, in bucket-jobs, in bombers, in those absurdly named Plexiglas droop-snoots, in little things the size of an aerial footbath; motoring; slogging through England, France, Italy, Belgium, Germany; talking to American, Russian, German, French, Belgian, English officers and privates and civilian men women children; at the unspeakable Buchenwald concentration camp; at gruesome Nordhausen; in the pale blue satin and snowy linen Ritz Hotel in Paris, I came to a conclusion irrevocably to be held by me for the rest of my life. No one likes war except husbands who are bored with their jobs and their wives. And generals. With generals, it is their profession. As is true of most people who enjoy their jobs, they are happiest when they actually are working at it full tilt. If this is treason, shoot me.

While I'm up I must add that no so-called civilized nation except Germany likes war. Germany loves it. They always have, they always will. It is their deeply ingrained method of expressing arrogance and relieving frustration. The chronic inferiority-sufferer compensates in combat. It is my utterly civilian opinion that Germany would fight tomorrow if it could; and that it will the moment the time seems propitious and when it is, in its own expert opinion, properly equipped to win.

This pompous statement is founded on nothing scientific or secretly knowledgeable. It stems from the instinct of an American-born citizen who has had a rather good news-trained look at war in its most hideously degraded aspects. My opinion is presented for what it is worth—which is nothing. Statistically and technically and politically informed giants of the international situation might well differ if ever they were to read this, which I'm certain they won't.

I only know that I don't really know. And they don't know. And you don't know.

Almost twenty years have passed since the mad May day of spring, 1945, that marked what was announced as the end of World War II in

Europe. V-E Day they called it. And where, by the greatest stroke of luck, was I landed in a plane from Germany on V-E Day? Why, in Paris, at the Ritz and I'll not forget that day and night as long as emotion and brain combine to form remembrance.

I never have heard anyone say to anyone, "Tell me about your experiences in the war."

They don't want to know, and the warrior doesn't want to narrate, and this is human and full of good sense. Except for just this. When a new post-war generation has grown to puberty and to youth and to manhood and womanhood, it should read, and it should be realistically told, of the futility, the idiocy, the utter depravity of war. For that matter, this instruction could begin at the age of six with the taking of those toy guns out of those toy holsters and throwing them in the ash-cans where they belong.

It is not that I fail to know that if our world had not risen to combat the Hitlerian madness that world would now be in Hitlerian slavery. And I, for one, certainly would have been good and dead these many years. The man in the factory, who has had to batter his way up through life in order to exist; the woman in the household, fending for her husband, her children; wary of deceit and false-dealing and bullying in the course of her busy day, know (and knew) instinctively that the bully must be met with instant repulse or he multiplies his own violence. A placated bully is a hand-fed bully. A Chamberlain, creeping home under the protection of his umbrella, tricked and ridiculed by the enemy, mouthing the peace-in-our-time fallacy, can cause the destruction of our world; and nearly did. One thing I've learned in life; you cannot placate the power-mad. You must—to paraphrase an old saying—take the bully by the horns. Early.

So, then, this will be no day-by-day account of my experiences in wartime during the Second World War; a sort of ludicrous mock-military account of my travels, resembling a parody of the post-Victorian diary entitled My Trip Abroad, bound in limp leather, with gold lettering. A half-dozen episodes, perhaps, and, I hope, a kind of over-all picture. I shrink from writing it. I must, because it loomed a gigantic thing in my life during those fantastic spring weeks in the Europe of 1945; and for almost twenty years it has remained locked in my memory and my emotions.

Each day I went to work at the business of seeing the War and recording what I saw and felt. It wasn't quite as simple as that, though badly stated, it was. But a gigantic human drama—inhuman, actually—cannot be digested hot off the griddle. Those weeks were crammed with the shocking, the ludicrous, the magnificent; the brutal, the nauseating, the exhilarating. Incidentally, I never had so little sleep, endured such searching cold and wet; worked so hard; experienced such physical discomfort at times, ate (occasionally) such badly prepared food, laughed so much, saw such savage sights, felt so gloriously well, in all the many years of my life. Bethesda or no Bethesda, I wasn't ill a moment. I never lost a spangle.

The magnificent Londoners walked the streets of their city on which, by now, the German bombs had ceased to fall. Yet, in many cases, out of force of habit or because of loss of their own accustomed housing, they continued to sleep by the thousands in the underground stations which we, in New York, call subways. The men and women whom I had remembered as being lean and sturdy and firm of skin and muscle, were markedly puffy now and on their handsome civilized faces a doughy pallor had taken the place of the clear ruddy color. For the war years they were, perforce, living on starches—spaghetti, potatoes, cereal, bread—with a few vegetables, practically no eggs, and perhaps a piece of beef or pork or mutton or lamb once a month if they were lucky. The women were dowdy, the men (those not in uniform) were shabby. Throughout my period in wartime England during this assignment I heard literally not one word of complaint or protest on the part of any English man or woman or child, whether waiter or Earl or actor or businessman or combatant or professional or private individual of any kind. I cringe, even now, when I recall those airy requests for food made to the waiter that first morning at the Savoy.

In and out of London and the English countryside; into underground mammoth caves, carefully camouflaged, where uniformed men and women eyed intricate precision instruments and machines or sat at charts or watched the tiny dial hands as they reckoned the course of British bombers, United States bombers, German bombers. A grim game, played for keeps. We went to parties at which beautiful and distinguished women wore with dignity dresses that looked as if they had been fashioned from old portieres. We went to the theatre, that imperishable panacea. We stood on platforms far afield and watched as fighters or bombers surged off in flocks, like mammoth birds, on missions fatal even before trial.

Sometimes living in comfort and even luxury at the Savoy Hotel, gratefully eating English wartime food and feeling guilty as we did so. Sometimes sleeping in barracks, sometimes in field hospitals. Two days after our arrival in England an early morning telephone call came in, and with it the welcome voice of Lieutenant Henry Goldsmith, husband of my actress niece Janet Fox Goldsmith who herself had been in Europe and in the South Pacific with the USO.

Glad cries from the amateur Amazons. "Where are you! We've tried everywhere. Are you all right? . . . Yes, we're great. But how did you know?"

"Elemental. Garson Kanin happened to run into Alfred Lunt in London. Alfred told him you were there at the Savoy. How about dinner?"

He was stationed at a camouflaged Intelligence point less than an hour distant by motor. So that was all right. And quite all right, too, was the belated arrival of our escort, Major Elliott, just in from Washington. The flight from Washington to London unescorted hadn't been too difficult, and bashing about England had been accomplished almost methodically on schedule, aided by a six-foot Irish-American from Brooklyn, blue of eye, bulging of biceps and bearing the courtly name of Melady; Major Melady. You felt as though you were a figure in a minuet, powdered hair, rose-patterned brocade, curtseying to a tough handsome American named, incredibly, Melady.

For three weeks now London had not been under bombardment. All England found this difficult—almost impossible—to believe. The hideous roar, the boom, the crash, the flames, the destruction and death had become too much a pattern of daily (or nightly) existence.

The classic eighteenth century houses in the West End were rubble. Now some one had placed amongst these dead ashes flower boxes brilliant with bloom. A gay gesture of defiance and hope, done in the there'll-always-be-an-England tradition. In the East End the docks were a shambles; and the workmen's cottages. If you were in great luck you ate Spam now and then, as a treat, and in the swank hotels and restaurants the menu snobbishly listed *Escalope de Spam*.

A kind of taut nerve-racked temporary semblance of peace hung over the battered English Island.

"But they're flying them out just the same," Major Melady had said. "The Eighth Air Force boys are taking off in those little ol' bombers and fighters like always."

"I thought they didn't like being called boys."

"Wait till you see them."

"Could we? Taking off, I mean."

"Why not? Anyway, it's on your schedule."

Up at dawn after a restless night in a billet far outside London near the airfield. It was intensely cold, as everywhere in Europe that spring. Into the briefing room. There was the huge map covering the wall at one end of the room and before it stood the Commanding Officer, pointer in hand. He was, I learned, twenty-four years of age. There, row on row, looking like college boys in a classroom just before a semester exam, were the fliers, their faces fresh, eager, pink-cheeked. Nineteen twenty twenty-one. Boys, certainly, we'd safely have said, back home. Their sheepskin-lined coat collars were turned up against the cold. They were bareheaded. The room was quiet, quiet. The colonel's pointer made a tapping sound against the heavy stuff of the map.

"Here . . . and here . . . and here . . . Berlin . . ."

A little derisive groan went up from the rows of attentive listeners. Berlin, known as Big B. The toughest, all but one.

". . . You will encounter snow and rain turning to sleet . . ."

They began to laugh a little, like mischievous schoolboys guilty of being rude to the Prof.

". . . Berchtesgaden . . . soandso many anti-aircraft on the ground . . . fighters . . . bombers . . . snow and sleet there too . . ."

But at this the snickers broke into a roar of laughter. These lads laughed and laughed and doubled over with laughter. It was a sort of hilarious hysteria, probably. They were being told that they were setting out to do that which could not be done, except through a miracle.

Then they filed out, but the laughter had ceased.

From the high platform overlooking the field we watched them as they walked toward their planes and took off for their rendezvous. Bundled helmeted strapped and buckled as they were, they walked jauntily and lightly as the young and healthy walk; with a spring, as the toe balanced the heel. Into the cockpit, and off. But off in formation, in clocked time, wheeling and returning for the final take-off. It was a glorious aerial ballet against the morning sky. They rose and swooped and lifted and were gone.

We counted them as they rose.

We stood again on the platform at sunset. And again we counted as they came in. The count did not come out the same.

They clambered out of their planes, stiffly now, and heavily, as though their flying garb weighed them down. Slowly they trudged toward the interrogation room. It was shocking, it was unbelievable to see these haggard furrowed faces of old men etched where youth had been.

An hour later, showered, refreshed, dressed in their pinks for dinner, they were boys again.

They had merely been to hell and back and knew they were lucky to be back at all. And today, probably, they have boys of their own—sons of fifteen or sixteen; and my bet is that they never even mention the dawn flights of fighters and bombers on their way to Big B and to the Monster's lair, Berchtesgaden. And if they ever did their sons today, busy in thought and talk of missiles and moon and astronauts and cosmonauts and four-million-mile swings around the earth, probably would say, genially, "Yeah, those old crates must have been a sketch."

Germany wasn't a sketch. Germany was a Dore horror—1945 version. The Germany we saw was a collection of ashes, for the English and American bomber ballets had not danced aloft in vain. But before Germany on our itinerary came Paris, and Paris had miraculously been spared. Paris, so recently liberated, was said to have been spared destruction by the German bombs because the Nazis fancied this exquisitely beautiful city as a future playground. Paris, they said, with its world-famous restaurants and cabarets, its avenues and boulevards, its museums, hotels, parks, would be just the thing for the moneyed Nazi on holiday. Certain of this prize, they spared it.

In London we had thought ourselves fantastically fortunate to have been billeted at the Savoy Hotel. Now at the end of our flight from London, we were ushered into the even more luxurious splendors of the Hotel Ritz. I had, in peace times, occasionally stopped there. We had thought to be billeted at the Hotel Scribe, Press Headquarters; or at some other less luxe hotel. Now our car drove into the Place Vendôme, there was the doorman, there were the velvet and silken hangings in the foyer, there at the reception desk was the quiet, steely polite staff in striped trousers and morning coats. Flowers bloomed in the garden.

I stared at Major Elliott.

"You too?" He had not been quartered at the Savoy.

"Me? No. How's if I come back for you in about two hours." He glanced around, his good kind face registering satisfaction. "Before our bunch moved into Paris this hotel was headquarters for Nazi higher-ups. Did they love it! The whole Ritz kitchen staff is here, just the way it was. Wait till you see what those chefs can do with U. S. Army rations. Invite me to dinner sometime—promise?"

"Every night."

"Careful with that. Everybody you meet is going to try to scrounge a meal off you here. Parisians and all. It's the top."

Striped trousers ushered us into two adjoining bedrooms on the garden side, free of street noises. Mina and I stared about the rooms; large, high-ceilinged, done in pale blue satin brocade and gilt; brilliant with sunshine, filled with the scent of flowers. Exactly as I remembered them.

"War, huh?" said Mina. "If Marie Antoinette's headsman had turned into a hair-dresser and had said, 'Permanent or just pin-curls?'—that's the way I feel about this."

"Don't trifle with your luck. Anyway, I promise you it's going to be worse; they're just softening us up. That bed was slept in by a Nazi officer, if you really want to hear something uncomfortable."

Paris, it turned out—and not only Paris but the Ritz in Paris—would be our headquarters at the end of various field trips. Belgium, and back to Paris; Italy, and back to Paris; Germany, and again the Paris Ritz. We were yet to learn how incredibly fortunate and pampered we were.

England was free of the German bombs. Much of Germany had been taken by the Allied troops. Italy too. Belgium. But the war was still raging with fury in much of Europe and in Africa and in Japan.

The threat of hidden and dreadful surprises hung over everything. Paris in the daylight was almost gay. Blacked out at night. Young Air Force captains and majors and colonels and generals were as charming and gallant as though we were guests at a West Point graduation. Only the higher rank United States Air Force officers were billeted at the Ritz and almost everyone had pangs of guilt about this luxury, even though tempered with the sweetening of treacly satisfaction. Lucky Ritz dwellers were issued cards to be shown at mealtime. A limited number of guests were permitted on payment (by the holder of the card) of an absurdly small sum. A few francs.

As an old kitchen habitué, amateur cook, and sister of the *Fannie Fox Cookbook* author, I was stunned by the Ritz Hotel cruisine in wartime Paris, 1945.

It was delicious. It was varied. It was luxe. And every bite of it was devised from United States Army rations. Oh, perhaps a dollop of *vin du pays* now and then, in the sauces.

American beef, tender and savory as it emerged from the Ritz kitchen. Bacon, ham, eggs, potatoes, coffee, hot rolls, butter at breakfast. Chicken, chops, roasts, vegetables, pastries, fruits. It was magic. Cardholders salved their guilty conscience by inviting not only their less fortunate fellow-countrymen but as many French people as they tactfully could, to dinner, to lunch.

In the days and weeks in other European countries visited after that first Paris wartime stay I was to encounter the same basic United States Army rations. But the difference was just about that which exists between, say, a beef stew served at a trucker's roadside lunchroom in a small Texas cowtown, and a beef ragout served at the Pavillon in New York. Same beef, same condiments, same cooking vessel. Only the artist makes the difference.

That Paris Ritz kitchen staff had first-rate basic ingredients with which to work. So did every other United States Army cook in Europe, country by country, base by base. The difference was incredible and the secret was talent. That Ritz chef could have made a delicate dish out of a Mojave Desert cactus, needles and all.

The Paris streets were thronged with servicemen in the uniforms of France, of England, of the United States, Belgium. Later, especially in Belgium, one saw many Russian soldiers. They looked much like the Kansas farm boys back home—tall, broad-shouldered, rugged, seemingly good-natured and somewhat naïve. In Paris the United States servicemen stood out like giants in height and shoulder. They towered above the British and the French. Steak, I suppose, and lamb chops and spinach and oranges and milk and bread-and-butter and hamburgers and ice cream. And milk and milk and milk. Their teeth alone would have marked them, so white, so sound-seeming compared to the broken or missing or discolored teeth one noted in the servicemen of other nationalities. When you asked the American soldier what he wanted when he returned home he said, "Fresh milk, ma'am."

On the wartime streets of Paris—true of Paris whether in war or in peace—one encountered more acquaintances and friends than in the course of months at home. In my case these ranged all the way from Mike Todd to Gertrude Stein.

Mike Todd, theatrical producer, was a well-known figure in New York theatrical circles. A decade or more later he was to be known throughout the world as the producer of the enchanting and preposterous film *Around the World in Eighty Days*. I've seen it twice. I'd like to see it again tonight. I'd like to see Mike, too; but three or more years ago he met a Jovian death in an ice-battered plane on a jaunt from Los Angeles to New York. Mike Todd came to wartime Europe with the firm and somewhat incredible plan to introduce organized American baseball into the lives of the millions of United States servicemen on duty.

Having arrived in Paris from the United States at some grisly pre-dawn hour he called me on the telephone at half-past seven A.M. to announce that he was downstairs at the Ritz and that he would meet me for breakfast at eight.

"Breakfast!" I croaked. "It's the middle of the night. I'm not even awake."

"Breakfast. Eight. I hear they'll give you pancakes if you want 'em. Is it true?"

The extraordinary thing is that, impelled by the outrageous magic of this dynamic human engine, I actually did dress and wobble my way down to breakfast at which he talked without pause about the necessity for baseball as part of the American war program in Europe. Exactly here I could lose thousands of readers (if any) by stating (which is true) that I have no interest in baseball even in the most peaceful of times. American baseball in Paris in wartime at the Ritz at breakfast at eight A.M. after having had five hours' sleep turned my excellent coffee and bacon to gall and wormwood.

Mike was wearing a perfectly plain darkish brown uniform consisting of trousers and battle-jacket. It resembled no uniform I had seen. Not a glint of metal appeared on it. He could have been a neatly garbed porter.

"Insignia," I said. "Where's the stuff you should be wearing?"

He glanced at my captain's bars. "Fourflusher."

"You go riding and flying up and down Europe with your baseball," I said acidly, "and no insignia on you anywhere, and some Nazi plane or something—you get lost or something—nips out and captures you, and you're wearing no insignia to prove you're an American and an officer, why, son, a big saftig Jewish boy like you, they'll boil you down for grease quicker than you can say soap."

When I encountered him later that same day he had visited the nearest PX. The front of that battlejacket looked like a bowl of alphabet soup. It was encrusted with every known English language letter malleable as metal and a few faintly resembling the Greek. He sported stars, bars, leaves, ribbons. No five-star general, heroic in history and in performance, ever staggered under such a load of hardware.

"Any sonofabitch of a Nazi catches me," Mike said, "he'll give me the VIP treatment, all right."

Restless, dynamic, improbable; amusing, preposterous, handsome; a disarming showman. His vitality was, after a time, almost exhausting to any companion. It was like being in the company of a high-voltage electric wire. You can't let go. You realize you'll be destroyed if you don't.

Gertrude Stein, at the extreme opposite end of the non-combatant war-picture, trudged the streets of her Paris, which was home to her, looking like a massive ambulatory Buddha. Accompanying her, on a leash, was a gray-white sheepdog the size of a pony. The eccentric American-born playwright and poet had adopted the entire United States Army. As the striking and somewhat macabre duo of massive woman and monster dog roamed the Paris streets—Place Vendôme, the Rue de Rivoli, the Left Bank, the Tuileries Gardens, the Ile St. Louis, Gertrude Stein stopped and talked with every man, young or old, in the uniform of the United States. She, like Mike Todd, had a formula. Hers was not baseball. She argued that the cure for war was love. If everybody loved everybody there would be no war. You couldn't argue this. As we stood talking on a street corner I agreed that her theory was a highly reasonable one but that it might be difficult to make it realistically workable. Miss Stein didn't see why, and I'm glad she didn't. She asked me to come to her apartment to tea and to look at her picture collection which was fabulous; and she assured me that there always were dozens of U.S. servicemen of every age color branch and rank in and out of the apartment every day. It was my bad luck to be leaving Paris next day and I had no available time in the interim. I never did make it, and I have never ceased, when reminded of this, to regret it. Even the United Nations Building and all its sessions haven't achieved International Love. But in a way, Gertrude thought of it first, and perhaps she somehow could have made it work. Eleanor Roosevelt was touched with a more realistic glow of the same. When Nikita Khrushchev, in a United Nations Session in New York, wrenched off his shoe and hammered on his desk with the heel of it in obnoxious rudeness while the representative of another nation was speaking, it was not the emotion of love that motivated the Russian dictator. I wish that some one—Eleanor Roosevelt could have managed—had quietly reprimanded him as you would a nasty little ill-mannered boy. In the unavoidable absence of Gertrude Stein, that is. A bully is a bully is a bully.

13

Not wishing to appear sentimental, it nevertheless must be stated that for sheer ingenuity under adversity—if the word adversity can be used as a euphemism for World War II—I never have encountered any human organization remotely equal to the United States Air Force. It was a mere novice who couldn't parlay ten American cigarettes into a nice little German Benz car. It was part of my assignment to write of the Air Force ground crews and enlisted men. But we often were politely herded off to the officers' mess, against our not-so-polite protests. We wanted to eat with the enlisted men. The food was better at the officers' mess, but the talk wasn't so nourishing. The serviceman showed you, always, the picture in his wallet. It was Butch, ten months old; or it was a girl who looked not so very much older than Butch and who turned out to be mother of same. In liberated areas that were former German bases it was a listless type indeed who had not acquired a collection of Lugers, knives, swords, cameras, coats, cars; all left behind by fleeing Germans. This accumulation routine was termed scrounging. The more realistic called it ghouling. It is one of the minor unattractive features of the hideous anachronism known as War.

But often the men were legitimately and most engagingly inventive and ingenious.

In liberated areas and on bases lately taken by the Allies, there was a deadly sort of lull in activity. The tide had turned. The world was holding its breath for the coming of the Day. Time hung heavy on the hands of these millions of young men, once the day's assignment was covered. Rome, Naples, Capri (a rest camp), Brussels, London again, Paris again.

At a Naples base, "Show you my radio I made."

"Made? Really!"

"Aw, it's nothing. Just out of parts I scrounged from the graveyard."

Your admiration became horror. "Graveyard!"

"Yeh, old airplane graveyard—condensers and coils, see. That wood is from a C-ration box, good. Speaker's one those old-fashioned earphones. That dial is just a piece of cardboard with the stations on it."

They were natural mechanics and as ingenious as only lads can be who had nosed around some sort of car or jalopy since they first learned to walk.

"Made me a scooter, see. Those tires are from the tail wheels of a midget plane. Frame is welded fuselage parts. Engine's from air compressors. Seats are parachute seats. I was kind of put to it for handlebars but they're real good, they're a bent piece of fuselage frame. . . . Windy show you his motorboat? He's always sounding off about his motorboat. He made it out of one of those 150-gallon belly tanks, split open and then he welded them together like pontoons so he won't tip over, kind of like a Hawaiian boat I've seen 'em in the movies. His vapor burner is from a 40-gallon drum, he remembered that out of chemistry in high school, Windy did. About heat from gas vapors, I mean. He's a smart cooky all right, Windy is. I wish I had me a motorboat. That Bay and all, out there."

"I'm about to make me a station wagon. Couple those old ammunition crates, you varnish and wax 'em real good, and cello-glass windows, why—"

A kind of uneasy semi-peace hung over the world. One kind of tension had been replaced by another kind, even more wearing.

End of the day. Cleaned up. Dressed in their pinks. Music on the radio; or even a base dance-band, and nothing amateurish about it; the horns, the drums, even a piano scrounged from who knows where?

"Dance, ma'am?" A little bow that he had learned back home in Columbus Ohio. I was old enough to be his mother—his grandmother. No other women in sight.

"Love to." And off we whirled, I used to be very good at it and it's like ice-skating, once you've learned early you never lose the knack. I told myself.

In Italy the small boys and girls stuck their tongues out at us, and spat. In Germany, as we toured escorted always by the omnipresent Major Elliott and two additional officers, guns in belts, the agate-eyed Nazi-indoctrinated young boys stared with such hate that the impact of their emotion seemed to jolt one's spinal nerves.

"Go home, kike-trained monkeys!" they said.

You argued with yourself, well, if the thing had been reversed, by some terrible mischance, and a plane-load of Nazi correspondents and escort had landed at, say La Guardia airfield, the American teenager doubtless would have normally reacted in much the same way.

For that matter, driving up the German Autobahn in a luxurious staff car, eating a K-ration lunch en route and looking from side to side at the broken ruins of cars, trucks—every sort of war vehicle piled in confusion like metal garbage, I thought how easily this German parkway called the Autobahn could have been the Merritt Parkway running its smooth ribbon through New York, Connecticut, Massachusetts. The whole thing in reverse. At that moment there approached from the opposite direction a fleet of open trucks. In each of these was a gray-green mass that resolved itself into men and men and men standing close-crushed together like lice. It was the gray-green uniform of the German Army. The wet-cold wind of the German spring season—a bitter spring it was that year—cut their exposed faces and must have chilled the bone marrow as they stood massed and defeated. They were German prisoners of war, bound for internment camps.

There, I said to myself, but for the grace of God, go I.

In Italy and England and France there stalked pure horror and tragedy, but always, somewhere in between, there were ludicrous happenings, pleasant moments or hours, even gay periods. But Germany was unadulterated horror. Personal discomfort in France Italy England went practically unnoticed; or, if remarked, was regarded in the light of adventure. Moments of laughter—some of this tinged, perhaps, with mild hysteria. Up in a droop snoot, for example. The technical name of the droop snoot was—I think—P-38, but it never was thus formally referred to. It may have appeared late in the war, or perhaps it didn't prove a success. Personally, I wished I never had met it. It resembled a glass bubble and was, really. Plexiglas. Its name was derived from the fact that the cockpit, all Plexiglas, drooped from the transparent body of the thing like an unsightly drop hanging precariously from the end of a runny nose. In this I sat, rigid with apprehension, nothing, apparently, between me and sky and me and earth but a transparent glaze of film. From this perch I viewed the ashes and crumbled stone of what had been the glorious monastery of Monte Cassino. This alone was blood-chilling enough; but the young pilot was a cut-up. He decided to take the old girl for a ride, and the process was known as cutting the daisies. He swooped to mere inches above the ground (the daisies) and then up with a *whoosh* into the blue. My jaw-muscles must have stuck out like clothes-hangers. If you can take this without squawking, I said to myself, and go on living, you can stand anything. And did and am. That rat boy.

With niece Mina on an inspection tour up in a P-47 fighter bomber, creeping precariously along the catwalk and, all unconscious of the absurdity, calling aunt-wise over my shoulder to her, "Don't lean on the bombs, darling!" A small sharp shriek of hysterical laughter, led by Mina, followed by me. To this day, at a word of unasked advice from me, I am likely to be met with don't-lean-on-the-bombs-darling.

Paris, by some miracle of good fortune, had been designated as base. There never was a luckier amateur War Correspondent. Perhaps health and nerves emerged unscathed because of this surcease at the end of each foray.

Wiesbaden was the first bitter bite of the German poison. In long past years I had traveled in Germany, I had once stayed briefly in Wiesbaden, it was not my dish—a stuffy handsome and orderly German spa full of stuffy people taking the cure. Now the city of Wiesbaden was more than one-third ashes. We were billeted in Press Quarters; a four-story apartment house that had no heat, no windows, no running water. The numbing cold of that spring of 1945 in Europe ordinarily would have made this combination formidable, not to say unendurable. We didn't mind. Perhaps it was the excellent Czech cook. Actually, this state of being oblivious to discomfort must have been due to the utter interest and even perverse fascination that was crammed into every moment. You went to bed wearing a sweater and the wool lining snapped out of your waterproof service coat. A tough tender young sergeant had scrounged two sheets for Mina and me. Rolled up in this, one each, we knew luxury. You went in to breakfast wearing all the clothing we could pile on and still navigate; coat-collar turned up. Breakfast wasn't Ritz but it was good Army ration intelligently cooked and I even learned to eat peanut butter with grape jelly, the one taking the curse off the other. An old-timer in the permanent Press Staff had managed to rig up an old stove, small, rusty and red-hot. When hands became too numb for the typewriter one could somewhat apologetically thaw out here for five ecstatic minutes.

You were driven from city to city; or were flown. The eye became so accustomed to ruin, devastation, horror that the glance grew glazed; rejected what it saw. That which had been an avenue was an ash-heap; that which had been a city was a monstrous ruin.

All Europe was afoot—fleeing or returning. One saw no vehicles other than war equipment; war on wheels. The continent walked.

As in Wiesbaden, I had last seen Frankfurt-am-Main about fourteen years earlier—a thriving commercial city of factories, shops, apartment houses, churches, hotels; its bridges spanning the Main; the old town quaintly contrasting with the modern.

We stood in what Major Elliott assured me was the center of Frankfurt. There was to me not one thing recognizable in this sea of debris. "If I could spot the Frankfurterhof," I said, "I'd know where I am. I stopped at that hotel years ago."

In the midst of this formless desolation I never found the Frankfurterhof. As far as the eye could see there was no dwelling, no structure of any kind in which a human being could live. The great bridges that had spanned the River Main were split in two like matchsticks; two ends sticking up in the air, two wallowing in the riverbed. And over everything there was the sickly-sweet stench of decaying flesh hidden beneath these ruined buildings. This was one city only of dozens through which we passed. Ruin and horror became so accustomed to our reluctant eyes that it took on the aspect of the commonplace. Or perhaps this was merely nature, protecting us from the unbearable.

One aspect of all this, though, was so remarkable, so portentous, that it never failed to strike a questioning note. It was a mysterious and sinister thing. In this Germany of crumbled walls and broken pillars and gutted basements and twisted beams walked a strong and purposeful people. Defeated, these yet were an undefeated people. Already they were preparing. Well-dressed and composed men and women walked these ruined streets through which American Army bulldozers had cleared a lane. The women's hair was modishly waved and coifed They wore silk stockings and smart shoes and excellently cut tailored suits and dresses. The men carried brief cases and walking sticks or umbrellas like London men on their way to the City in peace time. Their topcoats and shoes and hats were correct. Everyone carried a bundle of some kind, or pulled or pushed a cart. They were busy and intent as ants whose ant-hill has just been stepped on. In their smart clothes they were hauling wood picked from the rubble. In the country-side men and women were bent over in the fields, planting with their hands the grain, the vegetables, the fruit. The bomb-plowed fields now were being renewed by men and women hitched like animals to crude wooden plows. Busy, busy, busy, intent on their own lives, concentrating on the business of surviving, they ignored the strangers' stare. Frankfurt or Mainz or Weimar or Kassel, they were going about the business of reconstruction as though long ago they had been given their orders to be followed in case of unimaginable defeat. They were not working for that day only. They were working for the future. For now. Today. By the way, I'm told that steel is so much cheaper in Germany than in the United States that we're buying our building steel from Germany.

Two more incidents only. Who enjoys writing about the Second World War? Not I. Who enjoys reading about the Second World War? Not you. It must be written. It should be read.

Buchenwald Concentration Camp was situated just outside the city of Weimar. Hundreds of thousands of innocent men women children were cremated there or otherwise murdered in wholesale. And guess what? No one in Weimar knew a single thing about it. Didn't in fact, know it was there. As likely as your waking up some morning and not noticing an abattoir and glue factory sprung up overnight in your back yard.

In the two days spent in Weimar we were billeted in a requisitioned house which had belonged to a Nazi, now vanished. In opening a bureau drawer in my bedroom I came upon a man's celluloid collar. A harmless and dowdy enough article of male haberdashery, but so characteristic, so speaking, that it sickened me as strongly as some of the horrid sights I had seen and was to see. Sleeping in that bed was torture. Weimar, too, was busy planting and mending and building. A big thing about flowers went on in the little gardens nearby. Very flower-loving people, the German nation.

We were driven out to Buchenwald Concentration Camp on the outskirts of Weimar. It was afternoon. We were to have dinner with the

General in command, and his Staff Officers. This camp had only recently been liberated by American troops. Its ovens, its barred basement cells were idle now. Many recent occupants had been removed by transfer to rehabilitation if possible, or by death. Many remained, waiting for possible planning; or because they were too emaciated, too nearly dead to make moving possible. For the most part they lay on wooden bunks in the walls of enormous shedlike rooms, mere racks of bone from which the only recognizable living feature was the eyes and these were curiously staring, tortured and seemingly sightless things, asking an eternal question which no one could answer. On the skin of the wrist had been branded their prisoner's number and section. There were small skeletonlike children wobbling about and these, too, carried the identifying mark on their sticklike wrists. Their arms were the circumference of my finger; their fingers mere slivers, their heads skulls.

"And this," the soldier-guide said, as one to whom this now was an oft-told tale—not heartlessly stated, but by rote, now, through repetition and, perhaps, because otherwise he could not have survived this gruesome task—"this is the place where they herded the prisoners before they went into the crematory." He pointed to walls, to iron doors. On them were encrusted blobs of dried blood and hair. "This is a lampshade made from human skin. . . . Those? . . . uh . . . they're going to be moved out any minute now." Those were dead bodies, piled like orderly garbage waiting to be taken momentarily away; and so they were, tidily.

A man in the hideous striped pants and top of the Buchenwald prisoner's uniform—the liberation had been so recent that other clothing was not yet available—now yielded to an inner urge so antic as to chill the onlooker's blood even more than had the gruesome sights we had just beheld.

In health and in normal life he must have been a tall man, and hearty, fiftyish perhaps, and of dignified bearing. A businessman, a lawyer, or of another of the professions. He was stooped now. His shoulders and chest had slumped into his abdomen which was flabby, not fat at all. He resembled a walking withered gourd. In the chaos that followed the liberation of Buchenwald Concentration Camp, and in the scrounging that must have followed upon that, this once sedate and intelligent man had somehow come upon a high silk hat such as men sometimes wear to the opera or to a wedding, or another formal occasion. Perhaps a mischievous serviceman had come upon it, and given it to him. With it was a fine ebony and gold-headed walking stick. The man rubbed the nap of the foolish headgear round and round with the fore-sleeve of his striped and hideous jacket; round and round. He had owned one of these articles of headgear in a former day, and knew how to handle it.

Now he clapped it on his head at a rakish angle. He had got hold of a cigarette. He was shoeless. Thus accoutered, puffing the cigarette and flicking the ash elegantly, gold-headed cane in hand, he stepped down the dusty road toward the city of Weimar and its burghers who had claimed to be quite unaware of the presence of this man and millions like him; and of the stinking gas chambers and the ovens so near the lovely city of Weimar.

You knew that this man now was bereft of the dignity and sense which once had been his. He was grinning as he walked, but the face had, too, a kind of noble decency and you could no longer watch as the grotesque figure padded down the road in its futile gesture of defiance.

That night we had dinner with the Commanding Officer and his staff at the Air Force Base so near the hideous Buchenwald Concentration Camp. It was all very pleasant and decorous and not very stimulating. As touring temporary War Correspondent I had discovered that the higher the echelon the lower the pulse potential. A really good tough Brooklyn or Texas top-sergeant is my notion of nourishing copy.

As tactfully as I could I expressed a wish to visit the nearby Servicemen's Club rooms. This was not received with enthusiasm by the stars and bars group. I then argued, darkly polite but insistent, that part of my assignment was Air Base Ground Crews. The truth was that the hours spent surveying Buchenwald had resulted in a psychic depression so acute that it was like a physical illness. If, for only a few minutes, perhaps, I could see and speak with a roomful of young vital natural and even hopeful men to whom war was not a career but a dirty job that must be done as thoroughly, as neatly, as quickly and expertly as possible so that they could return home to the life they knew and wanted, then my own outlook on the human race might be less densely black.

We crossed over to the clubhouse. As we entered there was the sound of a piano and young male voices. The big room was warmly lighted, smoky, alive. Scores of young men were standing about or were seated at tables talking, playing cards or other games; reading, drinking I talked to a few here and there. Some of them knew that I had been on the base that day; some had read books I had written.

A young man crossed the big room and stood before me. He made a little bow, almost like a polite small boy. He spoke his name. The ensuing dialogue would have meant nothing to anyone but the two of us.

"You wrote *Show Boat*, didn't you?"

"Yes. Perhaps you've read it?"

"I know it by heart."

"How did that happen?"

"I'm stage-struck."

"So am I."

"That part about the audiences in the little river towns when the show boat docked there."

"I'm glad if you liked that bit."

"Listen: 'The curtain rose. The music ceased jerkily, in mid-bar. They became little children listening to a fairy tale. A glorious world of unreality opened before their eyes. Things happened. They knew that in life things did not happen thus. But here they saw, believed, and were happy. Innocence wore golden curls. Wickedness wore black. Love triumphed, right conquered, virtue was rewarded, evil punished.

"'They forgot the cotton fields, the wheat fields, the cornfields. They forgot the coal mines, the potato patch, the stable, the barn, the shed. They forgot the labor under the pitiless blaze of the noonday sun; the bitter marrow-numbing chill of winter; the blistered skin; the frozen road; wind, snow, rain, flood. The women forgot for an hour their washtubs, the kitchen stoves, childbirth pains, drudgery, worry, disappointment. Here were blood, lust, love, passion. Here were warmth, enchantment, laughter, music. It was Anodyne. It was Lethe. It was Escape. It was the Theatre.'"

He had recited from memory a full half of Page 104 in *Show Boat*.

In his Air Force uniform as he stood there, black-haired, rosy-cheeked, young, handsome, vital, this was the classic behavior of one who is a dedicated actor. I forgot for a time at least the gruesome day. My spirits rose. The human race was a non-destructible miracle. I had just witnessed a kind of magic.

Paris again. Articles to be written and filed and dispatched. You flew in whatever type of plane was assigned to you; a bucket-seat job, perhaps, in which everyone sat stooped forward in aching discomfort while the air vehicle plunged like a bucking bronco; or a tiny blob the size of a footbath in the diminutive center of which three people could just barely manage to sit with knees pressed close to the torso and feet tucked under one. I learned to drop (none too exquisitely) out of the belly of such midget conveyances, oblivious to the impish grins of nearby ground crews.

There was a little errand now in Paris that I had dreaded since Buchenwald. News of any correspondent's approaching visit to one of the liberated concentration camps brought agonized appeals from men and women one encountered; relatives who knew nothing, who had for long months heard nothing, of the absent ones. How these learned of one's intended visit was a mystery. "My father—my husband—my brother—my mother my sister—Buchenwald—Dachau—will you try to find—a record—some news—"

One of the reception staff at the Ritz Hotel—the steely-polite type in the correct striped trousers and morning coat who had greeted us on our first arrival in Paris—had motioned me quietly aside before my departure for Weimar and the Buchenwald inspection tour. The man's face was drained white, his voice was so low as to be just audible; he glanced quickly to right, to left.

"You are going to Buchenwald." It was not a question; it was a statement of fact.

"Yes."

"My father is there—was there when last we heard. Perhaps he is still there. Alive—perhaps. Can you—will you—records—"

He gave me the name. Approximate dates. It seemed so hopeless as to border on the absurd.

But the German nation of the Second World War was a tidy and orderly and businesslike people, and they kept careful records, unbelievable as this may seem. Neatly, in the books, were filed the names of every man woman child who entered the murder camp—and left it. So there I actually was to see the name and the proper date that had marked the arrival—and departure—of the father of the reception clerk at the Ritz Hotel in Paris. Dachau—the hopeless final Dachau—followed the notation.

We now faced each other, the Ritz office clerk and I.

"I found his name."

He waited, in silence.

"He—he was transferred from Buchenwald to Dachau." Another moment's silence. "That's all."

"That is all," the man repeated after me. I could no longer see his face, nor he mine, so we turned away in silence.

One more German trip only. Then back to Weimar; Weimar to Paris.

This final trip was to Nordhausen and it is almost literally impossible to set down in written words because Nordhausen bore absolutely no resemblance to reality. It defies description. It must, then, be set down in a kind of stark factual reporting.

Few people know of Nordhausen. Few, comparatively, have seen it. Few who labored there could have survived it, or did.

Nordhausen, to be brisk about it, was the place in which the V-2 bomb was manufactured—at that time the most deadly war weapon ever devised by man. But this was no mere factory with walls and windows and doors and chimneys. With fantastic ingenuity and superhuman pains (but then, slave labor isn't human, they would have assured you, and pains are meant to be taken) the vast plant that manufactured the V-2 bomb that so nearly caused the destruction of England and so nearly won the war for Germany, was situated inside a mountain. A mountain, literally, had been disemboweled to create this death-dealing weapon. Into the side of this solid stone mass they had blasted and gouged and picked; and once they had made a little headway and were safely inside they had camouflaged the scarred exterior with replacements of underbrush and trees. Like scientific moles they dug until a vast vaulted factory space lay safely inside the mountain's bone-structure and none but its builders and its burrowers knew—or even guessed—what that great granite tree-bedecked mountain concealed. Aside from its scientific, mechanistic and official staffs it was manned by slave labor. Slave labor was cheap in those days in Germany, like any other too-common commodity. It was elementally simple. One could work these slaves economically, with a minimum of food or rest or sleep, until they literally dropped. Then they were lugged off to the handy crematory just next door; and a new batch of prisoners brought in; an so on and on and on.

At the approaching end of the war the Allied Forces had come upon this hidden and deadly hive whose sting had so nearly destroyed our world.

Our staff car took us to the entrance. It wasn't actually a door. It was an ingenious secret opening in the mountainside. No daylight within; all the lights had been turned on now. We walked into a black and white hell.

The factory interior was two miles square. The stone walls and arched ceiling were whitewashed. They gave back the glare of electric lights so powerful that the eye could scarcely bear the assault. The floor was black. The machines were black. The shadows cast on the white walls were black. Not a living thing existed now within this horror of black and white. They had fled—the mighty and the abject. It was a dead hell.

As always had been the case during these weeks of our tour of work Mina and I were the only women in a group of men. Among these men, as we now stood surveying this gigantic death-factory, were men who knew war weapons and the machinery that produces the most effective and the most modern of these weapons. They looked at the German-made lathes that stood row on row and row on row as far as the eye could see; and they touched these lathes and all these magnificent precision instruments and the engines and tools that had made and perfected the V-2 bomb, and in their faces and in their engine-wise touch was an amazement and—yes—a dreadful admiration for perfection of achievement.

Their utterance was commonplace enough, they might have been describing a ball game; but their tone was awestruck.

"Say, look at this one! No wonder they could lob 'em over."

"I sure hope these birds never start another one. You got to hand it to the bastards when it comes to know-how."

Straw, matted and soiled, lay on the bare floor beside these exquisite instruments. Bits of worn and ragged clothing, too. Some tattered books. Scraps of letters, unbearable in their record of anguish. The slaves had not only worked here in this hell of black and white; they had lived here, slept here on these beds of straw, died here and been shoveled away to the ovens.

Mina picked up a little colored painting done on a piece of board. It was a sentimental painting of a cottage with a rose-embowered doorway and the housewifely figure of a woman standing there, and a child in the crudely portrayed garden; blue sky, a white puff-cloud;

pink flowers and blue. Not good at all. Merely great in what it represented of human suffering and longing.

Mina held it in her hand. "Could I have this?"

"Well, sure. Why not?"

So she put it in her suitcase and took it to Paris and a few days later
she developed an over-all skin eruption that necessitated a series of
visits to the doctor and also the most complete disinfecting process on
that suitcase and all its contents. Including the picture, which had to
be destroyed.

Out into the daylight now. There was the crematory, perched on a
little knoll near the mother mountain. It was rather a cosy-looking building; and cosily leaning out of an open window, her plump arms folded
on the sill, was a buxom blonde German girl, coquettishly talking and
laughing with a young man gazing up at her from the slope below.

We entered the crematory. It was plain and neat and clean. There
were the ovens. The doors for the moment closed. On the bare floor
before us lay row after row of flat statues that had been human beings.
They were partly covered with ineffectual pieces of thin gray linenlike
cloth. Only their feet protruded in those orderly rows on rows. There is
nothing more dead-looking than the feet of a dead human being; not
white, but a waxen gray-yellow and inert beyond bearing. We stumbled
out of the doorway and there passed us men bearing a crude stretcher
on which lay still another incredibly flat object under a nothing-colored
cloth. The outline of the figure seemed almost as non-dimensional as
a pencil sketch on paper.

In a stretch of trampled muddy meadow below the charnel house
there stood a sort of little cluster of dwellings hardly numerous enough
to be called a village. But one could not; in any case, have recognized
this as a group of houses because no one ever before saw habitations of
this description.

The Russian and Polish and Czech and Yugoslav and Greek slave
workers who had toiled in the V-2 bomb factory were free, now that
Nordhausen had been liberated by the Allied troops. Thousands had
started out on foot to walk the endless miles back to their homes from
which they had been pressed into slavery by their German captors.
But thousands could not attempt the journey on foot, physically de-
bilitated as they were. Some had found temporary refuge in improvised
huts or caves nearby. We now saw that hundreds actually were living

in the great metal fuselages of the V-2 bombs which they themselves had forged. These black metal monsters now stood all about in the yards. In their tunneled depths the liberated slaves had ironically set up housekeeping. They had rigged up ventilators for air. Patchwork stoves had been devised for cooking and for protection against the cold night. You could smell the food cooking for the evening meal. Bits and rags of their pitiful laundry were festooned in an almost gay frieze against the iron sides of their shelters.

As you saw again this gallant, this ageless struggle for survival you felt that there still was a dip of the scales in favor of the human race.

14

Wiesbaden. In contrast to what we had witnessed and felt—in Weimar, Buchenwald, Nordhausen—Wiesbaden loomed rosy and cosy in our memory; a haven of comfort and even luxury. As our plane nosed its way toward that battered city and the windowless heatless waterless Press Headquarters there, we felt like exiles returning to Eden. The faces of the hard-bitten kind War Correspondents billeted there took on the nobility of Roman Senators; the Czech cook was, at this distance, the equal of the Paris Ritz culinary magician; the tough sergeant would let us have a bucket of hot water from the kitchen stove.

It was to be Wiesbaden for one day only. Then Paris again. We barely made it into Wiesbaden. A pea-soup fog came down. It not only came down, it stayed down. After the first few hours of comparative comfort and rest we were prisoners of the weather.

"Just to Paris," we said cajolingly. "It can't take long."

"Sure won't take long if you hit a hard cloud," Air said, "over the Ardennes."

A day went by—two—three. We had dinner with the handsome and brilliant young General Hoyt Vandenberg at his headquarters in an imposing requisitioned Wiesbaden villa. I had tried to coax a ride to Paris through every possible Air Force source of influence—except this, the Top. Well, here was I, all dressed up in a regular black dinner dress and seated at the general's right. So I spoke up. What did I have to lose! Even Air can't break a make-believe captain back to a private. Anyway my tour would be over in ten days or two weeks.

"Uh—isn't there—couldn't some way be arranged to fly us back to Paris—it's sort of important for me to get back—"

"Yes, I know. A lot of people are waiting," he agreed, with the sympathetic charm that I ill-deserved. "And they feel it's important, too. But nothing's going out. Over the Ardennes in this stuff you might bump into—"

I knew how that sentence was to end. Hard clouds. It did.

"But," he went on, and he looked down at me with genuine kindness and concern, six-footer that he was, and a power in his vast field, "if anything turns up I'll let you know."

So that's that, I thought. Well, I tried, anyway.

Next day there came a message from General Vandenberg. He and his staff were leaving almost immediately. If we could make it they would take us aboard their plane and we would be flown to Paris.

I've been in scrambles, but never in one like that. Whatever we left behind, Wiesbaden can have, and welcome. The fog was as thick as ever, a drizzle added a redundant ingredient to the soup. The gray wet city lay like a corpse as we passed through it in the staff car toward the waiting plane.

Mina was muttering, "I don't see how a plane can make it simply because a general and a bunch of Brass happen to be on board. If we hit that hard cloud they're always beefing about it isn't going to soften up for a general, is it!"

"No. But think of the chic publicity and the stunning finale if we go crashing down in the company of a godlike general and all that lovely Brass."

Up into the gray-brown soup and over the treacherous Ardennes. The plane was again a C-54, a tried and trusty friend. Very bumpy, though. Take a deep breath. Try to think of something pleasant. Do I look as green as Mina, I wonder. Greener, I bet. Oo! No. Take a deep breath.

Then, mysteriously, we began to descend in orderly fashion and the Brass was assembling itself and the general evidently was preparing to emerge from his private section and I looked around me and said, "Paris already!"

No. No, it wasn't Paris. The general and his staff were stopping over, and we would proceed to Paris without them. And they did this. Luxembourg, some one said. The plane was strangely empty and somehow ominous, though when we reached Paris in our almost solitary splendor

228

the spring sun was shining and the Paris streets, to our eyes, so accustomed these past days to a dour and dreadful Germany, were brilliant.

The strain of those gruesome days in Germany; the delay in Weimar; the chancey flight over the Ardennes now was relaxed. Utter fatigue hit us as though we had been bludgeoned over the head with a lead pipe. Even dinner in the best Ritz war ration tradition was, after a few desultory bites, abandoned. Eyes already closed, we stumbled into bed and instantly were asleep.

It must have been—was, in fact—just about ten blissful hours later when I awoke to see a small American Air Force plane just about to enter my room through the window facing the Ritz garden. It changed its mind and whizzed by, with not an inch to spare.

One noteworthy leap toward Mina in the adjoining room. I wrenched open the connecting door to find that she had done the same on her side. With the precision of a trained duet we shouted, "Did you see that!"

At that moment another identical plane performed exactly the same impossible feat.

What we had taken to be an American fighter plane performing gymnastics within a few feet of the ground and in a space that would have irked an athletic bluebottle fly actually was an American fighter plane doing that which cannot be done except as a miracle.

It turned out to be a war world gone mad, and the American Air Force with it—and who had a better right! They were celebrating.

By a fluke of sheer dazzling fool luck we had stumbled into Paris on V-E Day. General Vandenberg and his staff had flown in spite of fog and had descended to sign the Peace Treaty.

Today—V-E Day—marked the end of the Second World War in Europe.

A city gone mad cannot be described and no attempt will be made at it here. We walked the Paris streets on wings. If, on that day, any man in the uniform of the United States Army went unkissed by a French girl he must have been asleep behind a pillar in the Tomb of Napoleon. Bands played. Men marched. Women marched. Flags flaunted the Tri-Couleur and the Stars and Stripes. Planes darted like mosquitoes, vehicles of war lumbered by, hidden by the swarms of Paris girls that bedecked them. If you ate at all you ate standing.

Night came. The lights of Paris were turned on. The lights of Paris,

City of Lights, bediamonded the exquisite boulevards and avenues, the bridges and the squares—the Place de la Concorde, the Place Vendôme, the Tuileries. Children, perched high on their fathers' shoulders, beheld the lights of Paris for the first time. Caught in an impenetrable bottleneck just around the corner from the Hotel Crillon, bashed up against the building and protected only by the endurance of the muscles provided by our sturdy Air Force escort, I saw a woman just next me faint standing up. She couldn't fall because there wasn't space to fall in.

Mina and I, each to the other, said, over and over:

"Suppose we'd been in Weimar!" We shuddered away from the thought.

"We could have been in Nordhausen."

"What if we'd been in Frankfurt . . . Capri . . . Naples . . . Brussels . . . Wiesbaden."

The War, we said exultantly, naïvely—the War was ended.

I wanted now to go to Berlin. I wanted to see this city, seat of the most infamous reign that the world had ever known. I wanted to see it in defeat. I wanted to reassure my eyes as well as my other senses and my emotions and my thinking, that democracy and decency and the spirit of man had triumphed over insane brutality and lust for power.

I never went.

In the beginning I innocently put in my request at the Paris SHAEF regular headquarters.

Not allowed to go to Berlin.

Soon I was cabling the State Department in Washington. Then— in a kind of desperation—the President. Not permitted.

I started all over again and finally I reached High Echelon—not the highest, but high—in Paris. High SHAEF said, "You can't go to Berlin."

This was no time for politeness and protocol I told myself in my innocence and ignorance. "But why why *why* can't I go?"

"No correspondents are permitted to go to Berlin. No one, in fact."

"But why? Why?"

"They won't let us."

This was maddening. "Who won't let us?"

"Russia. Russia won't allow us to go into Berlin."

It was no good just staring at him like that. He actually had said it. I had heard. I stood up. I suppose I was quietly hysterical.

"Look. This is appeasement. This is what the war was fought for. You can't do that. You can't do that. Russia was an ally of Germany. Remember? Until the day the Nazis invaded Russia."

Gently he said, as though talking to an unreasonable child. "We don't want war with Russia now."

Russia was cosily installed in Berlin. Winston Churchill, the wise, the intuitive, had unsuccessfully implored General Dwight Eisenhower and the high command in Washington to drive into Berlin. But Berlin, General Eisenhower said, is not a particularly important objective. So Russia helped itself to all it needed of the riches of Berlin and of Germany—machines, entire factory parts stripped to the boards; scientific instruments, and the scientists themselves. And these were sent out to Russia and the Russian command stayed in Berlin. So the Wall was erected, really, back there in May 1945.

That flight back to the United States and Treasure Hill was unique in one event at least—an event that even now, almost two decades later, I still cannot quite believe.

A fine flight. Same type of C-54. Same assortment of handsome Brass. Toward the end of the flight I had got hold of a flight map. I am not good at maps. We were supposed to come down in Washington, but a few hours before we were due to land the news had gone round the plane's cabin that certain High Brass on board preferred to come down at La Guardia in New York; and La Guardia it was to be.

This was good news, but it took a few minutes for the import of this to form in my mind.

"La Guardia? Wait a minute. Wait—a—minute." Then came the poring over the flight route on the map. My finger traced the line that ended in La Guardia Airport. During my years in the house on Treasure Hill I had seen and heard the big planes flying to the south or to the north of the house and sometimes, whether by mischance or deliberately, they had flown directly over us and had even seemed to skim the chimneys. Once, hearing the thunder of the engines, we had rushed out in panic to see the huge bird practically skimming the driveway.

Now, brashly, I put it to the C-54 pilot, long-suffering and kindly king of the craft. "Is this the flight course? . . . Well, my house is in

Easton. And it says Easton. Here. Do you think I could see . . . of course I suppose it's a foolish question . . . but do you think we might come anywhere near . . . of course it will probably be a mile or two off . . . but . . ."

"Just about where, exactly."

I pointed. "Just about there. The little sort of village is called Stepney. In Easton. A high hill and a long stone house."

"Uh-huh," the pilot said. "Couldn't say, really. You just stand over there by that window when I tell you and kind of stare around. Of course we could be a mile or two away, this side. Nearer Bridgeport, maybe."

I stationed myself at the window. Five minutes. Ten. Fifteen. I recognized nothing in the woods and the little lines or dots that were waterways; the tiny roofs of tiny houses. Lower. Slower. My face pressed to the window. And then I gave a shriek that must have made all the Big Brass on board decide to have me shot at dawn.

"My house!" I yelled. "Right smack over it. My house!"

There was the long line of Treasure Hill's rooftop. The orchard behind it. The walled garden. The sky-blue painted rectangle of the unfilled swimming pool. Curtiss's cottage. The white barn.

My house. I had been to the wars and was back again. And there was my house, sunning itself in the late spring afternoon light, welcoming me home.

La Guardia. It was packed with uniformed young men who were drinking milk. Never have I seen such a milk-drinking. There were women, young and middle-aged, at stands and counters all over the place and they were pouring glass after glass after glass of fresh cold milk and the belts of the milk drinkers seemed to tighten visibly as the stuff flowed down the throats. Not powdered milk. Fresh milk. The drink they had been parching for these months and months. Well, thanks; ma'am, I guess I will have another if you say so. She said so.

I had to go to New York directly instead of to Treasure Hill. But I telephoned Curtiss just as a mild joke.

"What were you doing sitting there under that apple tree at five this afternoon—with all those chores to do?"

New England is laconic. "Well, say! You fixed it up all right over there. Welcome home."

15

The thing to do—They say—when you've been thrown by a horse (or by life) is to scramble back into the saddle and gallop off. Otherwise you remain thrown forever. This is splendid advice for the huntin' set but it doesn't always apply to the ordinary pedestrian human. When I tried to climb back on the horse it threw me again.

I didn't write. For the first time in decades—since I was a seventeen-year-old reporter—I didn't write. It was bewildering. It was frustrating. It was horrible. The riderless horse galloped away, leaving me limping and ineffectual. It was June, and Treasure Hill was lovely almost beyond bearing (the lambs had been born and all but one were rams, so at least perfection didn't rear its haughty head on the Hill). Midsummer, autumn, winter. House, trees, garden, crops, stock, all went well. The family was flourishing. New York sparkled again, its luster perhaps slightly dimmed by the years of war and soot. I did not write.

The diary, always a mere two or three lines baldly set down, with an occasional word of comment thrown in, was as bare as a desert bone. From March 1945, when I had prepared to leave for Europe under the direction of the United States Air Force, until January 1, 1946—ten full months later—not one line, not one word, appears in the 1945 record.

Shocked, emotionally injured, I had resigned from the human race.

Yet on the surface everything in my life went on as usual. I even went through certain accustomed gestures of the writer. All writers experience good days, bad days, terrible days.

So now I still sent myself to my desk in the early morning after breakfast and a brief walk. Two forefingers, the left thumb, and the right middle finger are all I've ever used in picking out those hundreds of thousands—those millions of words on the typewriter. It was the crude method in which I had taught myself to type in order to hold that $3-a-week job on the Appleton *Crescent*. Those two forefingers, as a consequence, always have been stubbier than the other digits and their nails shorter through wear tear and necessity. Now, blankly, impersonally, almost as a feeble-minded person stares at her hands, I noticed, without satisfaction, that those two erstwhile stubby forefingers had taken on the tapering elegance of the idle. This really scared me. My humblest tools were already deteriorating from lack of use.

A medical man or a psychiatrist probably would have said, "You've been emotionally injured."

Instead, I silently argued with myself via imagined conversations with phantom specialists. "Injured! Not at all. I've just been a babe until now. Middle-aged babe. I used to be a reporter—a pretty good one. You'd think that would have taught me some of the facts of life. Not me. I had to cover police court and murders and dirty divorces and child-neglect and brutality and I was only seventeen to twenty-one in those years. That's considered young even in terms of today's teenagers. It was rough. But it was idyllic compared to what I've seen in these past few months in Europe. I've seen the absolute depths of wholesale degradation. I've seen the unspeakable horror that inhuman ferocity and power-lust can perpetrate upon innocent men and women and children; on great works of art, on whole cities; on an entire civilization. If man is capable of that—and he is and I've seen it—then I hereby tender my resignation as a member of the human race."

All this sounds deeply dreary, yet I was having quite a pleasant time in a ghostly way and perhaps because of this artless outward behavior my resignation never was accepted—even by me. Or perhaps the remains of my common sense took over.

I took long walks. I saw my friends often. I went to the theatre. I ate quite an impressive amount of steak, now that this protein provender was generally available. I slept and slept and slept. Slowly, like an animal that has been hibernating, I began to emerge from a long nightmarish lethargy.

The two forefingers became stubby-nailed again from picking out a short story on the typewriter as a ballet dancer practices bar exercises to keep in condition. The new novel, *Great Son*, whose background was the vast Northwest area of the United States—and the city of Seattle in particular—was published successfully. A collection of thirty-one old short stories, issued in a handsome volume entitled *One Basket*, was published. For this I had written a brief introduction. One paragraph from this introduction seems to me quotable here:

> All my writing life I have written to please first myself. Never, except in wartime, have I written to order on a theme or subject definitely requested or suggested. But war, to me, is not life at all. It is an excrescence, a cancer, on the body of civilization. . . . Of the period covering World War II only two stories are included here. One is *No Room at the Inn*; the other, *Grandma Isn't Playing*. The first was written because I wanted to write it out of my own indignation and burning sense of injustice. The second was requested as propaganda and it is included here purely as an example. In it everything turns out just lovely. This sometimes happens in life; but infrequently.

All this was undeniably the reverse of down-breaking, particularly as (and never mind all that lofty talk about dedicated writers and vocation and discipline and everything) I also earn my living by writing, and have for more than half a century.

Having been luck-starred in May 1945 at finding myself, by a mere fluke, in Paris on V-E Day, so now in September, instead of being up on Treasure Hill in splendid and dullish isolation, I was, again quite by chance, alone and bang in the middle of New York City on V-J Day. The news of the end of the war with Japan was flashed throughout the world.

With the old reporter's instinct I walked down Park Avenue from the Seventies, cut over to Fifth and emerged at 59th Street and the Plaza, opalescent and lovely in the early evening sunset over Central Park. The handsome square was almost peaceful. No din. Down Fifth Avenue then; and now the movement and undercurrent of excitement was evident. At Fiftieth and Fifth the massive doors of St. Patrick's Cathedral were wide open and the lights poured out upon the stream of worshipers pouring in. The broad stone steps flowed with people; a forest of lighted candles cast a golden glow upon the high-domed nave.

Men women children moved up and down the broad aisles. Sailors in uniform. Soldiers in uniform. Mothers with infants in their arms. Fathers with their five-year-old by the hand. There was no order, there was no disorder, they were here to offer up thanks; they had come naturally, spontaneously. This, I thought, is as it should be. This is what a church should be; open, and a refuge and a release for the emotions. Every church door in New York—Jewish, Protestant, Catholic—should be wide open now, tonight.

Out to a now crowded Fifth Avenue and cutting across town again and over to Broadway and 45th Street. Here, at last, was New York on the loose.

They were marching in the middle of that storied thoroughfare, Broadway. This was no organized parade. They were strangers suddenly united by emotion. They simply marched in clumps, men and women, boys and girls, parents with their children, dressed in their everyday clothes as they had come (as I had) out of their houses and apartments and offices and shops and had filtered, instinctively, into the famed Show Street, the street of Celebrations, Broadway. So they marched in groups and squads and masses in the middle of the street and no one tried or wanted to stop them. They were a force of nature.

Everywhere you saw soldiers and sailors in uniform. They were strangely quiet—or perhaps not so strangely. The stunned are quiet.

One man now clearly exemplified this state of mind and being. As I stood at the curb on Broadway, fascinated by this unrehearsed and dramatic parade, a young and handsome man in United States Army uniform made his erratic way, slowly and alone, in the street just at the curb's edge. He looked in our faces as we stood massed there, and we stared at him. His arms and hands were outstretched in a gesture of utter wonder and unbelief. His face would have seemed transcendent if his gaze had not been, somehow, unseeing, like that of a bedazzled child. He was revolving slowly as he made his way, round and round, but carefully, step by step. He was a little drunk and he repeated, over and over, in a quiet and awestruck voice:

"I'm alive. I'm alive! The war's over—and I'm alive!"

Perhaps we haven't, after all, learned much since then. But in some ways, at least, perhaps we have. In the diary for 1946 there is a grisly entry:

January 10. A party at Neysa's for flyers who dropped bomb on Hiroshima and Nagasaki. Very gay and pleasant. Bing Crosby sang. Life magazine took pictures. Freddy and Florence March drove me home.

236

Today I think a bomb-dropping, no matter how effective, would not be considered an occasion for a gay and pleasant evening.

In a family such as mine that had a record of bachelors and spinsters, of which I was one, the birth of a baby was a notable event. Among other pleasant emotions, it gave one a reassuring feeling of continuity. Not only were Henry Goldsmith and my niece Janet Fox Goldsmith a father and a mother, but they named their daughter Julie in compliment to great-grandmother Julia Ferber. Daughter of an actress and grandniece of a stage-struck (though dramatically frustrated) grandaunt, even then Julie must have felt the theatre stirring in her blood. The curt old diary makes an early prognostication:

July 21. To hospital to see baby Julie. Julie very active. Too much so I should think for her age. Probably already putting on a performance at the age of 24 hours.

Unproductive though I—and the majority of acknowledged writers —now seemed to be, Treasure Hill was busting out all over. Lambs calves chickens ducks. Apples melons grapes berries vegetables hay alfalfa. Roses lilies tulips chrysanthemums delphinium pansies pinks in the march of the seasons made a grounded rainbow and perfumed the air on Treasure Hill. The aftermath of the War was marked by a seemingly endless series of overseas movements—Drives, they were called. Clothing Drives for the war-ravaged countries of Europe. Food Drives. Book Drives. Medicine Drives. The United States experienced an emotional state in which relief and guilt mingled. Certainly the toll of American dead and injured was enormous. But the flower of Europe's young manhood had been almost mathematically destroyed. The generation between eighteen and thirty seemed non-existent. City after city after city; towns villages, farms were heaps of mortar and ashes. The United States of America, physically, as a country or continent, was untouched. The organized and uncounted flow from West to East began as it had done after the First World War a quarter of a century earlier. Money, food, materials wore a deep path, seemingly, through ocean and air, for a period of fifteen years, leaving the United States of America today in the position of the most hated country in the world. The giver is always resented and actively disliked which is understandably a human attitude. Who wants to acknowledge himself a dependent, a taker? And if he must, how natural to bite the hand that feeds you.

So then, Treasure Hill for nine or ten months in the year and New York and travel for the remaining months. But always travel had been merely a continuation of work or a necessary background preparation for work. I do not remember that I have ever had what is called a vacation; a holiday. There comes to my mind no time when I traveled without a typewriter or failed to rent one in whatever city I was to stay for more than a day or two. When not actually writing by means of a pen a pencil or a typewriter, a writer is writing in his head. There is nothing remarkable in this. I should say it applies to any writer whose work is recognized.

The balm of work now began again to apply its healing. Old novels began to be reissued in regular editions or in the paperbacks which were now beginning their enormous vogue. Again contract offers came in from the war-ravaged countries of Europe and from Asia and Australia and South America. There were sent me copies of my books in languages of which I never had heard a word; not only in languages to which my eye had become accustomed through the years of foreign translation and publication—French German Polish Hungarian Dutch Italian Swedish Norwegian Finnish Danish Czech Spanish—but in languages that were hieroglyphics to me as I encountered them on the printed pages; Japanese, Chinese, Urdu, Arabic. The American names as they emerged from the foreign text seemed so strange as to appear almost prankish; Yancey Cravat in a Japanese version of *Cimarron*; Parthy Ann Hawks of *Show Boat*, a name as American as Boston baked beans, emerging from a printed page of Urdu.

Now, in 1946 the musical play *Show Boat* which had been performed in every civilized country in the world, was presented in its third New York revival. It had originally been presented at the Ziegfeld Theatre almost twenty years earlier. Now again it was presented superbly at the Ziegfeld Theatre. Today, as I write of it, this musical play is thirty-six years old. Year after year it plays throughout the United States and in Europe. It will be presented in an Australian tour this year. Jerome Kern, composer of the *Show Boat* score, and Oscar Hammerstein, lyricist and librettist, both are gone. Their music and lyrics live on and will live on. Certainly "Ol' Man River" is secure as an American folk classic, it is the American Negro's too-patient realization of his life and his tragedy as portrayed in the period of a half century ago. That splendid and stirring folksong is a compassionate and terrible indictment of the white man's treatment of the Negro in the United States yesterday—and today.

I'm all for psychological help and psychoanalysis for others in need of this form of aid but I never have sought its professional benefits. When I find myself brooding, moody, frustrated, resentful because of a condition, real or fancied, about which I am unhappy or by which I am blocked, I always have managed to clear the impasse by way of the typewriter. Whether it has been anti-Semitism, political chicanery, national plundering, waste, callousness, carelessness, inhumanity, the air (for me, at least) has been cleared by bringing it all out into the open via the words on the printed page. With the exception of the romantic *Show Boat* this was true of every novel I'd ever written—*So Big, Cimarron, Come and Get It, American Beauty, Great Son, Saratoga Trunk, Giant, Ice Palace*—all of these and many others—and it accounts for the fact that the breath of life still exists in these books—and, I suppose, in me.

It explains, at least, why, in 1947, I became increasingly obsessed with the idea of writing about a group of European refugees in the United States, and in New York in particular.

There is no doubt that a wide open policy of emigration from Europe to the United States at the end of World War II would have resulted in the gravest consequences to this country. Millions upon millions of the homeless, the persecuted, the desperate, the disillusioned turned their faces toward the greatest and the richest democracy in the world. A tidal wave of humanity in search of refuge, given unrestricted entry, would have resulted in catastrophe. The land of the free and the home of the brave opened its doors to the extent of a slit so infinitesimal that only the wraith of the would-be emigration body could squeeze through. This policy of restriction met with public disapproval or approval, depending on circumstance. This editorial said political pressure; that editorial said powerful labor organizations; this group denounced it as blind isolationism; that organization denounced it as bigotry. The word reactionary was bounced back and forth. Right or wrong, wise or timorous, the fact remains that the record of the United States in the rescue and reception of Europe's desperate and homeless was almost incredibly meager in contrast to that of many smaller and less solvent countries, such as England, Mexico, Switzerland, Israel (at that time still Palestine) Brazil, the Scandinavian countries, and many others.

The Old Girl in New York harbor must have felt some embarrassment as her torch illumined the words engraved on the tablet set so neatly in her pedestal: Mother of Exiles, she was called, and her silent lips spoke eloquently:

> *Give me your tired . . .*
> *Your huddled masses yearning to breathe free . . .*
> *Send these, the homeless, tempest-tost, to me . . .*

So the cream of European culture had been thrown out upon a world frantic with post-war problems. It had been the intellectually courageous, the talented, the creative worker upon whom the Nazis and the Fascists had directed their most inhuman punishment. Millions had perished, but other millions remained—eager to work, willing to contribute their talents, asking only for freedom and the opportunity to use their abilities in a world that needed these. Over the face of Europe they wandered—the scientists, the churchmen, the musicians, the writers, the composers, the actors, the technicians, the teachers, the physicians, the businessmen, the designers, the painters, the architects, the lawyers, the craftsmen.

Occasionally you encountered these on the streets of New York and at once you recognized them as strangers in a strange land. It was nothing they wore or did; it was their eyes, the walk, the set of the shoulders, the absence of that certain cockiness which your accustomed American habitually wears all the way from the day laborer to the corporation president.

"What about a refugee play?" I said to George Kaufman. "A play about refugees in New York? What an obnoxious term—refugee."

"Terrible," George said.

"The word, you mean?"

"No. The idea."

"Why terrible?"

"You're always breast-beating about something."

"But it wouldn't be. I mean, it would be a comedy."

"It isn't a comedy background. Hitler and Mussolini and that gang weren't funny."

"Tragedy can be told effectively in terms of comedy."

"Uh-huh. The smile that hides the breaking heart."

"Look. This is what I mean. One of those old shabby rundown brownstone houses on the West Side in the—"

"That takes a cut. Either shabby or rundown."

"—in the Seventies or Eighties off Columbus or Amsterdam. They're not one family, see. A collection of Europeans who have come together, somehow, in New York and they've had a tough time and they're trying to fit in here somehow."

"Side-splitting comedy idea, as you say."

"I didn't say anything of the sort—side-splitting! Brightness! They all live huddled together in this old—"

"—shabby rundown—"

"—brownstone. There's a common kitchen and a common dining room and a living room—our one set is just the living room, full of *old shabby rundown* furniture and bits and pieces of heirloomy stuff they've managed to bring over. And a big old battered piano. One of them is a playwright, sort of Molnarish. And a woman, thirtyish, who was a distinguished actress of a distinguished stage family in Vienna. And a girl who was a Berlin ballet star. And a kind of deflated industrialist, and a professor and a brilliant young scientist. And assorted others, perhaps twelve in all. They have no money. They're doing any kind of menial work they can get. They pool the rent, the food. Each one has been through a special hell. Now they only want to take up their work and live again as human beings. Strangers in a strange land. At the rise the composer is seated at the piano trying to work and there's hell to pay all over the place because the—"

We wrote it. Finished, it read pretty well, rather rich though somewhat schmaltzy at times. Some of the parts actually were played by European refugee actors. This authentic touch was not as convincing as we had hoped it would be. Imported actors, like certain wines, sometimes do not stand the ocean trip. This can be as true of American actors in Europe as it is of European actors in America.

My niece, Janet Fox, played the part of the ballet dancer. This provided for me at least an additional fillip of excitement in the production.

Somewhat stormy rehearsals, with cast changes and the usual periods of alternate hope and despair. We called the play *Bravo!* (with the exclamation point). The year was 1948. Following a three-weeks' road tryout we were to open at the Lyceum Theatre, New York. The Lyceum had prestige and a success history; like the old Empire Theatre of Frohman fame it meant theatre to millions of New Yorkers and to many more throughout the country. Its interior was quietly and dowdily rich like the garments of a highly solvent old dowager who is so secure that she need not apologize for her somewhat gnawed sable scarf. For me there was an added aura of good omen in the Lyceum. My first play, entitled *Our Mrs. McChesney*, in which Ethel Barrymore starred successfully, had been presented at the Lyceum Theatre in 1915.

1915 . . . 1948. Thirty-three years. Well, I thought, you've done very little looking back, Miss F., so don't start now. Perhaps that's because you have so enjoyed the ride and the scenery and never mind those bumps now and then, and the rocks and the dust and the mud and an occasional spill. The Lyceum spelled luck for your first play thirty-three years ago. It can hold. Why not?

Bravo! opened. It was a flop. One of the New York critics in his review (prankish boy) substituted an interrogation mark for the exclamation point following the title that headed his column, thus: Bravo?

The play closed the week before Christmas. Because of the terrible hazard of uncertainty that is inherent in the actor's profession the untimely closing of a play always contains the element of tragedy. But to close just before Christmas is any actor's nightmare. I felt like a murderess. George Kaufman never once said I-told-you-so.

A good solid failure can sometimes have the same effect, psychologically, as a great success, just as too many sweets can result in acid indigestion. Now I recalled that winter of success in 1927 when the musical play *Show Boat* opened at the Ziegfeld Theatre December 27th and *The Royal Family* opened at the Selwyn Theatre December 28th. I didn't attend the opening night performance of either play; both were instant and enormous successes; I gloomed around all that winter, going nowhere, as though I had drunk the dregs of despair.

Now, in 1948, the flavor of failure, usually so bitter on the tongue, acted as a spicy appetizer, like a helping of big gray caviar bullets or smoked salmon sharpened by the piquant juice of lemon. Failure, perversely enough, seemed to impart zest for the meal ahead—and the meal ahead was the Texas novel, *Giant*.

Perhaps this conduct wasn't so eerie, after all. Other than the collaboration with George Kaufman on *Bravo!* I had accomplished less
creative work in the period since the end of the Second World War
in May 1945, than I in any similar length of time in my life as a
writer. Perhaps these three or four years of semi-idleness had replen-
ished the reservoir of energy and creativeness. Resolve and purpose
possessed me. A high-spirited relish for work ahead gave a tang to each
new day. I was conscious of feeling well and strong with the false but
effective strength that is born of anger. I was an Angry Old Woman,
thus beating the Angry Young Men to it by a couple of generations.
Mine was an anger which was directed not only at myself but toward
the hysteria of the United States in general and the Texas type of
behavior in particular.

Over the United States of America there was smeared a sooty disillusionment. The vast effort of war, the tensions of every sort of conduct—physical, spiritual, intellectual—had given way to a creeping
desuetude. The enormous land was untouched by the devastation that
had all but destroyed another continent. New riches poured into the
richest country on the globe as a war-paralyzed world clamored for the
goods which the industries of North America could supply. We gave
freely, lavishly. Good Time Charlie behaved almost exactly as he had
after the global catastrophe known as the First World War. The gesture
of sharing with the less lucky neighbor:

"See what the boys in the back room will have!"

And out spilled the dollar bills in the form of millions and of
billions. This was not only good but in a large degree sheer goodness,
and it was necessary and fruitful but it was not only misunderstood;
it was resented. The Rich Uncle, big-hearted, naïve, scarcely realized
(if at all) the sneering contempt with which his behavior was secretly
—and not always so secretly—greeted. "Take it. We've a right to it.
He'll never miss it. The old boy's loaded."

In a way they were right. The old boy was loaded, he was a born
war-hater and this largesse expressed in a measure his relief at surveying
for the second time in a quarter of a century a civilized world saved
from destruction.

A slackness, a carelessness, a slow paralysis of the spirit crept like
a miasma over the land. As the dazed soldier at the curb on that night
of the V-J Day celebration had scarcely dared to believe in his own

corporeal existence so we now revolved in an antic and exultant demonstration of semi-hysteria as we said, the one to the other, "We're alive. We're alive. The war's over—and we're alive!"

A forest of metal spikes that resembled lightning rods but weren't sprang up on roofs everywhere as the new communicator, television, began its ceaseless routine. A nation, free now of the outmoded custom of reading or conversing or moving or thinking, crouched in front of this new god. The chattering flashing box thought for you. It made your decisions.

Buy the Latest Fleet Heep Car with Built-in Disintegration. Guaranteed to Collapse Within a Year.

Own Your Own Home Solidly Built of Old Cigar Boxes and Grocery Crates Held Together with Chewing Gum and Spit.

Select Your Coat from Our Choicest Stock of Overbred Underfed Minks.

Smoke Sulfur Cigarettes They Build You Up.

Wash Your Clothes in Lily Lye. It Tears Them Down.

Buy Now. Pay Later.

It Is Later Than You Think—But Who Thinks!

Countless children, born during the war years, had been known to Social Service workers as Door Key Children. The mother was absent from the house during the day, being otherwise engaged in ammunition factory employment or other war work; the father was absent being otherwise engaged in war. The door key, attached to a longish piece of string, was worn around the child's neck, beneath the clothing. Between 1941 and 1948 these bewildered and self-raised children were well on their way to forming the nucleus of the night-blooming Beatnik Generation. Bewildered children, brash, resentful, disorganized; grown now into bewildered adults.

Inevitably I was reminded of one of those rather tiresome adages with which the old admonish the young—or used to. In the Appleton Wisconsin days there was always a barrel of apples in the cellar—or two barrels; enough, at least to outlast a winter of after-school crunching, and of apple sauce, apples pies and baked apples. It was my unwelcome task to sort this fruit in search of hidden decay; to separate the sound and firm from the soft and spotted.

Julia Ferber had said, "It only takes one rotten apple to spoil a whole barrelful."

16

Almost ten years had galloped by since that first trip to Texas. Novels, plays, short stories had transferred themselves somehow from my consciousness to the typewriter to the bookshelves. Through these years of war and peace and horror; exhilaration, work, travel, fun, the Texas novel idea and the Texas experiences never quite ceased to prick my consciousness with sharp needles of interest, remembrance and imagined scenes, characters, situations. Wisps of possible book material would drift into my thoughts, Texas-tinged; but I would shoo them out and slam the door on them. I had resolved that I definitely would not put myself through the gigantic task of familiarizing myself with this region, these people, the violent and dramatic background and foreground of this vast section of the United States. But the subconscious needling and nudging persisted. Strange odds and ends of facts and fancy, bits of behaviorism and dialogue and dress and food and psychic phenomena floated to the surface of this oil-soaked mass. Above all, the relation of this commonwealth to the rest of this nation took on definite form. I definitely did not want to spin the intricate web necessary to make a book of fiction read like reality. But just as certainly, I told myself, there was a terrific novel of Texas background to be written by some trenchant and courageous novelist. So far as I was concerned—no, thank you very much. Too tough and thankless a job. Texans are too touchy. Let some two-fisted male tackle it.

It was then that the subconscious took over completely. The woman of more than middle age had wisely rejected the whole idea. The compulsive writer went calmly to work. Viewed near and from afar, this

giant commonwealth seemed not so much a Southwest state of the
United States as a separate kingdom with its own laws, speech, mores;
and, above all, its apartness, other than geographically, from the rest of
the nation. It was insular, it was bombastic; naïve and brash. And
fascinating. Quite without conscious plan I read everything I could
lay hands on about Texas today and yesterday. Together with millions
of residents of the United States, I had read and heard incredible accounts of the goings-on in this almost legendary area.

Texas had even encouraged the outrageous stories. During the 1920s
and 1930s, the falsely quiescent period between two World Wars, the
fabulous became the commonplace in Texas. Fantastic stories occupied endless columns of print, described million-acre ranches; oil
wells spurting millions of gallons worth millions of dollars where only
barren desert had been; vaqueros complete with Mexican-Spanish chin-
straps and silver spurs and a foreign speech; strange new breeds of
cattle, humped and creamy-coated like creatures out of mythology;
bizarre palaces rearing their grotesque turrets on the plain; million-a-
week incomes; privately owned planes in a day when even public
planes were still a special mode of transportation; huge men in roll-
brimmed fifty-dollar Stetsons; bejeweled women whose fingertips had
only recently lost their washtub puckers.

The whole thing was larger than life. Notes and notes and notes
piled up and became notebooks. Magazines were read and stored
away. Newspapers. Photographs. Idiom. Clothes. Characteristics. Ten
or more years, really, had gone into this, for I had been Texas-con-
scious with a writer's instinct for the dramatic, the important and the
bizarre long before that first brief and rejected glimpse of Houston
Dallas San Antonio Austin Corpus Christi and all the rest of the giant
state.

Often, in these many years of my life as a writer, I have been drawn
to this or that section of the United States and even of Europe by a
compulsion that was stronger than mere curiosity. It was, unreasona-
bly, like an urge to return to something I never actually had known.
Reincarnationists may have an explanation for this. The places to
which I travel with a pleasant excitement born of anticipation I invariably enjoy with a double enjoyment of inexplicable recognition.
Love San Francisco, don't like Los Angeles; found Charleston enthralling, rejected Florida; think Canada dullish, crazy for Alaska; fascinated

by big burly Chicago, can't face Detroit; sometimes go to Boston just to be there, have no emotion about the rest of Massachusetts. The cities or countries in which I reluctantly find myself I dislike on sight and for no reason known to myself. I am wretched until I leave them. This was definitely true of Germany on my first visit in the spring of 1914 just before the brutal onslaught of World War I. It was true of the few days spent in Egypt in the '30s. The fields of that flat land were, in my imagination, fertilized with the dried blood of centuries; the smell of decay seemed all pervasive. My departure took on the nature of an escape. Perhaps, two thousand or more years ago, I was a little Jewish slave girl on the Nile.

My rejection of Texas on that initial visit had not been on the grounds of pre-formed opinion or inexplicable emotion. On the contrary, I had been vastly interested, astounded; confused and startled; repelled and attracted. I had found it as virile as it was vast. I had found it incredible that a whole people could possess such energy, such self-complacency, such lack of interest in the rest of the United States and such enthusiasm for living in the midst of this hurly-burly of heat, dust, glare, great distances and seeming discomfort. Deep deep down, I think I went back to Texas because I thought this strange commonwealth exemplified the qualities which must not be permitted to infect the other forty-seven states if the whole of the United States as a great nation was to remain a whole country and a great nation. This is pompous-sounding but not, in addition, naïve.

Back I went to Texas then. This assignment I had given myself was as difficult as the State of Texas itself was enormous and diverse. It was as Spanish as Mexico; it was as American as ham-and-eggs; it was as Neiman-Marcus as Fifth Avenue; it was as Western as long-horns and cactus. Its people were outrageous and delightful; and hospitable and resentful; and arrogant and insecure; and flamboyant and deprecatory; simple and complicated. Geographically and economically nature had thrown two hazards at the Texans; unlimited space, seemingly unlimited wealth.

Although the preliminary research for other novels—*Show Boat*— *Cimarron*—*Saratoga Trunk*—*American Beauty*—*Come and Get It* and others—had been arduous and time-consuming, they now seemed in retrospect to have been mere frittering compared to the labor of researching and authenticating this book in preparation. Yet the weeks spent in this great Southwest region of the United States were exhilarating and absorbing. Oddly enough, there was almost the impact of traveling in a foreign country. Certainly the Spanish language was common to south Texas. In spite of heat, cold, vast distances; insufficient sleep, fried food, Mexican food, humidity; over-exertion, new and strange situations, constant contact with strangers; and the swarms of doubts and fears that lurk in the mind of every writer as a new book is gestating—in spite of—and even rather savoring all these—I had on each Texas journey a sensation of refreshment and stimulation. Literally up and down this gigantic region I bounced; planes, automobiles, trains, afoot; from the Mexican border on the south to the Panhandle north; Corpus Christi to Dallas; Brownsville to Austin; Fort Worth to Lubbock; Kingsville to the Davis Mountains. Houston Galveston San Antonio. Theatres. Ranches. Hotels. Mexican shacks. Oil rigs. Grapefruit groves. Roundups. Barbecues. Dinner parties. Shocked. Enchanted. Repelled. Delighted. Locutions I never before had heard gave tang to conversation. In the beginning these phrases had sometimes baffled me.

You met a man with the look and manner of the region; big, bronzed, soft-voiced with the almost musical cadence of the male Texan's speech. "We'd sure like it if you'd come down to our country for a visit, ma'am."

"Oh. I thought you were a Texan."

"Sure enough am, ma'am. Nothing else but."

"You said your country—"

I soon learned that when they said "my country" they meant their own ranch—not Brazil or India or Canada but their own piece of Texas land perhaps a few hundred miles distant (distance means nothing to a Texan) and numbering five thousand (a mere patch) or fifty thousand or five hundred thousand acres. Come down for a visit to my country. An innocently feudal locution.

As you left a restaurant the head-waitress at the door chirped, "Come back quick!" Startled when first you heard this, you learned that this was *au revoir* in Texanese. To your return. We'll be happy to see you soon again.

Texas talk made two syllables of a one-syllable word. Thus "had" became "hay-ud." Louetta May's monolithic husband Ed was summoned to her side by a plaintive call of "Ay-ud!"

It was exhilarating to battle the stiff wind that buffeted you as you walked along the Corpus Christi waterfront facing the Bay and the Gulf of Mexico. That wind was oftenest hot and humid and breath-taking and the Texans, perhaps wisely, did not walk there. In fact, Texans didn't walk. They hopped into their private planes for a bit of shopping in Dallas or Houston or to visit the folks upstate or down. They drove their cars at eighty-ninety-one hundred miles an hour over the thousands of miles of flat country. They rode, but horses were no longer used as a means of actual transportation. They were for ranch work, for horse shows, perhaps for a quick dashing quarter-horse scamper over the range.

Huge ranches, middle-size ranches, north south and central, offered me hospitality. At some I spent a day, two or three days, or more. The famous King Ranch in Kingsville is so world-renowned that its owners, the Kleberg family, are constantly bedeviled by strangers, tourists, acquaintances and would-be acquaintances from Egypt to Alaska who innocently wish to view the vast and celebrated empire, view the mythological-looking Brahmans originally imported from India; and the Gertrudis breed of cattle, almost cherry-red and fabulous, scientifically originated on the Kleberg ranch itself.

Here at the King Ranch I had lunch with Robert Kleberg and his wife and his daughter and a few visiting branches of this famous far-flung family. I told Robert Kleberg about the curse of Treasure Hill that produced only male offspring, seemingly, and this interested him as a breeder of livestock. I had a half-hour ride jouncing in a station wagon over an infinitesimal bit of the gigantic ranch. I recall that a few head of the choicest stock intended for family consumption were kept in a small corral of their own and one of these was so overbred and overfed that it could no longer rise to stand on its own four legs. It lay sprawled flat on the ground and had to be raised by ropes and pulley in order to regain a standing position. Privately, I thought I'd relish no steaks from that cholesteroled carcass.

On my return to the main house Robert Kleberg queried me politely regarding the possibility of my writing a history of the King Ranch. With equal politeness I told him that I was a writer of fiction and that I hoped to write a novel of Texas background. The visit had been of two hours' duration, or less.

The so-called Benedict Ranch of the novel *Giant* was no one ranch but a blend of many Texas ranches I saw—and some that I not only never saw but that never existed.

The sociological and economic standards of Texas confounded me. The food I found to be the worst I had ever encountered in a general public way throughout my travels in the United States. Texas steaks are a test of tooth endurance. Texas fries everything but ice cream.

From the first I had made it clear that I had come to Texas as a writer. I did not pretend to be a visitor or a tourist merely. I intended to write about Texas as I saw it and felt it. When a Texan, in the hospitable tradition of that region, invited me to his or her home to dinner, to the ranch for a stay of a day or a week, I painstakingly made clear my position. "I am here as a writer to make sure that my background is accurate for the novel I intend to write about Texas people and Texas."

This was waved aside as though I had said I was about to write a colorful brochure for fast-selling Texas real estate.

On my final Texas foray I encountered an incident which illustrated the pattern of any serious creative worker's life. At the Dallas airport my plane was delayed. There was an unavoidable hour of waiting. I stood talking to an airport official about schedules when a familiar figure passed swiftly by. He was carrying a violin case.

"Jascha!" I called; and went to him. One doesn't expect to run into Jascha Heifetz in a Dallas Texas airport between planes. One thinks of him as being always in Paris or San Francisco or London or Buenos Aires or New York or New Delhi.

We chatted a moment. "Are you playing here tonight?"

"No," he said. "I'm here between planes. I'm playing in San Angelo tonight."

We parted. I returned to the conversation with the airport man. Jascha hurried on.

San Angelo Texas is a cow-and-crop town. It isn't large it isn't small. Just a prosperous central Texas town of something more than fifty thousand people.

I said, "That was Jascha Heifetz."

"I know," the airport official said. "I just arranged to give him a room to practice in."

"What do you mean—a room to practice in!"

"He's got an hour between planes. He's giving a concert in San

Angelo tonight and he wanted a place where he could practice. There's a kind of big empty room next to the restaurant, see, we hardly ever use it, so I told him he could practice there."

There may have been certain people in San Angelo Texas who would have known if Jascha Heifetz had not been playing the violin in top form. But it is certain that Heifetz himself would have known it. When he plays a concert—which he does practically every night—he is his own toughest audience. In a manner of speaking, any world-known musician writer painter sculptor actor dancer knows that that unexpected hour of leisure is forever committed to perfecting his performance in that big—or little—empty room, apart.

This weaving back and forth between the East Coast and Southwest Texas was accomplished at the close of 1948 and in the late winter and early spring of 1949. I had taken a furnished apartment in New York for two or three winter months and there I worked at the actual writing between trips. Those trips now were little more than brief jaunts for verification and reaffirmation. During this period of almost ten years the writer's conscious and subconscious were quietly drawing up the blueprints and assembling the stones and bricks and mortar and metal that must go into the structure of a novel. Now I knew that the theme, the background, the characters, the motivation, the flavor of speech of dress of temperament of food were firmly established in my mind. I knew my subject and I knew what I wanted to say.

To come from the white-hot heat and humidity of Texas to the tender springtime green of Treasure Hill and the cool verdant shelter of the Connecticut countryside was balm beyond description. True, Curtiss was no longer there; he had built a house of his own some miles distant and had returned to his craft as a carpenter-builder. But a capable enough young farmer-caretaker had come to take charge of the Treasure Hill acreage and all its problems from cows to swimming pool. It was a tough job and it was growing tougher by the year under that curious nameless malaise that had made the business of living more violently interesting throughout the world, and more difficult and hazardous at the same time.

It is a curious and perverse fact that when one is working hard and well at one major project all minor projects fall neatly into place and can even be handled without damage to the progress of the important task. Perhaps a too-simple explanation of this blissful state is that frustration is not present to sap the vitality; no drear-desolation of non-accomplishment is poisoning one with doubts and fears. This is a theory based on the idea that the more you do well the more you are able to do well. The glands and the juices released by contentment and enthusiasm doubtless have a hand in it, too. In any case, it is a theory not calculated to increase one's popularity with the do-nothing set.

"Looks like a no-apple year," the farmer would report lugubriously. "If we get half a crop we're lucky."

"Spray?"

"Sure we did."

"What are those mangey looking sheep I saw yesterday, crunching around. That isn't our stock."

"Oh. Man out Trumbull way asked if he could graze his spring flock I thought it would help maybe keep the place down—"

"Out. Off. We're not breeding our rams to second-rate stock."

Nothing seemed unsurmountable or even difficult. Things that went awry were fitted back into line. It wasn't that the fields outside and the rooms inside were filled with girlish laughter. It was just that the task of writing was going well and that, as always, cast a rosy glow over the dourest object.

The autumn and winter, the spring and now the present summer saw the pages sliding off the typewriter and into the little tidy stack that was growing so slowly—but growing.

The Fourth of July was just around the corner and Julia Ferber, the city slicker, was due to leave New York's hot stickiness for the duller but cooler Connecticut countryside.

I drove into New York to fetch her. At the main entrance of her apartment hotel the doorman stopped me with a message.

"The doctor wants to see you before you go up to your mother's."

A yearly checkup was Julia Ferber's sole gesture toward the medical profession, and even this was carried out in compliance with my request. Her health record throughout her life had been almost fabulous. Now, at eighty-nine, her step certainly had lost something of its buoyance, but step she did like a robust woman of fifty, up and down the tumultuous New York streets; church, theatres, dinner parties, bridge, shopping. There was no arguing with her, the family had long ceased to do so.

The physician saw me at once. He did not mince words. "Your mother has cancer. She may live two or three weeks."

In a kind of cold shock I said, "She'll live forever. . . . Operation?"

"Even if it's successful—in a temporary way—it could only be six months—a year at the most."

"A year is better than two weeks."

He was a realist. "Perhaps. Perhaps not. That is for you to decide."

It is a terrible thing to possess, even for a moment, the power of life or death for another.

Stubbornly I took Julia Ferber up to Treasure Hill. Five months of nightmarish procedure. Nurses. Doctors. Tests. Then the decision: To operate or death by starvation. The operation, then, and a kind of miraculous false recovery. There was Julia up at Treasure Hill again, dressed in cool summer garb against the glowing Indian summer days, being driven about the Connecticut countryside that was beginning to flaunt its scarlet-and-gold autumn finery. But October saw the end of all that temporary bravado.

During these past months the writing of the novel *Giant* had been put aside, perforce. With the approach of late autumn the ambulance carried her back to her New York apartment, high up and sunny.

She did not once speak during that seventy-five mile ride. I thought she was in a semi-coma induced by the pain-reducing drugs. We drew up at the entrance. The men prepared to carry the stretcher. She spoke, clearly.

"Edna, cover my face."

She always had had a wholesome pride and proper vanity in her own good looks. Her arrival today was expected, her apartment had been made ready, the hotel staff and perhaps some resident friends might be waiting there in the foyer through which she had passed so many times with a little rustle of silk and a discreet breath of perfume; her step firm, her handsome head held high. "Edna, cover my face."

So I untied the scarf that I wore and with it I covered the noble face, now reduced to a parchment-yellow mask.

After it was over and winter had come and gone, and the spring of 1950 found me again at Treasure Hill and hard at work on *Giant* with my back to the View and my face in the typewriter the decision that must inconsciously have been forming for months in my mind came to a final resolution. The summer and autumn lay ahead. I could see every step of the way with my eyes shut, May to November. The glorious rotation of color and scent in the garden; the rotation of crops; of stock, of cook's day out; of sun moon stars in the heavens; of the furnace-needs-cleaning the road-needs-mending; of the emotional struggle between the writer's compulsion to work work work and the feeling of guilt at not inviting those weekend guests to share the cool comfort of Treasure Hill. I was alone there now, from Monday to Friday, except for the household and farm helpers and an occasional guest or two at dinner. But writers do not work a five-day week. They work (by choice or compulsion) a seven-day week. Perhaps it is the one form of employment in the world of the arts professions sciences and business in which work is more exciting and exhilarating and sustaining than play.

But it was no such orderly reasoning that had brought the simmering decision to a final boil. A few scribbled notes on a pad of paper brought that about.

Many busy people know that a small note pad and a pencil on the bedside table can prevent a great deal of wear and tear in the accomplishment of next day's program. They also know that these vagrant nocturnal thoughts, unless nailed down on paper, have a trick of slipping away at daylight. What *was* that? you demand of yourself in the morning. It was wonderful it was important it was absolutely necessary—but what *was* it!

Ordinarily these gems, in my case, were related to next day's writing. A line for that character; the strengthening of a situation; a clarifying bit of description; perhaps even a whole new chapter. Sometimes a line whose exquisite wit, hastily jotted down at 11 P.M. had sent me into silent but appreciative laughter, had turned out, in the cold clear light of 7:30 A.M., to be no such sparkling stuff; dullish, if anything. Often, though, it was valuable—even important—to the work in progress.

Now, to my increasing horror, I realized that those typical writer's notes that tuck themselves so slyly into a recess of the creative worker's brain, waiting for a serene moment, for a change of tempo, in order to pop out and shout, "Surprise surprise! Look what I've got!"—these jotted reminders on my bedside table weren't writer's notes at all. They read:

"Tell John call Oscar about pump."

"Try get Blatch help cut hay."

"Remind John importance compost heap."

"Gus chicken manure."

"No broccoli next year loathe it."

"Prune program autumn." (This last didn't mean that I was planning a Prune Festival. It presaged a preliminary inspection tour for autumn tree-and-shrub pruning.)

Staring at these cryptic writings next morning I found myself as confused as Belshazzar confronted with the portentous Meme, Mene, Tekel, Upharsin. But I knew I must be my own Daniel in the translating of this written message. This, roughly, was the translation:

"You are giving time and thought and energy to something that actually is no longer important to you—at least, not that important. You are a compulsive perfectionist which means that you are uncontrollably compelled to do the best you can with everything you do from books to broccoli, from trees to Texas. And it's never quite as good as you hoped it would be and that makes for jitters and you're Jittery Jill all right. Listen: Do you want to be a successful amateur farmer and weekend hostess or do you want to continue to be a writer? You can't have it both ways. Come on. What do you say?"

The reply came sharp and clear: "I'd rather write one excellent novel than be the owner and manager of the Garden of Eden and all points east and west."

Treasure Hill was put up for sale. The truth was that I had had the realization of my childhood and childish dream of security. I had learned that security, like religion, is a thing of the spirit and that all the stone edifices and all the flowers and fruits and friends and audiences and congregations in the world cannot provide more than an outer semblance of the longed-for state of being. To be real and lasting security can only come from within oneself.

History attributes a famous line to Nathan Hale, a hero of the American Revolution. I hope it is not merely a tradition, that line, but actual. As he stood on the scaffold platform with the gibbet just above him he faced immediate death, yet he calmly voiced utter security:

"I only regret that I have but one life to lose for my country."

The characters in the guise of prospective purchasers who now rampaged through the gardens fields and house comprising Treasure Hill would—as non-writers say—make a book. It never will.

The real estate agents screened allegedly interested buyers but strange specimens slipped through. There were times when tourists seemed to have mistaken Treasure Hill for Yellowstone Park. It was not unusual, on glancing out of the window to see a clutch of strangers grouped around the pool or munching apples in the orchard or picking flowers in the walled garden. They were well-meaning people, they had heard about the place, they had a curiosity about it and, remote and secluded though it was, they had made their way to it. They were I-didn't-read-the-book-but-I-saw-the-movie people.

One family will remain forever green—in fact, verdigris as brass—in my memory. They were an attractive tweedy young couple accompanied by three small children, two boys and a girl, all seemingly of the same age. There had been no announcement of their coming but the houseman ushered them in on the strength of their pleasant appearance. With them, however, was a mammoth dog that was obviously a mixture of St. Bernard and Shetland pony. He was ejected, but not by his owners. The children immediately espied a covered glass jar of bright-colored hard candies on the hall table. Off came the top. One small fist—two—three were plunged in. The jar was emptied. Into the living room into the green-and-white dining room. The floor was covered in white rubber-like material. The candy was popped in and out of the relishing little mouths and by the time the troupe ascended the stairs to the upper floor the heavenly pale blue block pattern of the English wallpaper bore forever the flat imprint of fifteen sticky fingers. I could no longer witness the carnage. "Tell them the place is sold," I murmured to Jean. "Get them out." And fled. At the door, on leaving, they confided to Jean their address and the assurance that if he would come to work for them, together with his wife, the cook, whom they had seen in the kitchen, they would be paid in excess of whatever they now were receiving. As a final gracious tribute the behemoth dog was dicovered happily swimming in the pool that had just been vacuumed and chlorinated.

At the end of that summer Treasure Hill was sold to a man and wife and three sturdy sons who, like myself fourteen years previously, had fallen in love with the place. They would not take possession until late winter.

Faced with the turmoil of moving, my household couple then departed abruptly. I was alone in the big silent house. This did not dismay me. I had early encountered this situation in my childhood. Besides, John the farmer and his family were in the cottage just the other side of the driveway. But there was everything to be done; no household help to be snared at any price at that time of the year and in this remote community. The ghastly problem was the novel, *Giant*. Writers write in the midst of every sort of outer turmoil. But a measure of inner serenity or merely cool collectiveness they must have in order to set those right words down on that piece of paper.

New York was a maelstrom. Literally, there was no place in which to live. The city was crammed to bursting in this winter of 1950. Hotels wanted two-day transients only. Desirable apartments were for sale, not for rent. Co-operative was the word used. This Apartment Building Has Gone Co-operative the real estate agents said. You bought a hole in the air and then proceeded to pay monthly rent on this under the euphemistic term of Maintenance.

"Never!" I said. "Not me!" (Note: Never say never—or hardly ever. I am living in an apartment I bought in 1950.)

There was something eerie, with a tinge of fey gaiety about being alone in a big utterly quiet partially dismantled house on a remote hilltop in midwinter. From time to time, as if and when I could snare them, various people came in to pack china to pack glassware to roll rugs to unhang hangings. Part of the week was spent in New York, part at Treasure Hill. For the time at least, and certainly during Julia's illness and death, work on the Texas novel had been virtually abandoned. I now was a year, more or less, out of my original schedule. I should have been deeply upset but somehow I wasn't. It would be finished if I lived; and I meant to live.

A New York hotel had graciously consented to rent me two rooms for a month at an astral rate. Perhaps I could accomplish at least a little stretch of writing there. And, miraculously, two dear star-spangled friends, Richard and Dorothy Rodgers, telephoned to say that a six-room fifteenth-floor apartment in their building had been vacated and was for sale and that I'd better hurry over and look at it and grab it.

Obediently I hurried over and I looked and I grabbed. And here, to my surprise, I am still.

Throughout those final weeks on Treasure Hill I was usually too weary to be wistful. There was everything to do and practically no one to do it. The packers came.

"This goes into storage . . . That goes to New York . . . That's for the Thrift Shop . . . This has been sold to the new owners . . . Keeping that . . . Selling those . . ."

Objects that I had considered rather handsome took on a somewhat sordid aspect, now that they were snatched off their throne. But after a day of tough physical effort certainly the Connecticut winter sky at night had about it nothing sordid. You could stand out there on the terrace a moment or two and lean on the solid silence. The stars crackled just a little as they wheeled in a pageant; there were no dogs among them, or apes; or men either, in those days; or liquid food or bits of cracker crumbs.

Things were pretty well shut off and shut up that last night in the big stone house on Treasure Hill. Boxes crates barrels. The last of the movers were due early next morning. There was little or no food in the house; some eggs, bread, a bit of butter, a small hunk of cheese. Not exactly enticing; too tired to eat, anyway. This drawer, that cupboard, everything neat and tidy though the cleaners were due next day after the movers had left.

I came upon an improbable bottle—a full quart—of Bollinger '47 champagne. Not a drinker and definitely not a wine-drinker (grapes too acid-making for this alimentary tract) I break down when it comes to a single very cold very dry glass of that particular wine of that particular year. It is practically non-existent today. But there it was. I opened the back door and at the foot of the rear steps I plunged the bottle deep into the snow that lay piled all around. There I left it for an hour. I completed a few tasks—bag to pack, telephone call, reminder notes—and back to the kitchen. There I whisked up a bowl of eggs for scrambling, poured the mixture into the sputtering pan and stirred and stirred and plopped the golden mass out on the waiting hot plate; yanked the bottle out of its snow bed, eased it open carefully as I had seen it expertly done. And I ate all the eggs and all the cheese and all the bread and, so far as I can remember, drank all that champagne. Perhaps the poison of fatigue is an antidote for the poison of alcohol; even of such a wholesale libation. I only know that I felt refreshed and very talented and confident. I must have neated up the kitchen because there it was, spick-and-span, next morning. I went to the front door and out to the terrace and breathed deep and looked long and said (certainly this must have been the grape), "Goodbye sky, it's been lovely knowing you," went indoors and slept eight dreamless hours.

Curiously enough, that brief interval at midnight on the terrace that marked my final night on Treasure Hill was almost a duplicate of my first night on the Hill fourteen years earlier. I didn't think of this as I stood there.

Next day I said goodbye to my neighbors and drove down the hill toward New York and I never once looked back. I had lived out a childish romantic dream and I did not regret it. I knew I needed no mansion, no swimming pool, no orchard, no cows, no acres for assurance. I had created it, it had been beautiful, it still was beautiful. The time had come to leave it and I left it without a quiver or a backward glance. I had it in my mind's eye and could take it out and look at it forever.

17

It is my misfortune to be fascinated by the United States of America. Brilliant or dull, sordid or glamorous, vulgar or exquisite, it has for me a tremendous and compelling draw. Its people, their background, their beginnings, their habits, their failings, their moods; its rivers lakes mountains; its cities, its countryside, its shifting colorful panorama all communicate an excitement which no amount of travel in foreign lands can create in me. Completely absorbed I gaze as I walk, as I stare out of train windows, plane windows, automobile windows. Kansas prairies, Nebraska steppes, Colorado Rockies; flat monotony or soaring peaks; people people people white black yellow brown; their faces, though perhaps third or even fourth generation American, still plainly stamped with the background of Ireland Germany Egypt Italy England Sweden Greece China Japan and scores of other countries —none of this is boring to these bemused eyes.

This state of interest in and emotion about the United States of America is considered distinctly corny. Plaintively and publicly I have protested, "But I don't in the least think it's perfect. It is full of imperfections. I say it's unique. Potentially it could be the wonder-government of the world, if only it would grow up. Look, the whole thing was built from scratch just about three hundred and fifty years ago with nothing but an ax and a shovel and a pair of hands used in an utter wilderness by a couple of hundred people. No money. No influence. No protection. Show me anywhere in the world the like of that."

Naïveté in the very young may be charming. In the middle-aged it is embarrassing to the beholder—and certainly three hundred and fifty years is definitely middle-aged. The ax was replaced by the drill and the electric saw; the shovel was superseded by the bulldozer and the steam-shovel. The two hands were busy at the wheel of a car or the knob of a television box. The United States still believes that the big bad wolf will behave like a house-trained dog if you pat him on the head and say good doggy. From 1921, with the novel entitled *The Girls*, to 1961, a year or two after the publication of the novel *Ice Palace*, the novels I wrote were novels of protest. Loving protest, but protest nevertheless. However, they had vitality, they told a story and they were not symbolic. In theme background plot characterization dialogue, they were written in the idiom of their day, clearly and purposefully.

All this brought me mingled woe and happiness.

There is in the United States a cult or a stratum of book readers whose mental insecurity or whose lack of faith in their own taste and judgment has led them to this touchingly unadult standard: If a book is dull it must be good. If it is unreadable it's great.

For fifty years—since the book publication of the Emma McChesney stories entitled *Roast Beef Medium* in 1913—readers and even reviewers have taken the characters of my imagination as actual flesh-and-blood people; the events of my creating as solid facts. But I am a novelist, not an historian. Emma McChesney, chief character of these short stories, was a traveling saleswoman. Every traveling saleswoman in the United States laid claim to being the original Emma McChesney of the stories. I had never seen a traveling saleswoman in my life.

Many years ago I wrote a novel called *Show Boat*. On its publication every show boat on the rivers laid claim, belligerent or otherwise, to being the original Cotton Blossom Floating Palace Theatre of the novel. Some of these even threatened to bring suit for libel. As the book became increasingly popular and the musical play based on it was produced, followed (up to this moment) by almost four decades of steady production for both book and musical play, the attitude of the various show boat owners changed. They now were quarreling among themselves as to which could claim originality. They announced in local handbills newspapers and streamers up and down the rivers that this was the show boat of the novel and play; their leading lady was Magnolia, their leading man Gaylord Ravenal, this old character actor the original Cap'n Andy. Now each spring I received invitations to spend a few days floating down the Mississippi the Ohio the Missouri.

In 1929 the novel *Cimarron* was published. Its background was the State of Oklahoma from its territorial days up to the present. Scarcely a town in that incredible commonwealth failed to send me a message of burning hatred and contempt, claiming itself defamed. Local characters of whom I never had heard were announced as the original of Yancey Cravat. Incidents were argued and contested. But here, too, time spread a soothing balm. Newspapers and public-spirited citizens having written editorials and letters reviling me now urged me to attend monument-unveilings and other august public gatherings in Ponca City, Tulsa, Seminole, Bowlegs, Pawhuska and Oklahoma City.

This determination on the part of the reader to confuse the imaginary with the real became a bit irksome. Basically it was, perhaps, flattering. Following the publication of the novel *American Beauty* there blew up a storm of protest. Polish-Americans objected. New Englanders objected. A Boston newspaper published a full-page article, with illustrations, describing the New England mansion which was, it firmly stated, the house I had described in the novel. In order to make that imaginary house come alive on the printed page I had visited New England towns and villages throughout the tobacco-growing district from Amherst Massachusetts to Hartford Connecticut. The Boston newspaper named the village alleged by them to have been the original of the Oakesfield in my novel. It also named people, houses, dates. Staring-eyed, I read that the house I had described as having been built in 1700 had really been built in 1740 and that, consequently, I was a fraud and a fool. The Boston article was published throughout the country. In vain I cried, "But no! No! There never was a house such as the Oakes House. It is a composite of fifty houses—a hundred that never were. It was made of this cornice and that doorway and those old pink bricks described in architectural books on old New England houses, and shown in old engravings, and viewed by me on my travels through New England. I made it up out of my own head and built it in my mind in the year 1930 in New York. It is a beautiful house of my own imagining."

Perhaps I should have felt flattered by all this. Letters poured in. Here, in literal quotation, is a typical one:

I see that you have used our old family house in New London. I no longer live in it, but you have described it absolutely. It is true, as you say, that our family, through the years, has grown queer and twisted and decadent. I am really Temmie in your book. I only weigh ninety-eight pounds . . ."

Threatened lawsuits, recrimination, villification, reproach, insult, all are the lot of the imaginative writer. There was a measure of comfort in rereading Charles Dickens' original preface to *Nicholas Nickleby*. It reads thus:

> It has afforded the Author great amusement and satisfaction, during the progress of this work, to learn, from country friends and from a variety of ludicrous statements concerning himself in provincial newspapers, that more than one Yorkshire schoolmaster lays claim to being the original of Mr. Squeers. One worthy, he has reason to believe, has actually consulted authorities learned in the law, as to his having good grounds on which to rest an action for libel; another has meditated a journey to London, for the express purpose of committing an assault and battery on his traducer.
>
> While the author cannot but feel the full force of the compliment thus conveyed to him, he ventures to suggest that these contentions may arise from the fact that Mr. Squeers is the representative of a class, and not an individual. It is remarkable that what we call the world, which is so very credulous in what professes to be true, is most incredulous in what professes to be imaginary.

One can add little to that except to plead, somewhat plaintively, with reader and reviewer to believe that a writer of fiction, even today, may have an imagination.

Installed in the New York apartment (which now, twelve years later, I still own and occupy) I determined not to travel, not to flee New York during the hot and humid summer months with which the city is usually literally embroiled. Papers, books, notes, notebooks, first second third drafts of page after page, chapter after chapter, were piled and stacked on shelves, in drawers. The thought of attempting to move all this was madness. For another year—winter spring summer autumn and again into the winter—I worked at *Giant* daily seven days a week. It was a rhythmic and satisfying period. Hot, yes; cold, yes. It didn't matter. Friends fled the city's clammy heat. Weekends were soothing as the city streets became uninhabited canyons. It was as though

I alone, among seven million inhabitants, remained to savor the solitude and hush.

Hardened though I thought I was to literal-mindedness on the part of readers, I was not prepared for the violence of the Texas assault following the publication of the novel *Giant*. The virulence of this attack was so libelous in character that merely to start proceedings on the grounds of libel would have snared one forever in a mass of degrading filth. It was scarcely believable that such obscene matter would be permitted in a publicly distributed newspaper in the United States.

A motion picture was made from the novel *Giant* and a very dimensional and memorable film it was as directed by George Stevens. During some few weeks I was present at the filming of the picture. At least one characteristically Texan experience quite accidentally arose as a result. I had been conferring with the writer, Ivan Moffatt, and the director George Stevens. We had paused for lunch and were seated at a table in the patio restaurant of the hotel at which I was staying. I was paged for a message. My name was called at the pool, in the restaurant, the patio; now the message was delivered to me. We resumed our conversation whose subject was, of course, the picture script.

At this moment Henry Ginsberg, co-producer of the picture, rushed up to the table, his bathrobe billowing as he sped. He had been sunning himself at the swimming pool. The paging of my name came through the loud-speaker. At that a man just next to him who had been lying face down, at the side of the pool, uncoiled like a python.

"What's that!" he shouted. "Who's that he said?"

Affably Henry Ginsberg repeated the name to the stranger. This one now rose. It was an impressive footage. "I'll kill her!" he said. "Where is she? I'll kill her!"

He was a Texan.

Henry sped to announce my impending demise. We three at the table rose. Nothing was said. Ivan Moffatt, tall slim wiry Englishman; George Stevens, big brown brawny Westerner; Henry Ginsberg, medium, fiftyish; and I, five feet in height and enchanted at the prospect of meeting my prospective murderer.

At the poolside he was shrugging into a bathrobe and glaring about him. His stance, his expression, the slow movement of the head from side to side, reminded me of an angry and bewildered bull I had once seen in the arena at San Sebastian. We four advanced to him, the three men a solid wall just behind me. I held out my hand. I spoke my name.

"I hear you intend to kill me."

Before our eyes the bull melted and was reduced to the size of a bashful and rather engaging calf. "Well, say, you hadn't ought to have gone and written a book like that about Texas. We're real nice folks down there."

And so they are—with reservations. And so are we all—with reservations. Something, some little screw or bolt that holds the huge contraption together, seems to have been jarred loose. It could be the soul, or perhaps what is called the spirit, of a country. The contraption is lacking a vital part somewhere in its makeup.

We had dinner together, the big Texan and three or four of my friends, and I. In his late forties, a family man, the pictures of his wife and the kids in his wallet; friendly, colloquial; the IQ of an average high school boy.

There was, in the company that made up the cast of the motion picture *Giant*, when it was in the process of being filmed at the Warner studio in California, a young actor who was spectacularly talented; handsome in a fragile sort of way; and absolutely outrageous. He was an original. Impish, compelling, magnetic; utterly winning one moment, obnoxious the next. Definitely gifted. Frequently maddening. He was James Dean.

Occasionally—rarely—one encounters a dazzling human being who is obviously marked for destruction. Such a one was this young Jimmy Dean. Only two or three times have I encountered an example of the brilliant and ill-fated.

The fundamental lack, possibly, is the complete absence of the sense of caution. By this I do not mean fear, but the quality that prevents them from observing ordinary precaution; the common sense, really, of everyday physical behavior. William Allen White's brilliant young daughter, Mary White, was one such. Bill White used to say that if, when a child of twelve or thirteen, she had managed to climb up to the roof of a shed or barn on their place in Emporia Kansas she would not only walk about on the roof but seemingly with deliberation walk right off it into space. When she drove a car downhill she landed it in the ditch with the car on top of her. She died at sixteen after having been struck on the head by an overhanging tree-branch as she rode her horse on the town parkway. At a pell-mell gallop she had stood up in the saddle, her head turned over her shoulder, to wave to a friend passing by. The overhanging branch struck full force.

This sort of pattern was characteristic of the James Dean behavior. Aware of this, and knowing, too, of his passion for driving racing cars, the motion picture company had included in the Dean contract a clause to the effect that he was not to own or drive a racing car or to enter any automobile race of any description until the conclusion of the filming of *Giant*. Cast against type by the astute director, George Stevens, Dean was playing the part of the ruthless unpredictable young ranch hand Jett Rink who became the even more ruthless—and the doomed—wildcatter oil millionaire. He was, perhaps, miscast; yet enthralling.

During the shooting of the picture, and particularly when on location in open ranch country, his behavior was often intolerable; his performance always brilliant. There were times when he would absent himself for days, no one knew where. This is the unforgivable crime in the process of filming a picture. It means one of two things; work must cease if the sequence immediately requires the presence of the absent actor, thus creating a really gigantic financial loss to the company; or the filming may proceed, if possible, by the process known as "shooting around him"; that is, shooting scenes in which he is not immediately involved, while waiting for the missing actor's return.

This lad performed like a gifted angel and behaved like a juvenile delinquent. Everybody loved him including the Mexican extras on the set and George Stevens, the harassed and patient director, Elizabeth Taylor and Rock Hudson, the leading players.

Mercedes McCambridge, talented character actress, was playing the difficult part of Luz Benedict. In her kindness and warmheartedness she tried to be of help to this gifted and insecure young fellow-actor. He frequently turned to her for advice as one would to an older sister or a mother. She did not fail him. Usually he rejected any other counsel.

Giant, the picture, was finished. There were a few brief bits of additional work to be done, but these were mere repetition or perhaps fragments of scenes that needed strengthening; not vital, but enhancing to the picture.

The day following the finish of the main scheduled filming Jimmy

Dean bought his Porsche racing car. It was capable of a speed of more than one hundred and twenty miles an hour. He brought it round to the Warner studio and invited Henry Ginsberg to have a ride. The Warner lot in Burbank California is, in size and architectural planning, like a neat white cement town in itself, with wide paved streets and solid buildings. Up and down these streets one might in those days encounter anything from a truck towing Cleopatra's barge to an Alaska false-front saloon. To drive any vehicle on these streets was precarious. Jimmy Dean stepped on the gas and drove Henry Ginsberg up and down and in and out and around corners at Porsche speed. It was a ghastly experience. After a few minutes of this Henry stepped out of the car, his knees turned to liquid, staggered into the studio building on whose stage a scene was being shot, and clutched George Stevens' arm.

"Shoot those extra Jimmy Dean scenes. Quick! He's going to kill himself in that car."

Mercedes McCambridge, her work in *Giant* completed, was driving to San Francisco on a well-earned holiday. She stopped at a roadside gas station for a tank refill. Her glance was caught by a shocking mass of wreckage in the station lot. A twisted splintered lump of metal, leather, and wire, crumpled like an accordion and glistening with what looked like blobs of crimson paint but which turned out to be fresh blood.

"Good God, what's that!"

The gas station attendant was a woman. She did not glance round. "That's Jimmy Dean's car. They got him over there in the undertaker's across the street there, where the crowd is."

He had been driving to the auto races. A car came out of a side road. The driver, glancing up the road, must have gauged Dean's distance as being a safe half-mile or more. He could not have known the deadly speed at which that car was being driven. He emerged to make his road-turn. The Porsche came with the speed of a missile.

Just a few days before this I, in New York, had received in the mail a large photograph which he had sent me. It was inscribed and it showed him in character and in costume as Jett Rink, the ranch hand. It was not characteristic of him to send his photograph unasked. I was happy to have it and I wrote to thank him.

. . . when it arrived I was interested to notice for the first time how much your profile resembles that of John Barrymore. You're too young ever to have seen him, I suppose. It really is startlingly similar. But then, your automobile racing will probably soon take care of that.

I was told that the letter came the day of his death. He never saw it.

18

Following months or years of concentrated work in a single writing project the writer, task completed, is left dangling in a vacuum. The paradoxical mad orderly routine of the compulsive worker is broken. It no longer is necessary to awaken and immediately to say to oneself: "Up up up!" And a little later, again to oneself, "No, don't read anything but the headlines at breakfast . . . You know what happens when you get started on the *Times*. . . . The front page and Bergdorf's ads and the theatre and the obits and next thing you're plowing through the weather and the shipping news just to keep from working. . . . All right, take a little walk, but ten minutes flat. . . ." Then, to the understanding and infinitely patient housekeeper Miss Molly Hennessy, "Um—dinner?—well—lamb chops, I think, and carrots and string beans and a fruit Jell-O. . . . Yes, I know, it's baby food, but it's a mass of proteins and that's what I need to get work done."

This mental and emotional Simon Legree flogs the writer on mercilessly. Yet when the book or the play is finished and the shackles fall from the slave and he stands free he hugs his chains through force of habit or through fear of striding down the open road without the terrible voice of conscience and the snakewhip of ambition to urge him on.

The writer's antidote for this listless state often is found in travel. The open road toward which the writer turns is the West (if he is an Easterner) or the East (if he is a Westerner); or Spain or Japan or Switzerland or India or even that Trip Around the World. For those few weeks or months at least, he walks free. But never altogether free.

For the little voice of the Work Gremlin locked away in the creative attic claws at the barred windows and whines, "Let me out! Let me out! I want to tell you something. I want to tell you something important!"

If you listen for even a moment the shackles are on once more.

"Oh, you're home!" the family says; or your friends or somewhat disgruntled employees. "You said you'd be away until May."

"Yes, that was the original plan. But I have work to do that—I mean —that can't be put off."

Click go the shackles. Crack goes the bullwhip.

This travel interval was to be Spain. No reason—at least no reason based on a plan. I only felt that in Spain I would see a sort of beauty that would be strange and fresh to my eyes; and that, superficially at least, I would be mingling with a people I did not know, always a refreshing experience. My knowledge of Spain was limited to Christopher Columbus (who wasn't a Spaniard at all, but an Italian); to brief forays I had made with Louis and Mary Bromfield into San Sebastian to witness a bullfight (which I loathed); and the Spanish influence that remained in Mexico and in Texas.

The unique and somber beauty of the Spanish countryside astounded me. The olive groves, the purple-and-gold mountains, the deep green hills and valleys, the rust-red soil formed a landscape so utterly unlike the France or Italy or England I knew that it took on a dreamlike quality. That year, happily for me, was the last year before the great tourist influx into Spain. It was April and the streets, the roads, the hotels restaurants museums were uncrowded. Madrid was our point of arrival and departure, and there was not a day throughout my stay in that city in which I did not spend part of the time in that section of the Prado which held the work of the great Spanish painters.

Even more deeply than the Spanish landscape had held me enthralled, these paintings of Goya of El Greco of Velázquez had about them a compelling quality, an endless depth. In order to reach that part of the Prado which housed this collection one passed through the rooms on the walls of which hung the canvases of Titian, Rubens, Vandyke, Tintoretto, Raphael. I remember rushing past them with scarcely a glance. Toledo brought the same reaction, and Seville and Granada. Romantically, though, I was a bit disappointed in the visible Spanish folkways. Other than the historic buildings it all seemed astoundingly familiar. Madrid was a small Paris, modern, gay, clean. The gypsy dancing definitely was of the tourist-trap variety, though colorful and exhilarating. The more rural Spanish people one encountered while motoring through the countryside, the villages, had an impressive dignity and quiet affability. They were the peasants, the laborers, the stratum of Spanish life that for centuries had been oppressed by church and state. Yet they walked in proper pride and they acted in kindness to the stranger. You found yourself wondering how long this submission would persist. The new Workers Homes and the new University buildings were a sop, certainly. But a sop only.

It was hard to relinquish the too-girlish dream of mantillas, combs; and a rose between the teeth; the long flowing cape, the guitar, the balcony in the moonlight. But Spain wore the habiliments of Broadway New York, State Street Chicago, Market Street San Francisco.

Then, one day, just before the late lunchtime at the Ritz (adapting to Madrid meal times required considerable alimentary adjustment; lunch at three, dinner at ten or eleven) my sister Fan and I were passing through the hotel lobby on our way to the restaurant when I saw at last the romantic Spaniard of my girlish travel-dreams. There he stood, in the center of the crowded room. His back was turned toward me; tall, straight, he was wearing a full length black cape that hung in rich folds to his feet. On his head was a black beret at an angle only achieved by a Basque or a Spaniard. One corner of the sweeping cape was flung scarf-like, over the left shoulder. It was perfection.

I clutched Fan's arm. "There's one! That's what we've been looking for!"

There was a shift in the little group of which he was one. The tall figure turned toward us, slowly. I saw him full face. He was wearing Meyrowitz-type eyeglasses. It was Paul Gallico, well-known American writer, born in New York City.

In these decades of writing, a work-pattern evolved itself. Roughly, it followed a rhythmic sequence. Work. Work finished. Travel. The work might be a novel, it might be a play, it could be a cluster of short stories —though I haven't written a short story since 1945. Once finished, whatever form it might have taken, it no longer held me. There was nothing more I could do for it or about it. Usually, like all self-torturing writers, I wished it could have been better. But I had done my best at the time. So off to Spain, off to the Virgin Islands, to Europe, California, anywhere; but off. The idiotic part of it was that usually I carried a typewriter. And holiday or no holiday, this meant work; and what sort of holiday is a working holiday! Perhaps this explains why I usually travel alone. Besides, who wants to travel with a companion who is clacking away at a typewriter when she should be looking at the Taj Mahal?

Spain had been typewriterless for once; it had been enthralling. It had served as a dazzling change and refreshment but it was no integral part of my life as a writer. I had looked at it with various emotions as I had looked at the Goyas the El Grecos and as I had been content to leave them hanging in quiescent beauty on the walls of my memory; no more a part of my life, really, than a sunset seen and enjoyed.

It was a shock, then, after that Spanish spring, to hear the voice in the attic saying, "When are you going to Alaska?"

"Alaska! I'm not going to Alaska. You must be out of your mind."

"No," the voice retorted. "I'm out of *your* mind. Don't you remember?"

"I never thought of such a thing."

"O—yes—you—did. That friend of yours—Belle—who went to Alaska on a vacation and told you about the incongruity of the white-pillared Southern-style mansion that is the Governor's house in Juneau? And that Alaska book of Ernest Gruening's that you found so fascinating? And how about that little boat trip from Seattle to Victoria British Columbia? You got off at Victoria but the boat was full of men bound for Alaska. They were going there to work and to live there and they interested you so much that ever since that time you have regretted leaving the boat at Victoria instead of going on to Alaska. It's really rugged up there—tough and different and challenging. Ninety years ago it was Russia—remember? Now it's the last frontier in this country—or perhaps any country on earth. Just your dish."

"I had snow and ice and zeros enough to last me the rest of my life when I was a school girl and a reporter back there in Wisconsin."

"That's whimpering," said the Voice, with an undertone of malice. "What nourishment is a New York winter going to offer you? Theatre openings and Madison Avenue shop windows and dinner parties and walking walking walking—that's your New York. Or all that soft stuff in the South—Arizona or California or Florida—sunshine and flowers and patios and palms—"

"So what's the matter with sunshine and flowers in the winter?"
"That isn't your diet. You'll starve on it."

Perhaps no one since Vitus Bering, that daring Dane who discovered Alaska for the Russians and died doing it, ever was more inadequately equipped, mentally and physically, for Alaskan exploratory work than I. Some fragment of my Wisconsin winter memories—or perhaps a hint from my new-made friends, Alaska Ex-Governor Ernest Gruening or E. L. (Bob) Bartlett, Alaska Representative in Washington—caused me at least to equip myself with woollies and boots and a fur coat. In the spirit of true confession perhaps it should be stated here that that first trip was made in a mink coat. There's little or nothing wrong with mink coats, and quite a number of Alaska women citizens have them and wear them. But on that Alaska exploratory trip this garment was as inappropriate as pink satin and emeralds on a ski-lift.

Though I was born in the United States and have lived all my life here and would find it unthinkable to contemplate living in any other country; though I have scampered joyously up and down the land from Canada to the Gulf of Mexico, from the coast of Maine on the Atlantic to the coast of Washington State on the Pacific, I still find it difficult to believe that one country could contain two regions so fantastically dissimilar as the State of Texas and the State of Alaska. On this, my first visit, in the late '50s, Alaska Territory had not yet achieved statehood.

Texas, the background of the novel published in 1952, and Alaska, the scene of the novel on which now, in 1954, I was timorously embarking, were as unlike as the moon is unlike the sun. One thing only they had in common. Vastness. But even in this similarity the two regions differed. Texas, the big, the braggart, boasted an area of 267,339 square miles. Alaska, scarcely glancing up from its task of wresting a livelihood from this arctic semi-wilderness, never once spoke of itself in terms of size. Yet Alaska, of which the world knew so little and cared less, made Texas almost a pygmy in comparison. It's 586,400 square miles are twice the sum of which the Southwest state had so long boasted. Alaska is not only much more vast than the combined areas of Italy France England Wales and Germany; it is not merely a state, a country in size; it is potentially a seventh continent. No such statistical maundering is dinned into the ear of the traveler in Alaska. The native born Alaskan Eskimo, Indian, or white lives there, not only because he was born there but because he is in love with Alaska. The same might be said of the more recent residents dating from 1867 to 1963. If he didn't love her he couldn't live with her. She's a tough rough expensive girl; an extremist; blowing hot and cold by turns; unpredictable; dazzlingly beautiful; cruel; darkly glowering in an almost constant midnight from autumn until spring; incandescent with sunshine twenty-four hours round the clock in mid-summer. Snow and ice, snow and ice for six months; giant fruit, giant vegetables, mammoth flowers for six months under the sunlit spring and summer skies.

Giant is a much better novel than *Ice Palace* in theme characterization execution. I think that in order to write really well and convincingly one must be somewhat poisoned by emotion. Dislike, displeasure, resentment, fault-finding, indignation, passionate remonstrance, a sense of injustice, are perhaps corrosive to the container but they make fine fuel. The trouble with those Alaska trips was that while I often was physically uncomfortable and sometimes in actual danger I was as happy and carefree as a sailor on shore leave. There were various reasons for this, any one of which would have been legitimate.

The climate: Tough but exhilarating. The air was superbly dry. Being a low blood-pressure type normally, humidity destroys me. Given a really good 97 degrees New York humidity day and I feel like a walking typhoid case. No energy, no legs, no drive. Alaska air was my non-alcoholic martini.

The Alaskans: Tough but exhilarating. When I say tough I mean hardy, debunked, well-spoken, hospitable. They pretend not at all; they read books; they enjoy music when and however they can come by it; they join classes in French, ballet, cooking, and cultural subjects. Men and women, they work like ambitious pioneers—which they are. Politically, they are alive to and aware of what is going on in Alaska and in the rest of the United States of America and in the world outside this. Every day in Alaska is a kind of triumph of survival and if you don't believe it go and live there. Myself, I'd sort of like to.

The scenery: Blindingly beautiful from an airplane window, or, for that matter, as a vista on practically any street or village from Juneau, the capital, to Barrow on the Arctic Ocean; or along any road on which a car can make its way. The distances and the heights are almost frightening. The eye sometimes rejects them as being fantasy. Mount McKinley, for example, 20,300 feet, the highest peak on the North American continent. I defy anyone to view this breath-taking sight from an airplane window without hastily readjusting his estimation of his own personal importance.

Eskimos: Enchanting, mannerly and innately kind people. Their attitude and behavior toward children is more civilized than that of the white race. These statements are based on observation made eight years ago. It may be that statehood and enforced so-called civilization has changed the Alaskan Eskimo. His talents, like those of the neglected and abused American mainland Indian, are for the most part ignored or rejected by the United States government.

The food: Wildly expensive (in my day there, at least) and good. I don't remember having had a bad meal in Alaska, whether served me as a dinner guest at a private home in Juneau, Anchorage, Fairbanks or Nome; in any restaurant; or in an Eskimo village trading post lunch counter. Eggs, flavorsome ham or bacon, hot toast, strong clear coffee; steak, vegetables, ice cream, hot apple pie; fresh caught Alaska salmon, king crab. Well prepared, neatly served, this is good food in any language in any country. Alaskans know and like good food. This is almost invariably true of dimensional people. Instinctively I shy away from a person who says food-means-nothing-to-me. Such a one himself is almost certain to lack flavor, variety, and the power of vital communication.

If, from these somewhat sketchy observations, the impression unwittingly has been conveyed that Alaska, now or eight years ago, is or was a sort of deep-freeze Garden of Eden, I hastily add that my viewpoint was not entirely clouded by snow-blindness or infatuation. The Alaska crime statistics are appalling. Probably not as depressing, population-wise, as the crime records of New York City, which no longer is considered a frontier region—but horrifying nevertheless. Murder rape larceny robbery arson drunkenness wife-desertion crowd the meat-choppers of the Alaska daily press. This is strange only because, once you've committed a crime in Alaska, your chances of getting out of town are meager to the point of being practically non-existent. The exit transportation is via plane or ship. There is, of course, the fairly recent Alaska Highway. But that journey by automobile cannot be achieved without many stops and a certain amount of identification. For the fleeing criminal seeking anonymity this is not ideal.

The fact remains that once in Alaska you can't get out without your exit being known and noted. Steamship and airline carriers keep records of people transported to and from Alaska by sea and air. Both the United States and Canada record highway traffic on the Alaska Highway which connects the two countries.

Alcohol, loneliness, cold; and perhaps beneath and above all else, a strange and neurotic awareness of brooding crystal vastness of the arctic world around them; the knowledge that these hundreds of thousands of square miles are peopled by a mere handful of human beings; these elements combine to make Alaskans exhilarating but jumpy. Civilian and military population, spread over this gigantic area, was estimated in 1957 to be about four hundred thousand people. This is roughly the population of Dayton Ohio. Certainly Fairbanks and Anchorage are busy modern cities crammed with smart dress shops and household appliance stores and movie theatres and drugstores and bars and comfortable dwellings and automobiles and planes, both privately owned and commercially available daily in and out of Alaska. Yet there is about the entire gigantic region an other-world feeling for the visitor. Every day, every hour, seemed to me an adventure; and this was not true of that first trip only. Spring summer winter visits were made; I had long ago shed the mink coat and got down to business. Sixty degrees below zero in Fairbanks in January; ninety degrees above zero in Fairbanks in July. The midnight sun, like a knife-edged golden sword, cutting through the momentarily opened doorway of a dim Fairbanks night-club at 2 A.M. in the summertime. Darkness at 2 P.M. in the city's winter streets. A wall of black ice piled on the shores of the Arctic Ocean at Barrow in July. Nylon stockings and Sears Roebuck red velvet parkas on the Eskimo girls walking ankle-deep in the dark sand of the unpaved street of that farthest north town. White wales looking as mythical as the monster celebrated in *Moby Dick*, captured now and lying inert on the beach at Kotzebue while the Eskimo women skillfully cut them up for winter food. You nibble a bit of the raw slivered meat cut off the tail end, it tastes a little like an appetizer served you at a cocktail party in New York—slightly salty, faintly celeryish, chewy.

Here was a region sparsely inhabited by people who were daring, adventurous, rugged, resourceful. Frontier people surrounded by piercing mountain peaks, endless snow and ice, wild animals; motor cars television sets motion picture theatres sirloin steaks lettuce-and-tomato salad cocktail dresses sports coats paved streets parks museums colleges modern schools. If you foolishly decided to take a long walk outside the city limits you possibly might never return. I even remember driving with a friend down a beautiful country road, wooded on either side, and being confronted suddenly with two monster moose who sped lumberingly out of the dense wood to face us, blocking the way. The Alaska moose is the largest in the world. The massive heads were lowered, the antler-spread seemed to measure nine feet, the little hot eyes in the curiously oriental faces were like red coals. We backed the car on the otherwise deserted road, turned as soon as a wider patch of road permitted, and sped back with the accelerator pressed flat to the floor. A pair such as this had been known to demolish a car with their horns and hoofs, not to speak of the car's occupants. "Mean," the seasoned hunters say, in describing these great-chested creatures, "ornery, combative."

Here, then, was this Alaska, paradoxical, almost unknown generally; a prize, a treasure potentially for almost any country in the world other than wasteful careless over-fat North America. An unheeded stepchild this; vital, handsome, rugged, containing who knew what treasure; hard working, ambitious, resourceful. Neglected.

You soared in a battered vintage two-engine DC-3 over the twin islands nestling so incredibly side by side—the Little Diomede over which the flag of the United States flies; the Big Diomede under the flag of Russia. The pilot is careful not to fly near the border of this one. There, in the near distance, looms the menacing black cliff of the main-land shore. It is the shore of Siberia. Well, you think, the bear need only reach out with one big paw to grab the Little Diomede and the enormous mainland of Alaska itself.

So the novel with the Alaska background was written and published and a motion picture (which I never have seen) was made from it and distributed throughout the world.

There was nothing deliberate or sentimental in my having chosen to write novel after novel whose background was a distinct region of the United States. This was an absolutely unpremeditated process. As Hemingway had fallen in love with Spain and blood and bullfights; as Faulkner devoted his writing life to depicting the weirdies of the State of Mississippi in the county he chose to call by the jaw-breaking name of Yoknapatawpha; as Pearl Buck wrote of the China she had known in

her youth and young womanhood, novel after novel, so I found creative
satisfaction in writing only about the people and the land I knew and,
in a measure, understood. I never have ceased to marvel that a nation
made up of such dissimilar stuff—human stuff and geological and cli-
matic as, say, California and Vermont; or Mississippi and Minnesota;
or Iowa and Louisiana, could stick together for almost two hundred
years. These states might be, in point of difference, separate countries.
Here they are, welded with the metal of unity which now and then
shows rust and wear and at times appears to be held together only with
strips of adhesive tape. Perhaps it is true that only threatened disaster
and even possible obliteration—World War I, World War II—presses
the whole again into the mold of solid unity. A pity that peace and
prosperity cannot work the same magic.

So the regional novels simply happened, with no over-all plan in
mind. As I roamed up and down and across the United States I had the
refreshing sensation that comes of exploring. Everything interested
me—the people, the folkways, the food, the manner, the speech, the
social and economic and family and love life; the geographical peculiari-
ties. Curiously, politics never have bewitched me, good or bad. This is
a kind of game and, for the most part, a shabby one. Occasionally a
figure looms large, there is a performance so dramatic or so melodramatic that it holds the attention of even the most unpolitical-minded.
Such a one was that hollow shell, President Warren G. Harding at one
end; and that great and dimensional figure Franklin D. Roosevelt at the
other. The class, the period, the stratum that interested me was that of
the exploiter, the grabber, the shrewd ruthless operator who used his
country only for profit. And in novel after novel (of this, too, I was not
conscious at the time) women were the stronger sex.

From 1911 to 1921 there had been written and published three novels
and scores of short stories. Some of these were pretty good, some bad,
some good. Writers do not read their books, once they have been
through the process of writing, rewriting, correcting, proofreading, publishing. There is nothing more one can do about them. Their fate, their
life, has been decided. Yet I know, without looking at it, that in the
novel *Fanny Herself* published forty-six years ago (1917) and now out
of print, there is a chapter describing the Day of Atonement, called
Yom Kippur, the Jewish Holy Day and its observance in the congregation of a small Wisconsin town and the trial by fasting of the small girl,

Fanny Brandies, which is good and readable writing even in this tough and cynical day. Frequently this chapter appears in anthologies and textbooks. I myself copied it in *A Peculiar Treasure*.

But it was with the publication of *The Girls* (1921) and *So Big* (1924) that the regional novels quite unconsciously began. These two were of Chicago and its environs, the Midwest colossus. *So Big* will soon be forty years old. It is still published in the regular trade edition and has a sale of a comfortable number of thousands yearly. It is also published in the paperback edition. It is required reading in the high schools throughout the country. It has been translated and published in at least fifteen languages and countries. I am brash enough to say that if the world survives I think this book is likely to be read and readable fifty years from now because it is based on a fundamental truth of life. Perhaps a statement such as that isn't exactly sporting, because I shan't be around to have to prove it.

In any case I definitely never once said to myself, "There you are! The Midwest. Now how about a little number concerned with the North the Northwest the Southwest the West the South." But unplanned, unpremeditated, along came *Show Boat* (South); *Cimarron* and, later, *Giant* (Southwest); *American Beauty* (New England); *Saratoga Trunk* (East); *Great Son* (Northwest); *Ice Palace* (the far North); and others, North South East West Central. There was even a novel whose background was New York City, a region which defies complete capture by any writer; and it wasn't a novel, really, but what is stylishly called a novella, which is a word meaning a sort of half-portion novel in size. It is entitled *Nobody's in Town* and is a story of New York on a broiling July day when only about seven million people are in the city, including all those who actually make it function; the garbage collector, the waterworks employees, the food suppliers. It was written actually in the Rocky Mountains at a height of 6500 feet and had, consequently, a fey quality which is imparted (in my case) only by altitude. Very nice it was, too—and is. Practically no one ever heard of it.

The canny thing to have done, I suppose, was to stick to one region and keep hammering at it for fifty years. No thank you very much. The novels have ranged the United States in time and period all the way from 1875 to today, 1963; in background, North East South West Midwest Southwest Northwest Northeast.

Except as it could be viewed from a plane or a mountain top I never have explored, for writing background, the area known vaguely as Up. Science has not yet proved that the area in the stratosphere above the United States is peopled. A writer of fiction is concerned, not with geography, but with people. The rich diversity and numbers of these still make the United States a free frontier for those of the writing craft.

19

That same psychiatrist whose name escapes me for the moment because he never existed and I never, therefore, have consulted him—if this one actually had been my mentor he possibly could have told me why all the major women of my fourteen full-length novels have been stronger than the major men characters. If this quaint writing conceit had been deeply diagnosed, however, I might have become self-conscious about it and quite possibly would have been unable to write about either men or women. This would have deprived me of a vast amount of work and pleasure; also, of my livelihood.

The major women of all my novels, plays, and short stories written in these past fifty years and more have been delineated as possessed of strength, ingenuity, perception, initiative. This is because I think that women in general—and certainly the American female of the United States—is stronger in character, more ingenious, more perceptive and more power-possessing (potentially) than the American male.

How can it be denied that the vast majority of women in the United States have failed to claim their legal rights; to use their inherent powers; and to fulfill in any degree at all their great potentialities?

By this I do not mean that she can play better football; or more expertly hammer down all those nails about which the jokes used to be made; or kill more people in a war; or compose a grander opera or write a better book, paint a finer picture, run a faster mile. This she has not done. I mean that women are inherently tougher than men; they know this; and potentially they could rule the world if they wanted to. They may even have to, eventually.

This is a man's world. Look at it. You need only read the front page of the smallest newspaper published in the smallest town of the smallest country in the world—or, for that matter, the biggest—to know that men, as planners and rulers of the world, have failed; and that women, by accepting their privileges as females while failing to claim and use their rights as women citizens of the world, too have failed. The world, literally, is at the bursting point with wars, impending wars, hate, fear, apprehension, violence, insecurity. The reason for this is, quite possibly, that more than one-half of the population of the world has, for thousands of years, allowed the world outside the home to roll past and over it with with only an occasional shout of protest, only an act of defiance confined to a single country or class. Though women are tough and know they are tough they conceal this iron structure beneath a sugar-coated device which is a sort of old-fashioned homeopathic pill called femininity. If ever they decide to scrape away this dated confectionery façade to reveal the strong potion beneath, this world may yet be saved. A lovely world it is—or could be—and well worth saving.

There now are more women than men in the world. Statistics prove that this astonishing state of population is true for the first time in the history of the world. It even is true in the United States of America which used to be the spinster's paradise. So preponderantly male was this country that there was a saying (never quite proved, fortunately) that unless a woman was cross-eyed hare-lipped bow-legged and hump-backed she could leisurely shop around for a mate and snare one with little or no effort. The supply was greater than the demand.

At the moment there is no war between the sexes; not even an organized campaign is recorded. But skirmishes spring up constantly. This was accounted for in 1960 when a national survey proved that women make up one-third of the nation's labor force; own more than half of the wealth of the country; and could, if they were to combine as a solid sex unit (which heaven forbid!) elect in 1964 as President of the United States anyone they might choose.

In the use of the word tough the term is not meant to denote physical strength or muscular superiority. Women do, however, possess greater powers of endurance in pain, discomfort, illness. Women are less romantic, less sentimental, less gullible than men. This may be due to the fact that since earliest recorded history women have been relegated to the status of second-class human beings. Until only a few decades ago they had practically no legal civil or political rights as citizens here in the United States, and few rights as human beings. Perhaps that is why women as a whole are more practical than men. They have to be, in self-protection. The male shopper, seeking a gift for a woman, is welcomed by any woman clerk or shopkeeper; not with the idea of taking advantage of him but because the male shopper definitely is known as an easy sell. Men are not natural shoppers on a retail basis, though they may be formidable on a big scale. Gazing at the proffered gown or fur or lingerie or jewel he is likely to say, "Is that the kind of thing you'd wear to a party or to the theatre?"

"Any woman would be thrilled to have it," the saleswoman assures him.

"Well, if you say so . . . I guess you ought to know . . . Wrap it up." Almost sheepishly.

A woman selecting a gift for a man is a selling problem. Haven't you something like that only not so expensive? . . . I don't think he'd like that . . . Well, I don't like it and he usually relies on my taste . . . Show me something else, please . . . No, he'd never use that.

Four-legged animals are either male or female. Two-legged animals are not only male or female; they are boys or girls, men or women. A woman can be a female and a woman at the same time. Just here, perhaps, in order not to be involved in a mass of misapprehension, I might say that though I enjoy the company, the friendship and the affection of both men and women, I prefer, if given a choice, the company of men. They act more directly, they have not been obliged, for centuries, as women have, to dissemble, to resort to subterfuge. I find their company more stimulating, more challenging, no matter how young or how old. Having lived a somewhat adventurous life and since young girlhood the life of a worker, I am impatient of evasion and pretense as I would be of hoopskirts and pantalettes in a New York yellow taxi in the rush hour. Mine has been a long and eventful life in which the routine of work was not only accepted but sometimes fought for. More men than women live this sort of life. The male has been running up and down the world for thousands of years, bopping animals over the head, bopping other humans over the head, fighting foolish exciting wars in a kind of lethal game; exploring new continents, writing love poems, competing in politics, in fisticuffs and in business, the professions, the arts. So the masculine viewpoint is likely to be a refreshing one. No one has said to him, "Your place is in the home. Your place is in the office—the shop—the factory." His place was in the world. He had experience, he acted and spoke with incalculably greater freedom than the female. When he said, "Funny thing happened at the office today," it may not have been so very funny, but it was likely to be funnier than the funny thing that happened in the kitchen today.

My state of being irked by the present behavior of my sex in general is due to the fact that few women are even remotely fulfilling their potentialities. One can't hit high C constantly, but there is an occasional high C in the life of almost everyone. Most women never reach it even once, or try to reach it. The vast majority of women live their lives being female only, a role that is inadequate and tiresome for them, as well as unfair and uncourageous in a terribly troubled and hazardous world. Certainly small children require a mother in the home, and this careering does not apply to mothers whose charges are less than seven years old. With their children at school during fixed hours of the day millions of women who are young or of middle age represent a loss to their world of talent, of effort, of force.

In many important ways women are often—in fact, usually—smarter than men. The word smarter is deliberately used. They have had to be smarter in order to survive. There is little or nothing cerebral in this particular gift or trait. It is almost a reflex. They are smarter for the same reason that Jews are often considered smarter than non-Jews. They were held in subjection. The woman for centuries was held in subjection because she was a female; the Jew because of his religious belief in one God only, rejecting the Jew Jesus as a divinity. Hounded and bedeviled and persecuted, granted few rights and fewer privileges, they learned—the rejected Female and the rejected Jew—perforce to see through the back of their heads as well as through the front of their heads. The fundamental reason was the same. This special gift or trait came to be known as intuition. Wild things in the woods have learned it in order to escape the huntsman.

There have been women, despite this state of being, who became world famous and who, for centuries or decades, have remained a legend because they were in their day prescient, courageous; and because they actually fulfilled their potentialities almost to the limit. Elizabeth the First, of England, was one of these. A violent, ruthless, brave, frightened and terrible woman, she took England in her two over-bejeweled hands and made it a power without equal in her time. Not all good, certainly, but better than Henry the Eighth, her papa. One could, perhaps, say much the same of Queen Victoria and of Catherine the Great, though the first assumed a prunes-and-prisms exterior beneath which smoldered a banked fire that now and then broke into flames; the second rather overdid the snickersnee as she slashed her way through life. Of this small company there were, too, Joan of Arc, Madame Curie, Florence Nightingale, the Brontë girls, Sarah Bernhardt, defying custom, cant, false barriers. Certain women of today, too, have lived up to every ounce of their potentialities. One of these, widow of a President of the United States, could have sat back snugly, tending a house and garden in upstate New York, being Guest of Honor at an occasional creamed-chicken-and-peas luncheon at a downtown hotel. She chose to spend her energies, time, thought, resourcefulness in the interest of her fellow human beings. Jibes, insults, slander, libel were thrown at her. Calmly she went her way, she fulfilled her purpose, her potentialities. She is known and revered the world over. Her name is Eleanor Roosevelt. There was Jane Addams of Hull House, Chicago, that quiet spinster who revolutionized the pattern of living conditions of the city's immigrant population Back of the Yards, and whose example was copied by Social Service workers and establishments throughout the United States. These two have been met previously in these pages.

In the years closely following the American Revolution there was one of whom little generally is known, and less heard. So nobly wise, so original and determined in the face of opposition, one longs to have talked with her; to have known the exciting and nourishing quality of her mind. She is the only woman in the history of this country who was not only the wife of a President of the United States but also the mother of a President of the United States. Her name was Abigail Adams. Her husband was John Adams, second President of the United States; her son, John Quincy Adams, sixth President. A quiet sort, Abigail Adams, in a day when women were not only supposed to be quiet but ordered to be so. But she had a mind and she had purpose and she wished to combine the two.

The Constitution was being drawn up, and all those worthies in their white perukes were knotting their fine brows over the problems it presented. They made a superb job of it, but it would have been more splendid and perhaps the entire history of this country would have been more noble, had they heeded the famous three words of admonition spoken by Abigail Adams to her brainy husband John.

Bent over his homework brought from the office, as husbands are likely to be on occasional evenings, Abigail approached him. She well knew what the papers were over which he was working by candlelight; she was intelligent and perceptive enough to know their importance to the fledgling collection of erstwhile colonies that now was to be known as the United States of America. Not only that, her woman's prescience, her intuition, warned her that this document, so nobly phrased, could set an example in free government for the whole world to see; it could transform and enrich the status of women in the brave liberal-minded little new country, and from this, probably, the status of women the world over.

"John."

He did not look up.

"John, there is something I must say to you."

"Yes, my dear." Still he did not look up. "I'm very busy. There is a meeting tomorrow." He tapped the papers.

"I know. I know how important it is. I just want to say this: John, remember the ladies."

Testily, "How do you mean?"

"They are citizens. We are citizens. We can work for the good of the country. Put down our rights together with the men's rights. John, in that paper you call the Constitution of the United States of America —*remember the ladies.*"

But he didn't.

She could not and certainly did not vote for her husband John when he became the second President of the United States. She could not and did not vote for her son John Quincy Adams when he became sixth President of the United States.

This forward-thinking Abigail Adams has fascinated me for years; for decades, from year to year, I meant to write her biography, though already she has been the subject of biographies. The title of my book was to have been *Remember the Ladies.* Now I know I never shall write it. No reason. That exact electric moment somehow slipped by together with how many other unwritten book ideas.

Other women come to mind whose potential powers, freely used, have ennobled our day.

Who that has read the books written by Edith Hamilton can fail to regret the Morphean behavior of those committees who serve the Pulitzer Prize and the Nobel Prize; or any other laurel-and-gold-leafed decorations. Her book, *The Greek Way*, seems to me to be one of the few examples of definitely great writing in this century. It was her first published book. She wrote it at the age of sixty-three. Since that time Edith Hamilton has written six or more volumes.

To read *The Greek Way* is to forget, for the moment—for the hour —the formidable the frightening world of today. It is at once the purest and the most exhilarating spring of refreshment. One does not gulp it quickly. A few pages, a chapter at a time, only. It is a book about the great time of the Greek nation. Yet not that alone. It is a book so filled with the philosophy, the knowledge and the history of the whole human spirit that to know it is to know hope for the future if only the lesson can be applied to today.

In the preface to the present (reissued) volume, though originally written years ago, Edith Hamilton says this:

> I have felt while writing these new chapters a fresh realization of the refuge and strength the past can be to us in the troubled present.

This exactly is the power and charm and importance of her book. To read of the great past which she so masterfully presents is to be able more surely to understand and to endure the present.

I never saw or met Edith Hamilton. She lavishly and magnificently used, in these past thirty years, and doubtless for at least thirty years before that—her deepest potentialities.

Women are women and men are men and *vive la différence!* No normal person would argue that men should behave and appear like women, or that women should behave and appear like men. They are, and should be, as different as air and water; and each is as necessary to the continuance of human life. Occasionally a man does seem startlingly womanish or a woman mannish. A chemical or physical quirk somewhere in the intricacies of the human body can bring this about. Even an early sex experience or a trick of the mind can change the normal sex habits of a human being. This departure from the norm is regarded with a variety of reactions by the onlooking world. Some are repelled by it, some amused, others pitying or understanding.

Males and females are born of the union of man and woman. Men are predominantly male in appearance and characteristics, but usually with a definite dash of female in their makeup. Women are predominantly female, with a dash of the masculine. This, considering the origins of their conception, is sound. But as previously has been said, men sometimes are strongly feminine and women occasionally are predominantly masculine. At the other extreme, many men are almost completely male, if not entirely so; and many women are absolutely female.

For me there is no greater bore than a one hundred percent male or a one hundred percent female. Confronted by a massive two-fisted, heavy-breathing, barrel-chested all male he-man; or a fluttering itsy-bitsy deviously helpless, all-tendril female I run from their irksome company. Both are almost certain to be dull, unobservant, reactionary, gabby, and lacking in a sense of humor and of human. A sense of humor is a glorious gift which has nothing to do with jokes, but many people think it has. Actually, it is the rare quality which makes life bearable when it has reached the unbearable stage. It can make a tragic situation tolerable; it can bring understanding and even forgiveness into the emotions of one who is deeply hurt or resentful. It can make an affront seem ridiculous; a dull day luminous; a rebuff comic; hardship fascinating. It is salt, it is water, it is oxygen; occasionally it is like champagne and caviar before a surprisingly badly cooked dinner, so that the dinner itself doesn't really matter so much.

A man who is masculine with a definitely female streak of perception, intuition, and tenderness is a whole man; he is an interesting man, a gay companion, a complete lover. A woman who possesses a sufficient strain of masculinity to make her thoughtful, decisive, worldly in the best meaning of the word; fair; self-reliant; companionable—this is a whole woman. The feminine in the man is the sugar in the whisky. The masculine in the woman is the yeast in the bread. Without these ingredients the result is flat, without tang or flavor.

As I never have married and never have borne a child, any remarks that I might venture to make, sage or sour, could understandably be greeted with hoots of derision, particularly by thrice-divorced marrieds and Tennessee mountain couples with eleven children. I think every adult should marry and should, if possible, have children. This is our normally accepted pattern of life. Marriage and motherhood-fatherhood are two of life's four notable experiences. Being born into the world, and leaving it, are the remaining two. I do not regret not having married. I do not regret not having had children. They say that old age is a lonely state. Well, everybody's lonesome, particularly in crowds, and the more crammed the world becomes the lonesomer its inhabitants seem to be. Certainly I am by choice alone a great deal but I can honestly say that I am practically never lonely. The days usually are all too crowded with interest. Also, all these unrealized but insistent book-characters go rushing through my mind, slamming doors, stamping along corridors, poking their unruly heads out of the windows that are my eyes and yelling into the street, "Hi, I'll be down in a minute, wait for me!" And as for the world outside, just to be able to hear and see is enthralling.

I'd like to have the leisure to go out to lunch occasionally; to see dear friends oftener, talk with them, dine with them or they with me; travel more; work regularly in an organization for the less fortunate; buy a new dress before four in the afternoon at which time saleswomen are exhausted and stocks depleted. For that matter, I'd like to stay in bed for a whole day—not sick in bed—just in bed, resting, reading, napping, thinking unhurriedly, drinking warm milk and hot clear broth and cold orange juice. This would be a kind of eiderdown heaven.

During my preliminary visits to Alaska I met and talked with many women; nurses, doctors, clerks, secretaries, reporters, airline hostesses, waitresses, writers, shop managers, teachers, social service workers, college students. Some of these were full-time workers, some part-time. I do not recall having met any woman who did not have some sort of job or constructive working interest outside her own daily home interests and responsibilities.

These Alaska women seemed to me to be alert, healthy, outgoing, and certainly as happy as any of the more idle women I had encountered elsewhere. Life in Alaska is not easy, and actual material living is costly. Politically and sociologically they appeared aware and vitally interested.

Fairbanks Alaska is a populous and busy city. The City Coroner of Fairbanks during the period of my visits was a woman; handsome and intelligent. When an Alaskan crashed in a plane, was murdered, or otherwise done away with under strange circumstances, it was her job immediately to go by plane or car to view the victim and the situation professionally, and to act upon her findings. If she were not capable of fulfilling her job satisfactorily she could not hold it for a day. She has held it for many years. There may be other women coroners in the United States. It usually is thought of as a job only for men.

This state of the United States, though a territorial part of this country for almost a hundred years before it became a state of the Union, still is in many respects pioneer country. These women, smartly dressed, modishly coifed, well-informed, could, if occasion demanded, take their place, it seems to me, beside the women of the East the Midwest and the Far West in the day when those sections too were frontier country.

It is an historical fact that the earliest male settlers of this country brought their women along. Wives and daughters were there in the *Mayflower*; they were there in the covered wagon, in the log house on the plain or prairie, in the stockade. They pulled their weight, they did their share, if Indians had to be fought they fought them; if water and wood had to be hauled they helped haul them; but they were far outnumbered by the country's male population, they were a precious minority and so they remained for more than two centuries. Then, to the astonishment of a nation, it was announced that women were a majority bloc in the United States. Women outnumber men in thirty-nine of the fifty states. This, we were informed, was not due to a preponderance of girl babies over boy babies. It was merely that women lived longer than men, their health record was higher, their endurance probably greater.

Assertive, cocky, vigorous and self-confident, the American woman was a spoiled and pampered female. She worked, yes; she took part in local and national affairs; she was a member of clubs, societies and unions. She actually and astoundingly possessed more than half the wealth of the United States but she was, nevertheless, a spoiled pampered female. Millions and millions of her were no longer pulling their weight. It appeared that while the majority of the men of the country were living up to their physical potentialities at least, and often to their mental and even sociological potentialities, the majority of women were not. The fault could be laid at the doorstep of the men or of the women; no one seemed quite sure of where the blame lay.

Women were old-fashioned. For all their mechanical dish-washers and Laundromats and super markets and frozen foods and electric mixers and deep freezers and hair-driers and trousers they were old-fashioned. Though it no longer was necessary, they still covered themselves with the sugar icing of winning wiles and winsome ways. Sometimes, if the feminine female role became a thing no longer endurable they gave it up, like Marilyn Monroe. But for the most part they practiced ancient and outmoded ways, they submitted to the vagaries of the designers who yanked their skirts down or pulled their skirts up, commanded them to go sleeveless in winter or muffled in the summer in order, it was argued, that that whimsical state known as the National Economy might be preserved. Certainly it never occurred to designers and makers of male garments to order men to wear polka-dot suits one year and plaid suits the next; to wear short pants to the office and Black Watch kilts to dinner and sleeveless suits on the street. (By the way, if a sleeveless dress with a knee-length skirt sells at the same price as the sleeved and lengthier dress, which it does, how much material and money does the manufacturer gain on millions of garments?)

Fighting as a sport or as a means of attack or defense is supposed to be a manly performance. It is actually merely male. Except in self-defense against unwarranted attack it is an objectionable act. Most adults have seen hysterical women, boisterous women, drunken women, angry resentful unreasonable women. One can go through a lifetime without ever seeing a fighting woman. Women do not like to fight, physically. This is not because they are the weaker sex, or because they could not be trained to fight. They actually have fought effectively in battle with weapons, and in our day. Innately they hate fighting and are opposed to war. In this characteristic they are more civilized than men.

Perhaps it can be argued that a woman, confronted with what would be, for a man, a fighting situation, resorts instead to tears. If true, it still can be said that tears do not result in broken bones or broken countries.

Women behave strangely under stress, as do men. Women, like men, can be violent, cruel, intractable. I've yet to see a woman who behaved —or who by previous performance appeared capable of behaving—like a Kaiser Wilhelm, like a Hitler, a Mussolini, a Khrushchev, a Castro. Quite aside from the world-wide violence of these men, their actual personal performance, to my knowledge, never has been equaled by a woman. Hitler's screeching hysteria; Mussolini's pop-eyed arrogance; Castro's ludicrous antics. As for Khrushchev, what woman, if head of a nation, and seated in the midst of a United Nations session while the representative of one of the great and civilized nations of the world is addressing the assemblage—what woman would remove her shoe and pound her desk with the heel of that shoe thus creating a clamor which horrified, not only the assemblage but the civilized world. Such a woman would probably have been bodily removed from the auditorium and certainly regarded as mentally irresponsible. A child having behaved thus would have been hustled out and punished. I do not recall that any formal protest against this behavior was lodged with the nation represented by this apish character, nor that any apology ever was forthcoming from his associates in power. Boys will be boys. Or men will be boys.

The closest approach on the part of females to this type of behavior I saw only in newspaper and magazine photographs. I was not present actually to behold them. These photographs depicted the barbaric and repulsive behavior of white women in the South of the United States as they watched Negro women and children on their way to the classrooms of segregated or recently desegregated schools. The women's faces as they bawled obscenities of hate at the calm silent Negro would-be students were so distorted with venom as to appear sub-human. There was one photograph in particular which showed a group of young white girl students who appeared to be fifteen, sixteen, seventeen years of age. As they screamed their hate their lips were drawn back from their teeth, their eyes bulged with the poison of animal rage, they seemed no longer human, much less young, of decent family background, of American training. Though fascinated by this grotesquerie, the eyes of the reader turned away from the picture as they would from the sight of a mutilated corpse.

Women, perhaps perforce through the centuries, have developed a talent and an instinct for housekeeping. Men seem to have little of this same talent. There has evolved from this a series of trite jokes and stories about a husband's utterly haphazard housekeeping in the absence of his wife. I should like to see a female housekeeper as Mayor

of New York City. It needs a housecleaning. For years the city officials
have piled the dishes in the sink. The dust has been swept under the
rug until the foot stumbles over the bumps. The beds are unmade,
the curtains hang askew. Even if I were thirty years younger I wouldn't
apply for the job or even remotely want it. But in time—if there is still
time—there must be a woman between forty-five and fifty-five years
of age who is able and willing to take on this gigantic job of scrub-
bing, dusting, reorganizing, budgeting and politically grappling with
the conduct of one of the most—if not the most—dazzling exciting
culturally lavish and potentially beautiful cities in the world. From Harlem to the Battery, for rich or for poor, to live in it as a citizen is a
daily feat of survival. It builds and plans further to build entertainment
centers and so-called culture centers costing hundreds of millions of
dollars. A family of five in Harlem can—and does—pay $49.50 every
two weeks for two rat-infested scabrous rooms in an unspeakable tene-
ment. There are not enough schools for the children of New York
City and not enough teachers to instruct them. Free or very low-
admission recreation centers for young people between the ages of
thirteen and twenty-three, equipped with pools, gymnasiums, class
rooms, work-shops, social halls, libraries, low-cost restaurants definitely
would cost as many millions as those more elegantly patronized culture
centers that now are completed or proposed. After one look at New
York's juvenile crime record any New York woman citizen would
consider the schools and recreation centers cheap at the price.

In the early 1950s, a few years after the so-called end of World
War II, I returned to New York on the *Queen Elizabeth* after a few
interesting weeks spent in Europe. Reporters for various New York
daily newspapers came on board at Quarantine and they spoke to me
among other passengers. I am not good at being interviewed. This may
stem from my early years as a newspaper reporter. Even after all these
years I am self-conscious about answering the questions instead of
asking them. This is somewhat silly conduct on the part of an adult,
but there it is. I had nothing to say, really, and the newspapermen
were pleasantly non-insistent. But at the close of the somewhat bleak
interview one of them, knowing that I lived in New York, jokingly
asked a question which ordinarily is a stock interview query put to
strangers arriving for the first time in New York.

"Just what is your opinion of New York?"

To my own utter astonishment and later horror I told them.

For years I had been stamping dismally around the streets of the city muttering and shaking my head at sight of the dirt, the neglect, the carelessness that was evident from Park Avenue in the center of Manhattan to the glorious rivers east and west; from the Battery to the Bronx and including Central Park and every small park and square in the boroughs. I had just returned from seeing Naples Rome Paris London Madrid Zurich Seville Venice Florence. Perhaps the resentment I now expressed had been seething in me for years. Certainly I could not have predicted its sudden expression now.

Somewhere I may have a haphazard newspaper file that records the spontaneous and indiscreet reply made to the reporter's jesting question. If I have, I don't know where it is. Carelessness marks my own behavior in the matter of hoarding public notices. Roughly and fragmentarily it was this:

"New York is the dirtiest city in the world. I have just seen famous and great European cities, some of which were bombed again and again and in sections reduced to ashes. Through the years of war their man power has been reduced by millions. Financially these European countries are in desperate condition. The bombed and unbombed streets and cities are clean. The houses are neat. The parks are orderly, restful, cared-for oases of green and quiet. The people of these cities seem to have respect for their governments, their towns, their homes and for themselves as citizens. . . . New York is the richest city in the world. Its streets resemble open garbage cans. Its public places are defaced. Its buildings neglected. It is a disgrace to its citizens who are, perhaps, to blame for this condition—or partly responsible at least. Central Park, that once beautifully designed haven, is a goat-heap. New York is like a once enchanting and lovely woman now reduced to a bleary hag in the filthy garments of decay."

Well, this kind of utterance does not endear one to the municipal authorities. But I was speaking (with childlike naïveté) to newspaper reporters who had been joking genially. Certainly I did not say off-the-record because, first, I have no such immunity and, second, because I did not dream that this shrewish blast would interest anyone but myself. The idle amusing question, unexpectedly to me as well as to the newspaper group, had touched off a blast.

Next day every newspaper in New York carried this so-called interview. The reporters were quite within their rights. A question had been asked. I had answered it.

Throughout the United States, and in many parts of Europe, every newspaper of any appreciable circulation carried this story. By afternoon there was a small parade of women pickets on the sidewalk outside the apartment building in which I live. They carried home-made-looking signs on which was hand-printed in large letters this be-witching comment:

FERBER YOU NEVER HAD IT SO CLEAN

They were, I was told, wives of sanitation workers, incensed at the insult to their husbands' profession. But I had not considered the sani-tation workers as blameworthy. The villains were city government and us.

Hundreds and hundreds of letters poured in. Other letters were writ-ten to the newspapers. Strangers stopped me on the streets. There were interviews with New York City officials. These were published in the newspapers of New York. They were not admiring. One official, well known for his brilliant and indefatigable work for the betterment of the city—and for his high irascibility and low boiling point in angry vehemence—roared that I should go back to Mudville where, he said, I originally came from. As I had been born in Kalamazoo Michigan and had, at various periods of my early life, lived in Iowa, Wisconsin, and Illinois before residing in New York, I considered this a more whole-sale vituperation on the American scene than mine had been.

The letters sent to me came from every point of New York City. Invariably they were signed with the writer's name, and most of them bore a home or business address. They came from men and women. It is an unbelievable fact that, of the mass of mail, only three or four letters reviled me or disagreed with what had been published as my utterance. Evidently many of the seven million residents of New York had felt as I had. It took me a lifetime to learn that if you are feeling a national or physical discomfort it is a hundred to one that the people in the same position with you are feeling that same resentment and discomfort. They rarely confess this or act upon it. Shyness, insecurity, timidity; an understandable reluctance to be the face stuck through the curtain at which the rubber balls are being hurled in the amusement park sideshow.

For centuries men have said of women that they find them mysterious; that they are variable; that they have—and this has been so used and repeated that it has become a cliché—infinite variety; they have intuition but not much brain-matter; that they are unpredictable; unreasoning; not to be understood; above all, mysterious mysterious mysterious.

After all these thousands of years women are mysterious and puzzling to men. Men are not mysterious or puzzling to women. They see them with a clear and unillusioned eye. They have regarded the male in his public and private performances. They have loved him and resented him and hated him and accepted him. He definitely is no mystery to their loving but sardonic maternal eyes. They know him. They have taken advantage of this knowledge. Millions—even billions—of women yearly use a small percent of their energies, imagination, talent, constructive ability. It is almost as though one were to go through life creeping on all fours, never to walk, run, or stand upright.

The almost unused power is there in the unlimited wealth of intelligence, intuition, perception, the ability to endure vicissitude; in an astounding health record, adaptability, and an inherent cunning which makes a mere Machiavelli seem a bumpkin. Individually, this power is sometimes used. For evil. For good.

It sounds definitely ludicrous to say Women of the World, Unite! Yet if each woman from eighteen to eighty would quietly take stock, determined to live up to her mental and physical and spiritual potentialities for one hour a day—even for two hours a week—our frantic world of today could be saved from itself. A lovely world it is, worth saving.

Has anyone, I wonder, reminded the Negro citizen of the United States to look back to the year 1920. Today the Negro of this country is waging an heroic and, for the most part, a non-violent battle for his rights as a citizen and a human being. Though granted these rights just about a century ago he has, in many sections of this nation, been restrained from exercising them. Yet this state of affairs was not a solitary example of the denial of human rights. For almost one hundred and fifty years—from 1776 until the year 1920—an enormous segment of the United States, almost half its population in fact, was forced to accept a similar status of second-class citizen in the categories of civic, political, social and legal departments, among others. These many millions of the underprivileged citizenry in the United States were known as Women.

Here was a vast rich civilized country under a so-called democratic form of government. Yet until the year 1920 the women citizens of the United States were not even given a nation-wide right to vote in governmental political affairs.

Women were, even at that late date, in many aspects a form of chattel. They possessed in full few social cultural political human legal or property rights. They were restrained in these not only by custom but by law. A Federal Constitutional Amendment entitled the 19th Amendment was not passed until 1920.

In the United States and in Great Britain women increasingly protested these restrictions. The woman of spirit and determination marched, petitioned, spoke in defiance of her enforced handicaps. She manacled herself to lampposts, she staged sit-down strikes on the street. petitioned, spoke in defiance of her enforced handicaps. She manacled herself to lampposts, she staged sit-down strikes on the street. She She might be a woman of twenty, she might be a woman of eighty. She frequently was roughly handled, jeered, derided, ridiculed, arrested, jailed.

The American tea-room with its creamed-chicken patties, its fruit salad, its rubbery popovers and orange marmalade must have been born of the treatment likely to follow the attempted entrance of any lone respectable woman into a large conventional public restaurant. Not only might she be served after an intolerable passage of time; she might be refused a table in a room dotted with unoccupied tables.

A bigoted world said: "Votes for women! Women's rights! They'll turn masculine. They'll be wearing trousers next. . . . Property! they're too fuzzy-headed to manage property or money. . . . Women on a jury! Too sentimental too soft. Next thing they'll want to be judges or mayors or congressmen or even senators. Can you imagine! We'd be ruined. The country wouldn't be fit to live in."

Yet the following official statement was made at 9 o'clock on the morning of August 26, 1920: "The 19th Amendment has become valid to all intents and purposes as a part of the Constitution of the United States."

Even this battle for women's rights has not yet been fully won. But Abigail Adams, the farsighted, the prophetic, is at last justified. Today, as we read in our newspapers of the new revolt for first-class citizenship, it has a familiar ring.

20

Appleton Wisconsin was, in my day there, a civilized, intelligent Midwest town of then sixteen thousand population, it kept step with whatever was good and modern in that day. When, decades later, there actually emerged from that attractive city a would-be Führer named Joseph McCarthy it was as though a Loch Ness monster were to emerge dripping from Niagara Falls.

Through my years as a student at Ryan High School, Appleton, I sang every Friday night and Saturday morning in the choir at services in Temple Emanuel which was the place of religious observance attended by the Appleton citizens of Jewish faith. I had little vocal talent, no training, and small enthusiasm for this contribution. Friday after-school evenings and Saturday mornings offered more toothsome fare to a fourteen-fifteen-sixteen-year-old girl. But there I was in the choir loft weekly, nevertheless, bawling out the hymns and almost unconsciously learning quite a lot about the history of the religious sect known as Jews.

This baffled me. It still baffles me and I no longer am fourteen-fifteen-sixteen. I am quite an old party. In this rather charming and liberal place of worship in the beautiful Fox River Valley town, there was the proper acknowledgment of the man Jesus Christ as a Jew. I hadn't fully realized this before. Certainly it wasn't noised about in Ottumwa Iowa. I was deeply interested in the fact that Jesus Christ was born a Jew, remained a Jew until his death; that his family was Jewish, his disciples were Jewish, he had worshiped in the synagogue, observed the Jewish religious rituals and kept the Jewish Holy Days.

The Golden Rule that Jesus taught he learned from the rabbis of his time and the prayer of his composing, now known as The Lord's Prayer, was, in almost its entirety, taken from the prayer in use among the Jews of that day. It is part of the sacred Kadish prayer and is universally recited today in Christian and Jewish religious gatherings. Then why, I asked, all this screaming antagonism against Jews on the part of the religious sect called Christian? Jewish teacher called Christ. Christian. It didn't make sense.

Certainly I was young, but precocious as well and as excited and curious about the world as though I had just discovered it. Under the influence of that extra-sensory perception or perhaps merely hyper-sensitivity about which I knew nothing I dramatized everything and everyone; myself, my parents, ramshackle old Ryan High School, Appleton, life. A great stroke of luck for me, certainly, that the ability to write gave me, in the years that followed, a legitmate outlet for all this dramatization. Without this means of expression I might have degenerated into one of those touching creatures one occasionally encounters in New York and elsewhere, walking alone upon the streets while declaiming in loud oratorical tones some fancy of their own, embellishing the solitary production meanwhile with spacious arm-waving gestures, while the passerby stares with amusement or compassion.

The drama of this young Jew, Jesus Christ, seemed to me stupendous. In a largely pagan world of his century this youth was the most purely spiritual human being that his world had ever known. He gathered about him groups of people, for he possessed great magnetism. Especially did he inculcate with his philosophy of life a band of twelve men who went about with him or who went in his stead if he was busy elsewhere, preaching and teaching a strange and lovely and humane philosophy of life. It was a way of life he had learned in his home as a child and in the synagogue as a boy and young man. There were plenty of scoffers and threateners, but there were converts, too. In time, as his following grew, people began to attribute to him super-human qualities.

There was in this truly humble man no grain of arrogance. His God was Good. Good was his God. He never attached his own name to the tenets of the spiritual belief which he strove to make clear. The small and cruel world in which he now attempted to teach the acceptance of the Spirit of Man was engaged in idol worship as a form of religion.

They worshiped the elements Water, Fire, Wind, and Rain; they worshiped the Sun the Moon the Stars; or they bowed down before objects of wood or stone carved in the likeness of humans or of monsters or of animals. These seen or unseen gods were, it was believed, master spirits that had control over the fate of human beings. They had to be placated by gifts, petitions and human sacrifices.

That which Jesus Christ was teaching, spiritually and humanely, was the concentrated essence of the fundamental Jewish faith. Certainly he did not speak of his teachings and precepts as constituting the Christian religion—the religion of Christ. Himself. Not at all. In a pagan world, he was pleading for the acceptance of the purest possible form of his own religion—the Jewish religion.

In such a world it is small wonder that the man who went about the countryside preaching the God of the Spirit was considered a strange type indeed. As more and more of the everyday people listened to his teachings of love and brotherhood he came finally to the attention of the Roman governor Pontius Pilate. This fellow, Pilate said, is a nuisance and a menace. This carpenter, with his bunch of fishermen, yammering in the marketplace and in our temples, kicking up trouble and making everyone feel important—who does he think he is! Away with him! Out!

But the good and gentle teacher had left his mark on the minds and souls of hundreds and perhaps thousands of erstwhile idol worshipers. These now, after his death, made of him a martyr and then a Divinity. In a world of violence and lawlessness where the little man was a slave and the big man a law unto himself, a seed of hope had been implanted. There was, this man had told them, one true God only; a God of the Spirit. The belief in this one God, who could not be seen or felt, but whose spirit dwelt in every human being, could, this Jesus Christ had said, bring brotherhood, love, peace, justice, mercy to all human society. This was the God of the Jew, Jesus Christ, and of his humble disciples, and of all professed Jews. This man was one of them. Realistically and spiritually he was one of them. Jews, and the Jewish religion, are basically too realistic and too dedicated to the one God, the God of the Spirit, to accept as a Divinity a man, however truly good, who was one of them and who walked the earth as a man among them.

The young girl, now seventeen, working as a newspaper reporter on the lively little Appleton *Daily Crescent*, tried to understand the paradoxical world in which she found herself. She talked to Father Basilius —Father Basil for short—on her news rounds. He, in his rough brown robe, his bare feet thrust into sandals, was one of the Order affiliated with the Catholic church that stood across the lovely ravine in the district known as the Chute. She was attending to the job of garnering the church news from kindly shrewd little Father Basil, but they talked, too, a little, of the Catholic religion and of the Jewish religion. It was not argumentative talk. Neither was trying to convince or convert the other, certainly. Each had a decent measure of respect for and understanding of the other's views.

She attended an occasional Sunday night service at the Congregational church where Dr. John Faville, handsome, modern, perhaps a shade too charming, held forth in his liberal way. She sometimes attended Evensong at the Episcopalian (High Church) service. On Friday nights she went with her family to the Jewish service at Temple Emanuel.

She dropped into this church or that, then—Baptist, Methodist, Catholic, Unitarian, Jewish, Episcopalian, Presbyterian—as a sort of guest-observer, which was arrogant of her, perhaps. Puzzled, questioning, she was seeking knowledge. What was all this fuss and fury about Jews all these years and centuries? They're very little different from the Unitarians, she discovered; they think that character is the fundamental principal of religion; character, the spirit of man. I don't see anyone snarling at Unitarians, she thought, and insulting them and acting contemptibly toward them in many ways. What goes on here in the name of religion? A difference in dogma, a difference in ceremony, but what about the fundamental things that Jesus Christ talked about thousands of years ago? What about love and brotherhood and peace? What have trappings and ancient pomp and ceremony to do with these pure aims?

One dons a black robe. One turns his collar this way. One kneels to pray, and one prays but does not kneel; one serves wine and wafer, the other nothing; one has pictures on the walls, one has stained-glass windows; one has bare white walls; one uses Latin phrases; one speaks in occasional Hebrew, the ancient language of the Bible; one makes the sign of the cross; one pulpit has a seven-branched candlestick. What have these rituals and panoplied ceremonials to do with love and brotherhood and peace! How can this survival of a long past period now sustain the sick body of the human race? Processions no longer impress a distracted world literally tired and frightened to death and seeking only a sustaining Good.

This man Jesus, as he spoke his message of love, as he stood in the marketplace and on the village street, wore no splendid robes, was surrounded by no panoply. He wore the simple garb of any peasant or everyday citizen or student or teacher. Long before the day of the psychiatrist, the orator, the spell-binder, the pulpit-pounder, this traveling preacher said, quietly, "Come unto me . . . and I will bring you peace."

These questions, unanswered and perhaps unanswerable, marked the end of the young girl's observance of any formal religious worship. She believed only that Good was God and, interchangeably, God was only Good. She thought that the Jewish religion, with its simple ceremonies and its freedom from trappings other than the ancient Orthodox shawl which had been no part of the modern congregation she had known; its dietary laws which were health laws conceived thousands of years ago in a tropical climate where refrigeration was unheard of; its moral, social and civil laws; these seemed to her a simple and sound basis for faith and conduct, but the formal rites she now rejected . . . Prayer continued to be a fitting form for resolution and hope, whether humble or aspiring; but not phrased in the Biblical terms . . . Give us this day our daily bread . . . forgive us our trespasses . . . do unto others as we would have them do . . . lead us not into temptation . . . deliver us from evil . . .

These hopes and aims were uttered in the language of today, together with other more exigent and perhaps even more personal hopes and resolutions, and they were addressed, with no intent toward arrogance, impiety or vanity, to whatever the speaker possessed or could summon within herself of courage, fortitude and spirit.

Certainly she never sneered at formal religion or rejected it in others. Any religious faith, she thought, that brings a degree of comfort and solace and hope is good, probably. What does it matter? Why do they quarrel among themselves and rail at each other? So, fifty years later, she still liked to drop into St. Patrick's on Fifth Avenue just for a moment sitting quietly with the others scattered here and there in the pews, while the roar of the traffic sounded muffled and uninsistent; or at the vast Cathedral of St. John the Divine, uptown; or the Baptist church in Harlem; or Temple Emanuel at 65th Street; or, forsaking the stone edifices, listening while a courageous little Salvation Army band essayed to save souls in Times Square.

She had a whim to see for herself how they were making out in the old towns in which the young preacher, Jesus Christ, had held forth centuries and centuries ago; the old towns whose names fell so familiarly on the ear and which yet had a connotation of improbability. Did they actually still exist?—Jerusalem and Beersheba and Nazareth and Bethlehem and Galilee and Mount Zion. He had talked their langauge, he had preached their religion. How was it going with his people in that ancient modern country they now called Israel?

Together with that same niece Mina who had been such a delightful and perceptive traveling companion throughout Europe during World War II I took off in a big improbable jet plane for a small improbable country. Object: travel, information, the refreshment that comes with these. Nothing more. I had no plan or desire to write about Israel and never shall, other than these brief and superficial pages. On the way there was an overnight stop in Rome where we paid our respects as always, and like all tourists, to the Italian pasta, the Colosseum, the Spanish steps and whatever else of beauty and interest could be crowded into a handful of hours. I had visited Rome many times. The ancient city had never lost its infinite charm; even though it now was a mass of neon lights, automobiles, movie actors and knitted suits.

It had been in the 1930s that I had spent two or three days only in the desert land which then was Palestine. That jaunt was part of a somewhat jumbled Mediterranean cruise. Even a born observer with a reporter's training as a background cannot see much of a country, however small, in that brief time. In the twenty-five years or more that had elapsed since that trip I had found myself regarding this courageous and bumptious little nation, Israel, with a paradoxical emotion of admiration and exasperation.

Now, as our plane made little or nothing of the air miles between Italy and Israel. I remembered something of the barren dusty desert land I had so briefly seen a quarter of a century earlier. I recalled that the hills had glowed golden so that the lines of the old hymn "Jerusalem the golden, with milk and honey blest" took on actuality. I remembered how surprisingly close to earth the sky seemed to be, perhaps because of the clarity of the atmosphere, though I did not know this then. It was almost as though one could reach up and touch the blue. How astonishingly modern the King David Hotel; and the kibbutz in which the small children were being fed all the eggs and milk and butter while their parents, just in from a day's work in the fields, were content with a meal of tea and butterless bread; the size and honey-sweetness of the local oranges; the camels treading in their comically sneering way the dusty road between Haifa, the port town, and Jerusalem; the incongruity of a snatch of conversation between two men in a hotel lobby:

"How about a game of golf this afternoon?"

"Sorry. I'd love to, but I've got to go to Galilee on business."

October evening late twilight when we touched down at Lydda airport. It could have been any airport in any busy country in the world; jammed, noisy, a seemingly frantic but probably basically orderly rushing to and fro; white, black, brown faces; children; loud-speakers announcing destinations somehow anachronistically Biblical. There still lay before us the longish drive from the airport to Jerusalem, our destination. I still don't quite believe what I saw.

The Palestine of that long-ago visit had been an arid and almost treeless desert land. Now our car rolled along a paved road bordered on either side by forests and forests and forests. Hundreds of thousands of trees. They were not saplings. They were sturdy thick-branched specimens that towered, a tent of green, as far as the eye could see. I could think only of the false-front villages, hastily constructed by the Russian Commander-in-Chief and court favorite Potemkin during the reign of Catherine II whereby he completely fooled this usually astute Empress into believing that he had settled vast tracts of wild Russia. But these trees in Israel, these great forests, were real, these trees had been planted by the thousands; they flourished; they changed the very climate of the region in which they stood. This was only one of the many achievements, impressive sights and triumphs of man over adversity that I was to see in the next two weeks. I did see them; farms, factories, gardens; museums, universities, scientific laboratories; homes and workshops for the old; homes and workshops for the young; women drilling as armed soldiers; beaches, hotels, restaurants; roads, orange groves, towns sprung up where only a desert waste had been. White Jews, black Jews, brown Jews, yellow Jews; golden blonde, black-haired, red-headed, chestnut; tall, short, slim. It was much the same as I had seen all my life in my native United States; white Christians, black Christians, brown Christians, yellow Christians, red-skinned Christians, copper colored. Here in Israel, too, as in the United States, the people moved energetically, with purpose.

Before I had left for Israel an acquaintance had said to me, "I was there last year. It was wonderful—the feeling that everyone there is a Jew."

Rather waspishly I said, "How dreadful that anyone should feel as insecure as that."

Interested, impressed, and often fascinated though I was, I never, in all my travels, have felt as alien in any country as I felt in Israel.

As I drove and walked up and down this old-new nation, so gigantic in its aims and achievements, so tiny in area—270 miles in length, a mere 70 miles at its widest point—I had a strange and haunting feeling that somewhere sometime I previously had encountered in a definite region this same attitude of insularity on the part of its people toward the rest of the world; an arrogance, a braggadocio, an assumption of superiority.

The name of this region now came to me with a shock. It was an area so huge that tiny Israel could have been tucked into its smallest corner. Yet the temperament of its people, their disregard for the achievements or importance of all other geographical regions, was startlingly similar.

Israel was a sort of Jewish Texas; without oil wells.

In its brashness, its naïveté, its satisfaction in its own impressive achievement, the spirit of the country had an American quality. It lacked the American good-natured attitude, its relaxed temperament. Hedged geographically as Israel is by enemies, a relaxed attitude of general laissez-faire is perhaps not exactly practical.

Israel has no national type; there has not been enough time in its modern history to develop the typical Israeli. It is unlikely that this recognizable type will ever actually develop. An unmistakably American type never has developed in the United States. Israel, like the United States, is made up of émigrés from many countries. But the American emigrant over the centuries was preponderantly of English, Irish, Scandinavian, German, Polish, Czech, Hungarian, Dutch, Italian, Russian background. The nation of Israel now appears to become increasingly a refuge for the persecuted dark-skinned races of the Middle East,

Asia, North Africa. This fact is of increasing concern to the nation's government; it is this which accounts for some of the astounding and regrettable announcements and political statements put forth by Israel on the subject of Israel's alleged jurisdiction over citizens of other nations. Every Jew, they shout, meanwhile gazing covetously at the United States citizen, is an Israel national.

In these brash and offensive statements the government's conduct resembles that of Israel's younger generation. In its heroic fight for survival the citizenry of Israel—particularly its teenage to thirty range of citizenry—has had little time or opportunity to develop a liberal-thinking attitude toward the world in general.

Good manners are fundamentally nothing more than kindness and a recognition of the rights and privileges of others. Surrounded and threatened as they were and are by enemies situated at the country's actual borders, the amenities had to remain neglected.

These young people, whose conduct somewhat resembles that of our own beatniks, are known as "sabras." The actual sabra is a local plant, a cactus, which bears a fruit that is all prickles on the outside but sweet on the inside. One rarely penetrates beyond the prickles.

If the traveler from the United States chances to express a preference for his own country as a land in which to dwell in the future as he has in the past, the sabra—especially the young male sabra—is likely to say, "You don't know anything." This is disconcerting and definitely not engaging.

Occasionally, though, the frankness is rather endearing. In a restaurant, scanning the menu, you say, "I think I'll start with the soup."

"You're crazy," the waiter says.

"Why?"

"It's no good."

A newspaper woman came to interview me at my hotel. It was a pleasant hotel situated on the shores of the Mediterranean and about twenty minutes driving distance from Tel Aviv. The reporter was a young girl, attractive, intelligent seeming. She evidently had prepared her questions.

"Why do you write about the United States?"

"The United States and the people of the United States interest me. I know them."

"But you write about it as if you liked it!"

"I love it. I'd hate to have to live anywhere else in the world."

"I can't understand this," the girl said, quite simply. She wasn't being intentionally rude. She knew Israel only. Emotionally, she doubtless felt about it much as I felt about my country. But I had the advantage of first-hand knowledge with which to compare my country with many others—including her own. This I refrained from saying.

Her next question: "Do you have oranges in the United States?"

Israel's oranges are a paying national product; large, luscious, honey-sweet.

"Yes, we have oranges." Privately I thought of the miles of orange groves in Florida, California, Texas, Arizona.

"We have oranges even in the winter. Do you have oranges in the winter?"

"In the winter?" I thought of the bins and sacks of the brilliant golden fruit in every village and town and city; every supermarket and corner grocery; the golden glass at every breakfast table, every lunch counter. Certainly I would not describe to her a typical market or grocery or food-store window in December or January or February in New York, glowing and brilliant not only with oranges of every variety and size but actually with fresh pears, enormous fresh strawberries, grapefruit, ripe purple plums; nectarines; honeydew melons, Spanish melons; grapes jade, purple, red. Ripe peaches. Watermelons. Apricots. Persimmons. Pineapples. Cherries. Avocados. Raspberries. Blueberries. Tomatoes. Endive. Asparagus. All this spread in profusion. They were not exactly cheap but they were not out of the reach of the average middle-income.

"Yes we do," I said. "We have oranges even in the winter. Isn't it lovely to have oranges even in the winter!"

"We don't think it's so wonderful. We're used to them."

This I found rather touching; and the behavior, too, was understandable.

An invitation arrived for a late-afternoon tea at which I was to be the visiting guest. The group was made up of Israeli writers whom I did not know and with whose work I regrettably was not familiar. There were perhaps fourteen people seated at a large oval table. We had tea and cakes and talk.

The head of this organization was a man in his middle years. Under his leadership now the little supposedly informal gathering took on a surprisingly parliamentary and not quite friendly tone. The atmosphere was baffling.

Tentatively, I mentioned the young Israelis—their courage, their drive, their initiative. I ventured a suggestion:

The sabras, the new young generation of Israelis, are workers, students, and, when necessary, fighters. Their country is their world. They know—and many thousands of them have even taken part in—the Israel War of Independence in 1948. They are physically surrounded by unfriendly nations. From my balcony at the King David Hotel in Jerusalem I saw, a stone's throw distant, the barbed wire and the mounted guns facing Jordan on this side; the barbed wire and the mounted guns facing Israel on that side. Scarcely a reassuring or peace-promising view.

Courageous and determined as the young Israelis have been and are, isn't it, I asked, high time that they learned something of the manner in which other countries, even more handicapped at the beginning, have achieved freedom and independence for which they were willing to die, and still would die if needful?

These young people, perhaps only a selected few at a time, might learn a valuable lesson if it were made possible for them to visit the United States briefly, or perhaps even to study there, each group to be succeeded by another group through the year and through the years.

The United States, I reminded the gathering, had started its history of freedom under virtually unsurmountable handicaps. The first settlers had come with nothing but their hands and their hope and their courage with which to encounter and overcome the savage elements and the savage natives. They had come to this new continent, a wilderness, to escape religious persecution. But there were no gifts of millions of dollars or pounds to help them build a civilization in the wilderness. No donors, no societies or groups donated to these struggling pioneers their universities, their museums, hospitals, laboratories, playgrounds, machinery. These early Americans, needing a house, had to go into the forest and chop down a tree and from it build that house; and the chairs and tables and beds that must furnish it. Of money they had none. Of help, none. For food they lived off the woods and streams and such crops as they themselves could plant and tend. They built a great civilization and a magnificent nation with their bare hands. They fought savage tribes, they fought the trained armies of rich and ruthless European lands, they persisted, they survived, they were free.

I then made what I meant to be a realistic suggestion.

Israel, the courageous little land that it is, has received not only moral and spiritual encouragement, but millions and millions and millions of monetary gifts through these past years, and continues to receive this enormous largesse. Let the boys and girls and young men and women see what another country has done and is doing to preserve its freedom and the peace. Let them come here to observe and study, no matter how briefly. To this many Americans might subscribe.

No! thundered the head of the group seated with me around the big table. No!

But why not?

They might marry. They might meet and marry some one over there who is not a Jew.

Well, what of it! I know that strict Catholics and Orthodox Jews are intent on preventing inter-faith marriages each in its own religion. But most of the young people I've talked with here in Israel seem to have very few thoughts about their religion. The nation seems to be their religion.

No! thundered the man again. We must keep the race pure!

The six words simply did not register at first; or, if they did, their impact stunned me into unbelief.

What did you say! Will you repeat that, please?

He repeated the astounding assertion.

I stood up, somewhat shakily.

"That has a familiar sound. I've heard that statement before. I may not have got your name correctly. Is it, perhaps, Hitler?"

Certainly the most impressive and altogether delightful Israeli I met was General Yadin, hero of the 1948 Revolution; better known now throughout the scientific world as the archaeologist Professor Yigal Yadin. His name is associated with important archaeological findings and particularly with the Dead Sea Scrolls so recently and so dramatically discovered. Now the tourist regards with amazement these unbelievably ancient parchment fragments neatly and with incredible skill arranged in their protective glass cases in the magnificent new Hebrew University in Jerusalem. Here is a man worldly in the highest meaning of the word; gently humorous, wise, understanding. To talk with him and his wife and their two small daughters in their home in Israel is to know what the best of this new courageous country can be.

In appearance the younger generation Israeli is remote from the Jew as depicted in cartoons throughout the centuries. This young sabra is tall blond blue-eyed fine-featured. Gone is the tragic eye, the under-developed body of the ghetto dweller formerly forbidden in the despotic countries of Europe and Asia to own land or to work on the land. Huddled for centuries in the dark and airless tunnels of city slums their features their frames reflected the struggle of the undernourished human body to adjust to enforced adversity.

Now, in Israel, a physical miracle has been brought about by sun air freedom hope achievement. The handsome six-footer who was our guide and chauffeur during our visit might have been, in appearance, a Kansas or Minnesota or Iowa product.

This ancient-new land is an utterly fascinating point of observation for the tourist or the student. Here is one of the oldest—if not the oldest —of civilizations. Here recent excavations have disclosed treasures in architecture sculpture parchments dating so far into the remote past that they never before have been part of the recorded history of man. Here are to be found fragments of beauty equaled only in the ruins of Greece. Now, in unbelievable proximity, the tourist is confronted with the beautiful and scientifically important modern achievements. Univer-sities. Museums. Gardens. Laboratories. Farms. Planned forests. Roads. Hospitals. Nurseries. The eye almost rejects as impossible that which it actually beholds.

Certainly the visitor can be a source of important income to this new-old nation. Yet no country in the world except, perhaps, the United States of America, behaves with such casual lack of understand-ing toward its foreign visitors. As for its diplomatic behavior—certainly it should avoid such shocking statements as that recently made by its premier in which it was announced that Jewish citizens of other free and democratic countries were actually fundamental citizens of this foreign land simply because of their religious belief. This is a form of attempted dictatorship almost impossible to believe as emanating from a country made up, as Israel is, of refugees so recently escaped from dictatorship, persecution and even death.

Certainly the most magnificent achievement of this heroic little country lies not primarily in its economic, cultural or scientific achievements. Its triumph is that, through immigration, planned and persisted in despite almost insuperable handicaps, this tiny country has rescued millions of men women children who otherwise would have perished.

Perhaps one day this medley, this miscellany, may produce another Heifetz another Rubinstein another Spinoza another Einstein another Rosenwald—even another babe born, perhaps, in Bethlehem and growing up in the land of the modern prophets—a gentle compassionate and selfless Jew to lead this frantic world again into ways of peace.

Our westbound flight necessitated a change of planes at Rome. Between Israel and Italy there was scheduled a brief stop at Athens. Athens. Who—that cares about the theatre and its history—about the great art of writing—about sculpture—architecture—government—freedom—civilization itself—could actually come within sight of that monument to all culture—the Acropolis—and never gaze upon it!

Already overdue in New York, we resolved to have one stolen day in Athens. This idea was, of course, absurd, but not as hilarious as it actually proved to be in performance.

Down we touched at the airport and out we bounced in the late afternoon with twenty-four hours of culture as our program. The season was the end of October, twilight fell early, by the time we had reached the Grand Bretagne Hotel there was no possibility of dashing up the hill for a close view of the classic columns that now looked down on us as we stared at them from our balcony. The thing to do was to scamper around the town like the tourists we were. Athens! You're in Athens! Ruins. Statues. Monuments. Churches. I never have failed to experience that emotion of, perhaps, naïve enchantment and unbelief when I find myself in the midst of a world-wonder. Now there was just time for a walk in the city. An outdoor cafe. Dinner.

"Look," I said to Mina and Mina to me, in agreement, "hot or cold we'll have to be out of here early tomorrow afternoon. If we're going to see this heavenly hunk of architecture properly we ought to be up early early tomorrow morning. . . . Before the crowds begin to swarm up there . . . alone . . . in peace . . . to see it that way . . . no crowds of tourists . . . of course we're tourists but maybe no other . . ."

It was lighted at night, we had been told. Great spotlights, artfully placed, illumined the glorious façade, brought the classic columns into relief. It dominated the city below.

Darkness had fallen. Again we stood on the balcony that faced the noble hill. And there was the white light cast upon one of the most purely moving sights the world has to offer.

And there, just below it and around it, defacing it degrading it, were the red neon lights the green neon lights the blatant glare that has vulgarized the world. We might have been standing on a balcony looking at Detroit.

A hastily gulped breakfast next day and a scramble into the waiting car and up the magic hill early, early in the morning.

There weren't more than twenty-two tourist buses and seventy-nine cars lined up at the entrance booth at the top of the hill; and thousands of tourists like ourselves crawling over every stone, column, step and portico.

A woman near by stood staring thoughtfully at the fabulous face of the Parthenon. She called out to her companion, and what she said was the trite and tourist classic: "It looks just like the First National Bank back home."

It's no good rasping it out shrewishly, "But they thought of it first, don't you understand! No one had ever done a purely lovely architectural structure like that. Don't you see! They thought of it first, thousands of years ago. This is It!"

21

From my workroom window on the fifteenth floor of a Park Avenue apartment building I can view a small forest. This planting is, perhaps, not sufficiently lavish actually to be called a forest. A grove, then, a grove of bristling angular trees whose trunks are black metal, whose branches are black metal. They are television antennae and their limbs form a canopy that spreads over the entire area of the roof across the way and to the left. This sight is as nourishing and as stimulating to the eye, the mind, and the spirit as a horde of locusts.

Double French doors composed of glass form the east wall of the workroom. Just beside this door-window I sit and work with the light falling properly over the left shoulder; or I sit and stare, as is sometimes the zany habit of writers. When, thirteen years ago, I became a resident of this pleasantly perpendicular retreat there was nothing but sky to be seen from that window when the viewer was seated. For a writer this is perfection. Glancing to the left there it was; sky. It was blue sky or blue sky with white puff-clouds. It was gray sky or gray with gray-black storm-clouds. If I worked right through the day and into the late afternoon there might occasionally be a special treat as a reward for being a Good Girl—a rosy winter sunset handily reflected from the unseen western horizon. Literally there was no building high enough between me and the East River, a mile or less distant, to mar the soothing yet paradoxically exciting view of sky sky sky.

The little balcony's brick parapet and iron railing rebuffed the roar and squawk of traffic from Park Avenue below. Ten years of this. I had become quite smug about it. Who says a writer can't find a spot of serenity in which to work in New York! And then the enemy's horrid head appeared on the east horizon. He appeared noiselessly one night. Distance dulled his clamor. His metal arms reached up into the sky— my sky. He was encamped there, his minions swarmed the ramparts, his yellow-red eyes glowed now in the night like a monster cat's. Gradually, over a period of three more years, the monsters marched closer and closer. Evergreen shrubs against the balcony railing mask the gory head of one thirty-story giant. On the left the antennae forest can be seen only if I deliberately turn to stare at it. The others are still only mountain peaks in the near distance. But I know—as any experienced New York dweller knows too well—that one morning I shall awaken to the *bang!-boom!-crash!* that is the trumpet sound of the wrecking crew come to demolish the two handsome private dwellings which, just across the street, have preserved my sky for me; and from the dust will emerge a thousand-eyed monster to glare down at me as I cower in front of the typewriter.

"What are you doing here?" I demanded, as I have a hundred times before. "You're getting edgy," I cautioned myself. "Temper temper! Next thing you'll be walking along the streets, muttering; or writing Letters to the Papers or turning into one of those writers who don't write because the coffee isn't strong enough this morning, or the light isn't right, or the times are awry, or you didn't sleep eight hours, or there's too much noise in New York or in the world or in your own psyche. Pull the cover over your typewriter and take the cover off your routine and get out of here. A half-acre of TV antennae as a view indeed! You must be out of your mind. The Wide Open Spaces— that's the—but where are they? Between the Atlantic Ocean and the Pacific Ocean, fool! And nestled in there is a nice bit of ground known as the United States of America. It isn't fashionable to be in favor of this piece of real estate, especially if you live in it. In these past few years your traveling has been done by plane. You can't just step out of one of those when you want to look at a view or pick a daisy or buy a hamburger or stay overnight because the town looks pretty. But with a car as your vehicle, who's to stop you from sitting by the roadside, if you want to, with your shoes off. (State Police, that's who—though I've never tried it.)"

Ever since Henry Ford rigged up that little quivering contraption known as the Model T I have longed to climb into an automobile and to drive or be driven from New York to San Francisco. A half century had whisked by and I hadn't gratified this reasonable and—to me—enthralling urge. For this there were two reasons, one of which was fairly sound.

The sound reason was this:

Whenever a long pull of work was finished, every nerve artery bone and muscle—not to mention the mental and psychic anatomy—screamed to Get Away from It All. Limp, spent, lost without the compulsion of the daily task to be done; not at all sure whether the Thing was good or bad or both, one made for the nearest exit. In the early days that handy exit was a train; the *Twentieth Century* to Chicago, the *Chief* to California; the Whatever-it-was in railway speed to the Colorado Rockies. Then the escape hatch became a ship; a ship to England, to France, to Italy. Now it became a plane; two-engine, four-engine, jet. No need for special clothes. What you had would do. No elaborate plans necessary. Just a reservation on a train, a ship, a plane. Then a brisk leap down to Grand Central or Penn Station; or to the Hudson River docks; or to La Guardia or Idlewild airports. And off! Away! Free!

Though the garage in the years at Treasure Hill had been rather choked with good bad and medium cars—a neat but dated station wagon for utility, a handsome soft-running barouche-type for Julia's comfort; a tough little runabout for brisk errands and general slapping around. Here in New York I had and have no car, nor do I want one. It's bad enough to battle traffic on foot.

To drive or be driven across this vast country necessitates the use of a car. Since leaving Treasure Hill I have had no country place of my own. Myself, I wouldn't drive in New York City if I were presented with a fleet of Rolls-Royces, Bentleys and Cadillacs. Besides, mine is a sitdown job. When I stand up and walk away from that desk I prefer to keep on walking—a mile, two miles, three. For the necessary transportation there's always a taxi (or almost always); or a car to be had by the hour. My notion of a nightmarish existence in New York would be, on emerging from the building in which I live, to see confronting me always a car and driver waiting to deprive me of the air and exercise I need and long for, even if the air is polluted by foul gases and the path is concrete.

So much for the reasonable reason. The unsound reason was this:

Always, after about two hours of steady motoring, I want to get out of the car and stay out. I have no explanation for this. As the distance between New York and San Francisco is roughly three thousand miles, give or take a couple of hundred, to cover this mileage in two-hour jaunts would make old covered-wagon days seem like a whirl in a space ship.

The thing to do now was to buy or rent a car. Following this, the thing not to do was to yield to one's two-hour driving eccentricity, and certainly not to abandon the barouche in Ogallala Nebraska or Medicine Bow Wyoming, and walk back to New York.

Millions of good cars, millions of experienced drives. A combination of the two is not so easily brought about. Rent a good serviceable strong car, I decided; engage a good serviceable strong driver. That's all there is to it.

Finally achieved, the result turned out to be fairly fantastic. The route between New York and San Francisco is a matter of choice. One can make the journey over breathtaking mountain passes or across hundreds of miles of desert; through the richest farm lands in the world; through great cities or no cities; stopping to see the so-called natural wonders of the United States which actually are unnatural in their grandeur and their utter improbability—the Grand Canyon—Yellowstone Park—the Painted Desert—Yosemite National Park—the Dells of Wisconsin—Niagara Falls—the Mississippi River—Carlsbad Caverns in New Mexico—the Wind Caves of South Dakota's Black Hills—incredible mountain peaks—vast forests.

I did not want to see The Sights. (Most of which I had already seen.) No swarming national parks in August; no holes in the ground, be they ever so brilliantly bedizened; no caves waterfalls mountains unless they happened to be in the way. What I longed for, unspecifically, was to get out of New York and into the sort of environment which had been my early background. It was not the wish to Go Back. Thomas Wolfe and O. Henry and my own experience had taught me that you never can Go Back. A few years ago I spent part of a day in Appleton Wisconsin which I had not seen in decades. My girlhood school days there and my teens and every street and house and natural aspect were indelibly stamped on my memory.

They had vanished. Lost, I wandered around the strange streets like a ghost seeking surcease. Old Ryan High School was gone, Ferber's

Store was gone, the once fine old houses were gas stations; College
Avenue, like the main street of every city in the United States, re-
sembled a miniature Chicago. All this I saw and noted and rejected.
And now, when I take Appleton Wisconsin out of my memory and
look at it affectionately, it is exactly the town I knew when I was sixteen.
The new Appleton was wiped from my mind as completely as though
I never had seen the metamorphosis.

As I came away, dejectedly, I reasoned with myself in a falsely jaunty
vein, this: "That's Progress, Stupid. Don't you know Progress when
you see it! People who fight Progress have stopped progressing."

Though I did not analyze it thus, this too-luxurious jaunt of thousands of miles between the Atlantic Ocean and the Pacific Ocean,
across the vast country that was, physically and materially, the most
splendid in the world, was to be a refresher course. It was, I suppose,
Julia Ferber's stock-taking following the Christmas rush. Were the Iowa
cornfields still there, stretching away to the horizon? Was Nebraska
wheat and wheat and wheat as far as the eye could see? The factories
operating; the well-dressed well-nourished millions actually enjoying this
state of being; or was it only my girlhood state of fancy? I wanted to
see this with my eyes.

Out of New York into the reality of the land. On a vaster scale
this journey was probably motivated by the same emotion that had
caused me to establish myself on the crest of Treasure Hill. There it
was; the land; the fruits of the land; you could see it all, you could
touch it. It was real. Hadn't I learned that the only reality was the
spirit of man? Evidently not.

Perhaps the city of New York was the basic motivation for the entire touring plan. No born and bred New Yorker actually can appreciate New York City. Accustomed to it from infancy he must take for
granted this schizophrenic Bagdad.

It is the young cornfed wide-eyed naïve Middle-Westerner who meets
the impact of this half-sordid half-glittering city, head-on; is stunned
by it; and is forever stirred by love and hate for it.

Half palatial dream city, half foul slum. Rat-ridden tenements; rat-
ridden politics. Mountains, man made, walled by glass. Offering daily
the talent the genius of the world in music, the theatre, the dance
science, business, designing, architecture, merchandise, fashion. Days
and weeks of brilliant sunshine, Mediterranean blue skies, exhilarating

cold in the winter; salt ocean breezes in the summer; each autumn and spring a delight. The whole besmirched with dirt, crime, carelessness, greed, ignorance. Here were the matchlessly lovely rivers and bays put to no use for the millions who within their limited means, needed the haven of grass and trees and quiet and rest.

Out for a solitary salutary walk at 9 P.M., a reasonable enough hour for a pre-bedtime amble.

The building doorman says, "Taxi?" He has been there for years.

"No thanks. I'm walking."

"I don't think you'd better. This hour."

"It's nine o'clock!"

"You going far?"

"I'm walking a mile. Up Park, down Madison. What is this! A sanitarium or something!"

But I know he is right.

New York City the once beautiful enchantress, raddled now and grown careless and neglectful, is slopping about all day in soiled negligee and rundown slippers, uncombed, bleary-eyed. But at day's end she dons the flattering chiffons of dusk and of the kindly night. Her lines and wrinkles are softened, the marks of decadence hidden. She covers herself with jewels—the emerald and ruby and diamond lights, the silks and furs of the brilliant Fifth Avenue windows, she wears the tiaras of the flashing towers and the fountains. Again she is the beauty, the enchantress for a few hours until dawn reveals the wrinkles, the dirt, the grime, the decay.

To the sensitive ear the squawl of the chatterbox is everywhere. It is like the night-light which indulgent parents keep glowing for children who are afraid in the dark. The taxi driver listens all day to the yapping of nothing as it emerges from the mechanical box. You, the passenger, are subjected to the additional misery of that noise in streets already manic with sound. The yammer goes on in buses, on trains, in shops, in banks. You walk in Central Park and the metallic chatter comes to you from the postcard-size box carried in the hands of the frightened; frightened to be alone in the dark of daylight. Noise. A voice talking to you, singing to you the reassuring lullaby of the little metal box, your nurse, your mother, your drug. Often the actual content of this noise goes unheard. It is merely sound. The words, the notes, do not penetrate the listener's consciousness. That the sound probably actually comes from a room in which shirt-sleeved men or weary women sit in an over-heated smoke-filled room, fatigued, disheveled, talking into a metal gadget—this does not matter, even if the listener is aware of this. It is a sound, a voice, addressed to him, to her, the listener. I am here, it says. Mother is near you. Nothing can hurt you.

So then, a reassuring look at the fields and the forests and the towns. Perhaps America is still there.

Resolved to keep this firmly in mind, off we went, with my sights set for San Francisco and the Pacific Ocean. My two traveling companions were Oscar, the driver; and Miss Molly Hennessy, my housekeeper and friend.

As a driver Oscar was peerless. As a human he was stolid and uncommunicative, as a capable long-pull driver should be. From coast to coast he never lost a spangle, he ate steak and vanilla ice cream twice a day, daily. He never tried to pass a car on a hill or around a curve. When, as occasionally happened, a carload of road-happy beatniks with their legs hanging out of the open windows passed us in their quivering crate, hooting derisively on their way, Oscar made no attempt to outdistance them as they pressed forward for all their car would stand. He knew that his car need only maintain its pace, mile on mile, stuffily secure like a dowager among gamins, to outdistance anything on wheels.

Molly Hennessy, neat as a new silver dollar; possessed of initiative; alive to all that passed; intuitively quiet when one didn't want to talk; sage and observant when you waxed conversational; just the companion for a weary writer a-traveling.

The car itself, considering the purpose to which it now was being put, was absurd. In its majestic way it turned out to be as much of a person as any of us; and a gifted traveler. The search for a rentable solid serviceable middle-class dependable car (too much to expect of any mechanical vehicle) had proved fruitless and I now found myself on the tourist trail facing the Far West in a that year's hardtop Cadillac limousine, air-conditioned, pale gray upholstered, and of the kind one uses, if very solvent, for going to the opera, dressed-up; or to funerals. Certainly it was too regal for cross-country touring or for a self-supporting writer who is a battleground on which comfort and thrift are constantly at war with each other.

August; and all America was on wheels. Cars rolled ahead and behind and on either side. Coveys of children sprawled asleep in the rear of station wagons or trailers; or hung perilously from wide-open windows, their wide-open mouths and wide-open eyes greeting and staring at the passing fields, plains, prairies, mountain peaks, rivers, forests, valleys of an incredibly bounteous and unappreciated continent.

As they traveled they ate; ice cream cones, hot dogs, candy; fruit purchased from the lavish brilliant roadside stands.

The urge to be somewhere other than where you are is an American national characteristic. This, through the centuries, probably is inherited from grandfathers or great-grandfathers or great-great-grandfathers whose deep and desperate urge to come somehow to the United States had set the touring itch into the bloodstream in the first place. There never before was such a roving-footed nation. Perhaps, too, the size and the fantastic diversity of the great land titillated this tendency. If you wanted sunshine or cold; beaches or ski slopes; quiet or clamor; luxury or ruggedness; you filled up the gas tank and off you whizzed, leisurely or hell-bent, to Florida south, or northern Michigan; Maine or California; New York or Wyoming; New Mexico or New England. In any or all of these incredibly varied slices of American geography any United States citizen on wheels encounters the United States schoolteacher, industrialist, policeman, banker, houseworker, salesman, stenographer, clerk, lawyer, doctor, grocery delivery boy, mechanic. Into the car. Out on the road. Free!

Theirs was a modern and almost complete freedom from the everyday cares of the average human being. No house, office, shop, factory demanding hours of time and energy. No beds to make no meals to buy and prepare. No desk, no bench, no assembly line. No telephone. No school room. The sun, the moon, and perhaps a pleasant sort of road-weariness were the only clocks that nudged you. Free to roam up this road or that. Free to step out of the car at will. Free to look, learn, relax, and wonder. Free to litter with garbage and bottles and cans the lovely land through which they passed. Free to speed crazily toward nowhere seeing nothing. Some chose one way, some another.

For me, the journey began only in Chicago. The Midwest, the West, these were what I wanted for refreshment. Perhaps all these hundreds of thousands on wheels, westbound, were, like myself, seeking a kind of reassurance. A new apprehension poisoned the air. A Thing one could not see or feel or hear hovered over the great land, waiting. This Thing was like a monstrous hand, reaching, coveting, literally seeking to take a free nation by fear and force and use it as its own enslaved property. Perhaps just to see the land—thousands of miles of it—solid and serene and richly productive; to see the factories and the processing plants; the people, easy, comfortable, going about their daily business of living; working in the fields, up and down the streets of the small towns and the cities; there it all was, solid and seeable; this would dispel the poison of apprehension.

Through Iowa. The cornfields, mile on mile on mile, stretched away to the horizons, endlessly. You rode all the day, from morning to night, and the next day and the next, through Iowa and Nebraska cornfields and wheat fields, a solid green ocean of food. It covered the earth.

The world on wheels, rushing by, scarcely saw it, or if they noted it at all, took it for granted. Perhaps a man at the wheel of his good middle-class car, his wife and children snugly ensconced all about him, might say, over his shoulder, "Get a load of that! Ever see so much corn! Enough corn there to feed all the hogs in the world."

Or, through the Nebraska wheat and alfalfa, "That stuff's solid money. Old Khrushchev ever see that he'd bust out crying."

Gigantic trucks, diesel-engined, roared past, traveling the wide flat plain and prairie. Jalopy loads of hooting boys, catching sight of the big black glistening limousine, so incongruous among the cornfields, would pull up alongside and peer in, hoping to see the familiar face of a movie star or of some dazzling entertainer, Las Vegas or Reno-bound, would find curiosity cheated at sight of a gray-haired woman and the friendly merry face of little Miss Hennessy; and the stolid driver heedless of everything other than the road ahead.

"Yah!" they would yell, in their disappointment. "Lookit who's here! Nobody." And to emphasize their own importance they would step on the gas for a mile or two to put the cheats in their place.

Now I knew why the families had a sort of vacuity in their faces. In spite of trucks and traffic and the irresistible urge to arrive at the motel of one's destination before nightfall, there was about this entire coast-to-coast journey a sort of serenity, of peace that was almost hypnotic. Inside the car the unbelievable (to me) air-conditioning purred gently. Outside the sun shone. On the road ahead a glistening pond always turned out to be a mirage.

325

Each night there was a clean quiet motel and each motel, though occupied to the last room, was as characterless and impersonal as a deserted house. A face at the office desk. A key. No restaurant, no lunch room in connection except in one over-stuffed motel in Chey-enne Wyoming, of all places, where, in a state of shock, one paid twenty-one dollars a night for a room complete with incongruous ankle-deep carpet, engulfing plush chairs, empty unwanted refrigerator pur-ring its ice cubes to sleep; frigid air-conditioning, Roman bath, elec-tric baggage carts and steak steak steak.

There wasn't a really well-cooked plain or fancy meal between Chi-cago and San Francisco—except the breakfasts. In a country literally crammed with more food than it can consume, it was incredible that one did not once discover a well-served well-cooked major meal. To us, lunch was not important (except to our steak-and-ice-cream driver). I am a breakfast and dinner girl. That mid-day refreshment always has been a matter of just enough to keep the engine running; a cup of clear consommé and a saucer of stewed fruit; a glass of skim milk and a plop of cottage cheese on sliced tomatoes. To the motoring public with their quarters half-dollars and greenbacks in their pockets, the hotels, motels, restaurants, lunch rooms and cafes of the great open spaces offered the worst cooking I've encountered since I ate my way through the American Air Force bases in Europe during World War II. Again, as then, the basic ingredients were sound and good. Imagination and magic were lacking. Even the hamburger and the hot dog, now regrettably the backbone of the American diet, were just short of in-edible. But breakfast, inexplicably, was almost invariably good. As I could survive, if necessary, a lunchless and dinnerless day, but would expire by 9 A.M. if deprived of breakfast, this made for an agreeable start to each touring day. Inept as the continent seemed to be in every other department of cuisine, the United States early morning meal of orange juice and strong hot coffee, fresh hot buttered toast, eggs, bacon, or both, was briskly crashed down on the table or counter in front of you, inviting you by its familiar and reassuring scent, to break your fast.

It was miraculous to realize, day after day, in that fortnight of care-free leisurely travel through the August green and gold countryside of the richest nation in the world, not one major unpleasant incident disturbed the orderly progress of each day. It didn't even rain.

Certainly occasional sights or incidents irritated or annoyed or even somewhat inconvenienced me. But literally everything I saw interested me and much of it was fascinating. In a fashion, it was like having a rendezvous with a friend one has not seen in years; remembered, perhaps, with fondness but now, in prospect, regarded askance, fearing that this one had deteriorated with the years, or even that he or she actually never had been as gay or wise or warmhearted or companionable as you remembered through the decades. And then, at the meeting, to find that all these qualities still were there; and more.

The Iowa farmhouses, remembered from my childhood glimpsed since then from train or plane, actually were substantial homes, and not figments of fancy. Four-square, two-storied and white painted, set well back from the road and coolly tree-shielded from the blazing midsummer Midwest sun, I never had seen anywhere in the world working farmers' farmhouses as handsome and modernly habitable as these. The girls and women one encountered as one passed along the country roads, in the crossroads store or the small towns, were as modish as the Madison Avenue New York or the Michigan Avenue Chicago women I had seen a few days previously. Their dresses, their shoes, their nylons, the wave and set of their hair were triumphant copies of the edict issued by California, New York and Paris designers. The calico-covered flat-breasted sallow-faced farm drudge of the Midwest and Far West 1890s had vanished along with the buckboard.

If a Sight came into nearby view we viewed it but this route across the continent was not the route of the more obvious Wonders. Its wonders were, perhaps, lower-case (to use a printer's term) but as impressive and durable as the planet itself.

It was, for example, stirring and nostalgic and very important to find oneself ambling briefly through the grounds of Iowa State College in the smallish town of Ames Iowa. I had known Iowa State College teachers (to use that homely word) and Iowa State graduates. Farming land, this; rich to bursting. A freshwater college dedicated to agriculture, to husbandry, to science, the arts. Its very presence had direct influence on the State of Iowa, on the entire country, on the world, for that matter. India eats of Iowa; Africa too; the lands struggling throughout the world for freedom.

"Situated on the Skunk River," the tour map says, and no nonsense about it, "and bisected by rambling Squaw Creek."

That descriptive sentence was, somehow, as reassuring and sound and native as the college grounds and the State itself.

Feeling strangely spacious and serene, crunching peppermint molasses hard candies and staring out of the windows in a sort of trance as the Nebraska farmlands the towns the woods the streams the sky roll back and back and back you stop for the night at a small clean decent motel and go forth in search of a small clean decent dinner. The dinner is small, clean and just edible. The waiter, unconsciously, spoils your heretofore pleasant day.

The waiter was a high school boy; round-faced, fair-haired and almost touchingly inept. The old reporter's instinct surged to the surface.

"You—uh—been doing this work long?"

"Just part-time, summer vacation."

"School?"

"Starting junior high school next month. I'm going to college when I'm through high."

"That's great. I suppose that's why you're working now. College money."

"No, my folks are sending me. I just want a little extra money now, see."

"What course are you going to take at college? What do you want to be?"

He shrugged. "I don't know."

"But haven't you any plan? How do you happen to be going to college if you don't—I mean, after all—your parents are sending—"

"My uncle, he goes. He's twenty-one. You ought to hear him. He says living in the dormitory is a ball."

No. No! I thought. Somebody talk to him. Somebody talk to his parents. Aloud I said, only, "How old are you?"

"Sixteen."

Well, sixteen—that's young. Terribly young. But how naïve and thoughtless and young can you be, even at sixteen? Would an English boy, at that age, of hard-working parents; or an Italian, French, German, Dutch, African, Japanese, Russian, Latin American youth, look toward his years of adult education with such naïveté, such ignorance of values. Oh, don't be so priggish, I told myself, and don't take everything so big. The kid's only sixteen. You were no sibyl at sixteen yourself.

Next day, stopping briefly at a gas station in Wyoming, a seven-year-old boy canceled the waiter. The boy was dressed in the uniform of the young Western male; faded blue jeans, big roll-brim hat; boots. He was firm and plump of cheek, clear-eyed, and he regarded the massive car with almost professional interest. He peered into the engine. His eye traveled the foolish length of the vehicle.

"Are you going to be a mechanic when you grow up?" Patronizingly.
"No."

"What do you want to be?"

"I'm going to be a rancher." He said this with utter finality. You saw his range land, his grazing cattle. He belonged there.

I don't know why those six words made me happy. He didn't say, "I don't know . . . I'm going to be a space man . . . a policeman . . . a ball player . . . an aviator . . ."

I'm going to be a rancher. A simple declarative sentence that contained a fundamental and important promise for the continuance of a way of life.

It made my day.

Utah was a Sight; a Sight to Be Seen; it was, it turned out, two Sights. There were the tourists, hordes of them, clustered in Temple Square, and we joined them for the tour, eagerly. The Mormon trek across the wilderness of a continent, the courage, the resolution, the ultimate triumph of this almost bizarre little band of religious believers is unique and magnificent even in a country whose history is studded with unique and heroic migrations. We sat in the Tabernacle. We Oh'd and Ah'd the great domed roof; we listened and we heard the pin drop. We wanted to enter the Temple, but the Mormon Temple is not for tourists and not, for that matter, for the ordinary Mormon. I thought, well, a place of worship is not the place for a horde of the tourist and the curious and the unbelieving, so that's all right. And then I remembered St. Peter's in Rome, that noble edifice, with its endless throngs of tourists passing by the millions through its naves, up and down its aisles; quiet, respectful, awed as they gaze. I wondered if that, after all, wasn't the better way.

The days were hot, the sun was blazing, the American tourist, sartorially and pictorially, was not at his most winsome. He sweated copiously. His shirt-tail was out. He began to droop at the wheel. He still munched and munched as he went, but his heart no longer was in it. He and his wife and his small fry waded into that improbable body of salinity, the Great Salt Lake, and lay on it as on a mattress and sat on it as in a chair, and cavorted and splashed and shouted and coughed and were invigorated. Here, certainly, was a Sight to remember and that they could talk about when again they were back home. I had mildly looked forward to seeing this Sight. It lived up to its reputation, always a gratifying experience to a tourist. Perversely, I did not so much as dip a toe.

In my geographical ignorance I was not prepared for the Sight which was the Great Salt Desert. But then, I can't even bound New York State. The Great Salt Lake cosily tucked away in tour-memory we rolled on through Utah and suddenly were traveling on what appeared to be the planet Mars or possibly the Moon. In the half-light of the late August day I saw, to my shocked bewilderment, that we were surrounded as far as the eye could see, by a land of dully glistening white. It might have been white snow. It wasn't. It had no resemblance to white sand. Not a tree to be seen from the road to the horizon; not a shrub, not a weed, not a blade of grass. It was a world of white salt, ghostly, arid as the surface of the Moon. As the Great Salt Lake had receded and evaporated with the centuries it had left this white salt ghost to haunt the region forever.

We pulled up at the side of the road, got out, crunched our way over a stretch of salt field, stooped, wet a finger, brought it to the lips and tongue, gingerly. Then straightened and gazed again at what the eye rejected even as it marveled. A white world, surrounded by mountains. Mile on mile of snow-white salt, glistening, eerie, unreal.

Though the late August day still shimmered with heat, you shivered a little as you clambered back into the cosy familiarity of the cushioned car.

Other tourist groups dotted the spectral landscape. These, too, were stooping, tasting, staring. They were strangely quiet as they stared. So that's what chemicals and acids can do to a land, h'm? They seemed suddenly thoughtful.

Mountain country now, and Nevada just ahead. The flat farmlands of Illinois and Iowa, the prairies and plains of Nebraska, Wyoming, Utah were left behind; this was spectacular Western mountain land now; purple-blue and rose in the sunset; opalescent at sunrise. There was altitude now, too, very welcome and exhilarating for a low blood-pressure tourist. Five thousand, sometimes six thousand feet. Your spirits, serenely high since the journey's start, now rose with the aerial footage. Everything seemed bigger, clearer, rosier as the air became thinner and the perception more acute.

"I haven't heard anyone laugh," I remarked to Molly Hennessy, "since we left New York."

Molly Hennessy was no word-mincer. "I don't remember that anyone said anything very funny."

"I don't mean just this carload. I mean anyone. No one laughs; or even smiles. I don't mean grinning around. I mean—"

I didn't know exactly what I meant. Gayety. Perhaps that was the missing element. Not that I had expected to see the Merry Villagers dancing on the green; nor the thousands of tourists, westward bound, rollicking as they rolled along the roads. Holidaying, prosperous-seeming; eating well, sleeping comfortably in motels or trailer camps; viewing a lavish lovely world as they went—still they seemed not to be happy or even relaxed. Tense. Hurried. Accepting what they encountered but not moved or revived by it. That was it. An inexplicable joylessness.

This was nowhere more shockingly exemplified than in the two wide-open Nevada towns at which we made leisurely overnight stops on this, the famous California Trail of the 1850 Gold Rush period. Wide open was a term which meant gambling and what was termed night life.

Though a confirmed non-gambler—Monte Carlo, Nice, Carlsbad, Cannes, San Juan, Madeira, Saratoga, French Lick, New Orleans, all visited in the good old bad old days, never succeeded in infecting me with the fever—I now looked forward, nevertheless, to a dispassionate view of Elko and Reno Nevada as a spectacle.

With no sporting blood in my veins I nevertheless can understand the urge to bet on a horse, a ball game, even that savage manifestation, a prizefight. A human element is involved—at least, flesh, blood, muscle, training, mind enter into the contest. But commercial mechanical gambling in which neither intelligence nor physical prowess are involved, seems to me a dull pastime.

Here were two towns whose industries were mining, livestock, lumber, cattle and gambling. Business. Hard cold business. Yet all of these stemmed, certainly, from American frontier days. The cattlemen, the miners, the lumbermen of a past century after a day of intense toil and even danger, were grateful for the easy careless relaxation of the saloon and gambling place. For good or evil, it had a purpose. Crude whisky, sweat, comradeship, songs bawled into the smoke-choked air; oaths, lovemaking, tragedy, comedy, a kind of human animal enjoyment all went into it. This present cold mechanical process was the bloodless offspring of that long gone day. The rites were carried on in a mood of silent joylessness, win or lose.

Surrounding these wide open towns of pleasure were miles—hundreds of miles—of the fantastically glorious scenery which the Western United States lavishes upon its sated citizens. Vast national forests; the snow-capped Sierra Nevada Mountains; the desert, blazing hot under the August sun, cool and fragrant at night; roaring rivers such as the foaming Truckee tumbling out of the mountain snows; and in their depths the rainbow colors and the silver flash of the game fish; deer in the forests, mountain lions in the great hills. There they had all been in 1849. Here they were still in 1960.

The towns that had sprung up so casually from the original trading post and saloon and lodging were unlovely. Lunch rooms bars lunch rooms bars; and in these and in the barber shops the Laundromats, the shoe-shine stand, the market, stood the mechanical slot machine, comically incongruous in a workaday world.

The wide-open town motels were as decent, clean, and as quiet as those of the past week's experience. They even pampered the fleeting guest with food served on the premises; and actual walking bellboys.

In the big crowded strangely quiet gambling rooms nobody seemed to be having fun. A band was playing somewhere, very brassy. Weaving through and around and above all this was the sharp metallic click, clash, rattle of metal on metal. The slot machines, row on row. The five-cent slot machine; the dime; the quarter; the dollar. There, too, was the wheel; the card game. No attempt had been made to create the illusion of beauty or luxury. The guests or patrons or habitués were playing—as it is called—but in this there seemed to be no fun, no élan. Their faces were utterly joyless as they went about the grim business of asking the fates to grant them a dollar in exchange for a five-cent piece; ten dollars for one; a thousand for a hundred. Curiously—or perhaps not so curiously—it is not only the visitor whose veins feel fever of the infection. As, in the more conventional town, the delivery boy on his rounds or the man who reads the electric-and-gas meter stops in at the corner drugstore for a Coke, so the everyday citizen of the town slips his nickel his dime even his dollar into the machine perhaps daily, perhaps oftener.

In the dear decadent past, before two World Wars had made the whole world just one big unhappy family—when Russian Grand Dukes were not taxi drivers or dressmakers—when a chandelier was an iridescent blaze and not spectral indirect lighting—when basalt-eyed croupiers, not beatniks, wore little black beards—and the great plush and brocade rooms were heady with scent of flowers and perfumed bejeweled women of the world and the underworld—then the gambler, even the luckless one, in Monte Carlo, in France, Italy, got a sop of drama and luxury for his money.

Oscar, wearing his driver's cap still, was locked in combat with a small-change slot machine. Molly Hennessy had last been seen headed toward a row of five-cent slots, a cache of nickels as ammunition. Now she emerged, sagging a little to one side with the weight of the deluge of nickels that had dealt her beginner's luck. Morosely I dropped a shining Western silver dollar into a dollar slot machine as a sort of proper gesture as a guest; and started to walk away.

Klunk. G-r-r-r-r-r! Bang! Klunk-klunk-klunk-klunk-klunk-klunk-klunk-klunk-klunk-klunk. Ten silver dollars clashed into the metal receiver. The sporting thing to do was to feed it back. I gathered it up and gave it to the bellboys, feeling like Diamond Lil; or Marlene in one of those Westerns she used to enhance.

Each morning had seen us up at six-thirty and on our way in what the Westerners have so happily phrased as "the fresh of the morning." In this past fortnight these morning hours had literally been the freshest, what with the absence of strain and pressure, the almost dreamlike panorama of America, verdant, fulfilled, gliding past the windows of the car whose steady pace mile on mile, gave it almost the illusion of standing still.

This morning had a special quality. The "wide-open" towns with their joyless game rooms were now behind us. Two hundred and sixty miles, more or less, to cover. At the end of today's drive we would be at the end of the fortnight's journey. There, facing the Bay and the sky and the fog and the sunset and the Sierras would be San Francisco, the dazzler, the enchanter.

One thing only I share in common with Khrushchev: San Francisco.

In that first rude and rowdy visit to the United States he had sneered and clowned and bragged his way across the opulent continent but San Francisco, the unique, the iridescent, he could not even pretend to equal. So now, in the fresh of the morning, over the Nevada state line and into California, up and up and up on mountain roads, climbing steadily from an altitude of 4500 feet or thereabouts to the more than 7000 feet of tragic and historic Donner Pass.

Knowing the true horror story of that high plateau there was something deeply embarrassing about parking a Cadillac limousine on the spot where, little more than a century ago, scores of pioneers California bound, trapped and defenseless in the blinding blizzards and the numbing wind and cold, had perished, starved and frozen. And you shut your eyes as you gazed across the splendid valley below and tried not to think of the frenzied and grisly remnant who had survived by feasting off the flesh of their dead companions. A hideous and a piteous page in the history of a wildly melodramatic period. You turned and stumbled back into the luxurious car.

"Windy," Oscar commented. "But sure is a pretty view. They say even early as October you can get stuck in the snow up here."

Rolling downhill now and along the splendid highway whose towns and cities, as one noted their names, were a sort of primary lesson in the romantic Spanish-American legend and history of the region.

Sacramento! boasts the sign with a flourish as of pennants as you approach that thriving city.

Davis! crisply retorts the next town's signpost. Dixon! snaps the next.

Vallejo, croons the next sign. Rodeo and San Pablo the next and the next.

Berkeley. Oakland. Flat statements from the two following.

But romance has the last word.

San Francisco!

CONFIDENTIAL

World, you have not always been true to me. Though perhaps you have —in your fashion. You thought I didn't know. I knew.

Now and then I hear an ugly rumor that you may be planning to leave me. It is being whispered behind fans in Cape Canaveral and among the boys in Washington and Moscow and New Delhi and Peking.

Just lately, too, I've heard that you are making bold advances to the Moon. They say you and the other boys have been whizzing up and down in front of her house, blowing your horns as you pass by. The Moon, silly-faced thing, just sits there looking as though green cheese wouldn't melt in her mouth.

I'm not trying to interfere in your private life. I merely want to warn you as one who always has had your interest at heart. The Moon may be all right to visit but you wouldn't want to live with her. You know what the fellow said: "Swear not by the inconstant Moon."

All this may be merely rumor. But true or false, there is something I want to say to you whether you leave me first or I leave you. I've wanted to say it for years.

World, I love you. I have always loved you. . . . Or almost always.

NEW YORK
JANUARY 1963

E44